Agnes Moorehead on Radio, Stage and Television

Also by Axel Nissen
and from McFarland

Accustomed to Her Face: Thirty-Five Character Actresses of Golden Age Hollywood (2016)

Mothers, Mammies and Old Maids: Twenty-Five Character Actresses of Golden Age Hollywood (2012)

Actresses of a Certain Character: Forty Familiar Hollywood Faces from the Thirties to the Fifties (2006; softcover 2011)

Agnes Moorehead on Radio, Stage and Television

AXEL NISSEN

McFarland & Company, Inc., Publishers
Jefferson, North Carolina

Library of Congress Cataloguing-in-Publication Data

Names: Nissen, Axel.
Title: Agnes Moorehead on radio, stage and television / Axel Nissen.
Description: Jefferson, North Carolina : McFarland & Company, Inc.,
Publishers, 2017. | Includes bibliographical references and index.
Identifiers: LCCN 2017043914 | ISBN 9781476667584
(softcover : acid free paper) ♾
Subjects: LCSH: Moorehead, Agnes, 1906–1974—Criticism and interpretation.
Classification: LCC PN2287.M698 N56 2017 | DDC 791.4302/8092—dc23
LC record available at https://lccn.loc.gov/2017043914

British Library cataloguing data are available

ISBN (print) 978-1-4766-6758-4
ISBN (ebook) 978-1-4766-3035-9

Front cover: Agnes Moorehead, 1971 (Photofest)

Manufactured in the United States of America

McFarland & Company, Inc., Publishers
Box 611, Jefferson, North Carolina 28640
www.mcfarlandpub.com

To the memory
of Nils Axel Nissen, Sr.
(1920–2015)

Table of Contents

Introduction

Agnes Moorehead (1900–74) was unique among twentieth-century American actresses in making a major career for herself in all four entertainment media after the age of 40. Granted, she started out in radio when she was still in her thirties, but her star turn in "Sorry, Wrong Number" on the classic radio show *Suspense* didn't come until 1943; her film debut in *Citizen Kane* didn't happen till she was 40; her stage career began in earnest in 1951; and her fourth and final career, in television, didn't start until she was 52. It was as if she reinvented herself each new decade of her career, starting with radio work in the 1930s, moving into films in the 1940s, then adding leading roles in the live theater to her repertoire in the 1950s, and capping it all with a tremendous success in television in the 1960s. Who could match that trajectory?

Readers may be aware that I have devoted a book to Moorehead's screen career.[1] The present volume is meant to complement *The Films of Agnes Moorehead* and to complete the story by analyzing 25 of Moorehead's performances in radio, on the stage, and in television to give us a sense of the breadth and depth of her work as an actress in these media through more than 40 years. Yes, Moorehead got a late start, relatively speaking, but she more than made up for it by the almost unparalleled number and variety of her roles. Year by year, decade by decade, she added new strings to her bow. By the time *Bewitched* came along in 1964, she was an expert marksman in all four major entertainment media. *Bewitched* consolidated her position in the American entertainment industry and guaranteed her place in the popular imagination for many years in the future, but without all the talent, the versatility, and the professionalism she had displayed before Endora came along, she would not have gotten that part nor been so effective in it. Thus, *Bewitched* was one capstone of Moorehead's long career, which had already had many peaks along the way.

Naturally, in this book there are chapters devoted to major successes and classic series, such as *The Shadow*, where she originally co-starred with Orson Welles; and *Suspense*, where she gave her single most notable radio performance in "Sorry, Wrong Number," but she also played many other scintillating roles. I have also made room, though, for a more modest but still charming and enjoyable radio series called *Mayor of the Town*, in which Moorehead played an ornery spinster housekeeper called Marilly for seven years, making it her most important recurring role in a series prior to *Bewitched*. Among her stage performances, the original production of *Don Juan in Hell*, her one woman-show, and *Gigi* take pride of place, but I ended up making room for separate chapters on all her stage productions, because they were relatively few and little has been written about them.[2] The choice was the hardest to make among Moorehead's many interesting television performances. Here I was guided partially by availability and the intrinsic quality of the show, but also, I must admit, by my own personal tastes. Fourteen TV performances ultimately made it into the book, which is a relatively small number. I feel that in addition to her more familiar performances on *Bewitched*, *The Wild Wild West*, and *The Twilight Zone*, my choice to focus on shows like *Wagon Train*, *Adventures in Paradise*, *Rawhide*, *Channing*, *Burke's Law*, and *Custer* will represent her in a good way.

I must admit to being partial to the 1950s anthology drama series. For all their unreality, there is something raw and real about them. And they are all in glorious black and white. On the other hand, I can't stand the garish colors of the early 1970s TV series and TV movies. It doesn't help that their storylines are often equally garish. Thus, the reader will search in vain for a discussion of productions like *Frankenstein: The True Story* (1973), where the bonnet seems to be wearing Moorehead rather than the other way around; or *Suddenly Single* (1971), which like so many of her films for television, leaves us wondering what an actress of her caliber was doing playing such a tiny, inconsequential role.

Before we start, let us remind ourselves of some of the central facts about Moorehead's acting career in radio, the theater, and television. She graduated from the American Academy of Dramatic Arts in March 1929 and was finally ready to embark on the stage career she had been planning for and dreaming about for so long. For a newly minted actor, it was the worst possible time to be launching an acting career. The stock market would famously crash in October 1929. Banks began to fail a year later. The unemployment rate rose from 3 percent in 1929 to 25 percent in in 1933. In brief, Moorehead's stage career went nowhere. She later claimed to have been associated with six Broadway shows during her early years in New York, but she is not listed as having been among the original cast of *Marco Millions* (1928, 1930), *Courage* (1928–29), *Soldiers and Women* (1929), *Scarlet Pages* (1929), *Candle Light* (1929–30), or *All the King's Horses* (1934). This doesn't make her mendacious, though; it just means that she was probably employed in some modest capacity, as an understudy, standby, or extra or came in later as a replacement.[3] A 1933 feature article mentions that she was in several of these shows in New York and in *Marco Millions* "on the road with the Theater Guild."[4] In a note to her personal assistant and friend Georgia Johnstone, Moorehead wrote of these Broadway shows: "I was a Venetian flower girl in *Marco Millions*. Most of these I came in after the opening—naturally I wouldn't be listed in the original cast—some I understudied."[5]

Moorehead's professional acting career began and ended not with the theater, then, but with radio. Though she had done some singing on radio in the mid–1920s, she got her first foothold as a radio actress in 1930. Her last acting job 44 years later was doing two broadcasts as part of a new series called the *CBS Radio Mystery Theatre*, which hoped to recreate some of the magic of *Suspense* and similar old time radio classics. Without radio, Moorehead is unlikely to have had an acting career. Radio was her training ground. Radio gave her work during the Depression. Radio gave her a measure of recognition, if not celebrity. Radio brought her together with Orson Welles and many other industry players who would be useful to her in later life. Through all the twists and turns of her career and despite the diminishing returns, radio remained her comfort zone, her always loyal, low-key, and cherished friend.

The stage, on the other hand, was like an unrequited lover: it never loved her as much as she loved it. Towards the end of her life, Moorehead described the requirements for a theatrical career as: "The faith of an angel, the courage of a general, the hide of a crocodile."[6] Though she had trained to be a stage actress and made an unsuccessful stab at a Broadway career in the early 1930s, Moorehead's real career in live theater didn't begin until 1951. As such, it was her third career, following on from both her major years in radio in the 1930s and her glory days in the American film industry in the 1940s. With the end of her long-term contract at MGM in 1950 and radio work becoming more scarce by the minute, she needed a new source of income. The arrival of young dynamo producer Paul Gregory on the scene was timely indeed and Moorehead certainly knew how to take advantage of the openings life gave her.

When I take a somewhat sober view of Moorehead's stage work, it is because what little there was of it was of variable quality. I'm not thinking of the quality of Moorehead's performances themselves, which were always what the part required and included personal triumphs at the start, as Doña Ana in the landmark 1951–52 production of *Don Juan in Hell*; and at the last, as Aunt Alicia in *Gigi*. No, I say this because, out of the nine stage shows she did between 1951 and 1973, only Paul Gregory's production of *Don Juan in Hell* can be said to be lasting of importance and only *The Rivalry* among the remaining shows had any real artistic merit. Only half of Moorehead's Broadway-bound stage shows actually made it there: two productions of *Don Juan in Hell*, *Lord Pengo*, and *Gigi*.

Her first play *Don Juan in Hell*, then, was the only play of classic stature Moorehead acted in. As such, her stage career paralleled her film career: The best opportunities came early on. Phyllis Carlin calls Doña Ana her "most noted performance on the live stage."[7] She was certainly Moorehead's signature stage role; the only thing that could match it was her impersonation of a leading lady of the American stage in her long-running one-woman show. It is difficult to underestimate the importance of Moorehead's one-woman show to her career. It literally and metaphorically gave her a platform to stand on; it consolidated her position in the American entertainment industry as something more than a talented, versatile radio and film character actress; and it proved, if nothing else, that people were willing to pay good money to see and hear Agnes Moorehead alone and playing herself.

On the stage, Moorehead was given good opportunities in *The Pink Jungle* and *Gigi*, too, but both shows were deeply flawed and ended up being critical and commercial failures. Her parts in *Prescription: Murder* and *Lord Pengo* were unworthy of her talents. No other producer than her close friend Paul Gregory would ever have given her star billing and a salary to match for her minor roles as a wife who is murdered in the first act of *Prescription: Murder* and a devoted secretary who appears only intermittently in two out of three acts of *Lord Pengo*.

There is no question that Paul Gregory was to Moorehead's stage career what Orson Welles was to her film career. I once asked Gregory who he thought had been the most important to Moorehead of the two of them. He answered without hesitation that it had been Welles. "You always owe the most to the one who gives you your start," he explained.[8] As far as starring roles on the stage are concerned, Gregory certainly gave Moorehead her start and then some. He also gave her a new image. I will leave to another time the fascinating story of how he made a leading lady out of a film character actress with very little real stage experience. Suffice it to say, it was one of the deftest and most daring public relations exercises of the mid-twentieth century!

Moorehead's television debut in 1953 followed hard on the heels of her burgeoning new stage career. "Lullaby," which I discuss in detail in Chapter 5, is a low-key episode of the *Revlon Mirror Theatre*, a run-of-the-mill drama anthology series with middling script quality and production values, though it attracted some marquee names. Moorehead's work on the stage and the big screen prevented her from doing much television during the next few years, but by the late 1950s things had started to pick up and 1960 was her busiest year in the medium prior to her eight years on *Bewitched.* Out of her total output of eight TV roles in 1960, I have chosen to discuss her three very different performances on *The Millionaire, Adventures in Paradise*, and *Rawhide.*

Despite the money, the fame, and the success it brought her, Moorehead felt least at home in television, because of the hurried pace of production and what she saw as the lack of professional standards. She said in an interview in 1968, when *Bewitched* was in its fifth season, that she found working in television "very difficult, very tedious: Many times I enjoy a script as I read it. But when you're on your feet doing it, you can get bogged down. The pressures are so tremendous—time is the biggest problem—that you often let something go that could be improved. That is a great deterrent to a good performance."[9] Somewhat ironically, then, Moorehead's final performance was on television, in a segment of the TV movie *Rex Harrison Presents Stories of Love* titled "The Fortunate Painter," which aired on NBC May 1, 1974, the day after her death.

So, which of Moorehead's four careers in the entertainment industry was the most important? I've already given some hints of my assessment above. Devoting an entire book to Moorehead's film career, while treating her work in radio, live theater, and television together here is also an implicit answer to that question. Clearly, her work in film, particularly the films of the 1940s, is her greatest and most lasting artistic achievement. Our assessment of the relative importance of her work in the radio, theater, and television will depend on the criteria we base it on. I feel that both qualitatively and quantitatively, Moorehead's stage career, however important to her personally, has to take last place in the ranking. This is not to suggest that her stage career was unimportant, but she got a late start on the stage, she only did nine shows between 1951 and her death, and their quality was variable to say the least.

For various reasons, it's harder to judge the relative importance of her radio and television careers. Because of the visibility, longevity, and popularity of *Bewitched*, television as a medium has contributed infinitely more to Moorehead's posthumous reputation and lasting impact on American popular culture than radio, which certainly has its aficionados, but which does not generate the same degree of popular and critical interest. Certainly, the breadth and variety both of Moorehead's radio and television roles deserves to be better known. On the small screen, she was much more than Endora. Over the radio waves, she was much more than the harrowed heroine of "Sorry, Wrong Number." Moorehead herself balked when an interviewer suggested "Sorry" was her "most exciting radio performance," remarking tartly that "I've done loads of exciting radio performances. That just happens to be a memorable one."[10]

I'm am particularly grateful to Russell Beasley, Conrad Binyon, Norman Corwin, Paul Gregory, Judy Insel, Laurie Main, and Karin Wolfe for talking to me about the Agnes Moorehead they knew and worked with in radio and the theater. I would also like to thank the following individuals, who have contributed to my understanding of Moorehead's life and career or helped and inspired me in other ways: Don Bachardy, Kaye Ballard, Dr. Roderick Bladel, Ron Bowers, Scotty Bowers, Mary Grace Canfield, Clifford Capone, Fred Carmichael, Norman S. Chramoff, Beverly Jean Cooper, Michael Cooper, John Crawford, Wade Crookham, Richard Currier, Olivia de Havilland, Jone Devlin,

Tamela Dhority, Jean Porter Dmytryk, Dale Emery, Linda Myhre Enlow, George Gaynes, Kari Goodman, Harry Hart-Browne, Geoffrey Horne, Dean Jones, Lynn Kear, Brian Kellow, Gretchen H. Lainson, James Lashly, Mark Lashly, Jill-Marie Lehmann, June Lockhart, Vince Lynch, Ronald McClendon, Tom Margittai, Hank Moonjean, Katrina O. Nolder, Charles Miller Nolte, Carl E. Nord, James Robert Parish, Michael Pate, Cliff Pengra, Dame Siân Phillips, Carol A. Rodgers, Kasey Rogers, Boyden Rohner, Vanya Foster Rohner, Merri Jean Ross, Carol and Leon Schwartz, Marian Seldes, Craig Smith, Sam Staggs, Margery Stover, Charles Tranberg, David Tucker, Ann Wakefield, Tom Weaver, Charlotte B. White, Margaret Whiting, Hutton Wilkinson, Iva Withers, and Tom Wortham. Sadly, several of them have passed on while this book was in progress. Among those who have died, I have a special place in my heart for my friend Paul Gregory, who chose to take his own life in December 2015. Paul was in his 96th year when he died. He was one of the most fascinating individuals I have met and I am so grateful that Agnes Moorehead brought us together.

I have benefited from extended periods of research in several excellent libraries with collections relating to Moorehead or from the staff's willingness to copy and send me all the materials I needed. Let me thank the staff of the Wisconsin Center for Film and Theater Research and the Wisconsin Historical Society, particularly Harold L. Miller, Dorinda M. Hartmann, Dee Grimsrud and students Heather Richmond and Mark Ryan; the staff of the Billy Rose Theatre Division of the New York Library for the Performing Arts; Mark Gens at the Archive Research and Study Center, UCLA Film and Television Archive; the staff of the Charles E. Young Research Library, UCLA; Shannon E. Bowen at the American Heritage Center, University of Wyoming; Andrew Whitis and Sheila Ellenberger at the Muskingum University Library; and Sue Steiner at the Reedsburg Public Library. Moorehead's alma mater Muskingum University has kindly allowed me to use five photographs from their collection in the book.

This is the first book I have written since my father, Nils Axel Nissen, Sr., died in his 96th year on October 30, 2015. So much of what is good in my life comes from the fine start he and my mother gave me. He was the best father I could have had.

Note: Several abbreviations are used throughout the text to indicate the source of material. AHC refers to the Paul Gregory Papers, American Heritage Center, University of Wyoming; Muskingum refers to the Agnes Moorehead Collection, Muskingum University Library; Nissen indicates my personal collection; NYPL refers to the Georgia Johnstone Papers regarding Agnes Moorehead, Billy Rose Theatre Division, New York Public Library for the Performing Arts; and finally, WCFTR refers to the Agnes Moorehead Papers of the Wisconsin Center for Film and Theater Research.

1

The Shadow (Radio, 1937–39)

The New Amsterdam Theater is a slender slice of a building from 1903 in the Art Nouveau style, which stands at 214 W. 42nd St. near Broadway. In the 1930s, there was a 700-seat theater and radio studio tucked up under its roof. For six months from late September 1937 till late March 1938, that is where Agnes Moorehead and Orson Welles made the magic happen on Sunday afternoons at 5:30 p.m., as they gave voice and life to the elusive Shadow and his trusty mate Margo Lane.[1] Moorehead was fast approaching 37 (though she'd never admit it) and had been married for seven years to fellow actor Jack Lee. Welles was only 22, but already married himself to Virginia Nicolson. They would have their daughter Christopher only a week after the last *Shadow* broadcast Welles and Moorehead did together on March 20, 1938. Their close collaboration on the landmark series was not a long one, but it was a period pregnant with possibilities and one that would leave its mark on both their lives.

In the course of the 1930s and '40s, *The Shadow* developed into a multimedia phenomenon the likes of which the world had seldom seen. Through the pages of *The Shadow Magazine*, in comic books and comic strips, on radio, television and in films, the Shadow ultimately became "a pop culture icon" and "a major influence on the subsequent evolution of comic book superheroes, particularly Batman."[2] A figure called "The Shadow" first appeared in 1930, not as a fictional character, but rather as the mysterious narrator of *The Detective Story Hour*, a radio show designed to boost sales for the pulp magazine of the same name published by Street and Smith. A year later, in response to audience interest in the elusive Shadow, writer Walter B. Gibson was asked to develop this narrator figure into a full-fledged literary character, still to be known as the Shadow. As conceived by Gibson, "The Shadow was an Old Testament avenger, a ruthless slayer of the wicked, very befitting the Depression decade of his greatest strength."[3]

Our story really begins in 1937, when it was decided to turn the Shadow into the hero of his own suspense radio drama series. While the Shadow had several identities in the pulps, it was decided that in the new show he would simply be Lamont Cranston, "wealthy man about town." Welles biographer Frank Brady describes him as "a modern day Sherlock Holmes, who would attempt to solve any baffling mystery that the police were unable to unravel ... a sophisticated playboy and an amateur criminologist, who, because of a secret he had learned when living in the Orient, had the power to cloud men's minds—making himself invisible."[4] Cranston was to be joined on his adventures by his "friend and companion, the lovely Margo Lane," a character first created for this new radio series and the only person who knew that Cranston was the Shadow.

Enter Orson Welles and Agnes Moorehead. By this time Moorehead was a well-established and respected actress in radio. Welles, despite his youth, had done quite a few things, though mostly in the theater. We are accustomed to reading how much Moorehead owed to Welles, but a newspaper column from 1940 reminds us that there was a time when it was the other way around and Moorehead was in a position to help the younger actor. Here is the item in full:

> Agnes Moorehead taught Orson Welles the answers, and radio's fair-haired boy is still returning the favor.... Way back in 1934 Miss Moorehead ran into Orson Welles, he was hungry, lonesome and didn't know a soul in radio ... she knew everybody and was sitting on top of the world ... she gave Orson pointers and contacts with the right persons in radio and when Orson's star took off on its meteoric ascent, he didn't forget, and whenever he directs, Miss Moorehead automatically becomes a member of his cast if circumstances permit.... Orson still gets inspiration from Aggie's work and a lot of pats on the back for having such a capable actress on tap.... Aggie likes to think of him as a protégé, though she doesn't say so out loud, and is convinced he is the best director and actor on the face of the globe.[5]

The two of them had met on a radio soap opera in 1934 or 1935.[6] After working together for a couple of years on *The March of Time*, Welles had convinced Moorehead to lend her talents to his first independent venture in radio: his seven-part dramatization of Victor Hugo's classic *Les Misérables*, which premiered over the new Mutual Broadcasting System on July 23, 1937, and finished on September 3.

It was at this time Welles was cast as the Shadow/Lamont Cranston, largely on the merits of his work on *The March of Time*. According to Moorehead, he then requested that she be cast as Margo Lane.[7] From *Les Mis*, Welles and Moorehead segued directly into their new show, which was at the same network. *The Shadow* premiered with the episode "The Death House Rescue" on Sunday, September 26, 1937, on Mutual, which would carry it until it ended in 1954. According to *Shadow* historian Anthony Tollin, "the program was an immediate success."[8] Brady writes that it "became the most popular mystery show on the air" and radio historian John Dunning calls it "the epitome of radio crime drama," adding that "it remains one of the three or four shows cited by people as a synonym for 'oldtime radio.'"[9]

According to his contract, Welles did not have to attend rehearsals. "Not rehearsing," he told Peter Bogdanovich, "made it so much more interesting."[10] I wonder if Moorehead felt the same way! It must have made the broadcasts all the more nerve-wracking for her, his most frequent co-star on the series. In Moorehead's eyes, though, Welles could do no wrong, so what she would have viewed as a lack of professionalism in anyone else, she no doubt tolerated in Welles. Simon Callow writes that "Welles plays the wealthy young Cranston as rather leisurely and mild, with careless charm, in the more or less English accent then still synonymous with a private income; there is about the interpretation a suggestion of silk dressing gown and cigarette holder: this was his Noël Coward performance."[11]

Ultimately, Welles's tenure as the Shadow was brief, especially when compared with his immediate successor, William Johnstone, who played the role for five seasons, and Bret Morrison, who portrayed the Shadow on radio for a total of ten years. Tollin describes Johnstone as "a Scottish-born former reporter who was chosen over forty-five other aspirants."[12] As it happens, Johnstone was born in Brooklyn (in 1908); the Shadow and Judge James T. Lowell on *As the World Turns* would be his most recognizable roles. After the second season premiere, one critic noted that "Bill Johnstone ... does a thoroughly good job, up several notches from last season's interpretation by Orson Welles."[13] Paul Heyer, on the other hand, writes that Johnstone's "somewhat thinner, older voice proved adequate but lacked the panache that his successor, Brett [sic] Morrison, had in abundance. Morrison proved to be the quintessential Shadow—yes, better even than Orson."[14] According to Tollin, "Welles's departure had little effect on The Shadow's popularity."[15]

"Together, Lamont and Margo confronted the maddest assortment of lunatics, sadists, ghosts, and werewolves ever heard on the air," writes Dunning.[16] Their relationship is said to have been inspired by the chummy collaboration of the upper crust, amateur detective couple Nick and Nora Charles in the *Thin Man* films.[17] Nick and Nora were married, though, and Nick did not have hypnotic powers. Others have compared Lamont and Margo's dynamic to that of Sherlock Holmes and Dr. Watson.[18] The comparison is not unreasonable, as Margo often represents the voice of common sense and conventionality and serves to draw out Lamont's superior ratiocinative powers. Ironically, then, while Moorehead had finally escaped playing the stooge to male comedians, she was still playing the "straight woman" to a male star.

In the first season, Margo mostly stayed close to home and her radio transmitter, waiting for Lamont to signal to her. She acted as a liaison between the Shadow and the police and occasionally, if the investigation required a feminine touch, she was entrusted with talking to women involved in the case. Lamont's idea of a hot date was taking Margo to a trial of some wrongly persecuted individual he wanted to help, such as in "The League of Terror" and "The Silent Avenger," though she did get to accompany him to a swanky night club in "The Temple Bells of Neban."

Things looked up for Margo Lane in several ways in Season 2. She appeared in 23 out of 26 episodes (rather than 13 out of 26 in the first season), Lamont and Margo frequently traveled together to exotic locations (without the benefit of clergy), and Margo got more involved in the sleuthing, though not without dire threats to her life and safety.[19] Most of the time, Lamont blithely ignored the fact that he was putting his girlfriend at risk. He seemed to forget that, while he was capable of disappearing from his enemy's vision, Margo did not have that option. Tollin writes: "It seems amazing that the radio Margos lasted as long as they did when one considers the trials and tribulations that went with being The Shadow's girl Friday. Although the job had tremendous fringe benefits (including worldwide travels with a 'wealthy young man-about-town'), danger lurked at every turn."[20]

Lamont usually ignored the fact that Margo was a woman in most situations, not just those involving danger. He was so self-involved and, like Ibsen's idealistic hero Brand, so dedicated to saving the world from crime and iniquity, that it didn't leave much room for more carnal passions. All this has led Dunning to write that "they had a thoroughly asexual friendship" and Moorehead biographer Charles Tranberg to claim that Lamont and Margo weren't a couple at all.[21] Yet the fact that they are more than "just good friends" is signaled from the beginning, in the first scene of the first episode, where Lamont permits himself to call Margo "darling" (while also asking her to stop frowning). Later in the same episode, which features an unfortunate, jobless husband and father, who gets framed for a violent bank robbery, Margo is unusually candid in conversation with the poor man's wife, whom she has brought $1,000 and a message from the Shadow not to lose hope. ""I love him, but I wonder whether I know him," she says. "It's hard to tell whether I really know the man or only his shadow."[22] There's the occasional "darling" later on in the series, too, and neither Lamont nor Margo use that word casually.

Moorehead's years on *The Shadow* were chiefly marked by the death of her father, the Rev. John Henderson Moorehead. He collapsed and died of a heart attack during a Sunday service at his church in Columbus, Ohio, on May 22, 1938, and was laid to rest with his daughter, Moorehead's younger sister, Margaret in Dayton. *The Shadow* was on hiatus at the time and her father's death may have impacted on Moorehead's decision not to do the summer season of the show. Orson Welles was joined by Broadway ingénue Margot Stevenson as Margo Lane. As it happened, the character was named after Stevenson, who was dating one of the show's producers, Clark Andrews, at its inception in 1937.[23]

As fate would have it, Jack Lee's father, vaudevillian Robert Marshall Lee, also died in 1938.[24] Jack had been more successful on Broadway than his wife, though it wouldn't last. In mid–November 1937, he opened in *Too Many Heroes*, a new drama by Dore Schary, who years later would be Moorehead's boss at Metro-Goldwyn-Mayer. The play closed after only 16 performances at the Hudson Theatre. If you read the summary of this "meaningful" millworker melodrama in *The Best Plays 1937–38*, you can understand why.[25]

The Lees had moved in to Manhattan from Long Island in 1935. During her *Shadow* years, Moorehead lived in an apartment at 101 W. 55th St.[26] "Claridge's" is a vast neo–Renaissance apartment building from 1925 in the heart of the entertainment district and covers the western side of 6th Ave. between 55th and 56th St. Moorehead only needed to walk 13 blocks south and one block west to get to the New Amsterdam Theatre and the apartment was even closer to NBC studios at Rockefeller Plaza and the CBS studios at 485 Madison Ave. One feature article from 1936, where Moorehead complained about being "ZaSu Pitts on the radio," described her sitting room as "a huge, paneled white room, very modern and not at all ZaSu Pitts-ish."[27]

Moorehead's work on *The Shadow* marked the beginning of her glory days in radio; *The Mercury Theatre on the Air* and *The Campbell Playhouse*, *The Cavalcade of America*, and later *Suspense*, all followed in its wake. Finally, she had broken out of the straightjacket of comic female stereotypes; finally, she could get her teeth into meaty dramatic roles, rather than playing the stooge to male comedians. One reviewer noted after the premiere of *The Shadow* in 1937: "long associated with comedy parts, Agnes Moorehead ... proved that directors who attempt to 'type' actors make a mistake."[28]

On a personal level, the most lasting legacy of *The Shadow* for Moorehead was her friendship with William Johnstone's wife, Georgia. Georgia Brady Johnstone, a former dancer born in Pittsburgh in 1906, would play an important role in Moorehead's life, as her devoted and diligent secretary in Los Angeles in the 1940s and in New York from 1962 till Moorehead's death.

CREDITS: *Creators:* Edward Hale Bierstadt, William B. Gibson; *Directors:* Martin Gabel, Bourne Ruthrauff; *Producer:* Clark Andrews; *Writer:* Edward Hale Bierstadt; *Theme Music:* Camille Saint-Saëns, "Omphale's Spinning Wheel"; *Tag Lines:* "Who knows what evil lurks in the hearts of men? The Shadow knows"; "The weed of crime bears bitter fruit. Crime does not pay. The Shadow knows."; *Air Dates:* September 26, 1937–March 20, 1938 (Season 1) and September 25, 1938–March 19, 1939 (Season 2) over the Mutual Broadcasting System

CAST: Ray Collins (Commissioner Weston), William Johnstone (Lamont Cranston/The Shadow), Agnes Moorehead (Margo Lane), Kenneth Roberts (Announcer), Orson Welles (Lamont Cranston/The Shadow), Arthur Whiteside (Announcer)

2

Mayor of the Town (Radio, 1942–49)

The two constants of Agnes Moorehead's working life in the 1940s were her long-term contract with MGM studios and her weekly appearances on *Mayor of the Town*. The radio show did not tax her talents any more than her average MGM film did, but this work was the meat and potatoes of her career. Beyond that, the spinster housekeeper Marilly Jones was Moorehead's most important recurring role in a series before *Bewitched*. Marilly was an integral part of *Mayor of the Town* for its entire seven-year run from the show's premiere over NBC on September 6, 1942, during the four and a half years until May 1947 when it was broadcast from CBS Radio's "Columbia Square" studios on Sunset Boulevard, until its final seasons over ABC and Mutual, leaving the air for good on July 3, 1949.[1]

From *The Youngest Profession* to *Without Honor*, Moorehead acted in 20 feature films during her *Mayor of the Town* years, most of them produced at MGM, where she went under contract in the fall of 1942, after Orson Welles and his associates were thrown off the RKO lot. In the wake of her "succès d'estime" in *The Magnificent Amberson*, Moorehead surely could have stayed on at RKO, but opted for a future at Hollywood's largest and most prestigious studio. As a reminder of her precarious position even as a contract player, she was laid off for at least six weeks in July 1945 and was off the screen entirely in 1946, which must have made her income from radio all the more important. Yet these were Moorhead's glory days in American movies. She turned out stellar performances in films like *Jane Eyre*, *Since You Went Away*, *The Woman in White*, and *Dark Passage* and was Oscar-nominated no less than three times during her years on *Mayor of the Town*: for *The Magnificent Ambersons*, *Mrs. Parkington*, and *Johnny Belinda*.

On the domestic front, Moorehead's life during the 1940s was lived in three separate homes in Cheviot Hills. Though it did not have the cachet of Beverly Hills, Cheviot Hills was a quiet, comfortable, and affluent neighborhood located conveniently near MGM studios in Culver City. Moorehead and her husband, Jack Lee, first rented a house at 10268 Kincardine Ave., before buying their first home at 2702 Forrester Dr., a charming four-bedroom, 3,300 square foot home from 1928 on the corner of Monte Mar Drive.[2] In the spring of 1946, the couple moved just down the street to 2720 Monte Mar Terrace, a much grander, 21-room, Tudor Revival mansion, whose 0.63 acres backed directly onto the capacious grounds of the Hillcrest Country Club.[3] Without traffic, it would have taken Moorehead's chauffeur Frank about half an hour to drive the 8.8 miles from Cheviot

Hills to the CBS studio complex, which still stands at 6121 Sunset Blvd. in Hollywood.[4] Her *Mayor of the Town* co-star, Lionel Barrymore, drove in from his ranch in Chatsworth in northern Los Angeles.

Among the actors Moorehead worked with for a longer, consecutive period, Lionel Barrymore was certainly the most famous and respected in his own day. An actor since the age of 15, Barrymore would celebrate his 50th anniversary in the profession on a broadcast of *Mayor of the Town* on April 28, 1943, which also happened to be his 65th birthday. Unlike his equally famous siblings John and Ethel, Lionel had gravitated towards character roles even in his younger days. Like Moorehead, he has been called a "character star."[5] Never comfortable with stage acting, though he had notable successes in Broadway productions of *Peter Ibbetson* with his brother John in 1917 and *The Copperhead* with his first wife, Doris Rankin, in 1918, Lionel had been interested in acting in films since the earliest days of the American film industry and delivered many of his greatest performances on the big screen. As far back as 1911, he had asked D.W. Griffith for a job and ended up acting in more than 50 films for this director alone. After divorcing Rankin, with whom he had had two daughters who died in infancy, Barrymore married the actress Irene Fenwick in 1923. He retired from the stage, moved to Hollywood permanently in 1925, signed a long-term contract with MGM the following year, and would remain at the studio with "more stars than there are in the heavens" for the remainder of his film career: 28 years in all, making him the longest continuous contract player at Metro after Lewis Stone died in 1953.[6]

By the late 1930s, Barrymore had subsided into more or less benign grandfather roles on the screen, such as his eccentric Martin Vanderhof in *You Can't Take It with You* and the cantankerous but basically warm-hearted Julian "Gramps" Northrup in *On Borrowed Time.*[7] His film output in the 1940s would be dominated by the many "Dr. Kildare" films, where Lew Ayres played the title role and Barrymore his irascible mentor Dr. Gillespie, "everyone's favorite crotchety but essentially kind medico."[8] When Ayres was axed from the series for his pacifist stance during the war, the Dr. Kildare films became "Dr. Gillespie" films, though no less insipid and mediocre for all that.

During Barrymore's final years, he was also given some meatier opportunities in films like *It's a Wonderful Life*, *Duel in the Sun*, and *Key Largo*. He played a minister in *Since You Went Away*, his only screen performance with Moorehead, who played Claudette Colbert's self-involved, divorcee friend to great effect. Their *Mayor the Town* co-star Conrad Binyon even had a tiny role as a page. Barrymore made his final screen appearance playing himself in *Main Street to Broadway* in 1953, a film where Moorehead played a not very sympathetic theatrical agent, though they had no scenes together. At the end of the day, Lionel Barrymore had racked up more than 200 film credits, including standout roles in *A Free Soul*, which garnered him an Academy Award in 1931; *Grand Hotel*; *Rasputin and the Empress*, his only film with both his siblings; *Dinner at Eight*, *David Copperfield*, and *The Gorgeous Hussy*.

Despite professional advancement and financial success for Moorehead and, for Barrymore, the satisfaction of still being able to make a living after more than half a century as an actor, all was not easy during the 1940s. Beyond the challenges and strains of World War II, both performers had serious personal problems during the years they worked together on their mostly light-hearted, comical radio show. Moorehead's problems were marital, while Barrymore's were mainly financial. These years saw the slow, painful deterioration of Moorehead's marriage to Jack Lee, which they had entered on in 1930.

After a number of break-ups and reconciliations, they moved apart for good in mid–June 1949, just a few weeks before *Mayor of the Town* went off the air forever, though their divorce would not be final until 1952. Moorehead had already met her second husband, Bob Gist, on the set of *The Stratton Story* in late 1948.

The root of all evil in Barrymore's life was his owing a vast amount in back taxes to the Internal Revenue Service; so much, in fact, that MGM would hold back a large part of his weekly paycheck.[9] His income from *Mayor of the Town*, then, was vitally important to him. He may have been paid as much as $4,000 a week to do the show.[10] Charles Tranberg claims that Moorehead was initially paid $300 per week, rising $100 annually till she was finally earning $1,000 per week.[11] The total "estimated talent cost," that is the salaries of the cast, announcer, writers, and musicians, was estimated to be $7,500 per episode in 1947.[12]

When *Mayor of the Town* started in 1942, Barrymore had been a widower for five and a half years. Since his wife's death on Christmas Eve 1936, he had been making his home with three of her relatives from Minnesota: a widow his own age, Mary Ellen Wheeler, and her two unmarried daughters Benson and Florence.[13] With a keen eye to the main chance, the Wheelers had moved in on him as soon as Irene was dead, though the official version was that he had moved in with them. In the spring of 1939, Barrymore bought a 22-acre property in the Wheelers' name at 11050 Independence Ave. in Chatsworth, just south of the current Ronald Reagan Freeway, where the Sierra Canyon School is located today.[14] He lived there until his death. Barrymore still owned the Beverly Hills mansion at 802 N. Roxbury Dr. he had built in 1926. Staffed with a housekeeper, it stood unoccupied and unchanged as a shrine to his dead wife.[15] In 1952, Moorehead would move to North Roxbury Drive herself, just two and a half blocks up from Barrymore's house.

On the positive side, the 1940s saw Barrymore gain recognition as a composer with several of his pieces, including "In Memoriam"—a tone poem in memory of his brother John—being performed by professional orchestras.[16] Barrymore also composed the theme song for *Mayor of the Town*.[17] John Barrymore died in May 1942, just three months before *Mayor of the Town* premiered. Ethel moved out to the coast in 1946, though it wouldn't make much difference to her relationship with Lionel. "His solitary ways, his battered Olds, his rumpled ash-strewn clothes, his politics, his Wheelers—all alienated Ethel," writes the Barrymores' preeminent biographer, Margot Peters.[18]

To say that the Barrymores had addictive personalities was an understatement and Lionel was no exception. His particular poison was morphine, which he began to use medicinally to kill the pain in his legs and elsewhere and then became addicted to.[19] He also used cocaine on occasion and smoked avidly, though his major drinking days were behind him by the time *Mayor of the Town* came along.[20]

Apart from the smoking, which was ubiquitous, Moorehead probably did not know about Barrymore's addictions, nor do I imagine she'd heard the rumor in some quarters that he had syphilis.[21] She knew he had medical problems, though, telling her friend Warren Sherk: "I never heard him complain, even though he often was in intense pain."[22] The causes of his ambulatory problems were vague and varied with the telling.[23] Only one thing was certain: the old trouper was wheelchair-bound by the late 1930s and would be until his death. His battered-up Oldsmobile was specially fitted to accommodate his handicap.[24]

As a radio series, *Mayor of the Town* was generically diverse: part propagandistic war drama, part domestic comedy, even at times a mock-noirish crime drama. Radio historian

John Dunning describes it as a "comedy-drama."[25] The mayor of the title ruled benignly over Springdale, your average American small town in the popular imagination, which meant it had hardly any non-white people in it and hardly any genuine want, random violence, or social iniquity that couldn't be sorted out by the mayor's direct, paternalistic intervention. The mayor, who was never referred to by his proper name, was given to passionately patriotic monologues, grumbling, talking aloud to his dead wife, Ann, tending his rose bushes, and playing checkers with his friend Judge Williams. Being safely past the age of any combat use himself, he was always more than willing to encourage other, younger men to lay down their lives for their country. And not only men. When the young tomboy Amy Lou is torn between marriage to Jim, who is going off to war, and going off to war herself as a nurse, the mayor counsels her to use her "gift of healing." She follows his advice and is heroically but not fatally wounded. Naturally, no one ever really died on the show. Even the judge's son Tom, who went off to war on the mayor's encouragement and against his father's express wishes in the first episode and was promptly killed in the Coral Seas, turned out not to have died after all in episode 18.

During the first three seasons of the series, then, America was at war and storylines often centered around events and conflicts relating to the war. The focus was always on the mayor and his interaction with Springdale residents or visitors and helping to solve their problems, and the role of the mayor's housekeeper Marilly was really quite modest. Marilly was always threatening to quit, had an opinion about everything, larded her lingo with homely expressions likes "land sakes" and "stuff and nonsense," and had a certain malapropist tendency too (e.g., she calls grease monkeys "oil gorillas" in "Gone Fishing," which aired May 1, 1945).

Marilly did get a little romance, though, first in the unlikely form of a reformed forger, J. Morton Smith (Arthur Q. Bryan), whom she called a "wolf" for trying to hold her hand at the movies; and later in the shape of pool hall owner Clarence Jones (Lionel Stander), who wanted to marry her. In "The Mayor Recalls Scenes of Love in Springdale" (April 28, 1943), Moorehead and Stander even sang a little ditty during the interval to advertise the sponsor's "Rinso White" detergent. This was the same episode in which Barrymore's 50th anniversary as an actor and 65th birthday was celebrated on the air with cake and speeches after the main portion of the broadcast. Moorehead gave a speech in her most genteel, dulcet tones with rhetoric to match, so different from her harsh, grating voice quality as Marilly. James Cagney even stopped by to congratulate Barrymore on behalf of the Screen Actors Guild of which Cagney was then president.

MGM boss Louis B. Mayer, who loved sentimental, wartime films like *The Human Comedy*, heartily approved of two of his contract players contributing to this popular radio serial, which managed to ladle out as much patriotic gore as even the most lachrymose home front film. Barrymore was not allowed to do other radio series, while Moorehead certainly was.[26] She also appeared on *Suspense*, the *Jack Carson Show*, and the *Cavalcade of America* during these years.

The end of the war in 1945 was the only outward, historical event that impacted on the "timeless" quality of the plots and situations on *Mayor of the Town*. Peacetime naturally ushered in a more consistently comic spirit during the series' final years. Conrad Binyon has suggested that his casting in the third major role of Roscoe "Butch" Gardiner in 1945 "turned the plot line more into a family-like situation."[27] In truth, there had been various homeless or orphaned boys staying with the mayor and Marilly since the inception of the show, such as the plummy-voiced milksop Ronny in episode 5, "An 11 Year Old

As the youthful star of *Mayor of the Town*, Conrad Binyon (center) could not have known he was co-starring with a morphine addict and a woman in an abusive relationship. To him, Lionel Barrymore (right) and Agnes Moorehead were simply eminent actors and consummate professionals. In the second half of the 1940s, these three spent four years together creating domestic comedy on radio (courtesy Muskingum University Archives).

War Orphan" (October 7, 1942) and the mayor's 17-year-old nephew Jerry Turner, ubiquitous in the first season starting with "Finding Mary Meyer" (February 17, 1943). The addition of a youngster to the household allowed the three main characters to form an "alternative family" of mother, father, and child, even though the mayor was an aging widower, Marilly was an old maid, and Butch and his predecessors were orphans.

From the mid-1940s on, Marilly was more central to the action and got her own storylines. She acquired a sometimes friend in Abby Peters, who we hear a lot about, but never experience directly. The two women's rivalry comes to a head in "Marilly Runs for the School Board" (November 2, 1946), where Moorehead sounds more and more demented in her voice quality and interpretation of the role. Some of the best Marilly-centered episodes were actually from the show's latter years, such as "Sewing Circle Musical" and "Demetrius the Horse."

"Demetrius the Horse" is my favorite episode of *Mayor of the Town* and aired on February 20, 1949, as the series was winding down. The previous week, Moorehead had attended the wedding of her friend and interior decorator Tony Duquette to Elizabeth Johnstone, which was held at Mary Pickford's estate, Pickfair.[28] The week after this broadcast, Jack Lee's mother Susan Ping Lee O'Neill died in San Francisco at the age of 68.[29] In the episode, Marilly and the sewing circle are celebrating springtime by planting flowers in a park and Butch and the mayor have to get their lunch elsewhere. Marilly doesn't get back till after 6:30. It turns out she has been to the police station to complain about a "naked" horse in the park that had the audacity to eat the flowers. The ladies have had the horse arrested! The horse "Demetrius" belongs to a local flower peddler called Pete Griswold. Always a man of action and a problem-solver, the mayor clandestinely takes the horse from the alley back of the jail and puts it in his tool shed, but Marilly discovers what he's up to. "You planned to make this tool shed a horse's hideout. I should think you'd be ashamed," she says. The mayor finally gets around Marilly by suggesting that the peddler was planning to sell flowers named for the ladies of the sewing circle, such as the "Marilly Jones geranium" (in white letters right on the pot). When she hears of the peddler's ostensible plan, Marilly offers to try to get the "fickle girls" to withdraw the charges. She ends up making a nose bag for the horse with "his name right on it." Amusingly, in this episode Moorehead uses the tick of clearing her throat to indicate consternation, just as her "Aunt Cam" famously did (at least in the version of her Moorehead presented in her one-woman show).

As would later be the case with *Bewitched*, Moorehead did not appear in every episode. It sounds, though, as if she may have played other female roles in some of the episodes where Marilly did not put in an appearance. In "Amy Lou Goes to War" (September 20, 1942), she is probably playing a snooty lady who doesn't want her son Jim to marry the local tomboy and gets a talking to from the mayor ("I just don't like you"). In the aforementioned "Finding Mary Meyer," Moorehead actually gets a better opportunity than Marilly usually provided when she plays the diabolical Frieda, who frames her sister Mary Meyer for the murder of Mary's husband that she herself has committed. The put-upon sister, a famous novelist who has had to go into hiding, was played by Beulah Bondi, a top-tier Hollywood character actress with credits to rival Moorehead's own.

There is a Norwegian expression for the ease with which Lionel Barrymore could play the mayor: he could do it with his head under his arm and his arm in a sling. The same goes for Moorehead. Marilly was the kind of comic spinster stereotype she had been playing since her earliest days in radio. In artistic terms, she was right back where she started. In what is otherwise a positive review of the first episode, we can read in *Radio Digest*: "Agnes Moorehead, the housekeeper, will probably become a source of kitchen humor, though she is a bit weak as constant foil for the lead character."[30] Five years later, when the show had transferred to ABC, a writer for *The Billboard* wrote a scathing review of an episode that aired on November 19, 1947. About the show as a whole, Jerry Franken writes that it "adds lustre to none of the participants concerned" and is "devoid of merit: The entire affair on the evening caught was distressing, painfully so, and it is lamentable to observe the talents of a Lionel Barrymore (the mayor) and that sterling character actress, Agnes Moorehead (Marilly) being frittered away in so disgraceful a manner. From its very inception, almost every phase of *Mayor of the Town* is the most palpable of contrivance; stock characters, stock plot and the lowest grade of corn." Franken continues: "Miss Moorehead, who has given memorable performances both in radio and films, plays Marilly with a leaden hand; the character emerges as a shrew and a harpy, with a grating, irritating nasal voice." "As the mayor," Franken concludes, "Barrymore plays his part down his nose, as usual."[31]

Despite its stereotypical characters and situations, ideological blind spots, and simplified view of reality—maybe because of them—there is still something charming and idyllic about the series. Was life ever that simple? Were good and bad ever so clearly demarcated? Of course, they weren't; not then and certainly not now, but to quote the final line of Hemingway's *The Sun Also Rises*: "Isn't it pretty to think so?"

Radio Life assured its readers in a May 1946 feature article that Moorehead "adores working with Barrymore and always, with husband Jack, accompanies him to dinner at the Colony House on Saturday night after the broadcast."[32] The article even included a photo of the two of them at the restaurant, Moorehead and Barrymore that is. "Husband Jack" may have been cropped out. Conrad Binyon doubted the magazine's claims about the weekly dinner. "Mostly we all just went home," he recalled.[33] Moorehead would probably not have adored Barrymore's infamously foul mouth.[34] Binyon could confirm that he "often used salty language."[35] Long after her Barrymore's death, Moorehead kept a signed photograph of him on a table in her home and called it one of her "treasured photos."[36] She credited him with having invented the "overhead boom for radio." "He got the idea ... while fishing," she said.[37] Barrymore called Moorehead "one of the greatest actresses in the business."[38]

There is no sign that Moorehead and Barrymore kept in touch after the show ended, though they may have seen each other from time to time on the MGM lot, where Barrymore had a suite of rooms in a bungalow next to the school house until his death.[39] Moorehead's long-term contract with the studio ended in 1950. Barrymore died in 1954.

Not many people could say they had spent several teenage years acting with Lionel Barrymore and Agnes Moorehead. Indeed, there was only person in the world who could say that truthfully and that was Conrad Binyon. On May 10, 2007, Conrad, who was then 76, and his wife, Cathy Campbell, picked me up at the UCLA Guest House in Westwood, where I was staying during my first week in Los Angeles.[40] They lived in an apartment in Encino and drove me out to a favorite restaurant of theirs in Malibu. On the drive, I sat up front with Conrad; Cathy, a former nurse from Missouri and Conrad's wife of 22 years, sat in the back and formed an accompaniment to our walk down memory lane.

Conrad Ambress Binyon was born into an ordinary, working-class family in Los Angeles on January 30, 1931.[41] His father, William Ambress Binyon, had been born in

Chico, Texas, in 1906. During the 1930s and into the '40s, he is listed in the Los Angeles city directory as a cook. During the war, Conrad told me his father worked for Consolidated Steel Shipyards, before moving on in 1945, the year Conrad joined the *Mayor of the Town* cast, to a job as a utility worker at Paramount Studios.[42] Conrad's mother, Ann Dorothy Zelichovics, had been born in Hungary in 1910 and immigrated to the United States when she was 12. Prior to devoting herself full-time to marriage and motherhood, she worked at the Community Laundry in Hollywood.[43] She became a naturalized American citizen in 1943.[44]

Conrad's parents had met and married in Los Angeles. Ten months after their wedding on April 2, 1930,[45] Conrad was born, followed by his younger brother, Hugh William, in 1932. During Conrad's childhood and youth, his family lived in various modest homes in central Hollywood, which meant that he could walk or bicycle to CBS studios on Sunset Boulevard and to the movie studios in the neighborhood. Conrad had about 30, mostly uncredited roles in Hollywood films between his debut as an unnamed little boy in *Life Begins with Love* in 1937, when he was 6, and his final role playing an elevator boy in *My Blue Love* in 1950. He co-starred as Grisha in *The Boy from Stalingrad* and had named, credited roles in *Good Luck, Mr. Yates* and *The Underdog*, all three released in 1943.

Conrad was better known, though, for his recurring roles in two widely popular radio series: *Mayor of the Town*, where he co-starred from 1945 till the series' end in 1949; and the record-breaking, three-decade long, NBC soap opera *One Man's Family*, where he played the recurring character Henry Herbert "Hank" Murray from 1939 till 1950.[46] As a boy, Conrad Binyon was no pretty, delicate Dickie Moore type, nor was he a comically cute George "Spanky" McFarland. Rather, he was your typical skinny, straight-haired, fresh-faced boy next door. Not that it mattered what he looked like in radio…

When he was 14, then, something quite extraordinary happened to him, which would prove one of the formative experiences of his life. He was cast as Butch in *Mayor of the Town*, which had been airing over CBS since 1942. Even after 60 years, he still had vivid memories of his years spent on *Mayor of the Town*. Conrad told me that "The character of Butch didn't stem from the show's beginning: I seem to recall about three years or so playing the character, who was introduced as a boy who lost both his parents in an auto accident. Prior to that, the story line involved the mayor in city administrative plots, police investigations, and fraud schemes against citizens. The Butch character became the mayor's ward and turned the plot line more into a family-like situation."[47] He attributed the show's continuing appeal to "the diverseness of the storyline plots. The mayor ran a city where all sorts of activity could generate intrigue. The mayor had a family-like household for plots regarding relationships."[48]

About Lionel Barrymore, he had this to say:

> I was in his sphere as a co-worker and that was about it. For one thing, I was about 15 years old when doing the show and I hadn't seen any of his work other than what he'd done in the MGM Dr. Kildare series. I hadn't seen his *Captain's Courageous* role, or his Rasputin role with his brother and sister John and Ethel. Had I seen any of his earlier works, undoubtedly I would have asked the questions that would have peaked [sic] my curiosity about them. I held Lionel Barrymore in a sense of awe due to his stature in the business and his celebrity history. Yes, for sure I liked him.[49]

Conrad went out of his way to help the old man when he arrived at the studio for rehearsals and broadcasts. Conrad would be waiting "at the CBS Station back building area where he'd park his car":

> I had the studio wheelchair for him to use and I'd wheel him to his microphone and table stage location, where he'd stay the entire time of the show's broadcast (save for bathroom breaks). I'd like to think he appreciated the fact that I was always there to assist his entrance into the studio and that he didn't have to crutch himself all the way inside. I did have a continuing tease with him though. I once mentioned the Tower of Babel and pronounced Babel to rhyme with "Babble." He corrected me with "Bayble" and following from then I always said "Babble" and he'd come back with "Bayble" in an admonishing tone. I rather hope he caught on to my little leg pull and did not think I was that dumb.

"Other than that," Conrad concluded, "we didn't have a lot of conversations. When we did have anything to say, we were cordial."[50]

Conrad is the only person I've interviewed who knew Jack Lee well, keeping in mind that he was only a teenager at the time. He had no idea, for example, about Moorehead's marital problems. As he said to Charles Tranberg: "Of course I didn't go around prying into her private life, for it was none of my business, but she never said that to me."[51] To me, Conrad said: "When I realized the guy I usually saw hanging around her was her husband Jack Lee, I asked myself why she hadn't picked a more handsome guy."[52]

While working on *Mayor of the Town* with Moorehead, Conrad also got to know Jack. He would visit the couple at their "Monte Mar home," where he remembered Jack had his own bedroom "masculinely decorated."[53] He and Jack shared an interest in aviation. Jack would have friends with planes and would go on trips with them. Jack gave him an E6B computer, which is used to navigate planes. It had been used and was probably one he didn't need anymore. Once Jack came by in his jeep on which he had painted "Marilly" on the side. When Jack took the wheel down a straight stretch of road in Cheviot Hills, he drove so fast Conrad feared for his life. He also recalled that Jack had a bit part in a film called *Berlin Express*.[54]

Conrad remembered Moorehead's second husband, Bob Gist, as well. His take was that Gist had married Moorehead to further his career. Conrad had never thought of her as a sexual or sensual creature, thus he had to reassess her when she got into a relationship with Gist. As he remembered her, Moorehead was not beautiful or glamorous, but she was elegant. She had a trim, slim body, as he noticed once when she came down in a leotard in the Beverly Hills house. He never heard the lesbian rumors, nor thought of her in those terms. She was a woman very focused on her career, he said. He never met Moorehead's foster son, Sean.

As we were driving back to Westwood, Conrad hit upon a word that he thought best described Moorhead as he remembered her from the '40s. That word was *whimsical*. She was playful and willing to play along with you and see the comic aspects of life, he told me. Once when a secretary to the sponsor used the "F" word quite unexpectedly in reaction to some story in the studio, Moorehead said "Barbara!" is such a comical way it cracked everyone up.

After he graduated from Hollywood High School, Conrad joined the air force and was commissioned on March 16, 1954.[55] His more than 20 years of military service would take him to several overseas postings in Japan and in Europe. While in France, he met and married Renée Valsaque. Moorehead was invited to their wedding in Nancy on March 31, 1962.[56] She was performing in *Prescription: Murder* at the Fisher Theatre in Detroit at the time.[57] Conrad remembered that she once performed part of her one-woman show for the soldiers at his camp in Georgia. He could also recall that he had driven her from one venue to another when she was touring in *The Rivalry*. She referred to her co-star Raymond Massey as "Mr. B.O."

As her scrapbooks amply show, throughout the 1960s Conrad sent her post cards, Christmas cards, and letters from Europe; bases in Sumter, South Carolina, and San Antonio, Texas; and from Vietnam, where he spent a year in 1965–66 as a reconnaissance officer.[58]

He wrote to congratulate her on her Emmy win in 1967: "I just loved it when you said, 'I don't believe it!'"[59] He asked her to write to a dying child, Judith Ann Guerra, the daughter of his friends.[60] She did.

Indeed, Conrad kept in touch with Moorehead till she died and she was always happy to hear from him: "Whenever I felt an urge to visit Agnes, and for the life of me I don't know why they ever came up, I'd call her phone number to see if she was busy. One day she said she was having to have a 'Bewitched' rehearsal and I should come meet her at the studio. I drove down and did just that and she introduced me to all the 'Bewitched' cast."[61] In later years, he would visit Moorehead in Beverly Hills when he was in town and they would sit in the living room and talk. He remembered seeing her Emmy there. She also gave him the tour of the house, which included her bedroom decorated in lavender. He thought the last time he saw his old friend was at a read-through for an episode of *Bewitched* in the early 1970s. Conrad couldn't recall how he heard of her death.

CREDITS: *Director:* Jack Van Nostrand; *Producers:* Murray Bolen, Don Clark, Knowles Entrikin; *Writers:* Howard Blake, Howard Breslin, Jean Holloway, Erna Lazarus, Leonard St. Clair, Charles Tazewell; *Sound:* Joseph Cohen, Mary Ann Gideon, David Light, Al Span; *Musical director:* Gordon Jenkins, Bernard Katz, Frank Worth; *Theme music:* Composed by Lionel Barrymore; *Advertising agency's secretary to the producer:* Barbara Smitten; *Air dates:* September 6–27, 1942 over NBC; October 7, 1942–May 31, 1947, over CBS; October 8, 1947–January 30, 1948, over ABC; January 2–July 3, 1949, over Mutual

CAST: Lionel Barrymore (mayor), Conrad Binyon (Butch), Agnes Moorehead (Marilly); Robert Bailey, Edgar Barrier, Bea Benaderet, Sidney Blackmer, Beulah Bondi, Arthur Q. Bryan, Marjorie Davies, Sharon Douglas, Carl Esmond, Stan Ferrar, Jerry Hausner, Bob Hope, Joseph Kearns, Cy Kendall, Irvin Lee, Diana Lynn, Priscilla Lyon, Fred MacKaye, Gloria McMillan, Eddie Marr, Frank Martin (announcer), Gerald Mohr, Ken Peters (announcer), William Roy, Charles Ruggles, Lionel Stander, Claire Trevor, Lurene Tuttle, Ted Von Eltz, Janet Waldo, Harlow Wilcox (announcer), Paula Winslowe, Jane Withers, Will Wright

3

Suspense (Radio, 1943–60)

By any measure, qualitative or quantitative, *Suspense* was the most significant radio program Agnes Moorehead acted on, not simply because it was "one of radio's glamour showcases,"[1] but because it so uniquely showcased her particular talents. Moorehead had many talents: for mimicry, for wearing clothes, for dialects and sociolects, for the telling gesture. In *Suspense*, "radio's outstanding theater of thrills," she was able to exhibit to the full her talent for projecting extreme psychological states and what we today would call "personality disorders" (in addition to her legendary screaming). It was a show that trafficked in terror, paranoia, imposture, ambiguity, sadism, venality, meddlesomeness, and just plain evil; moods and states Moorehead was supremely suited to projecting and enacting. When she was good, she was good, but when she was bad, she was better!

While J. Alfred Prufrock measured out his life with coffee spoons, one might say that Agnes Moorehead measured out her life with episodes of *Suspense*; or more specifically, with broadcasts of her most famous *Suspense* episode, "Sorry, Wrong Number." For anyone unfamiliar with the plot of this drama, here is Louella Parsons's concise summary: "A woman picks up a telephone, discovers she is on a crossed line and is just about to hang up when she realizes she's listening in on a murder being planned. What she doesn't know—until too late, is that it is her own murder."[2]

By the time the landmark first broadcast of Lucille Fletcher's thriller hit the airwaves on Tuesday, May 25, 1943, Moorehead had been living in Los Angeles for about a year and a half. She had been a contract player at MGM since the fall of 1942. At that time, she also began supporting Lionel Barrymore on the radio series *Mayor of the Town*, which was broadcast from the same CBS studios on Sunset Boulevard as was *Suspense* for most of its 20-year run. Moorehead, who was 43, was married to fellow actor Jack Lee and the couple lived in Cheviot Hills, near MGM in Culver City.

When "Sorry, Wrong Number" aired for the second time in August 1943, Moorehead was just done with *Government Girl* back at her first studio, RKO, and was playing "Calliope Aggie" in Orson Welles's *Mercury Wonder Show* in a tent on Cahuenga Boulevard. The papers were already referring to her efforts as "one of the memorable performances of radio history." "Miss Moorehead's playing of this extraordinary role has rarely, if ever, been equaled on the air," we can read in one article she cut out and kept until her death.[3]

On the day of the third broadcast on February 24, 1944, *Variety* wrote that she was to have the second lead role in *Mrs. Parkington* at MGM.[4] Moorehead had campaigned vigorously for the role of Aspasia Conti, which would lead to her second Academy Award nomination in 1945. The fourth time "Sorry, Wrong Number" aired was on September 6, 1945, and coincided with the New York premiere of *Our Vines Have Tender Grapes*, which Moorehead was unlikely to have attended. Moorehead was touted as "the Metro-Goldwyn-Mayer star, Miss Agnes Moorehead" in the introduction to this episode, which was ironic, as Metro had laid her off that summer. She would not act in her next film,

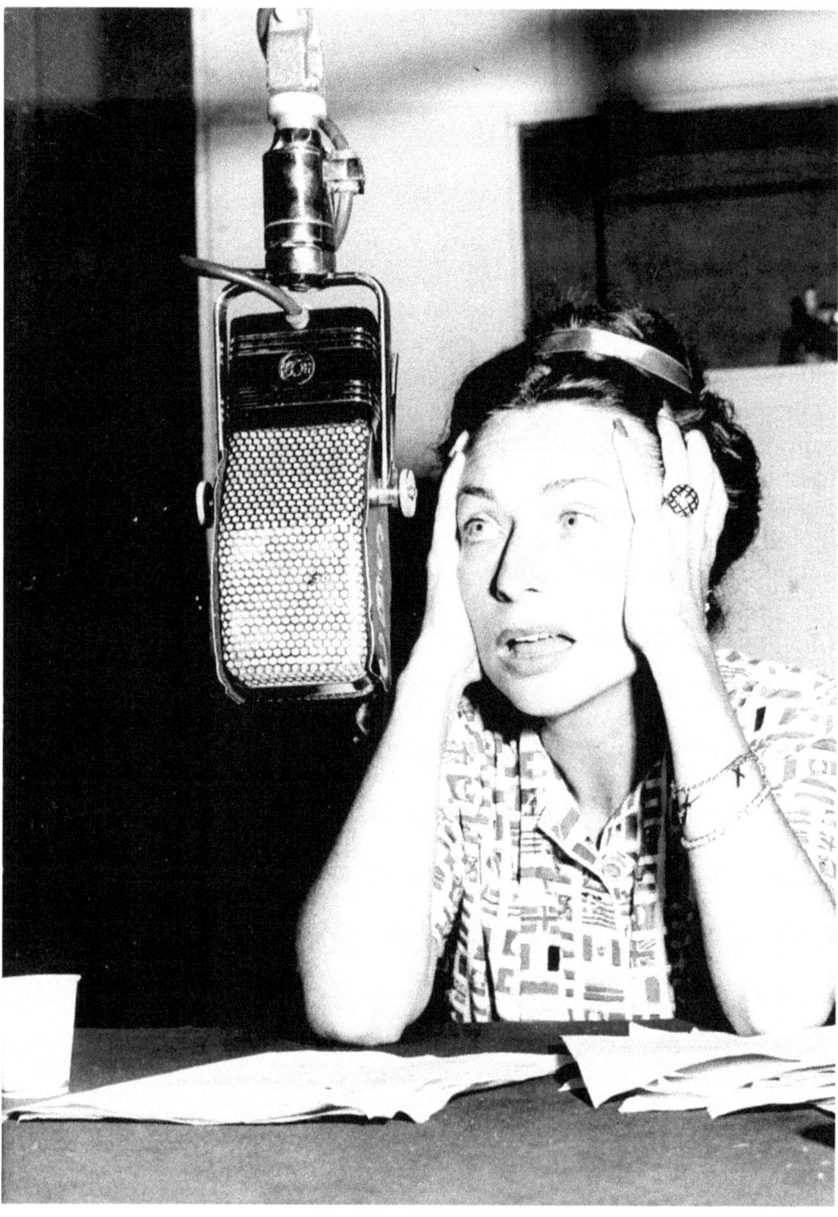

Agnes Moorehead performed her tour de force drama "Sorry, Wrong Number" no less than eight times on *Suspense*. This press photograph shows her after the fourth broadcast on September 6, 1945. *Suspense* was broadcast from CBS studios at Columbia Square on Sunset Boulevard, where Moorehead also did *Mayor of the Town* for many years.

The Beginning or the End, until the spring of 1946 and, to make matters worse, her part in that film was cut entirely. She would be off the screen all through 1946.

The fifth "Sorry" broadcast was on November 18, 1948, while Moorehead was busy filming *The Stratton Story* at MGM with James Stewart and June Allyson. Her marriage to Jack Lee was in deep trouble by this point and she would meet her future husband, Bob Gist, on the set of this film, where he had a small supporting role. News items about the forthcoming broadcast referred to "Sorry, Wrong Number" as "radio's most famous play," "the most exciting radio drama ever written," and "the world's most famous radio play."[5] According to a columnist writing in 1951, Moorehead was "the most requested star among 'Suspense' listeners."[6]

By the time Moorehead performed "Sorry, Wrong Number" for the sixth time on September 15, 1952, she and Jack Lee had divorced and she was living with Gist and her foster son, Sean, in her luxurious new home in Beverly Hills, which she called "Villa Agnese." The day after the broadcast, the fourth and final national tour of Shaw's *Don Juan in Hell* opened in Santa Barbara.[7] The seventh version of "Sorry" was recorded on a day off from touring in *The Rivalry* with Raymond Massey and Martin Gabel in October 1957.[8] During the 1950s, work on the stage and in television would more and more take over for work in films and on radio. Moorehead had filed for divorce from Gist in April 1957.

When *Suspense* aired her eighth and final performance as Mrs. Elbert Smythe Stevenson on Valentine's Day 1960, Moorehead had just received her star on Hollywood's "Walk of Fame." This turned out to be her swan song on the series, which lasted another year and a half. Each and every time, Moorehead did the performance live and from scratch, though there were no major changes in the script down through the years. James Robert Parish observes that "she would always do the show fresh through, never memorizing her lines, for fear it would remove the spontaneity of her changing characterization."[9]

On the anecdotal level, I want to remind my readers that Mrs. Stevenson's address is 53 Sutton Place in New York City. Today at least, there is no such house number, but there are two narrow, old-fashioned row houses at no. 31 and no. 33 and we might well imagine the beleaguered invalid living in one of them. The ramp of the Queensboro Bridge looms over Sutton Place just north of this block, on the other side of E. 59th St. You recall that the murder is timed for 11:15 p.m., so that a train crossing a bridge drowns out Mrs. Stevenson's dying screams. Funnily enough, Moorehead had lived in Sutton Place herself in the summer of 1934.[10]

If it hasn't been made clear enough already, "Sorry, Wrong Number" was one of Moorehead's most famous and recognizable performances. Orson Welles called the 30-minute drama the "greatest single radio script ever written."[11] Moorehead's other important mentor, Charles Laughton, told a friend "with a grimace half angelic and half impish: Until you've seen Aggie Moorehead playing her own special bit of dramatic caviar, 'Sorry, Wrong Number,' you haven't lived, old boy."[12] *Seen* might seem an odd choice of words about a radio play, but Laughton was referring to the fact that for several years Moorehead included a shortened version of her tour de force performance in her one-woman show *That Fabulous Redhead*.[13]

From her home in Santa Barbara, renowned German soprano Lotte Lehmann wrote "the first 'fan letter' which I have written in my life" to thank Moorehead for "a shuddering experience and unique excitement." "Acting has always been for me the most interesting and most important part of my opera career," she added, "and therefore I appreciate your art perhaps more than I can express."[14] Even Louella Parsons, who bore a grudge against anyone even remotely connected with that travesty of her boss William Randolph Hearst's life *Citizen Kane*, had words of praise for Moorehead's performance. "It's the finest of all radio dramas and if you haven't heard Agnes Moorehead do it—you've missed the greatest radio chiller of all time," she wrote in her column in 1947.[15] Norman Nadel pulled out all the stops in a feature article on Moorehead in 1949: "on a May night in 1943, the phrase ["sorry, wrong number"] embarked on an entirely new career. It signaled a major achievement in the field of radio entertainment. It stood for a dramatic performance by which all others were to be measured."[16] A dissenting, contemporary view is expressed by John Dunning, who writes in his magisterial encyclopedia of old-time radio, that he finds "Sorry, Wrong Number" "rather boring: the remarkable performance by Agnes Moorehead is lost in its unbelievable premise."[17]

For better or worse, the powerful and lasting impact of "Sorry, Wrong Number" has tended to overshadow Moorehead's many other fine performances on *Suspense* and on radio in general. Moorehead herself recognized this. In a lengthy interview with Chuck Schaden in 1971, she reminded him that "I played on *Suspense* many, many times. There were some marvelous shows in there." In answer to the question if "Sorry, Wrong Number" was "your most exciting radio performance," she responded adamantly: "No, no. I've done loads of exciting radio performances. That just happens to be a memorable one. I have done many of them."[18]

In the remainder of this chapter, I want to focus on the breadth and variety of Moorehead's performances during her 17 years on *Suspense*, which coincided with the major phase of her Hollywood film career. Between 1943 and 1960, Moorehead made 32 appearances on *Suspense* in 21 different dramas, including the eight times playing her signature role as Mrs. Elbert Smythe Stevenson in "Sorry, Wrong Number." As her radio career dwindled in the 1950s, *Suspense* remained one of the few radio programs she still appeared on regularly; in fact, the majority of her dramatic performances in radio in that decade were on *Suspense*. During the 1950s, too, when she was mostly mired in mediocre or downright ludicrous supporting roles on the big screen, *Suspense* allowed her to return to the type of unsettling or downright unsympathetic roles she had delineated so effectively in her films of the '40s, such as *Dark Passage*, *Since You Went Away*, and *Jane Eyre* and even in comedies like *The Big Street*, *The Youngest Profession*, and *Government Girl*.

On *Suspense*, Moorehead played both victims and victimizers. In her debut episode, "The Diary of Sophronia Winters," an old maid from Kalamazoo, Michigan, finally finds romance in St. Petersburg, Florida, only her husband turns out to be a psychopath haunted by his dead yet still detested sister-in-law. Hiram Johnson projects his hatred onto his wife, because she bears the same name and ultimately drives her mad. In a somewhat similar pattern, in "To Find Help" Moorehead was Mrs. Gillis, a widow who becomes a prisoner in her own home after her hired man, played to chilling effect by a 29-year-old Frank Sinatra, turns out to be mentally disturbed.

Josie Archer in "Post Mortem" is in mortal danger from her nefarious, grasping husband, who keeps trying to "accidentally" push the sun lamp into the bathtub while Josie is in it! Moorehead played this delightful, former actress flibbertigibbet with a fluty, genteel, high-pitched and ultra-feminine voice, creating her most memorable comically inflected character on *Suspense*. In "Death and Miss Turner," the amnesiac heroine Rachel Turner is slowly brought back to life, memory, and identity after a traumatic train wreck in which the man she was painting died, while she survived. They had switched places shortly before the accident to give her better light. Indeed, not infrequently in these stories, the protagonists' seemingly innocuous actions have unforeseen, disastrous consequences.

In "The Trap," an unmarried secretary's delinquent sister engineers a plan to imprison her in her own home in retaliation for being sent to reform school. The increasingly strident and fractious Miss Helen Crane is not a likeable woman, so the listener is left wondering who we are supposed to identify with in all this. We have the same problem in *Suspense*'s adaptation of Charlotte Perkins Gilman's classic feminist short story "The Yellow Wallpaper." In the story, we identify with the plight of the unnamed woman protagonist, who is being treated like a child by her husband, but Moorehead being Moorehead plays the role with a fussy matronliness and increasingly Grand Guignol histrionics—entirely convincing as far as the character's descent into madness is concerned—but it does not make us care much about her plight.

Moorehead also played her share of unsympathetic characters on *Suspense* who were decidedly *not* victims: killers, termagant wives, meddlesome spinsters, and con women. In "The Thirteenth Sound," Moorehead plays a murderous wife and her former *The Shadow* co-star, William Johnstone, a cunning sheriff, who manipulates a confession out of her; in "The Chain," a disgruntled, spiteful, and envious, lower middle-class Southern housewife sends a chain letter and unwittingly sets off a sequence of events that leaves several people dead, including her husband; in "The Evil of Adelaide Winters," the titular heroine is a bogus medium who preys on families who have lost their sons in the war. She does her job so well, she is almost annihilated by a zealous father, who wants to be reunited with his son in death and take her with him as his spectral spouse. It was on this broadcast, Moorehead was first called the "First Lady of Suspense," "a title I'll always cherish," she said in an on-air interview with announcer Harlow Wilcox after her performance.

Even Adelaide Winters pales in comparison with the iniquity, never proven, of likely real-life murderess Lizzie Borden, who Moorehead portrayed in "The Fall River Tragedy" in January 1952. My favorite *Suspense* villain, though, has to be Lori Rider in Moorehead's penultimate appearance "Don't Call Me Mother." A major entry in the long, proud American tradition of "silver cord" dramas, this radio play by the series' producer William N. Robson harkens back to such classics as Sidney Howard's play *The Silver Cord*, which gave the phenomenon its name, and Rose Franken's play *Another Language* and is reminiscent of a contemporary film written and directed by Clifford Odets called *The Story on Page One*. The phenomenon in question was the too cozy and co-dependent relationship of a mother and her son, in this case the aforementioned Lori and her foster son, Larry. Lori keeps saying to Larry "Don't call me mother," hence the episode's title.

"Don't Call Me Mother" employs retrospective first-person narration by Lori, which ties together a series of chronological scenes between her, Larry, and the third angle of this love triangle: Larry's love interest and later wife, Roberta. Before Roberta impinges on their domestic idyll, Lori and Larry Rider are often referred to as "a lovely couple." Then, out of the blue when Larry is 25, he announces that he wants to bring a "special friend" home for dinner, who turns out to be 28-year-old colleague Roberta. Lori feigns disbelief: "Why Larry, what's come over you? You've never been interested in girls." In a delicious scene, she does what she can to disconcert and undermine Roberta at the dinner, suggesting she is too old for Larry: "You're older than Larry, aren't you Roberta?" Finally, making no progress in splitting up the young couple, Lori's gloves come off and she warns Roberta outright: "If you try to take Larry away from me, it will be the death of you."

Larry and Roberta marry, even after Lori has had a fit at the mere idea and claimed she has heart trouble. They assure her she will be welcome to live with them and Larry will always take care of her. Lori has also claimed that Larry's father died insane and that Larry may have inherited the illness. After the wedding, Lori spreads the rumor that Roberta is mentally unstable and even plants a seed of doubt in Larry that the child Roberta is expecting may not be his. Finally, the two plan to kill Roberta by Larry driving the car off a cliff and jumping out at the last moment, but the plan misfires and Lori ends up pushing Roberta off the cliff herself. The police show up the next morning with Roberta's wristwatch, where unbeknownst to them she has engraved: "I have only one enemy in the world. If anything should happen to me my mother-in-law will be the cause." Larry cracks when confronted with the damning evidence, turning on Lori with harsh recriminations. She ends up shooting him dead, but is prevented from killing herself and being reunited with Larry in death. Lori's last line returns us to the opening: "Larry and Lori, such a lovely couple, people always said."

A common denominator for the many stories on *Suspense* is that they often deal with ordinary people in extraordinary circumstances. While that is true for many of Moorehead's episodes as well, I think some of her best entries deal more specifically with the individual who, from more or less benevolent motives, harms others even when intending to help. As we know, the path to hell is paved with good intentions. The young couple in "Uncle Henry's Rose Bush" only want to surprise the wife's aging aunt and uncle, but end up forcing the aunt to kill her deranged husband. In "The Death Parade," the discovery of a letter on the street by a meddlesome spinster brings about the very result she is ostensibly trying to prevent, that is the death of the addressee of the letter. Journalist Amy Sears in an adaptation of Charles Dickens's "The Signalman" only wants to interview the lonely railway worker of the title, but ends up indirectly being the cause of his death when her appearance reawakens traumatic memories from the past.

In order to offer what the famous tag line called "A tale well calculated to keep you in ... *suspense*," the 30-minute *Suspense* radio dramas used different storytelling strategies. "The Diary of Sophronia Winters," was, as the title suggests, in the form of a diary, which allowed the intermittent, first-person narration by Sophronia to stay temporally close to the ongoing action, while maintaining suspense as to what would happen next. The diary entries segue seamlessly into fully dramatized scenes, where we witness the heroine's experiences directly, especially her interaction with her increasingly erratic and threatening husband, Hiram Johnson, played by her old Mercury and *Magnificent Ambersons* colleague Ray Collins. It is only at the close that we learn that Sophronia is reading aloud from her diary to a nurse in a mental hospital, where she has been committed after killing Hiram with an axe to the head.

This diary form in "Sophronia Winters" is a minor variant of a common radio play structure, where the dramatized scenes are tied together through the narration of the protagonist. This form is found in several of Moorehead's *Suspense* dramas: in "To Find Help," "The Thirteenth Sound," "The Yellow Wallpaper," "The Trap," "The Chain," "The Evil of Adelaide Winters," "Death and Miss Turner," "The Signalman," "The Wreck of the Maid of Athens," and "Don't Call Me Mother." The character-narrator in these cases does not have a specific listener or audience in the world of the story. It is as if she is speaking aloud to herself and we, unacknowledged, get to listen in.

"The Death Parade," "Weekend Special: Death," and "The Fall River Tragedy" are structured in a related but slightly different way in the form of a dramatic monologue on the part of the main character to a specific human recipient, which creates a frame around the dramatized scenes we experience first-hand. In "The Death Parade," the dramatic monologue is told by the zealous spinster Miss Ellen Johnson to the police after she has been involved in the mysterious death of a young woman named Sheila Mannix. In the serio comic "Weekend Special: Death," the narration is conducted by Ellen's soul sister, the unmarried secretary Rita Dorsey, who starts out going grocery shopping on a Saturday evening after work and ends up being locked into the store and having to "take out" two burglars, before they finish her off instead. She relates her extraordinary experiences to her boss, Lee Stanley, who conveniently in this case is a defense lawyer. In "The Fall River Tragedy," we encounter Lizzie Borden in later life, grateful for the opportunity to tell her side of the story to a visiting journalist. In classic dramatic monologue style, we literally only hear her side of the story, as the newspaperman remains silent. Borden's monologue segues into dramatized scenes from the murder trial, where her arch nemesis, the prosecutor Mr. Moody, plays a dominant role. All these cases involve a large degree of after-the-fact self-justification, which the one-sided dramatic monologue is ideally suited for.

Beyond these various forms of character narration, we find some episodes that are fully dramatized from beginning to end, that is we enter the action *in medias res* and observe all the characters from the outside; no character narrates the story or gives us an inside view. This is the case in "The Sisters," which depends for its effect on a fundamental uncertainty about Lydia Haskell's motivation for ordering a coffin for herself three weeks before she dies; "Post Mortem," based on a story by Cornell Woolrich about a seemingly daffy actress-turned-housewife, who effectively foils her husband's plan to kill her and cash in on her insurance and a $150,000 winning sweepstakes ticket; "The Empty Chair," a modern morality tale about the dangers of driving too fast; and "Headshrinker," a rather tedious drama of the psychiatrist's coach variety, where a middle-aged woman is finally able to free herself from her unhealthy dependency on her therapist when he is forced to admit he needs her more than she needs him.

The most famous example of this fully dramatized, scenic form, where everything is dialogue, is "Sorry, Wrong Number." Indeed, this drama is not entirely the monologue it is often thought to be, because we also get to hear from Mrs. Stevenson's interlocutors—various operators, Sergeant Martin of Precinct 43, and a Western Union telegraphist—and, of course, the infamous conversation between the killer-for-hire George and the middleman for his "client," Mr. Stevenson. Thus, ironically, in "Sorry, Wrong Number" we are overhearing Mrs. Stevenson's conversations without the power to intervene, just as she overhears the two men plotting the murder without being able to influence the outcome either.

In "Sorry, Wrong Number," the choice of an external point of view turns out to be portentous. While so many of Moorehead's characters on *Suspense*, like Sophronia Winters, Mrs. Gillis in "To Find Help," the nameless narrator of "The Yellow Wallpaper," and the painter Rachel Turner in "Death and Miss Turner," live to tell their own thrilling stories, Mrs. Stevenson obviously does not. It had originally been intended that she should be saved by the police in the nick of time, but producer William Spier's wife, the writer Kay Thompson, "felt the happy ending was a yawn and jokingly suggested a more grisly denouement," according to Thompson's biographer Sam Irvin.[19] Radio historian John Dunning observes that it was a rare thing for crime to go unpunished on *Suspense*.[20] Among Moorehead's episodes, it only happened in "Sorry, Wrong Number" and a minor drama called "The Whole Town's Sleeping," where a killer is on the loose and finally murders Moorehead's character just when she thinks she has made it safely home from the movies.

Agness Moorehead's Appearances on *Suspense* (CBS, 1943–1960)[21]

"The Diary of Sophronia Winters" (April 27, 1943)

Synopsis: Sophronia Winters discovers that the Maine hotelkeeper she has married in middle age is a murderous psychopath, who mistakes her for his hated sister-in-law, and in self-defense she becomes a murderer herself.

Credits: *Producer:* William Spier; *Director:* Ted Bliss; *Writer:* Lucille Fletcher; *Musical director:* Lud Gluskin; *Composer:* Lucien Moraweck

Cast: Agnes Moorehead (Sophronia Winters), Ray Collins (Hiram Johnson)

"Sorry, Wrong Number" (May 25, 1943)

Synopsis: A bedridden, middle-class New York housewife accidentally overhears two men planning a murder over the phone and realizes too late that the intended victim is herself.

Credits: *Producer:* William Spier; *Director:* Ted Bliss; *Writer:* Lucille Fletcher; *Musical director:* Lud Gluskin

Cast: Agnes Moorehead (Mrs. Elbert Smythe Stevenson)

"Uncle Henry's Rose Bush" (June 29, 1943)

Synopsis: A young married couple, Paul and Carol Linden, pay a surprise visit to Carol's aunt and uncle on their farm and only understand the reason for Aunt Julie's eccentric, antisocial behavior, when it turns out she is trying to hide the fact that her husband, Uncle Henry, has gone insane.

Credits: *Producer:* William Spier; *Director:* Ted Bliss; *Writer:* Larry Roman; *Composer:* Bernard Hermann; *Conductor:* Lucien Moraweck

Cast: Agnes Moorehead (Aunt Julie), Ellen Drew (Carol Linden), Elliot Reid (Paul Linden)

"Sorry, Wrong Number" (August 21, 1943)

Credits: *Producer:* William Spier; *Director:* Ted Bliss; *Writer:* Lucille Fletcher; *Musical director:* Lud Gluskin

Cast: Agnes Moorehead (Mrs. Elbert Smythe Stevenson)

"The Sisters" (February 3, 1944)

Synopsis: Lydia Haskell orders a coffin ostensibly for herself, but her younger, simple-minded sister Ellie fears she is its intended occupant and does away with Lydia instead.

Credits: *Producer:* William Spier; *Director:* William Spier; *Writer:* George Wells

Cast: Agnes Moorehead (Ellie Haskell), Ida Lupino (Lydia Haskell)

"Sorry, Wrong Number" (February 24, 1944)

Credits: *Producer:* William Spier; *Director:* William Spier; *Writer:* Lucille Fletcher

Cast: Agnes Moorehead (Mrs. Elbert Smythe Stevenson)

"The Diary of Sophronia Winters" (August 17, 1944)

CREDITS: *Producer:* William Spier; *Director:* William Spier; *Writer:* Lucille Fletcher
CAST: Agnes Moorehead (Sophronia Winters), Ray Collins (Hiram Johnson)

"To Find Help" (January 18, 1945)

SYNOPSIS: A widow takes in a seemingly harmless young man to help her with the heavy work about the place and it turns out he is insane and comes close to killing her before she is saved by the timely arrival of a man from the telephone company.

CREDITS: *Producer:* William Spier; *Director:* William Spier; *Writer:* Mel Dinelli
CAST: Agnes Moorehead (Mrs. Gillis), Frank Sinatra (Howard Wilton)

"Sorry, Wrong Number" (September 6, 1945)

CREDITS: *Producer:* William Spier; *Director:* William Spier; *Writer:* Lucille Fletcher
CAST: Agnes Moorehead (Mrs. Elbert Smythe Stevenson)

"Post Mortem" (April 4, 1946)

SYNOPSIS: When a twice-married former actress wins the sweepstakes, she and a newspaper writer hatch a plan to reveal that her second husband actually killed her first and is intending to kill her.

PRODUCER: William Spier; *Director:* William Spier; *Writers:* Robert Tallman (radio play), Cornell Woolrich (story)

CAST: Agnes Moorehead (Josie Archer), Joseph Kearns (Stephen Archer); Howard Duff, Elliott Lewis

"The Thirteenth Sound" (February 13, 1947)

SYNOPSIS: A local sheriff suspects that a woman may have killed her husband and stages a number of repetitions of the screeching sound the murdered man's fingernails made against the wall as he fell to his death in order to drive her distracted enough to confess to her crime.

CREDITS: *Producer:* William Spier; *Director:* William Spier; *Writers:* Cathy Hewitt, Elliot Hewitt

CAST: Agnes Moorehead (Mrs. Skinner), William Johnstone (Jonathan Brown)

"The Yellow Wallpaper" (July 29, 1948)

SYNOPSIS: Instead of getting better from her postpartum depression, a young wife and mother is progressively driven out of her mind by the intricate, ugly wallpaper in her bedroom and the woman she imagines is imprisoned in it.

CREDITS: *Producer:* Anton M. Leader; *Director:* Anton M. Leader; *Writer:* Charlotte Perkins Gilman (story), Sylvia Richards (radio play); *Composer:* Lucien Moraweck; *Conductor:* Lud Gluskin

CAST: Agnes Moorehead

"Sorry, Wrong Number" (November 18, 1948)

CREDITS: *Producer:* Anton M. Leader; *Director:* Anton M. Leader; *Writer:* Lucille Fletcher; *Composer:* Lucien Moraweck; *Conductor:* Lud Gluskin

CAST: Agnes Moorehead (Mrs. Elbert Smythe Stevenson)

"The Trap" (June 16, 1949)

SYNOPSIS: A woman living alone in a large house suspects she is not alone after all and it turns out her delinquent sister is setting a trap to imprison her in her own home and take her place at work.

CREDITS: *Producer:* Anton M. Leader; *Director:* Anton M. Leader; *Writer:* Virginia Meyers (story), Walter Newman (radio play), Ralph Rose (radio play); *Composer:* Lucien Moraweck; *Conductor:* Lud Gluskin

CAST: Agnes Moorehead (Helen Crane); William Johnstone

"The Chain" (April 27, 1950)

SYNOPSIS: When a spiteful, abandoned wife sends out a chain letter, it has several unforeseen consequences, including her shooting her husband dead—or was that intentional?

CREDITS: *Producer:* William Spier; *Director:* Norman MacDonnell; *Writer:* Joel Murcott; *Composer:* Lucien Moraweck; *Conductor:* Lud Gluskin

CAST: Agnes Moorehead (Leonora Carpenter); William Conrad, John McIntire, Alan Reed

"The Death Parade" (February 15, 1951)

SYNOPSIS: When a meddlesome spinster finds a letter on the street and tries to warn the young female recipient that she is in danger, she only succeeds in scaring her to death.

CREDITS: *Producer:* Elliott Lewis; *Director:* Elliott Lewis; *Writer:* Antony Ellis (radio play), Shirley Gordon (story); *Composer:* Lucien Moraweck; *Conductor:* Lud Gluskin

CAST: Agnes Moorehead (Ellen Johnson); Jerry Hausner, Byron Kane, Joseph Kearns, Lou Krugman, Jack Kruschen, Lou Merrill, Jeanette Nolan, Jay Novello, Shimen Ruskin

"The Evil of Adelaide Winters" (September 10, 1951)

SYNOPSIS: Bogus mystic and con woman Adelaide Winters and her boyfriend prey on families mourning the deaths of their sons in World War II, including wealthy Edward Porter, but their plans go awry when Porter wants to marry Adelaide and take her into the great beyond to be reunited with his dead son.

CREDITS: *Producer:* Elliott Lewis; *Director:* Elliott Lewis; *Writer:* Arthur Ross; *Composer:* Lucien Moraweck; *Conductor:* Lud Gluskin

CAST: Agnes Moorehead (Adelaide Winters), Herb Butterfield (Edward Porter), Joseph Kearns (Robert McBain)

"The Fall River Tragedy" (January 14, 1952)

SYNOPSIS: In old age, Lizzie Borden tells a visiting journalist of how she experienced her trial for the murder of her father and stepmother and how the prosecutor, Mr. Moody, turned the whole town against her.

CREDITS: *Producer:* Elliott Lewis; *Director:* Elliott Lewis; *Writer:* Gil Doud; *Composer:* Lucien Moraweck; *Conductor:* Lud Gluskin

CAST: Agnes Moorehead (Lizzie Borden), Joseph Kearns (Mr. Moody); Herb Butterfield, Rolfe Sedan, Stuffy Singer, Peggy Webber, William Wright

"Sorry, Wrong Number" (September 15, 1952)

CREDITS: *Producer:* Elliott Lewis; *Director:* Elliott Lewis; *Writer:* Lucille Fletcher

CAST: Agnes Moorehead (Mrs. Elbert Smythe Stevenson)

"Death and Miss Turner" (November 17, 1952)

SYNOPSIS: A London doctor's treatment of an American expatriate painter with amnesia finally brings back the memory of the terrible train wreck she was involved in and the man she was painting, who was killed after they switched places to give her better light.

CREDITS: *Producer:* Elliott Lewis; *Director:* Elliott Lewis; *Writer:* William Spier

CAST: Agnes Moorehead (Rachel Turner), Joseph Kearns (Dr. Grice), Jeanette Nolan (Nurse Briggs)

"The Signalman" (March 23, 1953)

SYNOPSIS: A journalist returns to her home town after 20 years and wants to interview a signalman who has worked alone for 30 years, which ultimately stirs up unpleasant memories of a terrible train accident he was witness to and leads indirectly to his being killed by an oncoming train.

CREDITS: *Producer:* Elliott Lewis; *Director:* Elliott Lewis; *Writer:* Charles Dickens (story), Irving Reis (radio play); *Composer:* Lucien Moraweck; *Conductor:* Lud Gluskin

CAST: Agnes Moorehead (Amy Sears), Joseph Kearns (the signalman)

"The Empty Chair" (September 21, 1953)

SYNOPSIS: A school teacher boards with the family of her 17-year-old student Bobby, who likes to drive fast and furiously and almost kills a classmate in a race before he recognizes the error of his ways.

CREDITS: *Producer:* Elliott Lewis; *Director:* Elliott Lewis; *Writer:* David Friedkin, Morten Klein; *Composer:* René Garriguenc; *Conductor:* Lud Guskin

CAST: Agnes Moorehead (Barbara Warner), Sam Edwards (Bobby); Herb Butterfield, Michael Chapin, Joseph Kearns, Paula Winslowe

"The Wreck of the Maid of Athens" (November 30, 1953)

SYNOPSIS: When *The Maid of Athens* catches on fire and sinks off the coast of South America, Richard Wooldridge and his wife, Emily, have to resist a mutiny among the surviving crew members, who are being misled by a superstitious sailor, Lawson, to believe it is bad luck to have a woman aboard a ship and that the Wooldridges are to blame for the deaths of their fellow seamen.

CREDITS: *Producer:* Elliott Lewis; *Director:* Elliott Lewis; *Writer:* Gil Doud (radio play), Emily Wooldridge (book); *Composer:* Lucien Moraweck; *Conductor:* Lud Gluskin

CAST: Agnes Moorehead (Emily Wooldridge), Joseph Kearns (Richard Wooldridge), Ben Wright (Lawson); Jack Kruschen, Richard Peel, Larry Thor

"Weekend Special: Death" (May 24, 1954)

SYNOPSIS: Legal secretary Rita Dorsey finds herself locked in in her local grocery store after closing time, only to discover as well that the store is being burgled by one of her boss's shady clients and he and his partner want her out of the way.

PRODUCER: Elliott Lewis; *Director:* Elliott Lewis; *Writer:* E. Jack Neuman; *Composer:* Lucien Moraweck; *Conductor:* Lud Gluskin

CAST: Agnes Moorehead (Rita Dorsey), Tony Barrett (Tony), Joseph Kearns (Fred); Hy Averback, Whitfield Connor, Mary Jane Croft, Barney Phillips

"Death and Miss Turner" (May 19, 1957)

SYNOPSIS: A London doctor's treatment of an American expatriate painter with amnesia finally brings back the memory of the terrible train wreck she was involved in and the man she was painting, who was killed after they switched places to give her better light.

CREDITS: *Producer:* William N. Robson; *Director:* William N. Robson; *Writer:* William Spier

CAST: Agnes Moorehead (Rachel Turner); Raymond Lawrence, Richard Peel, Irene Tedrow, John White

"The Yellow Wallpaper" (June 30, 1957)

SYNOPSIS: Instead of getting better from her postpartum depression, a young wife and mother is progressively driven mad by the intricate, ugly wallpaper in her bedroom and the woman she imagines is imprisoned in it.

CREDITS: *Producer:* William N. Robson; *Director:* William N. Robson; *Writer:* Charlotte Perkins Gilman (story), Sylvia Richards (radio play)

CAST: Agnes Moorehead, Joe De Santis, Ann Hunter

"Sorry, Wrong Number" (October 20, 1957)

CREDITS: *Producer:* William N. Robson; *Director:* William N. Robson; *Writer:* Lucille Fletcher

CAST: Agnes Moorehead (Mrs. Elbert Smythe Stevenson); Norman Alden, Joe De Santis, Virginia Gregg, Byron Kane, Ellen Morgan, Jeanette Nolan

"The Chain" (March 9, 1958)

CREDITS: *Producer:* William N. Robson; *Director:* William N. Robson; *Writer:* Joel Murcott

CAST: Agnes Moorehead (Leonora Carpenter); John McIntire

"The Whole Town's Sleeping" (August 31, 1958)

SYNOPSIS: A young, unmarried woman is determined not to let a killer on the loose curb her freedom of movement and is finally killed in her own home, just as she thinks she has made it home safely from seeing a movie with friends.

CREDITS: *Producer:* William N. Robson; *Director:* William N. Robson; *Writer:* Ray Bradbury (story), Antony Ellis (radio play)

CAST: Agnes Moorehead (Lavinia Nebbs), William Conrad (narrator); Charlie Lung, Barney Phillips, Lurene Tuttle, Paula Winslowe

"Don't Call Me Mother" (January 4, 1959)

SYNOPSIS: A woman feels so threatened by her foster son's new wife that she is willing to go to any length to break up the marriage and ends up killing both her son and his wife.

CREDITS: *Producer:* William N. Robson; *Director:* William N. Robson; *Writer:* William N. Robson

CAST: Agnes Moorehead (Lori Rider); Norman Alden, Cathy Lewis, James McCallion, Barney Phillips

"Headshrinker" (August 23, 1959)

SYNOPSIS: A woman with a father fixation is finally able to break off with her psychoanalyst and lover after he admits in their last therapy session that he needs her more than she needs him.

CREDITS: *Producer:* William N. Robson; *Director:* William N. Robson; *Writer:* William N. Robson

CAST: Agnes Moorehead (Ruth Elander); Lawrence Dobkin, Patty Gallagher

"Sorry, Wrong Number" (February 14, 1960)

Credits: *Producer:* William N. Robson; *Director:* William N. Robson; *Writer:* Lucille Fletcher

Cast: Agnes Moorehead (Mrs. Elbert Smythe Stevenson); Norman Alden, Joe De Santis, Virginia Gregg, Byron Kane, Ellen Morgan, Jeanette Nolan

4

Don Juan in Hell (Stage, 1951–52)

Don Juan in Hell is a dream sequence, a play within the play, that takes up most of the third act of George Bernard Shaw's *Man and Superman*. It takes between 90 minutes and two hours two perform on its own.[1] In most productions of *Man and Superman*, *Don Juan in Hell* is simply left out, because the play is more than long enough without it. Thus, nearly half a century after its first performance in London and New York, *Don Juan in Hell* had never been part of *Man and Superman* as staged in the United States.[2] The Paul Gregory-Charles Laughton collaboration was the first professional production of the play in America.[3]

As the papers reported at the time, the production "grew out of Laughton's readings of excerpts from the Bible and Shakespeare on tour last winter."[4] In modern terms, it was a "spin-off" from the British actor's vastly successful reading tour under the aegis of the young dynamo producer Paul Gregory. "Laughton," according to one source, "had long believed this scene ... Shaw's finest work."[5] The actor described *Don Juan in Hell* as "a discussion of sex, life, economy and everything under the sun in extremely witty terms" and as "a cathedral of ideas."[6] As one reviewer put it, the play is "all concerned with the troublesome problem of whether it would be more fun to remain in Hell or to transfer into Heaven."[7]

More recently, *Don Juan in Hell* has been described as "a musical composition for human voices" and "a tennis match of ideas."[8] The musical instruments, or the tennis players in this set of intellectual mixed doubles, are Don Juan, the Devil, Don Juan's former paramour Doña Ana, and the latter's father, the Commander, who is also referred to as "the Statue." Laughton was slated to play the Devil, in addition to directing. The French movie star Charles Boyer, the English character actor Sir Cedric Hardwicke, and Agnes Moorehead were invited to play Don Juan, the Commander, and Doña Ana. It was the single most important casting decision of Moorehead's stage career and not far behind *Citizen Kane*, *The Magnificent Ambersons*, and *Bewitched* in importance to her acting career as a whole.

According to Hardwicke, *Don Juan in Hell* "contains the germs of virtually all [Shaw's] plays in one form or another." Maybe it's not surprising, then, that Shaw "had never encouraged *Don Juan*'s production, believing it to be more for the library than for the stage."[9] When I spoke to him in 2006, Paul Gregory agreed that Laughton had came up with the idea to do *Don Juan in Hell*, but reminded me that he was the one to go to

England to seek the author's blessing on the venture. Shaw did not believe in the idea, Gregory recalled.[10] "After listening to his plans, the 94-year-old writer warned him: 'It will never be a commercial success.'"[11] Shaw did not live to see how wrong he was, dying on November 2, 1950, less than three months before the U.S. premiere.

Admittedly, *Don Juan in Hell* was just about the most unlikely hit show you could ever imagine. It was wordy in the extreme and had no action to speak of. To make matters worse, they decided to stage it with no scenery, no costumes, and hardly any movement. As Cedric Hardwicke remembered it, "The inspiration of producing it as a reading, with the four of us perched on four stools in front of four microphones, developed spontaneously."[12] "We dispensed with stage movement so as to accentuate the rich, rolling words of the play," he explained in his 1961 memoir. "We brought in microphones to provide a visual reason for sitting together facing the audience and so tying it with invisible bonds of concentration to our performance."[13]

Such a pared down production meant that you only needed the four actors, a stage manager, and a crew of one.[14] One review described the result as a "philosophical charade," "presented without scenery and 'other distracting paraphernalia,'" where the actors "appear in modern evening dress" and the technical production is limited to four microphones and four spotlights.[15] "It wasn't divine inspiration"; according to Larry Swindell, "*Don Juan in Hell* had been similarly performed before and often, but not by players of such renown, and never before in America."[16] "Those damned stools," Hardwicke recalled "were as big a factor in our constant fatigue as anything. I cannot sit on a bar-stool today without an irresistible urge to burst into Shaw."[17]

Apart from Laughton and Gregory, there were others at the time who believed in the idea of staging *Don Juan in Hell* on its own. Frank Morriss, film critic for the *Winnipeg Free Press*, when asked by a local sponsor who was considering bringing the show to Winnipeg, "whether there was enough public interest" in *Don Juan in Hell*, assured him that "there'd be a lineup several blocks long to get tickets." Morriss felt that "the performers are all such movie names that the public would flock to hear them recite the alphabet. Coupled with a seldom heard Shaw play, the box office draw is irresistible."[18] His hunch was confirmed as soon as tickets were made available. Gail Plummer, manager of Kingsbury Hall at the University of Utah, one of the show's first venues, told the *Salt Lake Tribune* that "the ticket sale is getting more public attention than anything to visit Salt Lake in years."[19] By the time this landmark production had runs its course in late 1952, there had been three national tours, a tour of England, and two longer engagements on Broadway. Kurt Singer has calculated that they played in 52 cities in 42 states of the union. It was not unusual, Singer claims, to gross $7,000 to 10,000 in a single evening. The average weekly profits on the road were $30,000.[20] Paul Gregory told me it was the most profitable show he ever put on.[21]

Don Juan in Hell was both a commercial and critical success. The importance of the production was recognized immediately. John Houseman reviewed a Los Angeles performance in the Philharmonic Auditorium for *Theatre Arts Magazine*: "What the audience experienced, that evening, was pure theatrical pleasure of a kind that is seldom felt nowadays. Between that bare stage and the crowded house flowed the very essence of dramatic entertainment, the spoken word moving freely from author to audience, through the immediate, personal communication of the actor."[22] Little did Houseman know then that his own production of *Don Juan in Hell* would be opening in Los Angeles 21 years later. *Time Magazine* wrote in its review that "It is not only the finest thing in *Man and Superman*,

The First Drama Quartette during a performance of Shaw's *Don Juan in Hell.* From left: Charles Laughton, Charles Boyer, Agnes Moorehead, and Sir Cedric Hardwicke. For the remainder of his life, Hardwicke quipped, he couldn't sit on a bar stool without wanting to "burst into Shaw" (courtesy Muskingum University Archives).

but the most brilliant talkfest, the most glittering dialectical floor show of modern times."[23] The drama critic of the *London Evening Chronicle* called the show "A triumph of words over scenery."[24] According to *Variety*, it was "One of the most exciting experiences of this and any other season."[25]

In this chorus of approval, Sir John Gielgud is a lone dissenting voice. In a letter written aboard *The Chief* from Los Angeles to Chicago on October 19, 1952, he told his mother: "I went to *Don Juan in Hell* reading, with Laughton, Boyer, Hardwicke and Agnes Moorehead in Los Angeles before I left, but I found it a most affected exhibition of faked spontaneity and a terrific bore, as I am no Shaw addict anyway. However, it was packed to the roof and the audience adored every minute of it."[26]

In 1954, as Moorehead was touring the country in her one-woman show, one journalist reminded her readers that *Don Juan in Hell* had been credited with establishing and popularizing "the current trend toward dramatic readings in the American theatre."[27] Today "textbooks in readers' theatre include this production as an historic landmark in the development of oral performance."[28]

As a result of its importance both to American theater history and to the careers of all four of its performer, there are more published accounts of this production than any other stage show Moorehead acted in.[29] In the remainder of this chapter, I want to concentrate on what Moorehead brought to the production, why the role of Doña Ana was tailor-made for her, and the response her performance elicited from the critics.

Sometimes an actor and a role come together at just the right time in just the right place, resulting in a unique, indelible, once-in-a-lifetime performance that elevates both the performer and the show to new and maybe even unexpected heights. Such a performance was Agnes Moorehead's Doña Ana in Paul Gregory's legendary production of Shaw's *Don Juan in Hell* in the early 1950s. For Moorehead, who was making her final film under long-term contract for MGM at the same time as she was rehearsing *Don Juan*, the call from Gregory and Charles Laughton to take part in their new venture could not have been better timed. For eight years—nearly her entire film career, MGM had been her working home, supplying her with a steady and solid income and plenty of work, even if the roles were not always exciting. Now all that was coming to an end. Facing an uncertain future, Moorehead needed to find another leg to stand on in show business. Beyond the fine financial dividends that Gregory's production would bring, she would reap rich artistic rewards as well. *Don Juan in Hell* became the means through which, more than 20 years after graduating from the American Academy of Dramatic Arts, Agnes Moorehead was finally able to embark on a career in the live theater.

Madeleine Carroll, Beulah Bondi, and Laughton's wife, Elsa Lanchester, have all been mentioned as being in competition with Moorehead for the role of Doña Ana. Producer Gregory felt Carroll "didn't possess the sense of drama that the character needed" and besides, she wasn't available.[30] Gregory told me that they had considered Bondi "for about five minutes," but she just wasn't glamorous enough.[31] Laughton had pushed for Lanchester, but Gregory managed to dissuade him.[32] "I thought her voice was all wrong and that she possessed no romantic quality," he told Moorehead biographer Charles Tranberg in 2003.[33]

That left Agnes Moorehead. She was in the south of France filming *Adventures of Captain Fabian* with Errol Flynn, Vincent Price, and Micheline Presle, when she received the offer via cable in August or September 1950.[34] According to Charles Higham, "She replied with great enthusiasm from the Hotel Negresco in Nice, saying she would love to appear in *Don Juan in Hell*, but she would not be free until January." They decided to wait for her, because "both Charles and Paul Gregory felt that nobody else would be quite right."[35]

Gregory explained in 2003, that "she was bigger than life and could convey womanhood, rejection and love."[36] And he found her "extremely cooperative," always a bonus from a producer's point of view.[37]

In a backhanded compliment that was typical of him, Laughton once said that "We wanted not necessarily the best actors, but the best voices in America and we found them."[38] According to Larry Swindell, "Miss Moorehead ... possessed a refined, crisp speech that ideally complemented her brittle vocal quality."[39] She also "expertly used a skittish, rather hysterical laugh which expressed the girlish evasive hypocritical spirit of Doña Ana."[40]

Some evidently found the casting of Moorehead surprising. Laughton explained willingly: "She is with us because Anna has to change from an old wizened woman of 77 to a young lady of 27. The actress will only have her voice to convince the audience of this transition—Aggie will do it."[41] Despite his outward assurance, Laughton wasn't sure of Agnes's stage technique, according to Gregory, "so he spent 'weeks' working with her." Gregory recalled that "Charles strived to make Agnes become 'emotionally involved' rather than relying on 'phony' tricks such as a British accent she initially affected for her character."[42]

Moorehead herself was surprised at the opportunity she was given: "I sometimes wonder how they ever saw me in such a glamorous role for usually I am relegated to those dreary, drab characters that are completely void of charm and beauty."[43] As it turned out, her unglamorous screen image would work to her advantage when it came time to put in a "personal appearance" in *Don Juan in Hell.*

In that play, Moorehead also had the advantage of being the only woman on the stage. Even so, her role was the smallest and least interesting of the four. In his customarily dismissive and hyperbolic manner, Gregory claimed her part in *Don Juan* was "only about four minutes."[44] Charles Higham describes Doña Ana as "the voice of propriety, of rectitude," which doesn't sound like a lot of fun, though she did get to speak the famous last line of the play: "I believe in the Life to Come. A father! a father for the Superman!"[45] Moorehead described Donã Ana in 1972 as "a man's view of 'the embodiment of all women ... flirtatious, argumentative, sometimes very stupid about things.'"[46] In a way, Moorehead was once again playing straight woman to male comedians, as she had done so often in radio in the '30s.

When he heard that Gregory had cast Moorhead as Doña Ana, Orson Welles agreed that "she had what the part requires. No more, no less."[47] Yet out of all his productions that she acted in, Gregory thought Moorehead was best in *Don Juan in Hell.* She had a steadfast quality, he said in 2006, which meant that in a small part she could stay concentrated and intense. The role involved a lot of posing and reacting to the three men and she did that quite well. She posed to the words of one man and then the posed to the words of another.[48] The trouble, though, with Moorehead was that she was always trying to overshadow or one-up people. Gregory gave an example from *Don Juan*, where she would distract from one of Boyer's speeches by pretending to be primping in front of the mirror, something that had nothing to do with the performance. This was not very professional, according to Gregory.[49]

One might claim that the minimalist style of performance they had chosen was very like a live radio broadcast before a studio audience, including the microphones, and that was why Moorehead was able to do it so well. She had had extensive radio experience but little stage experience since graduating from AADA. Fortunately for her, you could say, this staged reading of Shaw's dream play did not involve any complicated blocking or hands-on physical interaction with her fellow players. They remained standing by their music stands and microphones or sitting on high stools.

Yet pointing out that this concert version of *Don Juan in Hell* was the best possible segue between Moorehead's radio and stage careers does not diminish her achievement, nor does it explain the strong *visual* impact Moorehead made on the audience. A friend from Reedsburg, Wisconsin, George E. Perry, recalled in a fan club publication in 1965 that "her visual and vocal transformation from the old woman of 79 to the young girl of 17 was a moment of incredible characterization."[50] In his 1983 memoir *Final Dress*, John Houseman recalled the original production more than 30 years earlier and the 1972–73 revival he had directed: "I can see her still, in both engagements, in a lilac gown of her own designing with a small gold crown set atop the flaming red hair that made her the equal, in authority and presence, of the three tall, handsome, formally clad males with whom she appeared onstage."[51] Bernie Kopell, a *Bewitched* "semi-regular" who did "The Warlock in the Gray Flannel Suit" episode with Moorehead in Season 8, saw her in *Don Juan* in his late teens: "There was Agnes, with her stunning red hair, decorated in this beautiful dress. That picture of her stuck in my mind every time I did *Bewitched*. She was such an over-whelming presence on that Broadway stage."[52]

But Moorehead was not just praised by fans, friends, and co-workers. During the original production, professional theater critics from Brooks Atkinson to Walter Kerr gave her some of the best notices of her career. Atkinson wrote in the *New York Times*: "Agnes Moorehead acts the respectability and propriety with tongue-in-cheek humor, and has caught the vivacity of the whole occasion."[53] Another New York paper said that "The actress has the crisp, clean elegance of a lily. She falls into exquisite poses and moves like a self-appointed queen, to give the play its chief visual distraction. It is a lovely performance."[54] Robert Garland in the *New York Journal-American* found "Agnes Moorehead, looking like some haunting Florentine painting I have seen, was always in the picture, even in her long sustained repose."[55] According to Elliott Norton in the *Boston Post*: "Miss Moorehead is all elegance and comic ease as the lady."[56] While the show was not a commercial success in England, the British critics were no less impressed than their American colleagues. One Birmingham paper wrote of Moorehead that "Her Donna Ana is a radiant, terrifying example of what we poor men are up against. She is magnificence itself."[57] Walter Kerr, then writing for the *Herald Tribune*, described her as "striking to watch."[58] To *watch*, not just to listen to.

Laughton best explained why Moorehead was such a success in this role. "Agnes Moorehead is great," he said, "because without being a dazzling beauty actually, she is able to create the illusion of queenliness, regal bearing, and sex appeal in its loftier connotations of magnetic femininity."[59] In Moorehead's retelling ten years later, "when he [Laughton] was casting the only woman's role in the first Drama Quarter's memorable presentation he wanted her because she so vividly projected the image of beauty.... 'He confided that that was the way he'd always seen me, that he didn't like to see me in so many ugly parts. I was surprised and touched.'"[60]

To enhance her visual image, Walter Plunkett designed a "magnificent dress" according to Moorhead's precise instructions, "low cut, tight bodiced, with yards of train sweeping from each shoulder: It looks from the audience like a richly gleaming shot taffeta; in fact, it is 'shocking'—or Schiaparelli—pink satin, with heliotrope net tightly drawn over it." "It gives just that iridescent look that I wanted," she explained. "Rather out-of-this-world—after all, we are supposed to be in Hell, aren't we?'"[61] Gregory remembered that she wanted the dress to emphasize her breasts.[62] As a finishing touch, on top of her braided hair twisted in the coronet style, she placed "a jeweled tiara that," according to Larry Swindell, "represented a substantial portion of the production cost, actor salaries apart."[63]

"As you know the roles that I play are pretty frightening and to see me look halfway attractive was rather shocking," Moorehead recalled with satisfaction in a 1953 lecture.[64] After performing at her alma mater the University of Wisconsin, the local newspaper wrote: "Known chiefly from her film performances in off-beat roles, Miss Moorehead blossoms out in the Shaw play as a glamorous, witty, and pulse-warming woman."[65] Edith Lindeman in the *Richmond Times-Dispatch* found her "unbelievably handsome and alluring for those who know her as a character actress in films."[66] According to T. Pearse

Wheelwright in the *Salt Lake City Desert News*, "Miss Moorehead was in fact, breathtaking. Hollywood should take a lesson and let her be her natural glamorous self."[67]

Given this overwhelmingly positive response, it was no wonder that in 1972, as she was touring with *Don Juan in Hell* once again, Moorehead told the *Chicago Tribune* that "the first time she played Doña Ana in the company of Charles Laughton, Cedric Hardwicke, and Charles Boyer was 'the happiest' of her life."[68]

CREDITS: *Director:* Charles Laughton; *Producer:* Paul Gregory; *Writer:* George Bernard Shaw; *Costumes:* Walter Plunkett (Moorehead's gown); *Premiere:* January 27, 1951, at Claremont College in Claremont, California

CAST: Charles Boyer (Don Juan), Cedric Hardwicke (Commander), Charles Laughton (Devil), Agnes Moorehead (Doña Ana)

Agnes Moorehead as Doña Ana in Shaw's *Don Juan in Hell* in the early 1950s. Her dress by MGM costume designer Walter Plunkett was so décolleté that it is barely visible here. Her hair is worn in the coronet style she favored in private life as well. The little crown on her head put quite a dent in the production costs.

5

The Revlon Mirror Theatre: "Lullaby" (TV, 1953)

Agnes Moorehead's television debut was as low-key as her screen debut was spectacular.

She is not on record has having expressed any great degree of skepticism toward the medium of television, yet more than two years would pass from the termination of her long-term contract at MGM after *Show Boat* in early 1951 until she did her first TV role. There were several reasons for this. In the early 1950s, Moorehead was still a sought-after film actress. As a freelancer for the first time in her film career, she could now pick and choose her roles. Her biographer Charles Tranberg suggests that "like many film actors in those early days of television…, she felt that appearing in a medium where people could see you for free would diminish her bankability and allure in motion pictures."[1] Equally significant, the early 1950s saw the emergence of Moorehead's new career on the stage. Most of 1951 and 1952 were taken up with tours of Shaw's *Don Juan in Hell* across the length and breadth of the United States and in England.

By 1953, though, *Don Juan in Hell* was behind her and her one-woman show *That Fabulous Redhead* was still in the planning stages. Moorehead did not appear on the stage that year, but continued to work in radio, including doing three episodes of *Suspense*. 1953 also saw the premiere of four films: *The Story of Three Loves*, *Scandal at Scourie*, *Main Street to Broadway*, and *Those Redheads from Seattle*. She only worked on two new films, though: the aforementioned *Redheads*, which was produced by Pine-Thomas from mid March to late April 1953 at Paramount Studios; and *Magnificent Obsession*, which went before the cameras at Universal from late September to late October 1953.

Sometime between those two film productions, she worked on her first television show: a 30-minute drama called "Lullaby," that was produced by Revue Productions, the forerunner of Universal Television, on a two- or three-day schedule at Republic Studios.[2] It premiered on CBS on October 3, 1953, while Moorehead was working on *Magnificent Obsession*. "Lullaby" was the third episode of the second and final season of *The Revlon Mirror Theatre*, a dramatic anthology series that ran between June 23 and December 12, 1953, and was sponsored by Revlon Cosmetics. During its first season in the summer of 1953, the series consisted of 30-minute episodes that were recorded live in New York City and aired over NBC, while the second season episodes, starting in September 1953, were prerecorded in Los Angeles and aired on CBS.[3]

It is worth asking why this fairly ordinary episode of a fairly ordinary drama anthology series was the vehicle Moorehead chose for her small screen debut. She had never worked with director Felix Feist before, nor would she again. The chance to star above the title would no doubt have been an inducement to take this first role on television. Also, Moorehead would probably have been aware that Joan Crawford was making her television debut in the same series in an episode called "Because I Love Him," which aired two weeks before "Lullaby" as the first episode of the second season. That a star of Crawford's magnitude would chose the *Revlon Mirror Theatre* for her television debut would no doubt have carried weight with Moorehead. Her friend Ronald Reagan was also going to do an episode in Season 2 called "Next Stop Bethlehem."

Apart from the obvious fact that this production could be fitted into her schedule, I imagine Moorehead would also have been attracted by the double challenge of acting in television for the first time and playing a non-seeing character for the first time. In "Lullaby," she was to play Mary Adams, quite an ordinary, middle-class woman, but for the fact that she has been blind since her son Ben was 15 and never leaves the house. Her husband is out of the picture and she lives with a paid companion. Plainly dressed in a print dress, cardigan, and often an apron, with her hair center-parted and fastened in a large bun, Mrs. Adams looks a bit like Mrs. Stratton in *The Stratton Story* or Mrs. Cosick in *Fourteen Hours*, as it happens, two other stories of mothers and sons.

So many of these TV dramas from the 1950s seem just a mite construed today and "Lullaby" is no exception. It sets up an unusual, to say the least, dramatic situation, which promises the maximum amount of suspense and roiling emotion, as a blind, reclusive, seemingly helpless woman must come to terms with the fact that her son is a bank robber and a murderer. After being away for three years, Ben Adams suddenly shows up unannounced with his "friend" Red Johnson and a third, nameless man, who has had an "accident." In her big scene in Ben's boyhood room, Mrs. Adams reminds him that his father was no good. If he continues to idolize his father, she warns him, he will end up just as badly as he did. Ben responds that "what you got here isn't living. It's just staying alive." Her son accuses her of having lived a sheltered existence out of touch with reality: "Look Ma, I don't want to live like you. I'd go nuts in a dump like this."

As far as troubled mother-son relationships are concerned, this portrayal forms an interesting counterpoint to the aforementioned *Fourteen Hours*. You'll recall that film starring Richard Basehart about a suicidal young man on a ledge, whose problems are at least indirectly traced back to his relationship with his overprotective, mentally unstable mother. Like *Fourteen Hours*, "Lullaby" hints in a vague, pseudo–Freudian way at the "unhealthiness" of the mother-son relationship and the dire consequences of the discord between the parents, leading to the absence of the father figure with all that implied to 1950s audiences. The "unnatural" closeness of mother and son is both symbolized and suggested by the latter's obsessive humming of a lullaby that Mrs. Adams used to sing to him when he was a boy.

Unlike Christine Hill Kosick, the mother in *Fourteen Hours*, Martha Adams is no neurotic and manages to keep a cool head in a crisis. Despite her handicap, or maybe because of it, Mrs. Adams stealthily removes the guns both of her son and Red Johnson and secretly locks the two men in their rooms. She is aided by the fact that they are uncommonly sound sleepers, especially as far as gangsters on the run go. The excitement is not yet over, though, as Mrs. Adams hasn't reckoned with the third gun belonging to the men's now dead partner in crime. Undeterred, Mrs. Adams survives a shoot-out where she also shows herself to be an uncommonly good marksman. Her son is not so fortunate.

As her co-stars, Moorehead had Tom Drake as her son, Ben, Lee Marvin as his fellow bank robber, Red Johnson, and Betty Lynn as her paid companion Mary. Moorehead and Drake were billed above the title with her name first. Drake was 35 and best known at this point for roles in *Mrs. Parkington*, where he had played Ned Talbot, the fiancé of Mrs. Parkington's great-granddaughter Jane; and *Meet Me in St. Louis*. He had worked in television since 1950. Lee Marvin was 29 and had only been acting in films and television for a few years. Betty Lynn was 27 and this was only her second television role, though she'd been working in films since 1948 with named, credited roles in quality pictures like *Sitting Pretty*, *June Bride*, *Cheaper by the Dozen*, and *Payment on Demand*. Lynn is best remembered today as Thelma Lou on the *Andy Griffith Show*.

It's a weakness in the script that Mary's role in Mrs. Adams's life and in the plot of "Lullaby" is so poorly defined. As it turns out, Mrs. Adams is perfectly capable of taking care of herself, even at the worst of times, leaving her companion largely extraneous to the action. There is also a very generic feeling about the mise-en-scène. Both the social and geographic background of Mrs. Adams and her son should have been fleshed out in Steve Fisher's teleplay. "Lullaby" was based on a short story from 1937 called "The Humming Bird Comes Home" by the prolific crime writer Cornell Woolrich, whose works gave rise to many film noir screenplays, including *Rear Window* and *No Man of Her Own*. His stories were also adapted for radio series like *Suspense*.[4] In 1946, Moorehead had appeared in an episode of *Suspense* based on a story by Woolrich called "Post Mortem."

On October 12, 1953, nine days after Moorehead's television debut in "Lullaby," something of almost equal significance occurred in her life: her husband, Robert Gist, opened in Paul Gregory's production of *The Caine Mutiny Court-Martial* at the Granada Theatre in Santa Barbara. After conducting a clandestine relationship for several years, Moorehead and Gist had finally married in Yuma, Arizona, on Valentine's Day 1953. By that time, they had secretly been enjoying their palatial new home on North Roxbury Drive in Beverly Hills for about a year. The *Caine* tour and lengthy New York run would keep Gist away from his wife and four-year-old foster son, Sean, for well over a year. He and Moorehead probably never lived together on North Roxbury Drive again. Premiering at a time when Bob Gist left the conjugal home for good, "Lullaby" marked the beginning of the end of Moorehead's life as a married woman, just as it signaled the beginning of her long and illustrious career in television.

CREDITS: *Director:* Felix Feist; *Writers:* Felix Feist (teleplay), Steve Fisher (teleplay), Cornell Woolrich (story); *Cinematography:* Gilbert Warrenton; *Film editing:* Richard G. Wray; *Art direction:* Martin Obzina; *Makeup department:* Jack Wilson; *Production company:* Revue Productions; *Air Date:* October 3, 1953, on CBS

CAST: Tom Drake (Ben Adams), Betty Lynn (Mary), Lee Marvin (Red Johnson), Agnes Moorehead (Martha Adams), Allan Ray (detective), Jack Shea (detective)

6

That Fabulous Redhead (Stage, 1954–73)

If *Don Juan in Hell* was the *Citizen Kane* of Agnes Moorehead's stage career, then her one-woman show was her *Magnificent Ambersons*. If *Don Juan* gave her a platform from which to launch a new phase of her career in the live theater, putting her on a level—literally and metaphorically—with stars like Charles Boyer and Charles Laughton, *That Fabulous Redhead* allowed her for the first time to stand on the stage alone. We can imagine that she relished the opportunity. Finally, she would be up front and center, not behind a radio microphone, not hidden under elaborate character make-up and costuming, not two steps behind a movie star. Finally, American audiences would be able to meet her face to face and, supposedly, as she really was. Building on the reputation she already enjoyed as a talented, versatile, and dependable character actress, in 1954 Agnes Moorehead began to craft what one might argue was her greatest and most long-lasting performance, as "Agnes Moorehead," leading lady of the American stage.

The impetus for what would become *That Fabulous Redhead* lay several years prior to the show coming to fruition in January 1954. The chief inspiration for this venture came from Charles Laughton, whom in combination with producer Paul Gregory had enjoyed great success with his own one-man show in many of the same venues that Moorehead would appear in. As early as June 1949, Laughton had written to her, referring to a previous conversation, that "I am almighty serious about this reading thing."[1] A month later, he reiterated that "I hope to goodness you persist with the reading thing," adding: "I am so terrified it gets into the wrongs hands. People like Ray Massey and Basil Rathbone could kill the whole bloody racket."[2] The following year, Hedda Hopper reported in her column that Moorehead was "preparing a reading program similar to that done by Charles Laughton" and would take it on tour that winter under the management of Paul Gregory.[3]

In a sense, then, Moorehead would follow in the path Laughton had staked out, playing to the same audiences Laughton and Gregory had created for serious, literary stage entertainment without fancy costumes, scenery, and staging, but with all the more emphasis on the beauty and dignity of the spoken word. Naturally, *Don Juan in Hell*, that Moorehead had been an integral part of, also played an important role in creating that audience. But the First Drama Quartet's success in an unlikely venture didn't necessarily mean that the public would pay to see Agnes Moorehead alone. To increase the chance of success, the initial plan was that the one-woman show would actually be a twin bill.

Most of the contracts for *That Fabulous Redhead* were signed during the spring, summer, and fall of 1953. All of them were signed for two performers: Agnes Moorehead and Robert Gist.[4] As early as January 1953, gossip columnist Erskine Johnson wrote that Paul Gregory was planning to co-star Moorehead and Gist in "Those Fabulous Redheads" in a nationwide road tour in 1954. Johnson took this as "further proof" of their "secret marriage."[5] On October 30, 1953, Sheilah Graham mentioned in her column that "Agnes Moorehead will do her famous 'Sorry, Wrong Number' sketch on tour for Paul Gregory. Her co-star is Robert Gist, her next husband."[6] Gist was actually already her husband, as the couple had wed in a secret ceremony in Yuma, Arizona, on February 14, 1953.

An early handbill for the show reads "Paul Gregory presents That Fabulous Redhead" above a sketch of Moorehead in profile. Below it continues: "Agnes Moorehead—featuring 'Sorry, Wrong Number' and Other Selections—also starring Robert Gist—program directed by Charles Laughton." On the back, we can read that "Miss Moorehead with Mr. Gist will also present scenes from Congreve's 'Way of the World,' Shakespeare's 'Merchant of Venice,' the story of Deborah from the Bible and selections from Guy de Maupassant and Damon Runyon."[7] None of these selections finally made it into the show and neither, as it happens, did Bob Gist.

We can imagine that the planning of the show and securing the contracts took place in the afterglow of Moorehead and Gist's Valentine's Day wedding. Moorehead no doubt welcomed the prospect of having her husband's company and support on this grueling and potentially lonely tour. Gist himself probably saw this as a career opportunity, if nothing else. So what happened? Well, a little show called *The Caine Mutiny Court-Martial*, that's what happened. For whatever reasons of his own and knowing full well that Gist had contracted to do his wife's one-woman show in more than 50 venues in the spring of 1954, producer Paul Gregory nevertheless decided to cast him in that soon-to-be spectacularly successful, Broadway-bound show. Obviously, Gist saw creating the role of Lt. Thomas Keefer in *Caine* as a better career opportunity than his modest supporting role in *That Fabulous Redhead*.

By early 1954, with *Caine* scheduled to open at the Plymouth Theatre in New York on January 20, it was clear that Bob Gist would not be part of *That Fabulous Redhead*.[8] Dorothy Olney, one of producer Gregory's assistants, explained to the Phoenix sponsor of Moorehead's show that they were "very desirous for [Gist] to stay in the play for he is excellent in the part."[9] Gist himself was understandably reluctant to abandon a ship bound for the Great White Way to paddle around in the wake of his wife through the outlying puddles of the American cultural landscape. Gregory found himself having to write to the nearly 50 sponsors of the tour he had already contracted with that they were not getting quite what they had signed up for. He gave a different explanation from Olney: "We found that in building of Miss Moorehead's program it was a much tighter program without an extra on-stage performer." This would also save money for the sponsors, he added, as Gist would have required a follow spot of his own and someone to operate it.[10]

Conflicting explanations were also given in the press. One report stated that "Charles Laughton ... found it impossible to replace Robert Gist currently appearing in 'The Caine Mutiny.'"[11] Another account quoted at length the circular letter Gregory had written to the sponsors, which concluded with the assurance that "By rearranging Miss Moorehead's program we have found that it is a sheer delight and we are positive that all her sponsors will agree that she is indeed 'That Fabulous Redhead.'"[12]

The first tour began in late January and extended into May. Moorehead was booked solid in February, March, and April and would perform in 25 states and Canada on her longest and most intensive tour with the show. A detailed itinerary follows. Her venues were high school auditoriums, university auditoriums, municipal auditoriums, the halls of women's clubs and other associations, and the occasional commercial theater. Her fee per performance ranged from $550 to $1,250; on average $750 per performance.[13] A second national tour was announced starting in early October 1954,[14] but there is only evidence of scattered dates in Berkeley, California; Huntington, West Virginia; and Oak Park, Illinois, during the remainder of 1954.

Moorehead's busy filming schedule in the second half of the 1950s meant that her one-woman show was more or less put on the shelf for the remainder of that decade. In the early 1960s, though, with her film career on the wane, Moorehead started going out with the show again and—even during her eight years on *Bewitched*—she tried to fit in as many performances as she could of what was now called *Come Closer, I'll Give You an Earful* or simply *An Evening with Agnes Moorehead*. Her appearance on a double bill with Christopher Fry's *A Phoenix Too Frequent*, directed by and starring Joseph Cotten at the Wharf Theatre in Monterey, was announced as "the beginning of her 1960 pre–Broadway tour."[15] Ten years later, Mel Heimer wrote that Moorehead was bringing her one-woman show to Broadway, "delighting all of us who have been Aggie's fans for so long."[16] The show never got there. The last performance I have documented was at a festival in Jacksonville, Florida, on April 7, 1973.[17] In the mid–1960s, we know she commanded $1,000 to $2,000 per appearance.[18] Her personal manager in the late '60s and early '70s mentions that during his tenure she received "Somewhere between fifteen hundred and three thousand dollars."[19]

Let us return to the beginning and look more closely at what Moorehead's one-woman show was made of. *That Fabulous Redhead* had its world premiere in Salt Lake City in the pseudo–Egyptian style Kingsbury Hall on January 30, 1954. Situated in the northwest corner of the campus of the University of Utah, Kingsbury Hall had first opened its doors in 1930 and remains the Performing Arts Center of the University of Utah to this day.[20] The auditorium can seat 1,913 patrons and, according to the university website, "There's not a bad seat in the house."[21] Moorehead was already familiar with the space, having done six performances of *Don Juan in Hell* there in February 1951.[22]

Producer Paul Gregory was on hand in Salt Lake City, in the words of University of Utah sponsor Gail Plummer, "to see the premiere of another hit."[23] Moorehead's director Charles Laughton was also meant to have been at the opening, but wasn't feeling well and promised to come to see the show on February 9 in Minneapolis.[24] In a front-page interview with *Winnipeg Free Press* film critic Frank Morriss at this time, Laughton said that Moorehead was "a fabulous person" and "the only woman he knew who could carry off such a demanding assignment."[25]

A press book article described *That Fabulous Redhead* as "an offbeat evening of unusual entertainment."[26] Reviewers described how Moorehead "ran an emotional gamut from life in the raw to the spiritually elevated and from comedy to suspense" and how "Her program ranged from the hilarious to the lofty, and her performance evoked tears one moment and laughter the next."[27]

Based on reviews, it is possible to piece together a fairly complete picture of what the audience saw and heard in 1954.[28] As originally conceived, the show lasted two hours and had one interval.[29] Moorehead got the ball rolling with a segment that would be known as "Household Hints Down Through the Centuries," which included a medieval recipe read with a mock Chaucerian accent, Mrs. Henry Ward Beecher's advice on "how to cure feminine withers bruised by horseback riding,"[30] and advice on how to cure a canary of asthma. Then followed in rapid succession the "These I Have Loved" section from Rupert Brooke's poem "The Great Lover"; Thurber's story about his mother, "Lavender with a Difference"; two Bible stories, the story of "The Flood" ("a masterpiece"—"the flattest part of the evening"[31]) and "Moses and the Bullrushes," or properly "Moses an' de Bullrush," a kind of aural blackface retelling of the story of Moses from the Bible "as told by a Negro maid"[32] ("southern dialect was flawless"—"one of the evening's high spots"[33]); before the first half concluded with the account from Proust's *Remembrance of Things Past* describing Madame Swann's daily drive through the park ("she created completely and convincingly a woman and an era"[34]).

The second half consisted of Queen Elizabeth I's letter to Richard Cox, Bishop of Ely (beginning famously "Proud Prelate"); Ring Lardner's short story "Some Like 'em Hot" ("the girl's laugh didn't sound in character, the man's voice wavered between a New York and a countrified accent"[35]); a short passage on Charles Laughton from Osbert Sitwell's 1946 autobiography *The Scarlet Tree*; "Sorry, Wrong Number"; and finally a passage from the first of the five plays in George Bernard Shaw's massive *Back to Methuselah* titled "In the Beginning: B.C. 4004," where "Mother Eve chides her son Abel for fighting and her spouse Adam for digging."[36] Moorehead tied it all together with appropriate personal patter; reminiscences about her childhood in Ohio, her loving father, and her straight-laced Aunt Cam, who approached any delicate or unpleasant topic with a characteristic clearing of the throat. "In this chatty, personal fashion," wrote the *Brooklyn Eagle*, "Miss Moorehead made friends with her audience and tied together her varied numbers."[37]

In a sense, given its reliance on impressing the audience with a wide range of voices, dialects, and literary genres, *That Fabulous Redhead* was a direct continuation from Moorehead's work in radio. It was symptomatic, then, that the chief draw and climax of the evening was her reenactment in live performance of her most important role in radio, the agonized heroine of "Sorry, Wrong Number." Opinions were divided on the success of transferring her radio classic to the stage. A reviewer in Sioux Falls, South Dakota, wrote that "Pointing out the highlight of Miss Moorehead's program isn't easy. But the tense, dread-packed 'Sorry, Wrong Number' had the edge."[38] In an otherwise glowing review, the critic in Oklahoma City wrote that "'Sorry, Wrong Number,' … left this writer a little cold. It is much more effective on TV, where closeups show the facial expressions."[39] Louis Shaeffer of the *Brooklyn Eagle* found two or three other numbers more entertaining than "Sorry, Wrong Number," such as Thurber's "fond yet unsentimental piece about his mother."[40] Bayard F. Ennis of the Charleston, West Virginia, *Gazette*, on the other hand, thought "Miss Moorehead's handling of the piece was gripping and intense."[41] Moorehead herself said in an interview that she would have preferred to do without "Sorry," "there are so many other great things," but had to include it due to popular demand.[42] By 1960, she had dropped it from the program.[43]

That Fabulous Redhead as a whole was universally praised. The show garnered Moorehead some of the most satisfying reviews of her career, because for the first and only time they were all about her. A local newspaper in Oklahoma City wrote:

> It takes a great artist to hold an audience of 2,000 persons spellbound for two hours, which is just what fascinating Agnes Moorehead did here Sunday afternoon. Many said it was the shortest two

> hours in their memory. Miss Moorehead's supreme artistry must be seen to be appreciated. Her facial expressions, her complete abandonment to each mood and her ability to live each part mark her as one of the "greats" of the stage today.[44]

After her performance at the Brooklyn Academy of Music, the *Brooklyn Eagle* commented: "Displaying an assured, attractive personality and a sense of humor which you could never guess from her many neurotic roles in films, as well as a distinguished, titian-hair beauty which is hidden generally under character makeup, the talented actress made an unqualified hit with the large audience."[45] According to the critic for the *Dallas Times Herald*: "This seems a late date to report that Miss Moorehead is carving quite a niche for herself in American theater; but, given two hours with the lady, one comes away with the impression that a great actress is being only really appreciated for the first time."[46] A reviewer in Middlesboro, Kentucky, thought "Miss Moorehead's performance was flawless in its entirety."[47] Finally, one Reno, Nevada journalist wrote: "Fabulous is perhaps the only word to do her justice."[48]

Moorehead's physical appearance also came in for praise. According to Louise Faulk in Ruston, Louisiana, "Those of us who had seen her only on the screen were totally unprepared for the impact of her personal charm."[49] Louis Shaeffer of the *Brooklyn Eagle* described her as "a striking figure with a tiara atop her elaborate hairdo and wearing a flowing mauve-colored gown."[50] Her décolleté, tight-fitting, filmy dress, almost a negligee, was an unusual choice, especially for a 53-year-old character actress, not to mention the fanciful little crown on her head, which had no connection with any of her readings. Clearly, Moorehead chose her outfit herself. Thus it reflected how she wanted to be perceived: as a queen of the American stage or, better yet, a princess.

Given the unanimous praise from the critics and the many large and satisfied audiences, it seems hard to understand why Wood Soanes would write in his column in September 1954, that Moorehead "wasn't exactly successful in her one-woman show last season."[51] Despite Soanes's sour grapes, the enthusiasm for the show among critics and audiences alike continued in the years to come. Virginia Shaw concluded an adulatory review in 1960 by saying that "800 people Tuesday night left the theatre dead in love with her."[52] One of her young fans, who saw the show in his home state of Idaho in about 1964, when he was 15, still vividly remembered the impact she had had nearly 50 years later:

> It was thrilling to watch her cast her spell over us. So many moods, tempos, characters. Tears of laughter, tears of sorrow. Shaw, Thurber, many more, as well as her own personal recollections—just the right mix of lilting wisps of reflection and silent wonder countered beautifully with raucous comedy replete with multiple characterizations and portraits of elaborate physicality, all painted on our imaginations by her bountiful skill as an artist.[53]

Granted, there were some dissenting voices. "Miss Moorehead's voice is pleasantly modulated, flexible and extremely easy on the ear," one critic wrote, "when she is not purposely trying to make it otherwise. She tends, however, to allow her own personality too much sway to the detriment [sic] at times to her material."[54]

Charles Nolte, who was in Paul Gregory's hit production of *The Caine Mutiny Court-Martial* on Broadway at the time, attended a rehearsal of *That Fabulous Redhead* at the Plymouth Theatre on W. 45th St. in New York on March 15, 1954. He wrote in his journal that "There are touches of coyness which aren't particularly attractive. And 'Sorry, Wrong Number' is a dead-end for her, being too long. It made me nervous to watch." He thought the most effective part of the show was "a bit of Proust: a scintillating description of

Mme. Swann, remarkable first as literature, and then for what Moorehead does with her voice."[55]

Several years later, an irate ticket-holder wrote in to his local Florida newspaper:

> Miss Moorehead was playing it safe for our community.... She was also playing it patronizingly. Her program was shadow—but no substance.... Miss Moorehead posed and arched her back, ... fluttered her eyelids and hands in hyperfemininity and played down to us.... Her program had no bite. It was sweet and sacchariney. She was pink on the outside and pink on the inside.[56]

This anonymous audience member was commenting on a performance from 1967. Paul Gregory himself thought Moorehead's one-woman show lost its charm and spontaneity in later years. In my first interview with him in 2006, he said that her show was wonderful in the beginning, because she was fresh and read everything as if she was seeing it for the first time. Later, he said, it simply became "an exercise in memory."[57] He felt that her performance deteriorated to the point that she was "bombarding the audience with sound and diction."[58] Listening to the recording of the show made by Moorehead's tour manager Quint Benedetti in 1969,[59] I can see Gregory's point with regard to some of the poetry, such as Rupert Brooke's "The Great Lover," but Moorehead's delivery of comic pieces like "Household Hints through the Centuries" and the little vignette about her Aunt Cam is still spot-on.

An article by one of Moorehead's most devoted fans, Claire Baker, titled "My Unforgettable Earful," gives us a clear idea of how the program had changed—actually how little it had changed—nearly a decade after Moorehead first started touring with the show. Baker attended a performance of *Come Closer, I'll Give You an Earful* at the Civic Auditorium in her hometown of Portland, Oregon, on Friday, November 1, 1963. The program according to Baker consisted of the usual "Household Hints" ("delivered with just the right amount of 'seasoning'"), followed by the Devil's speech from *Don Juan in Hell* ("the applause was deafening"), "Lavender with a Difference" ("manipulated with a great sense of timing"), "The Harp Weaver" ("There was complete and utter silence"), "Moses and the Bullrush" ("a highly animated sketch"), Proust's account of Madame Swann ("A short, spicy monologue"), "Mary's Ghost" ("a cold, eerie shiver passed through the audience"), and finally the story of the Flood from the Bible ("full of great feeling and deep sensitivity").[60]

Baker does not mention in her ecstatic account that Moorehead performed her show for a "rather tiny audience."[61] According to the *Portland Journal*, "It was all over in exactly 100 minutes."[62]

As Charles Tranberg has pointed out, in the Civil Rights era Moorehead found it desirable to change the storyteller in "Moses and the Bullrush" from a black maid to the performer's made-up Southern cousin Daphne, who we can assume is not African American and who sounds a lot like Velma Cruther.[63] The most significant addition to the program in later years was Edna St. Vincent Millay's "Ballad of the Harp Weaver," an audience favorite.[64] Her tour manager in the late 1960s refers to this poem as "the dramatic vortex of her show."[65] Her mother's Reedsburg friend George E. Perry described it as "on all counts the most memorable."[66]

Other texts that were added to the show in the 1960s were Rosemary Benet's poem about Lincoln's mother, "Nancy Hanks"; the Devil's speech on destruction from *Don Juan in Hell*, William Blake's poem "Little Lamb," Thomas Hood's ballad "Mary's Ghost," Ben Hur Lampman's popular poem "Where to Bury a Dog," and Robert Frost's famous lyric

Agnes Moorehead in a publicity shot for her one-woman show from the 1960s, by which time it was called "Come Closer, I'll Give You an Earful." Even during her busy *Bewitched* years, Moorehead tried to go out with her program of readings as often as she could (courtesy Muskingum University Archives).

"Stopping by Woods on a Snowy Evening."[67] The show varied in length from 70 to 100 minutes, depending on the audience and their paying power.[68]

In August 1967, it was reported that Moorehead had done her one-woman show 375 times.[69] Fan club president Roy Buchanan claimed her performance in Billings, Montana, in January 1969 was her 500th.[70] Lynn Kear estimated that Moorehead had taken her show to 200 cities in the United States.[71] I have been able to document about 125 performances in roughly 100 different American towns and cities plus Canada, Israel, Egypt, and Jamaica, so the estimates above are probably too high.

CREDITS: *Director:* Charles Laughton; *Producer:* Paul Gregory; *Writers:* Various (see above)
CAST: Agnes Moorehead

Performances of Agnes Moorehead's One-Woman Show, 1954–1973[72]

Date	*Place*	*Venue*	*Fee*
Jan. 30, 1954	Salt Lake City, Utah	Kingsbury Hall, Univ. of Utah	$750
Jan. 31, 1954	Rapid City, South Dakota	Rapid City High School Aud.	$750
Feb. 2, 1954	Sioux Falls, South Dakota	Coliseum	$1,000
Feb. 3, 1954	Sioux City, Iowa	RKO Orpheum Theatre	$1,000
Feb. 5, 1954	Port Arthur, Canada	Port Arthur Arena	$800
Feb. 7, 1954	Virginia City, Minnesota	Virginia City High School Aud.	$800
Feb. 8, 1954	Hibbing, Minnesota	Hibbing High School Aud.	$800
Feb. 9, 1954	Minneapolis, Minnesota	Minneapolis Woman's Club Aud.	$600
	Duluth, Minnesota	Denfield Aud.	$800
Feb. 10, 1954	Ironwood, Michigan	Ironwood High School Aud.	$800
Feb. 11, 1954	Marshfield, Wisconsin	Columbus High School Aud.	$600
Feb. 13, 1954	Wasau, Wisconsin	Wasau High School Aud.	$550
Feb. 16, 1954	Aurora, Illinois	Bardwell School Aud.	$550
Feb. 17, 1954	Neenah, Wisconsin	Appleton High School Aud.	$750
Feb. 22, 1954	Ottumwa, Iowa	Ottumwa High School Aud.	$750
Feb. 23, 1954	Lincoln, Nebraska	Nebraska Theatre, Univ. of Nebraska	$1,000[73]
Feb. 24, 1954	Manhattan, Kansas	Kansas State College Aud.	$750
Feb. 25, 1954	Kansas City, Missouri	Plaza Theatre	$800
	Wichita, Kansas	University of Wichita Aud.	$1,000
Feb. 27, 1954	Chickasha, Oklahoma	Oklahoma College for Women Aud.	$650
Feb. 28, 1954	Oklahoma City, Oklahoma	Municipal Aud., Civic Center	$1,000
March 1, 1954	Little Rock, Arkansas	Robinson Memorial Aud.	$750
March 2, 1954	Ruston, Louisiana	Howard Aud., Louisiana Tech Univ.	$1,500[74]
March 3, 1954	Shreveport, Louisiana	Municipal Memorial Aud.	$750
March 4, 1954	Natchitoches, Louisiana	Northwestern College	$900
March 5, 1954	New Orleans, Louisiana	Municipal Aud.	$750
March 8, 1954	Mobile, Alabama	Murphy Aud.	$750
March 9, 1954	Hattiesburg, Mississippi	Mississippi Southern College	$675
March 10, 1954	Jackson, Mississippi	Municipal Aud.	$750
March 11, 1954	Memphis, Tennessee	Ellis Aud.	$750
March 13, 1954	Brooklyn, New York	Brooklyn Academy of Music	$1,000
March 16, 1954	Scranton, Pennsylvania	Jewish Community Center	$750
March 17, 1954	Charleston, West Virginia	Municipal Aud.	$800
March 18, 1954	Cincinnati, Ohio	Queen City Club	$900
March 19, 1954	St. Louis, Missouri	Hotel Sheraton Aud.	$900
March 24, 1954	Ann Arbor, Michigan	Hill Aud., University of Michigan	$1,250
March 26, 1954	Bay City, Michigan?		
March 29, 1954	Akron, Ohio	Akron University Aud.?	
March 31, 1954	Kent, Ohio	Kent State University Aud.	$750

Date	*Place*	*Venue*	*Fee*
April 2, 1954	Fort Worth, Texas	Anna Shelton Hall	$750
April 5–7, 1954	Dallas, Texas	Coronet Theatre	65% ticket sales
April 9, 1954	Lake Charles, Louisiana	McNeese State College Aud.	$800
April 12, 1954	Harrogate, Tennessee	Duke Hall Aud., Lincoln Memorial Univ.	$750
April 14, 1954	Baton Rouge, Louisiana	Gym-Armory, Louisiana State Univ.	$850
April 20, 1954	Reno, Nevada	State Building Aud.	$650
April 21, 1954	Chico, California	Chico State College Aud.	$750
April 23, 1954	Fresno, California	Hardy's Theatre	$750[75]
April 24, 1954	Stockton, California	High School Aud.	$750
April 26, 1954	Phoenix, Arizona	Phoenix Union High School Aud.	$1,000
April 29, 1954	San Diego, California	Russ Aud.	
May 17, 1954	Los Angeles, California	Los Angeles City College Aud.	$800
May 19, 1954	Oakland, California	Oakland Aud. Theatre	$800
Oct. 1, 1954	Berkeley, California	Garfield High School Aud.	
Nov. 1, 1954	Huntington, West Virginia		
Nov. 8, 1954	Oak Park, Illinois	High School Aud.	
March 6, 1956	Tacoma, Washington	Pacific Lutheran College	
June 17, 1960	La Jolla, California	La Jolla Art Center[76]	
July 26–30, 1960	Monterey, California	Wharf Theatre and Opera House[77]	
March 7, 1961	Cairo, Egypt	Ewart Memorial Hall, American Univ.	
cJuly 19, 1961	Mershon, Ohio	Ohio State University	
Sept. 30, 1961	San Francisco, California	Masonic Temple[78]	
Oct. 26–27, 1961	Dayton, Ohio	Loewe's Theatre	
Nov. 3, 1961	Des Moines, Iowa	Drake University	
ca. April/May 1963	Boise, Idaho		
July 18–31, 1963	Israel	Israeli Festival of Arts, Tel Aviv	
Oct. 25, 1963	Alton, Illinois	Hatheway Hall, Monticello College	$1,000
Nov. 1, 1963	Portland, Oregon	Civic Aud.	$1,000
Nov. 6, 1963	Minneapolis, Minnesota	Minnesota Art Institute Aud.	$1,250
Nov. 14, 1963	Park Ridge, Illinois	Park Ridge Town Hall	$1,100
Nov. 21, 1963	Montreal, Canada	La Grande Salle, Place des Arts	$1,100
Nov. 26, 1963	Salem, Oregon	Willamette University Aud.	$1,250
Jan. 9, 1964	Casper, Wyoming	Natron City High School Aud.	$1,000
Jan. 12–19, 1964	Kingston, Jamaica		$1,750[79]
Jan. 25, 1964	Coldwater, Michigan	Tibbits Opera House	$1,000
Feb. 4, 1964	Pocatello, Idaho	University Aud., Idaho State Univ.	$1,000
April 2, 1964	Tacoma, Washington		
April 10, 1964	Medford, Oregon	Holly Theatre	$1,000
April 16, 1964	Richmond, Kentucky	Eastern Kentucky State College	
April 17, 1964	Berea, Kentucky	Berea College	
Mid-March 1965	Detroit, Michigan	Fisher Theatre	
April 12, 1965	Pittsburgh, Pennsylvania	Chatham College Chapel	
April 28, 1965	St. Paul, Minnesota	Macalester College	
Aug. 15, 1965	Kalispell, Montana	Flathead County High School Aud.	
Oct. 31, 1965	Beverly Hills, California	Beverly Hills High School	
Dec. 10, 1965	Palos Verdes, California	Marymount College	
March 12, 1966	Pasadena, California	Caltech?	
April 1, 1966	Chicago, Illinois		
April 7, 1966	Los Angeles, California	Brentwood–Bel Air Women's Club	
April 26, 1966	Hastings, Nebraska	Hastings College	
Oct. 30, 1966	Missoula, Montana	Mission Mountain College	
Nov. 6–7, 1966	Omaha, Nebraska	University of Omaha	$2,000[80]
April 1, 1967	Portland, Oregon	Lewis and Clark College	
April 6, 1967	Bethesda, Maryland	Walt Whitman High School	
Sept. 21, 1967	Columbus, Ohio	College of St. Mary of the Springs	
Nov. 28, 1967	Fort Walton Beach, Florida	Choctawhatchee High School	
April 6, 1968	Rock Island, Illinois		

Date	*Place*	*Venue*	*Fee*
1969	Madison, Wisconsin	University of Wisconsin[81]	
Jan. 26, 1969	Billings, Montana	Petro Theatre, Eastern Montana Coll.	
April 13, 1969	Norman, Oklahoma	Holmberg Hall Aud., U. of Oklahoma	
April 26, 1969	Phoenix, Arizona	Fox Chris-Town Theater	
May 1, 1969	Dayton, Ohio	NCR Aud.	
July 15–20, 1969	Traverse City, Michigan	Cherry County Playhouse	
Late July 1969	Chicago, New York		
Oct. 23, 1969	Scottsdale, Arizona		
Feb. 14, 1970	Eugene, Oregon	Central Presbyterian Church	
April 11, 1970	Nevada, Missouri	Rosemary Aud., Cottey College	
April 24, 1970	Zanesville, Ohio	Municipal Aud.	
Jan. 1, 1972	Arlington, Illinois	Arlington Park Theatre	
April 7, 1973	Jacksonville, Florida		

7

Schlitz Playhouse: "The Life You Save" (TV, 1957)

In October 1956, Agnes Moorehead received a script for a 30-minute episode of *Schlitz Playhouse*, which was titled "The Life You Save May Be Your Own." It was based on a short story by the Southern writer Flannery O'Connor.[1] The long, delayed production period on *Raintree County* was finally coming to an end at this time and Moorehead was already working on her new project, *The True Story of Jesse James*. The film had begun production at Twentieth Century–Fox in early September and wrapped in late October with retakes and additional scenes being shot from mid to late November. In mid–November, too, production started on *The Story of Mankind* at Warner Bros.' Burbank studios. After that, Moorehead was slated to do *Jeanne Eagles* at Columbia.

In the three years since her television debut in "Lullaby," Moorehead had been so busy in films and touring with her one-woman show that she had only found time for four further appearances on the small screen, three of them in 1956. In October of that year, despite her busy schedule, Moorehead decided to accept the role of Ma Crater in the TV drama that would ultimately be known by the shorter title "The Life You Save." While many of Moorehead's directors in television were new to her, there was a familiar face helming this effort, which may have had a positive influence on her decision. Herschel Daugherty had been the dialogue director on *The Woman in White* back in 1948. Recently, he had directed Moorehead in an episode of *Studio 57* called "Teacher" with June Lockhart, which aired on October 31, 1956.

That being said, the opportunity to co-star with Gene Kelly was no doubt the chief attraction of this project. Kelly was 44 and still a major star after his strings of hits *On the Town*, *Summer Stock*, *An American in Paris*, and *Singing in the Rain*. Yet his films of the mid–1950s had not been so successful. Now he was considering what television might have to offer this career. "The Life You Save" would be his television debut. Like *The Revlon Mirror Theatre* ("Lullaby") and *Studio 57* ("Teacher"), *Schlitz Playhouse* was produced by MCA's "series factory" Revue Productions on the Republic lot in Studio City, which in 1952 had become the company's first home.[2] This drama anthology series had been running on Friday nights on CBS since October 1951, sponsored by the Schlitz Brewing Co., and was originally called *Schlitz Playhouse of Stars*. The first 26 episodes were an hour long and broadcast live from New York. In April 1952, the show was shortened to half an hour and by the fall of 1956 all the episodes were prerecorded in Los Angeles.[3]

Moorehead's move into television in the 1950s certainly led to more leading roles, but not necessarily to more glamorous ones. Ma Crater in "The Life You Save" was certainly one of the least glamorous and can almost bear comparison with Velma Cruther. "Non descript" is probably the most neutral term one can use about the way she looks and dresses and "mannish" might also be the word to describe the baggy, amorphous shirts and overalls and slouch hats she favors. She is only referred to as "the old woman" throughout O'Connor's story and is described further as "about the size of cedar fence post." She wears "a man's gray hat pulled down low over her head" in the opening scene of the story, just as Moorehead does on television.[4] Moorehead's Ma Crater is not toothless, though, like the original character.[5] Moorehead is spared that indignity, though she would no doubt have been game even for that.

A widow for 15 years, Ma Crater has clearly given up. Yet the story revolves around her not giving up on the idea that she might find a husband for her 30-year-old deaf mute daughter, named Lucy Nell like herself; someone to care for her after her mother is gone. According to the narrator of the short story, "The old woman ... was ravenous for a son-in-law."[6] Enter Tom T. Triplett, the tramp and jack-of-all-trades played by Gene Kelly. He's "a man," as he points out, even if he only has one arm (the right one). A young actress from Norwood, Ohio, was cast as the younger Lucy Nell Crater. Janice Rule was 26, had been working in television since she was 20, and had racked up several credits on shows like *Campbell Playhouse*, *Studio One*, *Goodyear Television Playhouse*, and *The Alcoa Hour*.

It wasn't all that often Moorehead had a chance to work on TV scripts based on texts by major writers. Other examples are *A Tale of Two Cities*, *Frankenstein*, *The House of the Seven Gables*, and a first season episode of *Night Gallery* titled "Certain Shadows on the Wall" based on a short story by Mary E. Wilkins Freeman. Nelson Gidding's teleplay of "The Life You Save" follows O'Connor's story closely, including many lines of dialogue and most of the plot. In the short story, Tom Triplett is Tom *Shiftlet* (no doubt a play on "shiftless") and Mrs. Crater claims her daughter is 15–16 rather than 22–23, but otherwise the TV adaptation follows O'Connor's original to a remarkable degree.[7] In return for food and a bed in the garage, Tom makes himself useful by doing various repairs around the "plantation" and getting Mr. Crater's old car, which broke down the day he died, running again. Tom even teaches Lucy Nell to say "bird."

There is a scene which is typical of O'Connor's unconventional view of life and love, where Mrs. Crater and Tom negotiate the terms for his marrying her daughter. After haggling over the honeymoon, that sum turns out to be $17.50 both in the print and TV version. On a Saturday, the three of them "drive into town and get married," as Mrs. Crater puts it. It is only at the end that the televised episode veers off sharply, so to speak, from the original track. In O'Connor's story, Tom abandons Lucy Nell at a diner 100 miles from her home and takes off in the car bound for Mobile. In the TV version, he comes back and saves her from a belligerent proprietor who wants the 35 cents she is owed for pastries, giving quite a different and more affirmative meaning to the title "The Life You Save May Be Your Own." O'Connor would hardly have approved.

The original short story is vintage O'Connor and typical of her penchant for dark humor, ambiguous romance, itinerant men, and characters with missing limbs, most famously seen in the college anthology classic "Good Country People." Despite the fidelity to most of the original storyline and dialogue, there is very little of the grotesque humor, absurdity, and Southern Gothic atmosphere of O'Connor's tale in the televised version.

Gene Kelly (center) made his television debut as a one-armed hobo in the half-hour *Schlitz Playhouse* version of Flannery O'Connor's mordant tale "The Life You Save May Be Your Own." Appearances to the contrary, Kelly had the full use of both his legs in the role. The hayseed ingénue of the piece was played by Janice Rule (right).

Moorehead delivers her more or less standard rustic rube performance and sunny-faced, middle-aged dancing man Kelly seems an odd choice to play a 28-year-old, one-armed tramp on the move and on the make. Granted, he is only referred to as being 28 in the story, not in the teleplay.[8] Janice Rule is touching and suitably angelic as Lucy Nell in this strange mixture of *Johnny Belinda* and *Tobacco Road*.

By the time the episode aired on March 1, 1957, Moorehead was nearing the end of the *Jeanne Eagels* shoot and looking forward to Paul Gregory's new stage production, *The Rivalry*, about the Lincoln-Douglas debates, where she would co-star with Raymond Massey and Martin Gabel. As for Gene Kelly, ultimately he didn't do much work in television. After this show, it would be five years until he appeared on TV again, starring in the series *Going My Way*, based on the Bing Crosby film. Janice Rule, on the other hand, worked steadily in the medium until 1992. She also acted in films like *Bell Book and Candle*, a precursor of *Bewitched*; *The Chase*, *3 Women*, and *Missing*. She died of a cerebral hemorrhage in 2003.

CREDITS: *Director:* Herschel Daugherty; *Producer:* Frank P. Rosenberg; *Writers:* Nelson Gidding (teleplay), Flannery O'Connor (story); *Cinematography:* John L. Russell; *Film editing:* Michael R. McAdam; *Art direction:* George Patrick; *Makeup department:* Jack Barron (makeup), Florence Bush (hair stylist); *Costume and wardrobe department:* Vincent Dee; *Production company:* Revue Productions; *Air date:* March 1, 1957, on CBS

CAST: Buddy Joe Hooker (as Buddy Hart) (hitchhiker), Gene Kelly (Tom T. Triplett), Agnes Moorehead (Ma Crater), Barbara Pepper (Miss Buell), Janice Rule (Lucy Nell Crater), Paul Smith (George)

8

The Rivalry (Stage, 1957–58)

On Saturday, January 11, 1958, Agnes Moorehead wrote a letter to her friend and producer Paul Gregory from Burlington, Vermont, where she was just starting the final stretch of a long tour with *The Rivalry*, a new play by Norman Corwin. In this play about the 1858 Lincoln-Douglas debates in Illinois, she was co-starred with Martin Gabel and Raymond Massey.

> Paul dear,
> I've rubbed myself with Vermont Maple syrup in order to sweeten my disposition but that was pretty sappy of me for Ray [Massey] has started already—everything wrong—honestly—he has given me such depression—he even started out and on about the Jungle location—I know it must be pretty rough—but the continual screaming and snobbery is creating such loathing that it even surprises me! We had a run through at Martin [Gabel]'s home. Ray came in higher than two kites—I did my bit and left. Norman [Corwin] didn't come with us. He had a bad throat but he is to meet us in Boston.

She went on about some other, unrelated matters and signed herself "Agatha."[1]

Moorehead was a good hater. Never one to seek open conflict on a film set or in other professional situations, she enjoyed giving vent to pet peeves and repressed resentments in letters to close friends and confidantes, often in a teasing or satirical tone.[2] As the letter quoted above indicates, one individual she came to dislike intensely was the gaunt, gangly, Canadian-born actor Raymond Massey. Among his more than 80 roles in film and television, Massey is probably best known today for playing the murderous Brewster sisters' equally homicidal nephew Jonathan in *Arsenic and Old Lace*. In his own day, though, Massey's forte and chief claim to fame was playing Abraham Lincoln, most famously in the stage and film version of *Abe Lincoln in Illinois* and later in *How the West Was Won*. In the words of one small town reviewer of *The Rivalry*: "He *is* Lincoln."[3] On Broadway off and on since 1930, Massey had starred in Gregory's production of *John Brown's Body* there in the spring of 1953 with Judith Anderson and Tyrone Power.

Moorehead and Massey had not worked together previously, nor would they again, but during the period of rehearsing and touring with *The Rivalry* from late August 1957 till late January 1958, through nearly 70 towns and cities in 32 States of the Union and Canada, they were stuck with each other. Massey irritated Moorehead, as we have seen, by whining about the rigors of touring, but we also know she resented his giving the impression that he was *the* star of the show.[4] The rivalry, indeed.

In *The Rivalry*, Massey played Abraham Lincoln, Martin Gabel was his political adversary Stephen A. Douglas, and Moorehead played Douglas's wife, Adele Cutts Douglas, who would only have been 22 at the time of the seven debates, which all took place in Illinois between August 21 and October 15, 1858. Moorehead and Gabel had been friends for more than 20 years, since they both worked in radio in New York in the 1930s. More recently, Gabel had directed Moorehead in an ill-conceived filmatization of a classic tale by Henry James, *The Lost Moment*, and had made his film debut as Dr. Strauss in *Fourteen Hours*. He was a frequent guest panelist on the game show "What's My Line?" where his wife, Arlene Francis, was a regular panelist for many years.

Brian Donlevy, the customarily black-hatted villain of classic westerns such as *Destry Rides Again* and *The Virginian* and Oscar nominee for *Beau Geste*, had been slated to play Douglas, but withdrew for "personal reasons" only a few weeks before the opening. Gregory recalled how Donlevy had come crying into his office with the $5,000 wig that had just been made especially for him, begging to be let out of his contract. His drinking made it impossible for him to remember his lines.[5] Gregory let him go and hired Gabel at $1,750 a week for the first eight weeks, rising to $2,000 for the rest of the tour and $2,500 for the New York run.[6] In comparison, Donlevy had contracted to receive $3,000 on tour and $2,500 in New York.[7] Moorehead was paid 10 percent of the weekly gross box office receipts up to $2,750 per week. In addition, she was allowed to bring a secretary or maid at a salary of $100 a week.[8] Her stand-in Kathy Ellis was hired as assistant stage manager at $175 a week.[9]

The author and director of *The Rivalry* was radio Renaissance man Norman Corwin. Corwin had held listeners in thrall with his broadcast celebration of the Allied victory in Europe *On a Note of Triumph* in 1945 with Gabel in the cast and had written scores of radio dramas, including *Ann Rutledge and Lincoln*, where Moorehead played Rutledge's mother. Corwin had left radio in 1955, but kept on writing. *The Rivalry* was his stage play debut. He had constructed a 90-minute play based on a sampling of the transcripts from 30 hours of the famous Lincoln-Douglas debates a century earlier. When I spoke to Corwin in March 2008, he was nearly 98, but still full-voiced and clear as a bell. Seventy years after he first had gotten to know Moorehead when he was a director and writer at CBS radio and she was a successful radio actress, he was still full of admiration for her professionalism and versatility. He never had any trouble working with her, he recalled, nor had he picked up on any animosity between her and Massey when they were rehearsing and touring with *The Rivalry*. He thought, though, that Massey was possibly more insecure playing Lincoln in the context of Corwin's play, as he had two such expert co-stars vying for attention on the stage. He recalled overhearing Massey backstage just before their opening night in Vancouver muttering to himself: "You've done it before and you can do it again."[10]

Rehearsals started on Monday, August 26, 1957, in the Rainbow Studios at 1627 Cahuenga Blvd. in Hollywood.[11] The show opened at the Georgia Theatre in Vancouver on September 23 and wended its way down the west coast to San Diego and Long Beach, California, before moving across the country via Arizona, Texas, Oklahoma, Kansas, Nebraska, Iowa, Minnesota, South Dakota, Illinois, Wisconsin, Missouri, Indiana, Ohio, Kentucky, and West Virginia, ending up in Pennsylvania, Connecticut, Delaware, Virginia, North Carolina, Maryland, and New Jersey in December. After almost a month off, they resumed the tour on January 12, 1958, in Burlington, Vermont, moving down to New York, Massachusetts and Connecticut, where *The Rivalry* closed in New Haven on January 25. Originally slated to open on Broadway on January 27, according to Paul

Gregory's telegram to Moorehead this failure to come in was "due to our inability to get the proper house in New York."[12] *The Rivalry* would not be the last of Gregory's Broadway-bound shows not to make it there. Moorehead would not be back on the Great White Way until the fall of 1962.

The play was generally well received. The effectiveness of the simple staging was frequently remarked upon, in addition to the fine acting and the timeliness of the topic. "By what lucky prescience," one reviewer asked, "did Paul Gregory, a year, two years ago, complete his plans for a play based on the Lincoln-Douglas debates, that was to reach the American public so close upon the events of Sept. 6th and Little Rock?"[13] The *Vancouver Province* wrote after the world premiere that "much of it is so topical Mr. Corwin could have been using today's segregation headlines as source material."[14] The topicality of the play's racial theme prompted Gregory to warn his actors on September 17, that they should "guard very carefully what is said by any of you outside the theatre pertaining to these issues: All of our passions pro and con for the subject should be spent in the performances."[15]

Notoriously hard-to-please *Chicago Tribune* critic Claudia Cassidy was not impressed by *The Rivalry*, though, when it played the cavernous Anshe Emet Auditorium in Chicago on October 29–30, 1957. She thought Corwin had made the historic debates "drab and dull, partly as a dramatist and partly as a director: His so-called 'Rivalry' is about as exciting as a fight you know is fixed or a poker game with stacked cards."[16] Moorehead's diplomatic response to Cassidy's review was recorded by an interviewer. "'We were disappointed,' Moorehead said, 'but Miss Cassidy has always been very kind to me, and we can't hope to please all the critics all the time.'"[17] Thus she deftly suggested that the faults of the production probably didn't lie with her.

Corwin had designed the narrator-figure of Adele Douglas to provide the necessary context for the fiery words of the two famous orators, to give them an on-stage listener, and to provide a link between the debaters and the audience. As one review described it, Mrs. Douglas served as "a sort of Greek chorus to comment, foreworn, fill-in and lead-on, a loving feminine foil to these two bears of men, long and short."[18] One newspaper got a headline out of the fact that "Curtain Will Not Be Lowered When Actress Dons Costumes." It was not as risqué as it sounds. Walter Plunkett, on loan from MGM to design a costume for Moorehead, explained: "It is interesting to know that Miss Moorehead never leaves the stage, and, although wearing only two different costumes, she effects eleven different changes without the lowering of a curtain."[19] Plunkett had designed the costumes for several of Moorehead's MGM films, including period films like *Summer Holiday*, *Show Boat*, and most recently *Raintree County*, and he had also designed her gown for *Don Juan in Hell.*

Adele Douglas was a less showy and, certainly, less wordy part than those of her male co-stars, but the critics were unanimous in their praise of Moorehead's handling of a difficult assignment. A review in the *Vancouver Sun* of the premiere performance remarked that "Agnes Moorehead won honors hands down. So great was her vitality, it was impossible to ignore her even when she sat silent for minutes at a time."[20] Another reviewer noted that she played her part "with charm and deep understanding: She is presented as a woman of insight and one who appreciates greatly the qualities of both her husband and Lincoln and their ideals. She is a balance wheel for her husband, noting his short-comings and where he excels. Her imitation of her husband's interview with a reporter on the tariff is one of the gems in the play."[21] An even more ecstatic critic referred

It was rare for Moorehead to express such a strong dislike for someone as she did Raymond Massey (left), her co-star in *The Rivalry*, Norman Corwin's play about the Lincoln-Douglas debates. Massey played Abraham Lincoln, Moorehead played Mrs. Douglas, and Martin Gabel (right), Moorehead's old friend from her days in radio and the director of *The Lost Moment*, played Stephen A. Douglas.

to her as "the beautiful and always brilliant Agnes Moorehead"; but not only that, the critic found her "wholly captivating," "a figure of immense usefulness and adornment to the play," and "always, in herself, ample justification for being put on any stage, anywhere."[22] A student critic in Bloomington, Indiana, who found the play "Paul Gregory's least impressive production to date," nevertheless found that "When Miss Moorehead is at the helm, the stage takes on an added glow."[23] A reviewer in Boston wrote: "She lightens and brightens and stirs *The Rivalry* with a feeling of human warmth."[24] According to the *Freeport Journal Standard*, "she makes the play."[25]

Variety reviewed a performance of *The Rivalry* in Seattle, Washington: "It is in the asides and shorter scenes featuring Agnes Moorehead as Mrs. Douglas that Corwin brings the rivalry to life. The actress fairly steals the show in a charming performance as the shrewd but very feminine Adele Cutts Douglas."[26] Moorehead's scene-stealing tendencies were noted by several critics. One found that "Agnes Moorehead was so vital that she stole the show on occasion and was a moving force even when in the background."[27] Not everyone approved. A reviewer in Waverly, Iowa, where they played October 27, 1957, wrote: "Miss Moorehead, who held the spotlight only about a fourth of the time, tried to counteract the situation by constant attempts at scene-stealing. Straightening her wig and waving her fan, Miss Moorehead distracted the audience while Lincoln was delivering his speeches."[28]

A fan from Big Spring, Texas wrote to Paul Gregory after Moorehead's appearance there at the Howard County Junior College on October 12:

> One of my fondest wishes has just been realized. I have seen Miss Moorehead in a personal appearance. I wish to express my appreciation to Gregory Enterprises for the opportunity. Everyone here is as enthusiastic as I. It was a wonderful production. The play is a splendid vehicle and the actors were magnificent! I love that Moorehead! Thank you! Thank you! Thank you![29]

Even Gregory himself—in retrospect never one to dole out praise for his erstwhile friend—had to admit that Moorehead was "wonderful" in *The Rivalry*.[30] To Norman Corwin, she was "a perfect Mrs. Douglas."[31]

CREDITS: *Director:* Norman Corwin; *Producer:* Paul Gregory; *Writer:* Norman Corwin; *Costumes:* Walter Plunkett (Moorehead's costume); *Premiere:* September 23, 1957, at the Georgia Theatre in Vancouver, British Columbia

CAST: Martin Gabel (Stephen A. Douglas), Raymond Massey (Abraham Lincoln), Agnes Moorehead (Adele Douglas)

TOURING SCHEDULE: Washington state, Oregon, California, Arizona, New Mexico, Texas, Oklahoma, Kansas, Nebraska, Iowa, Minnesota, South Dakota, Michigan, Illinois, Wisconsin, Missouri, Indiana, Ohio, Kentucky, West Virginia, Pennsylvania, Connecticut, Delaware, Virginia, North Carolina, Washington, D.C., and Maryland, closing December 14, 1957, in Newark, New Jersey; resumption of tour January 12, 1958, in Burlington, Vermont, followed by dates in New York state and Boston, Massachusetts, closing January 25, 1958, in New Haven, Connecticut

9

Wagon Train: "The Mary Halstead Story" (TV, 1957)

Wagon Train was a big deal. Not only was it the first hit drama series Moorehead guested on, but Mary Halstead was one of the best dramatic roles she would ever get in television.

Wagon Train was also significant in Moorehead's television career for being her first of many Western series. It would be followed by guest appearances on *The Rebel*, *Rawhide*, *The Rifleman*, *The Wild Wild West*, *Custer*, *Lancer*, and *The Men from Shiloh* (aka *The Virginian*), but none of these could match *Wagon Train* in prestige, popularity, and longevity.

Moorehead had a nineteenth-century look about her that made her well suited to "sprigged muslin roles" in Western costume dramas. She played a few such characters on film, including Mrs. Caslon in *Station West*, Mrs. Samuel in *The True Story of Jesse James*, and Rebecca Prescott in *How the West Was Won*, but it was on television that she really came into her own as an actress in Westerns. In episodes like *Wagon Train*'s "The Mary Halstead Story" or *The Rifleman*'s "Miss Bertie," the story was finally all about her.

Wagon Train ran on NBC and later ABC for eight seasons from September 16, 1957, till September 5, 1965. Moorehead was the "Special Guest Star" on the 10th episode of the first season, in other words, early in the series' long run, when it starred Ward Bond as the wagon master Seth Adams and Robert Horton as the frontier scout Flint McCullough. "The setting," Brooks and March remind us, "was a California-bound wagon train in the post–Civil War days, starting out each season from 'St. Joe' (St. Joseph, Missouri) and making its way west until reaching California in the spring." "What made *Wagon Train* work," they add, "were the characters who passed in and out of its episodes. The program was actually a series of character studies."[1]

The plot of "The Mary Halstead Story" has more tortuous twists and hairpin turns than a game of snakes and ladders. In brief, this episode tells the story of dying woman who has joined the wagon train seeking the son she abandoned 12 years earlier, when he was only six years old. Mary Halstead is too late to be reunited with her son Earl, now better known as the outlaw "Laramie Kid," who is shot and killed as the episode opens. She finds a kind of replacement son, though, in Tommy Nichols, a 17-year-old boy found seriously wounded on the trail, whom she nurses back to health. In a plot twist of epic proportions, it turns out that Tommy was the "punk stray" who shot and killed her son.

After a struggle, Mary finds it in her heart to forgive him and successfully pleads for his life when the members of Earl's gang want to lynch him. She expires from her exertions after uttering the dying words: "Thank you, Major, I found all I was looking for."

Wagon Train was distinguished by an excellent cast both of regulars and guest artists. Ward Bond had been one of the busiest character actresses in Hollywood films since 1929 and since 1950 also on television, but by some fluke he and Moorehead had never worked together before. Bond's co-star Robert Horton, 21 years his junior, who played the scout Flint McCullough, was not given much to do this time. Two other regulars also seen in this episode were Terry Wilson as the assistant wagon master Bill Hawks and Frank McGrath as the cook Charlie Wooster. There is a comic subplot involving Wooster, who amazes Major Adams by sprucing himself up for the benefit of Mrs. Halstead and her maid Paula (Ruth Lee), first by shaving and later by having a bath and changing his shirt.

A young, rising star named Tom Pittman played Tommy Nichols, the 17-year-old boy Mrs. Halstead takes into her wagon and into her heart. Pittman had been born Jerry Lee Alten in Phoenix, Arizona, in 1932, the son of the Austrian-born actor Frank Alten and Beulah Dahlia Cory. Despite only having acted for a year, he had already racked up an impressive list of credits both in film and television. Pittman had an uncredited role as Hughie in *The True Story of Jesse James*, played Tom Burleigh in *The Proud Rebel* with Olivia de Havilland and Alan Ladd, and had even larger roles in TV series like *Suspicion*, *Gunsmoke*, and now *Wagon Train*. Pittman had married Carole Arlyn Johnson in 1952, when he was 21 and working for the U.S. Coast Guard and she was only 18.[2]

Mary Halstead ranks as one of Moorehead's best performances on television. Through all the emotional ups and downs, and coincidences more numerous than you can shake a stick at, she nevertheless was able to create a coherent, credible, well-rounded portrait of a fatally ill yet determined woman, a mixture of good and bad as most of us are, taking stock of her life and doing what she can to find forgiveness and atonement before she dies. She is particularly affecting in a scene with Ward Bond's Major Adams, when he discovers her precarious state of health and she is afraid he will send her home. Visibly squirming, Major Adams becomes a reluctant listener to Mrs. Halstead's confession of how she was "married too young to a man I scarcely knew" and left her husband and six-year-old son for another man.

Indeed, one of the strengths of this episode is the fine rapport Moorehead develops onscreen with her co-stars Ward Bond and Tom Pittman, but also with her chief antagonist, the shady, self-serving Mr. Ferguson, played with supreme smarminess by 46-year-old Vaughn Taylor. Mainly a television actor, Taylor is probably best remembered today as Deacon Davis in *Cat on a Hot Tin Roof* and Janet Leigh's boss in *Psycho*. Ferguson strings Mrs. Halstead along with promises that he will find her son. Despite himself, he is ultimately instrumental in saving Tommy Nichols's life, when Mrs. Halstead strongarms him into showing her where the outlaws have taken Tommy.

A script for this episode dated July 10, 1957, among Moorehead's papers suggests that she was probably offered the role about this time.[3] We also have a shooting schedule that shows that she was on the set at Republic Studios Monday to Friday, August 19–23, 1957, and Monday, August 26, 1957.[4] August 26 was the day rehearsals started on Moorehead's new play, *The Rivalry*, at the Rainbow Studios in Hollywood.[5] Thus she would have gone directly from playing this demanding television role to rehearsals for the play, which opened in Vancouver, British Columbia, on September 23. Unless she had a TV

We see an uncommonly pensive Ward Bond in this still from an episode of the long-running western series *Wagon Train* titled "The Mary Halstead Story," in which Agnes Moorehead was given one of her best dramatic roles in television as the title character. Moorehead would have appreciated Bond's rugged masculinity and right-wing politics, but there was no suggestion of romance either on or off camera. This was the only time these two Hollywood veterans acted together.

in her dressing room, Moorehead would not have been able to see the original broadcast of "The Mary Halstead Story." When it aired over NBC on Wednesday, November 20, 1957, at 7:30–8:30 p.m., she was getting ready to go on stage in *The Rivalry* in the Keith Albee Theatre in Huntington, West Virginia.[6]

At the age of 26, Tom Pittman met a terrible end. He disappeared on October 31,

1958, just about a year after "The Mary Halstead Story" aired, and wasn't found until almost three weeks later. As his father had feared, Pittman had driven off the road and his body was finally found lying half in and half out of his sports car at the bottom of a 150 foot ravine in Benedict Canyon.[7] There was no way of knowing whether his death was instantaneous or whether it was prolonged and agonizing without a soul to help him. He died like his idol James Dean three years earlier.

Playing Major Seth Adams on 133 episodes of *Wagon Train* was Ward Bond's final role. He died of a heart attack in Dallas on November 5, 1960, at the age of 57. His co-star Robert Horton died in 2016 at the age of 91. He was the last surviving original cast member of *Wagon Train*.

CREDITS: *Director:* Jus Addiss; *Producers:* Boris Ingster, Richard Lewis; *Writers:* Leo Lieberman (story and teleplay), Robert E. Thompson (teleplay); *Cinematography:* Herbert Kirkpatrick; *Film editing:* John Hall; *Art direction:* Howard E. Johnson; *Makeup department:* Jack Barron (makeup artist), Florence Bush (hair stylist); *Costume and wardrobe department:* Vincent Dee; *Production company:* Revue Productions; *Air date:* November 20, 1957, on NBC

CAST: Ward Bond (Major Seth Adams), Fred Coby (deputy), Walter Coy (Tracey), Craig Duncan (Peters), Robert Horton (Flint McCullough), Jack Lambert (Creegar), Tom Laughlin (Earl/"Laramie Kid"), Ruth Lee (Paula Wallace), Frank McGrath (Charlie Wooster), Agnes Moorehead (Mary Halstead), Gregg Palmer (Groton), Robert Patten (Kermit), Tom Pittman (Tommy Nichols), Paul Sorenson (Marshal Crocker), Vaughn Taylor (James Ferguson), Terry Wilson (Bill Hawks)

10

Shirley Temple's Storybook: "Rapunzel" (TV, 1958) and *The Shirley Temple Show*: "The Land of Oz" (TV, 1960)

With there being an even greater preponderance of witches on television than on the big screen, it was probably inevitable that Agnes Moorehead would sooner or later play a witch. This happened for the first time in an episode of *Shirley Temple's Storybook* based on the fairy tale "Rapunzel," which aired on NBC October 27, 1958.

"Rapunzel" is one of *Grimm's Fairy Tales*, originally published in German by folklorists Jacob and Wilhelm Grimm as *Kinder-und Hausmarchen* in 1812.[1] As we recall, the "initiating event" of the tale is when a young, pregnant woman gets a strong hankering for rampions, *Campanula rapunculus* in the Latin, a species of bellflower with leaves like spinach and a parsnip-like root.[2] These plants only grow in the witch's vegetable garden. When the witch catches the husband red-handed, she extracts a promise from him that he and his wife must give her their first-born child if she is to spare his life. She names the little girl "Rapunzel," another word for rampion.[3] Later, we know, a prince shows up and saves Rapunzel from her captive existence in a tower, but not before being tried and tested by blindness. In this rendering, Moorehead was cast as the witch, Philip Abbott and Marian Seldes played Rapunzel's parents, Carol Lynley ("a cornfed Brigitte Bardot"[4]) played Rapunzel, and Don Dubbins played Prince Peter.

There were some concerns in advance of this production. Producer Alvin Cooperman had received "critical letters from protective parents" in connection with previous episodes of *Shirley Temple's Storybook* based on "The Legend of Sleepy Hollow" and "Beauty and the Beast." TV and radio columnist Hal Humphrey quipped: "Parents who see nothing wrong with TV's Wyatt Earp beating some badman into a bloody pulp will scream in protest when Washington Irving's headless horseman goes trotting through the glen." According to Humphrey, Cooperman was "taking great pains to see that no kid gets even a heartburn from this one. His witch, in the person of Agnes Moorehead, will be shrouded in a high-fashion gown and spell chic from head to toe. 'You will notice,' says Cooperman, 'that she has no moles or warts and even wears lipstick. We made sure that her long fingernails looked fake. In other words, she is a stylized witch and this takes her out of the typical horrendous category.'"[5]

Despite these attempts to give the witch a makeover, Moorehead is given a traditional witch's peaked hat, a voluminous black cloak, a false nose, and long nails very much in the Wicked Witch of the West tradition. She also has quite a cackle. Almost as a counterpoint to the ugliness, Moorehead makes beautiful, almost balletic movements with her arms and hands that contribute substantially to the effectiveness of this larger than life portrayal. Under the significant subhead "Witch Is Really Quite a Dish," reviewer Hal Humphrey concluded: "I think I'm safe in recommending it ['Rapunzel'] for all but the most neurotic of toddlers. Of course I'm no kid anymore and even the witch looked pretty good to me."[6]

I want to dwell on that final phrase: "looked pretty good to me." You see, Humphrey wasn't the only reviewer who found Moorehead attractive in this role. While *Variety* mentioned "the wretched witch they have made of Miss Moorehead,"[7] UPI's reviewer William Ewald wrote in his mostly negative review: "Agnes Moorehead was also in the piece and I rather liked her. She played a witch and a beautiful witch she was—maniacally fiendish with just the right combination of intelligibility and cuckooness."[8] Moorehead's agent Lillian S. Small wrote to her in Boston, where she was staying with a friend: "I hope you saw Rapunzel last night. I must say, you were the prettiest witch I ever saw. It was a wonderful performance."[9]

Despite the talon-like fingernails and prosthetic nose, several viewers and reviewers found Moorehead strangely attractive in her first performance ever as a witch in a TV version of the fairy tale "Rapunzel," part of *Shirley Temple's Storybook*. Her agent thought she was "the prettiest witch I ever saw." It was a harbinger of things to come.

In general, Moorehead received a lot of press attention for this performance and all of it good. Matt Messina in the *New York Daily News* thought she "hammed up gloriously."[10] Another reviewer wrote: "Agnes Moorehead is the first really wicked witch we've seen on this program."[11] Hank Grant in the *Hollywood Reporter* found the episode "well calculated to keep the kiddies on the edges of their seats for all scenes involving Agnes Moorehead as the witch who ruled the Forest of Evil." On the other hand, "when Miss Moorehead wasn't around, interest lagged."[12] "Rapunzel" got a rave review in *Variety*: "The show is a tour de force for Agnes Moorehead, whose gymnastic witchisms easily surpass the run-of-the-broom interpretation. Hers is an evil spirit of boundless vigor, an outstanding portrayal."[13]

By the time Moorehead returned as a guest star on Shirley Temple's show in the fall of 1960, it had undergone some changes. *Shirley Temple's Storybook* was now called *The Shirley Temple Show* and it was being produced in color. As the first installment of the new, second season, "The Land of Oz" was a dramatization of L. Frank Baum's sequel to *The Wonderful Wizard of Oz. The Marvelous Land of Oz: Being an Account of the Further Adventures of the Scarecrow and the Tin Woodman* had been published in 1904. In the television version's relatively "free" adaptation, we are told the story of the liberation of the boy Tip (Shirley Temple) from domestic slavery in the household of the witch Mombi (Moorehead) with the help of *Wizard of Oz* regulars Scarecrow (Ben Blue), Tin Woodman (Gil Lamb), and Glinda (Frances Bergen) and new characters Jack Pumpkinhead (Sterling Holloway) and Sawhorse (Mel Blanc), after it turns out that Tip is really the Princess Ozma, rightful ruler of the Emerald City. This storyline segued in the TV version with the plot of the nefarious Lord Nikidik (Jonathan Winters) to start a revolution that would bring him to power in the Land of Oz.

Again, Moorehead delivered a standout performance as Mombi, an unabashedly ugly and comic witch whose only external similarity with the "Rapunzel" witch was her talon-like nails. With a huge cotton cap, hooked nose, bushy eyebrows, peasant dress and apron, and lime green shoes, and not a half bad Cockney accent, Mombi looked and sounded like a mixture of Madame DeFarge and Eliza Doolittle before her transformation by Professor Higgins. Like the witch in "Rapunzel," Mombi could materialize instantly in a puff of smoke.

In an interview in the *New York Times* published the day "The Land of Oz" aired on September 18, 1960, James P. Shanley opened with the observation that "After playing on thousands of radio programs, many television shows and in a long list of films, Agnes Moorehead has reached a point where bizarre characterizations don't trouble her at all." He continued: "Miss Moorehead believes that in playing parts of less substance she is properly extending her range as an actress." One such part was apparently Mombi the Witch in "The Land of Oz." "'An actress, after all, is someone who can make the audience believe what she's doing,'" Moorehead was quoted as saying. "'I've tried to be faithful to the book,' she said. 'I didn't want to do a trick-or-treat kind of witch. Mombi is, I think, a wicked witch, but she has a sense of humor. She gets a great deal of glee out of the things she does.'"[14] We can certainly think of another witch who fits this description perfectly.

It is possible to see the witches Moorehead played in "Rapunzel" and "The Land of Oz" as precursors of Endora in some ways or, to put it differently, as an intermediate stage between the Wicked Witch of the West and Endora, between haggish, warty gruesomeness and sophisticated, cosmopolitan elegance, between the fear-inducing and the humorous witch. As I will discuss in my chapter on *Bewitched*, Endora was a novel and unique portrayal in the history of representations of witches in Western culture, but she didn't materialize out of nothing. She was a three-dimensional witch, a real-life witch, if you will, not just because she could dress and act like a mortal, but because she incorporated and amalgamated so many different features of the witch stereotype.

In the 1960 *New York Times* interview, Moorehead said: "'I just want to keep going along like this. I'm not particularly floored by anything."[15] Prophetic words, indeed. Though she could not have known it at the time, her first two appearances guest starring on Shirley Temple's show constituted the best possible "auditions" for her future role on *Bewitched*. "The Land of Oz" was even produced by William Asher. If nothing else, her performances in "Rapunzel" and "The Land of Oz" proved that Moorehead could be scary, funny, and even strangely attractive playing a witch. In 1964, she would fully prove the truth of the saying that "the third time's the charm."[16]

Credits: *Directors:* James Neilson ("Rapunzel"), William Corrigan ("The Land of Oz"); *Producers:* Alvin Cooperman, Shelley Hull, Norman Lessing ("Rapunzel"); William Asher, William H. Brown, Jr. ("The Land of Oz"); *Writers:* F. William Durkee, Jr. (teleplay "Rapunzel"), Jacob Grimm (story "Rapunzel"), Wilhelm Grimm (story "Rapunzel"); L. Frank Baum (novel "The Land of Oz"), Frank Gabrielson (teleplay "The Land of Oz"); *Cinematography:* Henry Freulich ("Rapunzel"); *Art direction:* William Flannery ("Rapunzel"), E. Jay Krause ("The Land of Oz"); *Makeup:* John Chambers ("The Land of Oz"); *Costumes:* Bob Carlton ("The Land of Oz"); *Production company:* Henry Jaffe Enterprises; *Air Date:* October 27, 1958 ("Rapunzel") and September 18, 1960 ("The Land of Oz") on NBC

Cast, "Rapunzel": Philip Abbott (husband), Don Dubbins (Prince Peter), Carol Lynley (Rapunzel), Agnes Moorehead (witch), Alexander Scourby (king), Marian Seldes (Widow Enga), Shirley Temple (host). "The Land of Oz": Frances Bergen (Glinda the Good), Mel Blanc (voice of Sawhorse and The Book), Ben Blue (Scarecrow), Charles Boaz (colonel), Maurice Dallimore (The Gump), Sterling Holloway (Jack Pumpkinhead), William Keene (Royal Army One Soldier), Gil Lamb (Tin Woodman), Norman Leavitt (Lightning Bug/Repairman), Mari Lynn (Jellia Jamb), Louis Merrill (court doctor), Agnes Moorehead (Mombi the Witch), Shirley Temple (host/Princess Ozma/Tip), Arthur Treacher (Graves the Butler), Jonathan Winters (Lord Nikidik)

11

The Pink Jungle (Stage, 1959)

On Friday, May 8, 1959, as Agnes Moorhead was shooting her starring role in *The Bat*, producer Paul Gregory announced that she and Ginger Rogers were headed for Broadway in Leslie Stevens's new "comedy with music," *The Pink Jungle*.[1] The 35-year-old Stevens was the author of *The Marriage-Go-Round*, "currently flourishing at the Plymouth Theatre under Gregory's sponsorship," with Claudette Colbert and Charles Boyer in the leads. The director of *The Marriage-Go-Round* was Joe Anthony, who signed on to direct *The Pink Jungle* as well. The 47-year-old former dancer had directed, written for, and performed in a number of Broadway shows since 1934 and had been the dance partner of Agnes de Mille in the early 1940s. The male lead in Stevens's spoof of the cosmetics industry went to Leif Erickson, who had had a big hit opposite Deborah Kerr in *Tea and Sympathy* both on Broadway and the silver screen in the mid–1950s.[2]

Moorehead signed her *Pink Jungle* contract on August 29. She was to receive $1,500 a week until the production costs of the show had been recouped, when her salary would increase to $1,750 a week. The producer would also pay a salary and transportation for her maid. Moorehead was to receive star billing.[3] She was to portray Eleanor West, the "shade" of an Elizabeth Arden–like cosmetics queen who must do one good deed before she can gain entry to heaven. It was the most showy stage role she ever got. Ginger Rogers's name may have been above the title, but just below the title and in just the same size type was the name of the de facto star of the show: Agnes Moorehead.[4] Dressed to the nines in a variety of gorgeous gowns by Jean Louis or disguised as any number of comical characters, on stage nearly continuously and with all the best lines, this was the part and the play that was going to bring Moorehead triumphantly back to Broadway. It would form a fitting finale to a decade where she had established herself as a force to be reckoned with in live theater.

Well, it just didn't happen. There were many reasons for this and, ironically, one of them was Moorehead herself. According to Paul Gregory, her long-term producer and one of her closest friends, she contributed to her own and the play's downfall by forgetting one of the cardinal rules of performing: you're only as good as your weakest link. The force of her charismatic performance could not carry the show, if it made the rest of the cast—and not least of all, the official star—look bad. Gregory had warned her about this. Nearly 40 years later, he still remembered vividly how Moorehead had enjoyed Ginger Rogers's increasing inadequacy and insecurity. She positively reveled in it, saying to Gregory that this was her chance finally to get her own back after two decades of playing second fiddle to more or less talented stars on the big screen. "Paul," she said, "I'm going to be the captain of this ship." With reference to her co-stars Rogers and Erickson, Gregory responded that you needed all three sails on the ship to be working.[5] He called her a "five foot termite," because he meant she was eating away at the fabric of the show.[6] Something she once said to her friend Fred Carmichael might be cited here in her defense: "Those who work for the good of the production I'd do anything for, but those who work for themselves alone, they'll just have to look out for themselves."[7] Clearly she felt Rogers belonged in the second, self-serving category.

Moorehead was particularly amused, in Gregory's recollection, when it turned out Ginger Rogers couldn't really dance.[8] Fred Astaire had warned Gregory that she would ask for a dance-in and she did before rehearsals had even started.[9] There was no open conflict between the two leading ladies, of course, they were both too subtle and proud to engage in any kind of cat fight, but Rogers knew that Moorehead knew that one half of a legendary dance team couldn't dance. Nor could she sing. Moorehead would stand in the wings making fun of the star struggling to learn Vernon Duke's songs and Matt Mattox's routines.[10] Guaranteed to be in the wings, too, was Roger's legendary mother, Lela. To the extent there was any hostility backstage, it was between Moorehead and Lela Rogers. The stage mother of all time asked Gregory to "build up Ginger," adding that "there was only way 'to strengthen Ginger's part' and that was to cut Agnes's practically out of the play."[11]

For impressions of the show as performed, we must turn to the critics. With a few exceptions for critics who adopted a hopeful "wait and see" attitude as the play was still being worked on intensively through the pre–Broadway tour, the reviewers turned three thumbs down. Under the heading "Talent Wasted in 'The Pink Jungle,'" Theresa Loeb Cone, drama editor of the *San Francisco Tribune*, panned the show after its world premiere at the Alcazar Theatre on October 14, 1959. She found the plot, characters and dialogue "distressingly lame: We actually cringed at some of the vapid speeches such talented people as Leif Erickson and Agnes Moorehead are compelled to deliver." She had found it difficult to tell "exactly what 'The Pink Jungle' was all about. Midway through, we no longer cared." On a positive note, "the show's principal sparkle came from the contributions by Agnes Moorehead. But she, poor dear, completely charming was utterly wasted." Cone provides us with a summary of what Moorehead's role involved:

> She really played a variety of roles like someone with special talent who lends his services to a college end-of-term revue. With great good cheer she was at various times: a living picture in a frame, a lady cop, a telephone operator, a jack-in-the-box, a gum-chewing stenographer and a waitress. At the very end, this game performer permitted herself to be wafted skyward on a pulley arrangement a la Peter Pan. What more could she do for producer Paul Gregory?

Cone did not blame Ginger Rogers for the show's failure: "there is just so much one can do with that material and she did it." "Her singing was not overwhelming, to put it kindly, but then neither were those blah Vernon Duke numbers." Cone concluded that *The Pink Jungle* was "A disappointing hodge-podge" and "nothing short of a fabulous fiasco in its present state."[12]

Variety's review began by neatly summarizing the play's problems, which included "inordinate length," a simple plot made confusing by being played on several levels, and leading players who couldn't sing. The show's strengths were, primarily, "A marvelously funny performance by Agnes Moorehead," "stunning costumes and elaborately beautiful staging," and "Ginger Rogers' amazing youth, luscious figure and delightful, though too scarce, dancing." All in all, "it was obvious director Joe Anthony has a huge job to do in getting more virile performances from everyone but Erickson, a pleasant straight man for the girls." Among the performers who weren't virile enough, apparently, were Buck Class and Ray Hamilton who "played too coyly" Eleanor West's two ne'er-do-well younger sons.[13]

Emilia Model, drama editor of the *News-Call Bulletin*, was one of the critics who chose to give the show the benefit of the doubt, given that it was a work in progress. Under the somewhat ambiguous heading "'Pink Jungle' Looks Like Hit," Model noted that both Rogers and Moorehead enhanced the show: "The play, though, goes to Miss Moorehead. The audience fell in love with her ridiculous, wicked glee as a ghost spying on humans."[14] Another critic described how Moorehead "With her crisp, sardonic style of comedy and her voice that cuts like a knife, really steals the show."[15]

Several weeks and numerous changes later, it was time for veteran Boston drama critic Elliot Norton to bring his experience to bear in analyzing the show, still keeping in mind that "it is not yet in final form." Whether it would "ever reach a final acceptable form" was to him "a matter of grave doubt." Norton traced the play's genesis:

> Leslie Stevens set out to write "The Pink Jungle" as a satire on the cosmetics industry, a likely subject, with five incidental songs by Vernon Duke to make it more agreeable. Somehow this good idea got lost in a conventional love story of no account, and then somebody in the management decided to increase the number of songs from five to fifteen and to convert what the producer had originally called a "comedy musical" into a "musical comedy."

This conversion process had begun two or three weeks previously in Detroit. Norton found that while Rogers looked wonderful and had an occasional chance to dance, "she has a small, weak singing voice and the role of a naïve beautician does not fit her personality." When she danced, though, "Every line of her movement is as true and perfect as though she were a great ballerina." Norton felt Moorehead was "often too stern and too formal to suit what is still meant to be a comedy," though she did have "some fine scenes." Singled out for praise were her impersonations of a "jaunty Irish policewoman in Central Park" and a "gum-chewing telephone girl." Director, choreographer, and composer had done no credit to themselves, while Leif Erickson "is lost in the cast as a he-man of a she-industry." The settings were "opulent," but Norton was forced to conclude that the show needed more than opulence: "It needs a quick injection of wit and humor."[16]

By the time *The Pink Jungle* had opened in Detroit on November 12, director Joe Anthony had thrown in the towel.[17] Three days after they opened in Boston, his replacement, author Leslie Stevens, was ready to do the same. On December 5, Stevens sent a long telegram from Boston to Gregory at the Algonquin Hotel in New York. He started by quoting extensively from Elliot Norton's review. "As you know," he wrote, "Norton is considered the Boston Brooks Atkinson and I am afraid his discerning eye has laid bare the show's fundamental flaw. The more improvements we give Ginger the more visible her acting, comedy and singing shortcomings become." He continued:

> Directorially speaking I cannot wring a star performance out of her and I must ask you to call in a director who can. Also I have written close to 50 pages of script changes and added 3 entirely new production sequences. All adding up to making Ginger more visible and less likable. I will cooperate to the bitter end but as the critics keep telling us I do not see my script changes leading to a hit show. You are therefore free to call in another writer.

He concluded: "The show lives or dies by the star performances and you cannot turn it into a Gwen Verdon dance recital nor can you breathe magic into an unmagical love interest. I leave it to you to proceed wisely."[18]

Photographs from *The Pink Jungle* are hard to come by, making this one of nominal star Ginger Rogers (left) and de facto star Agnes Moorehead all the more fascinating. We can see that Rogers is styled very much as she might have looked in private life, while designer Jean Louis has pulled out all the stops in his costume for Agnes Moorehead, playing the ghost of cosmetics queen Eleanor West, who must do one good deed before she can go to heaven (courtesy Muskingum University Archives).

The star herself was in open rebellion. In an interview published in the *Boston Evening American* on December 8, Rogers insisted that she was staying with the show, but "It isn't the play I contracted to play in." "Originally, it was an intimate, little comedy," she added. "Now, with the same cast, it has been transformed into a comedy musical. There's not a singing voice in the company." When she had first read the script, she had believed the role of Eleanor West "inadequate for Miss Moorehead's formidable talents." "Since then, Miss Moorehead's role has been considerably fattened and … the deceased cosmetics tycooness comes down to earth in at least a half-dozen busy incarnations during the evening. In her satiric fashion, she contributes the only wit in the comedy musical which is as short on comedy as it is on good tunes."[19]

Faced with near total breakdown of the show, Gregory had little room in which to maneuver. As he remembered it, Equity would not let him fire Rogers and she would not bow out graciously. He had given her "every opportunity in Detroit to quit," but she would not, saying she liked the money.[20] On December 7, Gregory notified the company he was closing the show at the end of the week. "It has become quite obvious," he said, "that the amount of work necessary to bring the play up to a taut, exciting[,] fully rewarding evening in the theatre could not be done while playing regular performances."[21]

In the aftermath of *The Pink Jungle*'s sad demise, the major players inevitably got involved in the blame game. The potential culprits were many, but Rogers was a prime suspect. Since most everyone seemed to blame her, including the writer, director, and producer, it is interesting to examine first whom *she* blamed for the disaster. Well, Ginger Rogers primarily blamed the author, Leslie Stevens, but in retrospect also Paul Gregory, whom she claimed was an absentee producer.

On the day the show was to have opened at the 54th St. Theatre in New York, the *Schenectady Star* printed an article by Bob Thomas titled "Cast Friction Reported: Ginger Blames Author for New Play's Failure." Rogers was quoted as saying that "The play was light and fluffy as a meringue, … but it had no substance. It was a big nothing." They would have been foolish to come into New York with it. "The problem," she continued, "was the writing. The author made a lot of changes, but he never attacked the real problem." In her version of events, the author finally refused to do anything more and under Drama Guild rules they couldn't bring in another writer without his permission, so they had to close. Stevens responded to this attack with his own diagnosis of the play's ills: "I think the problem was that one actress (Agnes Moorehead) got rave reviews for her part, written by the same author [i.e., Stevens], while another actress (Ginger Rogers) drew pans for hers." Rogers denied rumors that there had been a feud between her and Moorehead: "The fact is that I have the greatest admiration for Miss Moorehead as a performer and a person. There was never anything but good feeling between us." Stevens got his ten cents worth in here too. "No," he agreed, "there was no friction between Miss Rogers and Miss Moorehead, but there was enormous friction between Lela (Ginger's mother) and Miss Moorehead." There was no comment in the article from Moorehead.[22]

In her autobiography, published more than 30 years after *The Pink Jungle*, Rogers gave a more detailed account of what in her opinion had gone wrong with the show. She explained that author Stevens had a sick wife and "was understandably not as responsive as he might have been." Producer Paul Gregory had left the show in Detroit to return to Hollywood where he was producing a movie: "That's all I needed to hear. The writer wasn't writing, the producer wasn't producing, and the show was standing still. A traveling show without its producer is like a saddle on a wooden horse." In her version of events, "I emphatically said that if the show was not ready for a proper New York opening by the time we reached Boston, they could forget about my being in the cast." Rogers claimed to have given her notice the day the show opened in Boston on December 2, 1959, though in her December 8 interview in the *Boston Evening American*, she had said: "Of course, I'm staying with the show. I've never walked out on a show yet."[23] Thus memory plays its little games with us, bringing past experiences more neatly into line with present needs.

In addition to the telegram from Leslie Stevens to Paul Gregory quoted above, three letters from Gregory reveal that Rogers's recollection of events is fanciful at best. In a letter to her agent, Gordon Youngman, setting out in detail the extra expenses incurred through having to hire a dance-in and an extra dance partner for Rogers, which she had said she would pay for, Gregory reminded Youngman "that it was because of the general inadequacy on the part of Miss Rogers that *The Pink Jungle* eventually closed. She was getting lousy reviews, she could not keep up with the work. It was impossible for either Joe Anthony or Leslie Stevens to substantially improve the piece with her in the role, and she would not quit."[24]

On January 19, 1960, Gregory wrote a three-page letter to Rogers herself. After berating her for her tardiness, her blatant disregard for the other members of the company, and her inability to learn the new material and outlining her mother's meddling in the whole proceedings, he got to "the fact of the matter: the load in *The Pink Jungle* was just too much for you." He continued: "if your performance had been sufficiently up to standard I believe you would have gotten far better reviews, comparable to those of Agnes, the evaluating of the property would have been much easier and, consequently, the process of improvement far less hazardous."[25]

Gregory's letter of February 3, 1960, to the Actors Equity Association makes it clear that he thought Rogers's behavior sufficiently unprofessional to report it to her union. Gregory's charges were that she was never on time for rehearsals and had no excuse to offer when she arrived up to 40 minutes or even an hour late. They also found that "she either could not or would not perform the lines as written, the music and lyrics as written nor the dances as choreographed: her lack of knowing the lines up until the very night of opening in San Francisco contributed greatly to confusion and frustration so far as the director was concerned." She had refused to dance with her leading man, Leif Erickson, so choreographer Matt Mattox had to be hired as a dancer at additional expense. Even then, the choreographer found her incapable of learning the steps to her dance. The composer had found it "utterly impossible to write a number she could do. Taking into consideration the attitude as well as the obvious inadequacies displayed by Miss Rogers," Gregory continued, "the management decided, even though we had a tremendous advance sale in Philadelphia and New York City, that in order to protect and not defraud the theatregoing public ... we would close the show." Gregory asked that charges be brought against Rogers through her Equity association.[26]

This is all damning evidence. One wonders what prompted Ginger Rogers to such unprofessional behavior. Clearly, being teamed with a performing powerhouse like Agnes Moorehead brought out all her latent insecurities. She felt, and probably rightly so, that she was being upstaged in her own show. One reviewer, for example, noted that "Agnes Moorehead commits grand larceny scene stealing."[27] In Rogers defense, too, the problems with *The Pink Jungle*, as the scripts and the reviews indicate, went far beyond her role and performance.[28] To say that the play had the weight and consistency of a powder puff would be giving the play too much credit. Rogers's part and her storyline as Eleanor West's Girl Friday, Tess Jackson, who struggles to win both recognition for her business talents and the heart of West's eldest son, are about as interesting as watching nail polish dry. Even had she sung like Mary Martin and danced like Ginger Rogers, there would still have been myriad structural problems with the show. Likely as not, though, with Rogers performing to full capacity they could have gone on to Broadway and been a commercial, if not a critical, success. The tour had been practically sold out in advance and the advance sale in Philadelphia and New York was, as we have just read, "tremendous."

The Pink Jungle, Gregory recalled in 2007, was the only one of his many shows to lose money.[29] The sole participant to emerge from this debacle still smelling like a make-up counter was Agnes Moorehead. Her staunch ally, the *Detroit Free Press*'s longtime film critic Helen Bower, published an article titled "Agnes Moorehead Is Tops at the Box-office" on December 5, 1959, a week before the show closed. In her opinion "the 'Fabulous Redhead's' elegance, style, wit and manner in the new comedy-with-music-and-costumes ... needs being brought to studio attention." After mentioning Moorehead's forthcoming appearance in *Pollyanna* and reminiscing about her own campaign to "get Agnes Moorehead out of those baggy sweaters and into something stylish—and in Technicolor," Bowers had a suggestion for "somebody in Hollywood smart enough to take it: How's about a remake of *The Shanghai Gesture* for Agnes Moorehead? Or a picture in which she could be the famous Chinese Empress Dowager?" Peter Fleming's new novel *The Siege at Peking* was partly about the empress and "could be written into a great character part for A.M."[30]

For Moorehead, it was a pyrrhic victory. She had won the battle, but lost the war. She would have to wait another three years for her return to Broadway and then she wouldn't be wearing diamonds, satin, and furs.

CREDITS: *Director:* Joseph Anthony; *Producers:* Paul Gregory, S.S. Krellberg; *Writer:* Leslie Stevens; *Music and lyrics:* Vernon Duke; *Choreographer:* Matt Mattox; *Scenic and lighting design:* Donald Oenslager; *Costumes:* Jean Louis (gowns); *Premiere:* October 15, 1959, at the Alcazar Theatre in San Francisco, California

CAST: Buck Class (Simon West), Leif Erickson (Brian West), Gavin Gordon (Harvey West), Ray Hamilton (David West), Maggie Hayes (Chris Taylor), Lisa Jonson (Annette), Agnes Moorehead (The Shade of Eleanor West), Louis Nye (Dr. Prescott Alcott), René Paul (Pierre Aubusson), Ginger Rogers (Tess Jackson), Marilyn Watson (Suzy Harkness)

TOURING SCHEDULE: Fisher Theatre, Detroit (opening November 12, 1959); Shubert Theatre, Boston (closing December 12, 1959)

12

The Millionaire: "Millionaire Katherine Boland" (TV, 1960)

Given Agnes Moorehead's vaunted versatility and deserved reputation for playing characters that looked and sounded very different from herself, it is easy to forget that she played several roles in which she dressed and styled her hair very much as she did in private life. I'm thinking of characters like the intellectual mission doctor's wife, Beryl Sigman, in *The Left Hand of God* and the lady authoress Cornelia Van Gorder in *The Bat*. The woman played by Moorehead in one of the last episodes of the long-running anthology series *The Millionaire* outwardly resembles both Beryl Sigman and Cornelia Van Gorder and, I would argue, has Moorehead's own "look" at this time in her life.

The storylines in *The Millionaire*, which ran on CBS from 1955 to 1960 and climbed to ninth place in the Nielsen Ratings in its first season, were all about how various characters reacted to receiving a check for one million dollars from an anonymous benefactor and what they chose to do with the money.[1] Katherine Boland (Agnes Moorehead), a 50-year-old unmarried woman from a prominent family ruined by the 1929 stock market crash, has taken her brother's orphaned daughter Beth (Tuesday Weld) into her family home, that she has been able to hold on to despite the family's financial reverses. Beth is kept busy fixing pots of tea for guests and seems to be some sort of unpaid maid. She has a boyfriend, the grocery clerk Tom Smith, whom her aunt deems unsuitable.

Miss Boland receives the news from the eccentric millionaire's "executive secretary," Michael Anthony (Marvin Miller), with a great deal of skepticism and concern for appearances. Once she realizes the check comes with no strings attached, though, and that the whole arrangement will be a closely guarded secret, she decides to use the money to renovate the family home and to give her niece as spectacular a coming out party as she herself had had 30 years earlier. When Beth finally elopes with her boyfriend, Miss Boland realizes that she has been selfish in not considering her niece's own wishes; that, as Beth has said: "It's not my party, it's yours." In the final scene, Katherine seeks comfort and understanding from Max Goodson (Jerome Cowan), the contractor who has renovated her home and who was present at her debut as a busboy. There is romance in the air as they waltz around her parlor.

The cast of this episode was a curious mix of seasoned veterans and beginners. At 16, Tuesday Weld was one of the veterans. She had been an actress and model since her mother put her to work supporting the family when she was three, following her father's death. Weld graduated from Hollywood Professional School as class valedictorian in 1960, moved out of her mother's house, and won a Golden Globe Award as "Most Promising Newcomer" for *The New Pennies*. Bob Newkirk, who plays Weld's beau Tom, was a singer who was making his television debut at age 24. In 1968, he became the father of the singer Anastacia (Anastacia Lyn Newkirk). He died in 2005.

Moorehead's love interest in *The Millionaire*, veteran character actor Jerome Cowan, was born in 1897 and is best known for playing Sam Spade's murdered partner Miles Archer in *The Maltese Falcon*; District Attorney Thomas Mara in *The Miracle on 34th Street*, who is in the sticky situation of having to prosecute Santa Claus; and for an episode of *The Twilight Zone* he did with Ida Lupino in 1959 called "The Sixteen-Millimeter Shrine." He received a star on the Walk of Fame for his television work just a few months before acting in *The Millionaire*.

The script by Marvin C. Johnson, his only writing credit, is full of visual and verbal references to films and plays of the day, such as *The Glass Menagerie*, and including films that Moorehead herself had acted in. For example, the opening scene where Michael Anthony comes to the house and Katherine first speaks to him through a small opening in the door is clearly an allusion to the important scene in *Dark Passage* where Madge Rapf does the same with Humphrey Bogart's character Vincent Parry. There are shades of the "Jealous Lover" segment of *The Story of Three Loves* in the relationship between the older, upper-class spinster and her more clearly heterosexually orientated, rebellious ward. The scene in the bedroom between Katherine and Beth is very "Tennessee Williams" with its suggestion that Katherine Boland has stopped really living and the mention of "gentlemen callers." I wonder, too, if it's a coincidence that Katherine is called "Boland," when we remember that the sterling comedienne Mary Boland starred in the 1932 anthology film comedy *If I Had a Million*, which was the precursor of the series.

We know the production schedule must have been tight. The revised script is dated March 8, 1960, and the episode aired on CBS April 19, 1960.[2] *The Millionaire* was produced at Desilu Studios at 9336 W. Washington Blvd. in Culver City, co-owned by Moorehead's friend and neighbor Lucille Ball. The lot with its characteristic Colonial Revival mansion headquarters, modeled after Mount Vernon, was leased for many years from RKO by Selznick International and many famous films, not least of all *Gone with the Wind*, were produced there.[3] Moorehead did *Since You Went Away* on this lot in 1944, which was close to her home at the time in Cheviot Hills.

The production values on a series like *The Millionaire* were not quite up to *GWTW* standards. Ralph and Richard Berger's sets for Miss Boland's home aim for a *Magnificent Ambersons*, 1870s Gilded Age look and achieves the effect of a particularly tasteless antiques store with grotesque knick-knacks encrusting every wall space and surface. There is an impressionistic painting of Miss Boland over the fireplace and producer Don Fedderson's wife Tido, who appeared, usually in a cameo, in every one of the 206 episodes, is seen in a photograph in the parlor.[4]

The hair styling, makeup, and costuming in this episode is also less than ideal. Moorehead is wearing her usual coronet hairstyle and her favorite gold filigree earrings, that show up in a vast number of her film and television roles. We also see her wearing a large, ornate diamond pin shaped like a crest or coat of arms, which she would later use on *Bewitched*. Moorehead rather looks her age in this, which was 59, with a sallow complexion and big bags under her eyes, probably due to the combination of rudimentary

The lighting, makeup, and costumes on Agnes Moorehead's episode of the popular, long-running series *The Millionaire* were under par. She was 59 at the time and, for once, she looked it. Here she is seen with her co-star, Tuesday Weld, who was sweet 16, though already an industry veteran.

lighting and amateurish makeup. Her clothes are not flattering. Tuesday Weld is having one long bad hair day and looks like she's auditioning for *Tobacco Road* or *The Beverly Hillbillies*. It helps to be 16, though, in lighting as bad as this.

CREDITS: *Director:* Dick Darley; *Producers:* Don Fedderson, Fred Henry, Milton Merlin; *Writer:* Marvin C. Johnson; *Cinematography:* Robert H. Planck; *Film editing:* Charles J. Van Enger, Jr.; *Art direction:* Ralph Berger, Richard Berger; *Makeup department:* Charles Blackman (makeup artist), Anna Malin (hair stylist); *Costume department:* John Zacha; *Production company:* Don Fedderson Prod./MCA TV/Columbia Broadcasting System (CBS); *Air Date:* April 20, 1960, on CBS

CAST: Jerome Cowan (Max Goodson), Paul Frees (John Beresford Tipton), Marvin Miller (Michael Anthony), Agnes Moorehead (Katherine Boland), Bob Newkirk (Tom Smith), Tuesday Weld (Beth Boland)

13

Adventures in Paradise: "The Krismen" (TV, 1960)

The episode of *Adventures in Paradise* called "The Krismen" can certainly compete with *Dragon Seed*, *The Conqueror*, and *Custer*, as one of Agnes Moorehead's most absurd and deliciously camp performances. Indeed, it might well belong at the top of the list. Any program beginning with the line "Cocoanut oil, rub it on his body," especially when uttered in a robotic, mock Chinese accent that makes Ona Munson in *The Shanghai Gesture* sound like a Method actress, is promising indeed. When in addition Moorehead is made up and togged out like a mixture of Wilma Flintstone and Mother Gin Sling, things can hardly get better. Unless, of course, the body in question happens to belong to one of the great male beauties of the twentieth century...

Adventures in Paradise aired on ABC from October 5, 1959, till April 1, 1962. According to William Froug, who produced eight *Adventures* episodes and wrote nine, the series was "about a young ex–Korean War veteran named Adam Troy who ran a freight and taxi service among the islands of the South Pacific aboard his sail boat *Tiki*."[1] Gardner McKay starred as Adam Troy. The star himself admitted that "the elements were uncomplicated; a boy and a boat in the South Seas." According to McKay, the show's success might partially be explained by the fact that "At the time, there were fifteen Western series on television: *Adventures in Paradise* came as a relief. No shootouts. No sheriff. No posses. There was nothing like it."[2]

Adventures in Paradise was the first TV series produced at Twentieth Century–Fox studios.[3] James Michener created the show as his first contribution to television and then had nothing further to do with it.[4] McKay recalled that "Fox was the last major studio to recognize television as a valid form of expression and when *Paradise* was brought to them their conception was to create a feature film each week."[5] During the first season, 30 episodes were filmed on an eight-day schedule at a cost of about $90,000 per episode.[6] Several of Moorehead's friends and former co-stars were seen in Season 1. Joseph Cotten's future wife, Patricia Medina, starred in the first episode to be filmed, "The Black Pearl" (#1.2); Ricardo Montalban was in "The Derelict" (#1.5), Eva Gabor in "Peril at Pitcairn" (#1.9), Murray Matheson in "The Archer's Ring" (#1.14), Vincent Price in "The Color of Venom" (#1.18), and Moorehead's *Tempest* co-star Geoffrey Horne was seen in the season finale, "Whip Fight" (#1.30).

Come the second season, which began airing on October 3, 1960, it was Moorehead's turn. By that time, it must have been clear to her that her film career was winding down and that the future lay in television. She only had one film released that year, *Pollyanna*, and didn't work on any new ones, but appeared on eight TV series: *Startime*, *The Millionaire*, *The Chevy Mystery Show*, *Adventures in Paradise*, *Rawhide*, *Harrigan and Son*, two episodes of *The Shirley Temple Show*, and *The Rifleman*. In fact, 1960 was Moorehead's busiest year in television up until that point.

As Adam Troy, captain of the *Tiki* and star of the hugely popular early 1960s series *Adventures in Paradise*, Gardner McKay was called "one of the most handsome men in the world" and received more fan mail than Marilyn Monroe. McKay quit the series, which had no future without him, in 1962, after three seasons and 91 episodes, to devote himself to writing, teaching, and world travel. He died of prostate cancer in 2001.

Moorehead reported to work on the Fox lot on Friday, September 9, 1960, and spent the entire following week completing this episode.[7] She had worked at Fox before, of course, having done films like *Fourteen Hours*, *The Left Hand of God*, and most recently *The True Story of Jesse James* there in the early to mid–1950s. "The Krismen" was filmed on Stage 3 and Stage 9 (where there was a mock-up set of the schooner *Tiki* with a painted backdrop[8]) and on the fabled Fox back lot "in a studio-built lagoon on a studio-built schooner."[9] William Froug recalled: "The Fox lot was unlike any other in the world of motion picture studios. It was spacious with great areas of open lawns dotted with huge pine trees and sweeping concrete walkways, lushly landscaped.... This was a truly insulated world of great natural, as well as theatrical, beauty."[10] The studio at 10201 Pico Blvd. was located just on the other side of the Hillcrest Country Club and the Rancho Park Golf Course from Moorehead's three former homes in Cheviot Hills.

The director of "The Krismen" was Justus "Jus" Addiss, who was the life partner of Moorehead's friend and co-star in *All That Heaven Allows*, Hayden Rorke. Rorke is best remembered today as Colonel Alfred E. Bellows on *I Dream of Jeannie*, perpetually foiled in his attempts to uncover the causes of Larry Hagman's strange behavior. Addiss did a total of seven episodes of *Adventures* and also directed Moorehead in her episode of *Wagon Train*, "The Mary Halstead Story" in 1957. Behind the camera this time was Lloyd Ahern, Sr., who was cinematographer on a total of 70 episodes of *Adventures*. He would show up again in Moorehead's life as the director of photography on the *Bewitched* pilot in late 1963, but did no further work on that series.

"The Krismen" is set in Mindanao in the Philippines. Moorehead is cast as Jikiri (pronounced JEE-kuh-ree), who is described in the final script as "an old Datu woman of wealth, eminence and power, an eagle among lesser fowl."[11] Jikiri is the leader of a rapacious band of Moro pirates, who kidnap the daughter of an American lumber baron and one of Captain Troy's young "native" crew members off the *Tiki* and demand $50,000 in gold for their safe release. Malcolm Atterbury played the rich Minnesotan Lars Olafson, Whitney Blake was his kidnapped, very blonde daughter Carol, and Lani Kai the abducted Pacific Islander crewman "Kelly" Kalimakaha.[12] Dressed up like one of the Pirates of Penzance, character actor Al Ruscio enjoyed an early standout role as Jikiri's henchman Sayid.[13] The episode also included James Holden as the Tennessee hayseed first mate Clay Baker. Clay, Kelly, and the hard-drinking, wheeler-dealer hotel owner Trader Penrose (George Tobias) had all come aboard as regular characters in Season 2. Unfortunately, the future Mr. Kravitz is not seen in the "The Krismen." Local color was provided by jungle drums and ominous gongs, scantily clad natives, a dance routine performed by nubile beauties with stiletto nails, and plenty of exotic foliage.

By the time she did *Adventures*, Moorehead was used to working with the great male beauties of the 1950s, such as Rock Hudson (*Magnificent Obsession*, *All That Heaven Allows*), Montgomery Clift (*Raintree County*), Geoffrey Horne (*Tempest*), and Jeffrey Hunter (*The True Story of Jesse James*; Moorehead was also credited as his dialogue coach on *King of Kings*). Gardner McKay could compete in pulchritude with any of these. He had been born George Cadogan Gardiner McKay in New York City in 1932. Before he rocketed to stardom in *Adventures*, he had had some uncredited film roles (including making his screen debut as a bearded soldier in *Raintree County*) and worked on television series like *The Thin Man*, *Boots and Saddles*, and *The Silent Service*.

When McKay and Moorehead worked together in September 1960, he was 28 years old and about one third of the way into the series, which would last for three seasons and 91 episodes before he called it quits in 1962. Executive producer Dominick Dunne writes in his photo memoir *The Way We Lived Then* that "Gardner was a forerunner of male cheesecake: every time he took off his shirt on camera, the ratings went up." He claimed that McKay received more fan mail than Marilyn Monroe, "then at her peak."[14] Froug writes that McKay was "widely publicized as one of the most handsome men in the world. It was not an unreasonable appraisal."[15]

According to Froug, McKay "disliked Hollywood and its trappings and wasn't comfortable with his life in the spotlight.... [H]e tended to be moody, withdrawn, and even disinterested, but he did his job with a minimum of fuss.... It was as if someone had put a gun to his back and ordered him to star in a television series."[16] McKay himself would have enjoyed this description. In his remarkable memoir *Journey Without a Map*, that he worked on up until his death from prostate cancer in 2001, McKay reflected: "I never liked the word actor. Couldn't get past it. In theater-writing I learned to love actors. Not to be one. I love dogs. I don't want to be one. The very soul of an actor is vulnerable to anyone. A glass heart. Vanity based on clarity."[17]

Not surprisingly, McKay quit acting in the late 1960s to pursue his interests in writing, the arts, and world travel. Truly a man of many talents, he was a prize-winning playwright, novelist, drama critic, teacher, sculptor, photographer, and animal lover. He spent the last 25 years of his life in Hawaii with his wife, Madeleine Madigan McKay, and their two children.

The Fox back lot was sold to developers in 1961 and became what is known today as Century City. The Century Plaza Hotel on the corner of Constellation Boulevard and Avenue of the Stars stands on the site of the sleepy, palm-lined lagoon where the *Tiki* once moored.[18] Yet the schooner will sail on forever in immortal episodes of *Adventures in Paradise* like "The Krismen." Beg, buy, borrow or steal, but do what you have to do to get a copy of this one!

Credits: *Director:* Justus Addiss; *Producers:* Richard Goldstone, Martin Manulis, William Self; *Writers:* Rolf Bayer (story and teleplay), James Michener (series creator), George Worthing Yates (teleplay); *Cinematography:* Lloyd Ahern, Sr.; *Film editing:* Robert Belcher; *Art direction:* Duncan Cramer, Charles Myall; *Production company:* Martin Manulis Prod./Jaymar Prod./Twentieth Century–Fox Television; *Air date:* October 31, 1960, on ABC

Cast: Malcolm Atterbury (Lars Olafson), Whitney Blake (Carol Olafson), Frank de Kova (Captain Bultian), Michael Ferris (Jutamentado), Luis Gomez (Lopez), James Holden (Clay Baker), Lani Kai ("Kelly" Kalimakaha), Gardner McKay (Adam Troy), Agnes Moorehead (Jikiri), Ernest Raboff (elder), Al Ruscio (Sayid), Leonard Strong (Alibon), Tony Terry (Moro boy)

14

Rawhide: "Incident at Poco Tiempo" (TV, 1960)

Rawhide, which ran from January 1959 till January 1966, was the fifth longest-running American television Western.[1] It starred Eric Fleming as Gil Favor, the head of a gang of cattle drovers, and Clint Eastwood as Rowdy Yates, one of the young, hot-headed, and indeed "rowdy" drovers. Fleming was not in the Season 3 episode titled "Incident at Poco Tiempo," which only featured Eastwood and Steve Raines as fellow drover Jim Quince among the regular characters. Because of its grueling weekly production schedule, one source notes, creating episodes that featured only a few of the regular characters was the only way cast members could get time off.[2] So "Poco Tiempo," which was taped in the second week of June 1960, meant a vacation for every regular actor save Eastwood and Raines. The 1960–61 season saw *Rawhide* placed sixth in the Nielsen Ratings, its highest placement.[3]

Most of the storylines in *Rawhide* were limited to one episode and consisted of the drovers encountering people on the trail or in town and getting involved in solving their problems or needing to be rescued themselves. Each episode, then, in addition to the regular cast members, had its roster of guest artists; in "Poco Tiempo," primarily Agnes Moorehead and Gigi Perreau, but also Stewart Bradley, Lew Gallo, Carolyn Hughes, Ken Mayer, Allan Nixon, Frank Puglia, and Gregory Walcott.

In "Incident at Poco Tiempo," a man named Payton (Bradley), leading a group of vigilantes, accuses Rowdy (Eastwood) and Jim (Raines) of having murdered a priest and stolen money from a mission at Poco Tiempo in Texas. Moorehead first appears as Sister Frances when she corroborates the boys' story, saying she has never seen them before. It turns out the padre, Father Sebastian (Puglia), is alive and being kept hostage by two gunmen, Mara (Walcott) and Colley (Gallo), in a secret basement room in the mission. Mara and Colley coerce Sister Frances and young Sister Joan (Perreau) into taking the stolen money to Blanesville for them on the stage coach or they will kill the priest.

Rowdy and Jim, who have lost their horses and need to get new ones to be able to rejoin their herd, end up in the stage coach with the two nuns. The suspense and narrative interest in the remainder of the episode is tied to whether or not the nuns will succeed in their mission and save Father Sebastian's life and whether or not Sister Joan will be led away from the narrow path by Rowdy's sexual appeal. In the latter context, Sister

Frances has a particularly fine scene with Sister Joan about a nun's vocation; and one with Rowdy, where she explains that the young nun's crisis of faith really doesn't have anything to do with him.

Prior to *Rawhide*, Moorehead had played a nun on the screen only once and only for about a minute. That was in the lackluster last pairing of Greer Garson and Walter Pidgeon in *Scandal at Scourie* back in 1953. Moorehead's Sister Josephine was chiefly characterized by her "Flying Nun" wimple and her standard French accent (the film is set in Quebec). Five years after *Rawhide*, Moorehead would play Sister Cluny in *The Singing Nun* with her friend Debbie Reynolds in the title role. Sister Cluny provides much needed comic relief and some salt in this sickeningly sweet concoction, but as a portrait of a nun it doesn't get us further than your standard *Sister Act* type comic stereotype.

Out of Moorehead's three nun roles, then, Sister Frances in *Rawhide* is my favorite. I like the clean, scrubbed-down realism of her face here, as compared with the overly "colorful" treatment she was given in *The Singing Nun*. As already indicated, there's some of the same thematic here as in the Debbie Reynolds vehicle, where a young nun's vocation is tested when she encounters the magnetic force of a member of the opposite sex, but the treatment is much more realistic and interesting in the *Rawhide* episode. I dare say, too, that bad boy Rowdy Yates represents more of a threat to Sister Joan's celibacy than clean-cut Robert Gerarde (Chad Everett) does to Sister Ann in *The Singing Nun*.

As fate would have it, all three of Moorehead's nun roles were filmed on the MGM lot in Culver City, a lot she knew well, as it had been her professional home as an MGM contract player through most of the 1940s. But this was a different age and MGM certainly no longer had more stars than in the heavens. In June 1960, Moorehead was returning to her old studio, but she wasn't finding many familiar faces there. Most of the cast and crew working on "Poco Tiempo" would have been new to her. This was her only common credit with Eastwood, Raines, and Carolyn Hughes, who gives a fine performance as a saucy saloon girl and counterpoint to saintly Sister Joan.

This was not Moorehead's only credit with 19-year-old Gigi Perreau. Funnily enough, at the age of three Perreau had played Hume Cronyn and Jessica Tandy's infant daughter Annie in *The Seventh Cross*, where Moorehead had a small but beautifully acted role as the seamstress Madame Marelli. I wonder if they made the connection. Perreau married a 35-year-old business executive only a few months after being on *Rawhide*. Director Ted Post, who helmed 24 episodes of *Rawhide*; writer Buckley Angell, who retired after writing 13 episodes of the series; cinematographer John M. Nickolaus, Jr.; and makeup man Jack Dusick, the father of actress Michele Lee, were all working with Moorehead for the first and only time.

The only "old timer" onboard was Frank Puglia, born in Sicily in 1892, whose film career went back to the silent screen days of D.W. Griffith and who is probably best remembered, if at all, as the Moroccan rug merchant in *Casablanca*. Puglia had played the servant Pietro in *The Lost Moment* and also had minor roles in *Journey into Fear* and *Dragon Seed*, but he and Moorehead had not had any significant on-screen interaction until *Rawhide*.

In 1965, Clint Eastwood wrote an article where he reminisced about *Rawhide*, which was about to enter its final season, and the "dozen beauties who have brightened the life of Rowdy Yates, the character I play in the series—and my own too." The actresses mentioned—Julie Harris, Dina Merrill, Mary Astor, Ruta Lee, Miyoshi Umeki, Agnes Moorehead, Kim Hunter, Julie London, Debra Paget, Elizabeth Montgomery, and his own wife,

Agnes Moorehead gave her finest performance as a nun on an episode of the long-running Western series *Rawhide*. Here she is seen with one of the series regulars, Clint Eastwood, who played the cattle drover Rowdy Yates. Eastwood fondly remembered their collaboration on the episode "Incident at Poco Tiempo" and was impressed by Moorehead's professionalism, sense of humor, and general knowledge.

Maggie—are certainly a motley crew. Despite the misleading title "Beauties Brighten Lives of Drovers," it turns out that Eastwood is more concerned with these women's inner qualities. He remembers Moorehead in the following way: "Agnes Moorehead had the greatest sense of humor of any woman I have worked with. She's 100 percent actress before the camera and real fun the moment she sits down to chat with you. And I never cease to be amazed about how well informed she is on so many subjects."[4] After *Rawhide* was cancelled in mid-season in 1966, Eastwood never acted in television again.

CREDITS: *Director:* Ted Post; *Producers:* Endre Bohem, Ernest J. Nims, Charles Marquis Warren; *Writer:* Buckley Angell; *Cinematography:* John M. Nickolaus, Jr.; *Film editing:* James Baiotto; *Art direction:* John B. Goodman; *Makeup department:* Jack Dusick; *Production company:* Columbia Broadcasting System (CBS); *Air date:* December 9, 1960, on CBS

CAST (regular): Clint Eastwood (Rowdy Yates), Steve Raines (Jim Quince). Guest: "Incident at Poco Tiempo": Stewart Bradley (Payton), Lew Gallo (Colley), Carolyn Hughes (Emerald Carney), Ken Mayer (Swanson), Agnes Moorehead (Sister Frances), Gigi Perreau (Sister Joan), Frank Puglia (Father Sebastian), Gregory Walcott (Mara)

15

The Twilight Zone: "The Invaders" (TV, 1961)

On October 19, 1960, Hedda Hopper concluded her weekly column with the lines: "Agnes Moorehead is doing a Twilight Zone show on television. I don't know why she isn't always working in pictures."[1] As we know, by 1960 the major phase of Moorehead's film career was over, and 1961 would be the last year she worked on more than one feature film. It was an unsettled, transitional phase of her career, where money was increasingly tight, as she pondered how to make up the lost income from films. Throughout the 1950s, film work had always been her top priority for financial rather than artistic reasons, while the stage was closer to her heart. Now she no longer had the choice, with opportunities in the film industry getting harder to come by for actresses of her age and background. Her first love, radio, was no longer a reliable source of income either. Little did Moorehead know that television would prove the saving of her career in more ways than one.

Hopper's snobbery aside, it wasn't as if *The Twilight Zone* was just any old TV show. "The Invaders" was the 15th segment of the second season of the groundbreaking and vastly popular science fiction series that ran from 1959 to 1964. Historians of the series Don Presnell and Marty McGee have observed that *TZ* "was near its creative peak in its second season: actors were scrambling to snatch up juicy and prestigious *Twilight Zone* roles." Director of photography George T. Clemens recalled: "That second year, I can't think of anyone who turned down a chance to do the show."[2] In terms of visibility, originality, and popularity, the 25-minute episode that aired on CBS on January 27, 1961, is arguably the most important single program of Moorehead's career. Today *The Twilight Zone* is the most popular television series Moorehead ever acted in followed by *Bewitched*.[3]

"The Invaders" has been called by *Twilight Zone* aficionados "one of the greatest *TZ* episodes ever filmed" and "also one of the best-remembered."[4] Apparently, it was one of series creator and executive producer Rod Serling's two favorite episodes.[5] In a tour de force pantomime performance with no spoken dialogue, Moorehead plays a woman alone in a rural cabin, whose preparations for dinner are rudely interrupted by two spacemen landing their flying saucer on her roof. Or so it seems.

"The Invaders" was directed by Douglas Heyes and written by Richard Matheson, *TZ* mainstays both, who created some of the best episodes of the series. Born in 1919, Heyes had directed the popular "Eye of the Beholder" episode earlier in the season. With a total of nine *TZ* episodes to his credit, he has been called "one of the finest directors ever to work on the series."[6] Though he remained mainly a television director, Heyes would go on to direct the hit films *Kitten with a Whip* and *Beau Geste*. A writer for film and television since the early 1950s, Heyes would also go on to write the screenplay for *Ice Station Zebra* and ended his career as a co-writer on the popular mini-series *North and South* in the mid–1980s.

Richard Matheson was 34 when he wrote "The Invaders" as the seventh of 16 episodes he would write for *TZ*. He was the author of both the original novel and the screenplay for *The Invisible Shrinking Man* and wrote the novels on which the popular recent films *What Dreams May Come*, *Stir of Echoes*, and *I Am Legend* were based. Matheson died in 2013.

In Moorehead's papers at the Wisconsin Center for Film and Theater Research, there is a 25-page typescript of "The Invaders" dated August 6, 1960, probably sent to the actress when she was asked to do the show. It is not marked in any way, as it would have been had she used it during production. At any rate, it allows us to compare the finished version of "The Invaders" to writer Richard Matheson's original conception. The cast list consists of the "The Woman" and "The Invaders." The woman is described as follows: "she has been alone for many years; a strong, simple person whose existence is primitive and whose only problem is acquiring enough food to eat." The invaders are described as "from another planet; two individuals, never seen clearly."[7] The last three words are significant. Matheson felt that in the finished episode the spacemen were visible too soon and seen too clearly. He also felt they weren't menacing enough. "Those little figures wobbling around looked like windup dolls," he said.[8] Director Heyes has explained why the figures look the way they do: "The reason I made them this kind of bulky round shape is that, first of all, they should not look like human beings, but secondly, after the fact, you had to say they *were* human beings. Ah hah! Then therefore, they were in inflated spacesuits, right?"[9]

In the script, the sets were simply specified as three exteriors—"Bleak landscape," "Simple, primitive house," "Roof top"; and one interior, consisting of "House/Kitchen area/Main area/Sleeping room."[10] The episode as aired follows the script closely up until the point where the woman catches one of the spacemen in the blanket from her bed. From that point on, the episode as shown is considerably simpler than the complex close combat Matheson had envisioned in his script. For example, he had the bed catching on fire and the spaceman getting out of the blanket and making a temporary escape, before the woman uses a box to the block the hole in the door and cunningly recaptures him in it. She then casts the box into the fire. Originally, too, Matheson had envisioned that the spaceman's gun would leave bleeding wounds on the woman's skin and that she would pick out two small bullets after their first attack on the roof. In the final version, the gun leaves wart-like protrusions on her skin, but there is no blood.

It is interesting in the context of these differences between the teleplay and the episode as produced to read in *A Critical History of Television's The Twilight Zone*, that Matheson "has never been overly fond of this episode." "Agnes Moorehead was wonderful," the writer commented, "but the direction just dragged its feet." According to Matheson, his version "had many things going on that really kept the story going: much more involvement and incident."[11] This is just the difference I noted in the struggle between the woman and the ostensible "invaders," which has been considerably simplified in the episode as aired compared with the original teleplay. On the other hand, Matheson felt the opening as filmed was "much too long: It seemed like Moorehead was cooking a whole meal before she hears the sounds on the roof. But she was marvelous."[12]

This image from the celebrated "Invaders" episode of *The Twilight Zone*'s second season captures the strangeness of Moorehead's character, simply referred to in the teleplay as "The Woman," and also shows one of the ostensible "invaders." Writer Richard Matheson thought the spacemen were seen too soon and too clearly and he also felt they weren't menacing enough. He had high praise, though, for Moorehead's wordless performance.

The surprise ending of "The Invaders," where the Martians turn out to be the humans and the woman is the alien, is justly famous and has been called "one of the most genuinely surprising twist endings in *Twilight Zone* history."[13] In the teleplay, the planet the woman is living on is explicitly identified as Mars. On the other hand, it is never said explicitly that the so-called invaders are human beings from earth. Serling's closing voice-over narration is considerably shorter than in the finished episode. As originally scripted, the narrator simply says: "This is one of the out-of-the-way places; until now, one of the unvisited places in our solar system—the planet Mars. Bleak. Wasted. Dying. But not *quite* dead yet."[14]

In "The Invaders," the lighting is so flattering and Moorehead's make up so well done, that she looks preternaturally young, as if she were 40 rather than 60. Or maybe it would be better to describe her as uncannily ageless, which only serves to foreshadow the discovery of her alien identity. Even a seeming inconsistency—her long, perfectly manicured nails—may be seen in retrospect as a sign that this is no ordinary farm woman. *TZ* aficionado Douglas Brode describes how Moorehead's performance also suggests that all is not as it seems: "She performs in a style that occupies a middle ground between the realistic approach we expect and a mime-like effect to convey emotional reactions and thoughts through exaggerated body language. The way in which this 'person' reacts to what happens is not as a normal human would. We don't need to hear the woman speak in a foreign tongue to grasp that she's not of this Earth."[15]

Veteran actor Jack Warden, who did two episodes of *TZ* and the excellent "It Shouldn't Happen to a Dog" episode in Season 1 of *Bewitched*, recalled that Rod Serling "created such a great situation for performance. That was one of the reasons so many actors wanted to work with Rod."[16] What is most remarkable to anyone who has been a close observer of Moorehead's acting technique, particularly during this relatively late stage of her career, is the extent to which she delivers a performance in "The Invaders" which is radically unlike anything she had ever done before or would do again. Being deprived of her most pliable and familiar instrument—her voice—forced her to reinvent herself and her technique as an actress.

Director Douglas Heyes explains how they worked: "I would rehearse for about half a day with her and the camera for one piece of film, and then we would do it. It would take like four hours of rehearsal and then four minutes to shoot it. Then another long, long period of rehearsing and then a short piece of film."[17] Heyes had specifically wanted Moorehead for this role. He admitted that there was "an element of mischief embodied in her casting," since she was so well known for her "virtually unstoppable" monologue in "Sorry, Wrong Number," where she only had her voice to work with.[18] Moorehead's initial reaction, Matheson recalled, was to ask where her part was, "Because actors and actresses, to them their job consists of dialogue or monologue, and it didn't have either one."[19]

For those who know Moorehead's acting career well, "The Invaders" is not just an ironic inversion of her verbal histrionics in "Sorry, Wrong Number." It is also possible to see the nameless woman in her rustic cabin as a wonderful send-up of all those homespun, stalwart, rural women Moorehead played on film and television. There's just a touch of Ma Stratton here, not to mention Aggie McDonald from *Johnny Belinda* (with her niece Belinda's muteness) and Jessie Crain in *The Blazing Forest*. In her ornery, unwashed unkemptness, the woman of "The Invaders" also looks towards the Grand Guignol of Velma Cruther. Watching Moorehead being "just plain folks" is always entertaining. She has the makings of a champion bowler, the way she knocks out that little spaceman with her torch on the first throw!

Regrettably, there is little sign that this renewal in Moorehead's technique in "The Invaders" had any lasting effect on her screen acting. In the four feature films that were produced soon after *The Twilight Zone* episode in 1961—*Twenty Plus Two*, *Bachelor in*

Paradise, *Rebecca*, and *How the West Was Won*—Moorehead is for the most part up to her old tricks. Always a staunch supporter, Hedda Hopper wrote after "The Invaders" had aired: "Agnes Moorehead should be adding another Emmy to her trophies for an amazing TV performance in Twilight Zone."[20] She was not nominated for this performance, which may have been because her role didn't fit neatly into any of the existing Primetime Emmy categories.

CREDITS: *Director:* Douglas Heyes; *Producers:* Buck Houghton, Del Reisman; *Writer:* Richard Matheson; *Director of photography:* George T. Clemens; *Film editor:* Leon Barsha; *Art direction:* Philip Barber, George W. Davis; *Set decoration:* H. Web Arrowsmith, Henry Grace; *Sound:* Franklin Milton, Charles Scheid; *Music:* Jerry Goldsmith; *Production company:* Cayuga Production/Columbia Broadcasting System (CBS); *Air Date:* January 27, 1961, on CBS

CAST: Douglas Heyes (voice of astronaut), Agnes Moorehead (woman), Rod Serling (narrator/host)

16

Prescription: Murder (Stage, 1962)

Two years after *The Pink Jungle* closed in Boston, a new Paul Gregory production starring Agnes Moorehead finally went into rehearsal. The play was originally called *RX: Murder* and dealt with a noted psychiatrist, Dr. Roy Flemming, murdering his wife, Claire, with help from his mistress, Susan Hudson, only to be investigated to the bitter end by a police lieutenant with the now familiar name Columbo. The young co-authors were William Link and Richard Levinson, both born in Philadelphia in 1934 and friends since junior high school. In 1959, they had started out on a prolific writing career in television that would culminate with the hit series *Columbo* and *Murder, She Wrote*. The 46-year-old Australian, Myles Eason, was set to make his directorial debut, having been an actor in London and New York and assistant director to Peter Brook, John Gielgud, and Nigel Patrick.

Prescription: Murder had no less than four stars and was bound for Broadway after a cross-country tour. In addition to Moorehead as the murdered wife, Claire, Joseph Cotten would play Dr. Flemming, his real-life wife, Patricia Medina, would play his mistress, Susan Hudson, and Thomas Mitchell would create the now classic role of the investigator Columbo. Cotten recalled in his autobiography that Moorehead and Mitchell had already been cast when he and his wife signed on.[1] The couple had never acted together before, in fact this was Medina's first stage play. When they were reunited for *Prescription: Murder*, the old friends Cotten and Moorehead hadn't worked together since filming *Since You Went Away* in 1943–44. From there, Cotten had gone on to be Jennifer Jones's leading man in three high-profile films produced by her future husband, David O. Selznick: *Love Letters*, *Duel in the Sun*, and *Portrait of Jennie*. According to Paul Gregory, Selznick liked to use Cotten to focus the audience's attention on Jones. In Gregory's salty phrase, you used Joe Cotten if "you didn't want the star to scratch her cunt."[2] Cotten had Broadway credits extending back to 1932, including shows like *Jezebel* (1933–34) with Miriam Hopkins; Orson Welles's productions of *Julius Caesar* (1937–38) and *Danton's Death* (1938); and Katharine Hepburn's comeback vehicle, *The Philadelphia Story* (1939–40), where Cotten played C.K. Dexter Haven, the role that went to Cary Grant in the film version. Though Cotten had worked steadily in film and television throughout the 1950s, the vehicles and the roles were more modest.

Cotten's wife of nearly 30 years, Lenore Kipp, died in 1960. Moorehead paid frequent visits to the grieving widower.[3] Maybe she entertained the idea she might become the second Mrs. Cotten. On October 20, 1960, that assignment went to a 40-year-old English actress of partially Spanish extraction called Patricia Medina. Medina's film career had begun in England in 1937 and later in Hollywood consisted chiefly of playing damsels in distress in period costume dramas such as *The Three Musketeers*, *Desperate Search*, *Botany Bay*, and *The Black Knight*. After a decade away from the silver screen, she would return in 1968 in the lesbian classic *The Killing of Sister George*, as Susannah York and Beryl Reid's neighbor, a florid lady of easy virtue called Betty Thaxter.

Thomas Mitchell was best known as Scarlett O'Hara's father in *Gone with the Wind* and had started in movies in 1936. Other of his most familiar screen roles were Diz Moore in *Mr. Smith Goes to Washington*, Uncle Billy Bailey in *It's a Wonderful Life*, and Mayor Jonas Henderson in *High Noon*. He had won an Oscar for Best Supporting Actor in 1940 for playing Doc Boone in *Stagecoach*. His Broadway career went as far back as 1916. He had replaced Lee J. Cobb as Willy Loman in the original Broadway run of *Death of a Salesman* and had won a Tony for Best Actor in a Musical in 1953 for *Hazel Flagg* with Helen Gallagher in the title role. Mitchell's last feature film would be *Pocketful of Miracles* with Bette Davis, which was released the day before rehearsals on *Prescription: Murder* started.

Moorehead was apparently less than impressed by her co-stars in this production. In October 1961, we find her writing to her producer in a poison pen mode from Chicago. "Save these notices for me," she writes, "I put them in my tour book—of course I'm not saving T.M.'s [Thomas Mitchell's]—when I get the other notice of T.M., I'll send it to you—but it's something to think about—for I know how jittery you get when an actor begins to throw a play out of the window—from too much talk (in the south) or falling down drunk!" She insists that "I couldn't let you go on without finding out the attitude of people who make up box office." Evidently, Thomas Mitchell was beginning to talk publicly about *Prescription: Murder* before the show had been announced. Moorehead wanted to know when she was getting the script. "You're the only person in this mad world that I say 'yes' to without reading a script! Who know's [sic]—the part may have been written for E.G. Robinson?" The latter was an allusion to the fact that Orson Welles had originally wanted Moorehead for the role of the war crimes investigator in *The Stranger*, which ultimately went to Robinson. She got in a jab at her coming co-stars, when she wrote: "Don't put the group before your old friend—it might be worse than Ginger R[oger].'s. At least none of them have ever stood on a stage by themselves with one exception T.M.—and he better stop it before they sandbag him." In conclusion, she sighed: "I wish you were here—I'd at least have some fun—what am I doing? Looking at a corny movie—'Pink Fuzzy Nightgown'—oh dear—."[4]

Not long after he received Moorehead's barbed letter, Gregory was ready to go public with his new production. "I have made the deal with Don Loper to do your clothes," he wrote on October 18, "and he is just wild about his opportunity to dress you, particularly in boudoir trappings!"[5] Loper and his partner Charles Northrup had recently designed a new gown for Moorehead's one-woman show for $1,400.[6] Gregory promised her a copy of the script within 48 hours: "In the meantime, darling, rest assured old Gregory is in your corner and we'll beat our enemies to death."[7]

Moorehead signed a preliminary contract on October 18 and a final contract on December 19, the day before rehearsals started. She would receive the same terms as for *The Pink Jungle*: $1,500 a week until the show recouped its actual production costs, then $1,750 a week. In comparison, Joseph Cotten was to receive $4,000 a week and 10 percent of the gross box office receipts, Patricia Medina $1,000 a week, and Thomas Mitchell $2,000 a week.[8]

Prescription: Murder had its world premiere at the Curran Theatre in San Francisco on January 15, 1962. The box office was strong, but the reviews were negative; so negative, that Gregory swore he would never open one of his productions in San Francisco again. He would stick to that resolve.[9] The company stayed in San Francisco for 12 days, before embarking on an extensive and exhausting tour that would take them to 24 states and Canada. Playing only one or two nights in most places, they wended their way from Denver to Syracuse and from Ottawa to Jacksonville in the course of the four and a half months the tour lasted. When the show opened in Minneapolis on February 12, it had a new title: *Prescription: Murder*.[10] Gregory was hoping to parlay the script into a film deal, but there had already been a movie called *RX: Murder*.[11] Cotten and Medina had an agreement with Gregory that they would reprise their roles in the film version.[12]

The original plan was to open on Broadway in April, but by late February Gregory had decided to postpone the New York premiere till the fall. During their run in Philadelphia, Thomas Mitchell had to undergo an operation and was replaced permanently by his understudy, Howard Wierum.[13] By mid–April, Gregory stated openly to the press that though the New York opening was scheduled for September 22, he would be happy not to take the show to New York at all. "I produce for the road," he said.[14] Cotten recalled that "the play seemed to lose its spine without Tommy."[15] While they were playing at the Royal Alexandra Theatre in Toronto, Moorehead received word that the show would close at the Shubert Theatre in Boston on May 26.[16] For Moorehead it was *déjà vu*, as *The Pink Jungle*, which had also been Broadway-bound, had closed at the same theater in December 1959.

On June 20, 1962, Gregory wrote to the investors in *Prescription: Murder* that he was disappointed they had not "reached pay-off" and to explain what had gone wrong with the production. They had hoped to tour through June, he wrote, ending in Seattle, but that had not been possible due to lack of available air-conditioned theaters and an inability to arrange consecutive bookings. He put the poor box office on parts of the tour down to Thomas Mitchell's illness and the hot weather, particularly in Toronto and Boston, with temperatures in the nineties. It did not improve mattes that the Toronto critics had given them a verbal roasting as well. Gregory alluded to problems with the two writers when he regretted the "inability to secure sufficient quality re-writes to improve the major weakness in the script."[17]

Link and Levinson, who were jokingly referred to by the cast as "Leopold and Loeb," were "very young and quite determined not to change a word of their script," Patricia Medina recalled, nor would they allow other writers to make changes or additions without their approval. On a telegram from the two writers' lawyers "to protest your presenting this unauthorized version of the play," Gregory has penciled in a response:

> Every word as now played has been approved by L+L. It is common knowledge within the confines of this production based on re-write submitted to date by L+L that they [are] not competent to re-write sufficiently to make further contributions [to] this play—there [sic] refusal to approve other usual procedure for salvation of this play is a direct and tragic disregard of the expected standard set by this our profession. They leave me no alternative than to advise the League of New York Producers of their obstinate attitude in the hopes no future producer will be frauded [sic] by their protestations in the future.[18]

We know Link and Levinson had made a number of changes to be inserted in the play in Minneapolis in mid–February, but that they felt hampered in their efforts by limitations in Joseph Cotten as a performer. Making the love affair between Dr. Flemming and Susan Hudson more believable was "complicated by the fact that there are certain things that would improve the play that our leading man cannot do":

> With Cotten, he must be given spare dialogue so that his tendencies toward grandeloquence [sic] will be tempered. With another actor, one who can underplay with tenseness and conviction, the dialogue can be more ornate—but at all times, when making additions at least for now, we must consider if Cotten can play it.

They added that "The pacing is slow, and the leading man does not have the stage presence to command excited interest."[19]

On the whole, the reviews had been middling at best. The worst thrashing was given by the reviewer for the *Toronto Globe and Mail*. Under the heading "Old-Fashioned Mystery: When Actress Died, So Did Play," Frank Morriss analyzed its deficiencies in excruciating detail: the murder melodrama intrigue was "old-hat" and utterly banal; Wierum was out of his element in Mitchell's role, because "he was trying for the Mitchell manner and only succeeded in giving the Mitchell mannerism"; Link and Levinson had "written some of the most old-fashioned dialogue since Lady Audley's Secret"; Joseph Cotten was wasting his time; Patricia Medina was "amateurish"; and the director had been little help to the actors and merely kept the play going. Only Moorehead received laurels for her efforts: "she did wonders with a portrait of a disillusioned, jealous, but basically likeable woman."[20]

Moorehead's limited role was universally regretted. It must have been satisfying for her to read that "It is a crying shame to waste Agnes Moorehead on one act of a three-act play" and that "one act of Miss Moorehead's controlled histrionics is worth an entire evening of some lesser thespians' emotions."[21] After noting that "Miss Moorehead, with her splendid red hair and her splendid pink gown and her splendid black coat, is not seen again until the curtain calls," one reviewer wondered "why a woman of such talent wastes her time in such a small role in such a weak play."[22] A reviewer in Savannah, Georgia, sounded a similar note. The "Biggest disappointment," he wrote, was that "They killed off Agnes Moorehead in the first act." According to the same writer: "The audience never recovered. This great actress swept her audience with her in the all-too-brief role of unwanted wife. But Cotton [sic] strangled her so soon as to cause the viewer to wonder: Why was such talent touring so far for such a small role?"[23] When asked directly, she responded that she "did it as a favor to Gregory and that she believed even the smallest role should be played by the best talent available."[24] She didn't mention that this small role came with a big paycheck.

The reviewer for the *Omaha World-Herald* wrote that the four stars "undoubtedly provided the greatest attraction for the largest single-night drama audience here in years—1,236 patrons." As the wife, Moorehead was "convincingly crabby and perverse." Like so many reviewers, he remarked that she was wasted in the play and missed after she was gone.[25] In a review rare for taking a more upbeat view of the play, Bob Goddard of the *St. Louis Globe-Democrat* was one of many sorry to lose Moorehead so early. He observed that the play was not a traditional whodunit, but rather a "how will he catch him" and "fairly predictable for the most part." Yet Goddard found it "just about what the doctor ordered for an entertaining evening." After repeating that it was a "downright shame" to have to lose Moorehead so early in the game as the "brittle, jealous wife," he added: "However, even one act for Miss Moorehead is magnetic doings, and I am beholden to her, and the authors, for that."[26]

Once again, it fell to the respected Boston critic Elliot Norton, to provide a sober summing up. His prescription for the play was simply to "pick up the tempo"; either the writers or the director were to blame for the play sagging and dragging. Beyond the problem of pacing, it was never really made convincing that the psychiatrist should be in love with his young actress patient: "Theirs is hardly a crime of passion, yet passion is advanced as the cause, and you need to believe in it." Wierum, in Norton's opinion, did very nicely in Mitchell's role. Of Moorehead as Claire Flemming, he wrote: "Why anyone would want to do away with such a woman is hard to understand."[27]

Despite being strangled in the first act, then, audiences seemed to hope and expect that Moorehead would make some sort of miraculous and spectacular return. She neither returned in the course of the play, nor did *Prescription: Murder* ultimately provide her longed for return to Broadway. Fortunately, she had not long to wait. Paul Gregory had another show in the works. Less than six months after *Prescription: Murder* closed in Boston, Agnes Moorehead would be performing on the stage of the Royale Theatre in New York.

CREDITS: *Director:* Myles Eason; *Producers:* Paul Gregory, Amy Lynn; *Writers:* Richard Levinson, William Link; *Costumes:* Don Loper; *Scenery and lighting:* James Trittipo; *Premiere:* January 15, 1962, at the Curran Theatre in San Francisco, California

CAST: Joseph Cotten (Dr. Roy Flemming), Raleigh Davidson (delivery boy), Lucille Fenton (Miss Petrie), Patricia Medina (Susan Hudson), Thomas Mitchell (Lieutenant Columbo), Agnes Moorehead (Claire Flemming), Raymond Parker (Dave Gordon), Howard Wierum (Dave Gordon; Lieutenant Columbo)

TOURING SCHEDULE: Colorado, Kansas, Nebraska, Iowa, Minnesota, North Dakota, Wisconsin, Illinois, Pennsylvania, North Carolina, Virginia, Ohio, Michigan, Missouri, Georgia, Tennessee, South Carolina, Florida, Louisiana, Maryland, Connecticut, New York, and Canada, closing May 26, 1962, in Boston, Massachusetts.

17

Lord Pengo (Stage, 1962–63)

On May 19, 2007, I found myself walking down from my comfortable hotel on Hammond St. in West Hollywood to meet one of Agnes Moorehead's old friends at Starbucks on La Cienega Boulevard near 3rd Street. Despite the gloomy predictions about the impossibility of walking in Los Angeles, there was a neat sidewalk to guide my footsteps along the way, as I sauntered down San Vicente Boulevard, past the toylike green and blue cubes of the Pacific Design Center and alongside the imposing bulk of the Cedars-Sinai Medical Center.

My appointment was at two o'clock. As I entered the characteristically nondescript coffee shop, I recognized the beige-clad, mustachioed, and bald-pated figure of Laurie Main ordering his coffee at the counter. I tapped him on the shoulder, introduced myself, and we seated ourselves outside on a small terrace to conjure up a part of his colorful past in the midst of an asphalt jungle.

Originally from Australia, Main made a career for himself in the United States as a character actor on stage and screen and narrating the popular Disney series *Welcome to Pooh Corner*, which ran from 1983 till 1995. He first met Agnes Moorehead in 1962, when she came backstage after a performance of *Camelot* on Broadway and complimented him on his portrayal of King Pellinore. They remained friends until her death. He turned 40 the year he and Agnes met, making him 22 years her junior. Now he was 84, long retired and enjoying life's small pleasures, such as his daily excursion by motor cart from his home on North La Jolla Avenue to his local Starbucks. In addition to the usual people watching, coffee, and his favorite cigar, there would today be a chance to talk about a dear friend long gone and a show they did together nearly 45 years ago: *Lord Pengo*.

At the time I interviewed him, Laurie Main was one of only three surviving cast members from *Lord Pengo*, veteran dramatist S.N. Behrman's penultimate Broadway show.[1] Born in 1893 and dying on his 80th birthday in 1973, Behrman is chiefly remembered today for his brittle drawing room comedies of the 1930s, including *Biography* and *End of Summer*. He had contracted to write *Lord Pengo* for producer Paul Gregory as early as 1953.[2] On June 9, 1961, we find mention of the play in a letter Gregory wrote to Moorehead while she was shooting *How the West Was Won* on location in Paducah, Kentucky. Gregory was still having trouble about the exact rehearsal dates for *Lord Pengo*, he said. "In any event," he assured her, "you are my star #1 concern and I won't let you down." In closing, he mentioned that Behrman was working on the play and that the part of Primrose was "growing and growing."[3]

It appears, then, that Moorehead was involved in the project early on and had been promised a starring role. Gregory kept his word, though the size of the part never quite justified the billing. The only real star of the show was Charles Boyer in the title role. *Lord Pengo* did not really begin to come together until he signed on on May 9, 1962.[4] Later that month, Gregory and Behrman were at the Hotel du Cap in Cap d'Antibes conferring with their star about the play. It was inspired by "The Days of Duveen," a series of sketches Behrman had written for the *New Yorker* about the art dealer Joseph Duveen. Though playwright and lead actor did not get along according to Gregory, they shared a fascination for the legendary Duveen, who died in 1939.[5] Boyer was ready to take on something meatier after his long Broadway run in *The Marriage-Go-Round* with Claudette Colbert, but he declined to invest in the production.[6] The play was very much centered round him as a charmingly manipulative art dealer, who is forced to take stock of his life as it nears its end. There was to be a plotline about Pengo's relationship with his son Derek, who refuses to follow in his father's footsteps; a faithful secretary, Miss Swanson, with a yen for her boss; and a number of incidents generated by visits from wealthy clients looking for art to fill their souls (and empty their pocketbooks).

On his return from the Riviera, Gregory signed a contract to stage *Lord Pengo* at the Royale Theatre in New York.[7] He was still looking for a director and told Moorehead on June 20 that he would not formally announce the play until he had one, so as not to weaken the director's position. He promised to have a script for her soon. In answer to her question if he missed her, he replied:

> Miss you? Indeed I do! But the trouble is you insist on being in the lousiest, bastardly business in creation. If you would just agree to be a beach bum and forget all this other crap I might be agreeable to going with you to an isolated island where we could eat cocoanuts, papaya and fish—no pressures, just you and me and the son. But alas, dear Ekbert, you won't do such a thing—not with that fabulous hairdo—and I can't say I blame you for life with me could be pretty dull. I am like the stock market, I gain and then I drop.[8]

On June 22, Peter Glenville wrote Gregory declining to direct the play. He would rather "work on something a little more challenging from a director's point of view."[9]

The man who finally took the assignment was Vincent J. Donehue. Born in 1915, Donehue had been nominated for a Tony for directing *The Sound of Music*, which had opened on November 16, 1959, and was still running. His most recent Broadway show, *Daughter of Silence*, only ran a month, but before *The Sound of Music* he had had great success with the original production of Horton Foote's *The Trip to Bountiful*, starring Lillian Gish, and with Dore Schary's play about the Roosevelts, *Sunrise at Campobello*. The latter garnered him a Tony for Best Director in 1958 and ran for 556 performances.

Gregory wrote to Donehue on July 5 that he wanted to use his usual backstage crew for the production and that casting should be their first concern when he arrived in New York.[10] Five days later, Gregory sent the long-awaited script to Moorehead. He wrote in the accompanying letter: "By no means is it all I hoped for from the standpoint of Miss Swanson; however, I think you will be able to do marvelous things with it. And further, before we even get into rehearsal I feel there will be additions which will strengthen considerably your part as well as the whole play." He imagined that a great deal of what was left of the role of Primrose would be cut. Director Donehue was concerned with the character's lack of real belonging.[11]

The aging socialite Primrose Drury, then, was the role Moorehead had originally been slated to play, but somewhere along the way she opted for Miss Swanson, Pengo's devoted secretary, instead. At this stage, Gregory's chief concern was to keep Moorehead happy. She was worried, it seems, that another actress would steal her fire in the role of Mrs. Drury—one of Pengo's many rich clients—a spoiled dowager, who wants to win back her estranged husband, but ends up marrying her analyst instead. Jessie Royce Landis, Mary Astor, Rosemary Harris, and Colleen Dewhurst were among the actresses being considered for the role.[12] Moorehead's competition finally turned out to be the talented Ruth White, born in 1915, who after a late start due to caring for elderly parents had made a name for herself on Broadway since 1949 in shows such as *The Ponder Heart* and *The Happiest Millionaire*. She would be nominated for a Tony in 1968 for creating the role of Meg in the original Broadway production of Pinter's *The Birthday Party* and died of cancer the following year at the age of 55.

Veteran actors such as Henry Daniell, Cliff Hall, and Betty Sinclair were cast in other of the play's many roles. Daniell had made his debut on Broadway as far back as 1921 and had acted in countless films in addition to his stage work. In 1929, he had triumphed as Lord Ivor Cream in Berhman's comedy *Serenda Blandish*, starring Ruth Gordon. The role of the Primrose's ex-husband, the industrialist Enoch Drury, would be his last. Laurie Main recalled that Daniell died in 1963, while they were filming *My Fair Lady*.[13] Comedian Cliff Hall, who would do an episode in the second season of *Bewitched* titled "A Bum Raps" in 1966, played a millionaire who comes to buy a gift for his wife after a quarrel. Pengo sells him a Settignano sculpture he had intended to give his own wife. Betty Sinclair had only one scene as Lady Winfield, an impoverished aristocrat wanting to sell a family portrait. When Sinclair was found collapsed in her dressing room one night, understudy Constance Carpenter went on. Because she suited the part better, she got an unexpected number of laughs, throwing Boyer off. Laurie Main remembered having to explain to the star that this was because Carpenter looked the part, something buck-toothed Sinclair apparently did not.[14]

Lee Richardson played Wilfred Oliver, described in the script as "a very attractive, somewhat epicene American, about 35 years old."[15] He pays court to Primrose and then goes off and marries her daughter. Gregory wrote to Boyer that they had to be careful in casting this role as "any slight evidence of swish would be bad."[16] Finally, the central role of Pengo's would-be artist son Derek was given to the talented young actor Brian Bedford. Born in 1935, he had gone to RADA in the same class as Albert Finney, Alan Bates, Peter O'Toole, and Richard Harris and made his Broadway debut as Jessica Tandy's son in Peter Shaffer's *Five Finger Exercise* in 1959, a role he had created in the London production. Robert Donat's son Peter Donat had been in the running for this part, but was in Gregory's opinion "a little powder puff blue like the English can be (without being queer): I do think we have to guard against the slight possibility of this for it could just knock our play cockeyed."[17]

With the casting and the script finally in place, rehearsals began in New York on Tuesday, September 11th.[18] One month later, *Lord Pengo* had its world premiere at the New Locust Theatre in Philadelphia. During the ten-day run, Moorehead stayed at the venerable Warwick Hotel. The company moved on to Detroit and opened at the Fisher Theatre on October 22. After a week, a new first act was introduced. Mary Martin had come round after a performance and told Boyer that the start of the play didn't make a good entrance for him. Thus the comic scene where he coaches his faithful valet Filbert

(Laurie Main) in what to say to help make a sale to a wealthy client was replaced by a similar scene between Pengo and his son. Boyer was grateful to Main for not making a fuss about losing one of his best scenes, Main recalled, adding that Boyer generally was a cold man.[19]

The revamping of the first act did not affect Moorehead, as she only appeared in the second and third acts set in Pengo's New York gallery. Her part was the familiar one of the not unattractive yet unmarried older woman, who for years devotes herself wholeheartedly and selflessly to a powerful man. She secretly carries a torch for him; he does not even know her first name. While realizing that her employer has his faults, she remains steadfast in her devotion, thus serving to indicate to the audience that he is basically lovable. Moorehead could have played this sort of role with her head under her arm and her arm in a sling, as we say in Norway. One wonders why she took it. Well, the answer is simple: she needed the money, which in the case of *Lord Pengo* was $1,500 a week.[20] Further inducements were the opportunity to co-star with Charles Boyer, whose star power was still shining forth at age 63; and the chance for a return to Broadway after long absence. Despite the fact that her role was "transient,"[21] she received star billing second only to Boyer.

Lord Pengo also gave Moorehead the opportunity to live in New York for the first time since 1941. In June 1962, after the end of the *Prescription: Murder* tour and as things were falling into place with the forthcoming production, she had moved in with fellow actress and *Pengo* understudy Constance Carpenter in the latter's apartment at 135 E. 54th St. After the show, Laurie Main would often escort her home on his way to his room at the Selwyn Arms Hotel. He also recalled that they frequently had a bite to eat at the Brasserie restaurant in the Seagram Building at 100 E. 53rd St. near Park Ave. and only one block down from Moorehead's apartment.[22]

Four years younger than Moorehead, Carpenter was a voluptuous bogus Englishwoman, according to Paul Gregory, and the former mistress of King Farouk of Egypt.[23] She was also a close friend of Joseph Cotten's wife, Patricia Medina, who may have introduced her to her future flat mate. Carpenter had replaced the dying Gertrude Lawrence as Anna Leonowens in *The King and I* in 1952, and her Broadway career since then had been spent as an understudy. She was currently understudying Moorehead, White, and Sinclair in *Lord Pengo*. On June 17, Moorehead reported to Gregory that "Con-Con and I are not getting in each other's way and she is quite a generous, kind gal—so it's all very serene—and strangely enough rather funny."[24]

Moorehead appears to have gotten on well with her fellow cast members. Her blue scrapbook for the spring of 1963 contains a souvenir program with autographed greetings next to each actor's profile. From Boyer, "Dear 'Anna' Dear 'Edna' Aggie darling, 'Jamais deux sans trois' as we say in Paris! With fondest admiration and love, Charles"; from Ruth White, "Dear Agnes It was an honor + pleasure to work with you. May it happen again real soon. Good luck! Ruth"; from Betty Sinclair, "Thank you for being the best 'cheerer-upper' I ever knew! As well as my favourite actress!!—All good wishes always, Betty"; and finally, "Oh Edna! How we did laugh! Still what more could we do with V.D. always around! Laurie Main."[25]

The person Main referred to by his initials was the director, Vincent Donehue, who appears not to have made a favorable impression on the cast. Main recalled him as the only director in his long career he had not gotten on with. In retrospect, he blamed him for the show's failure, claiming that the play was really a light comedy (albeit with serious

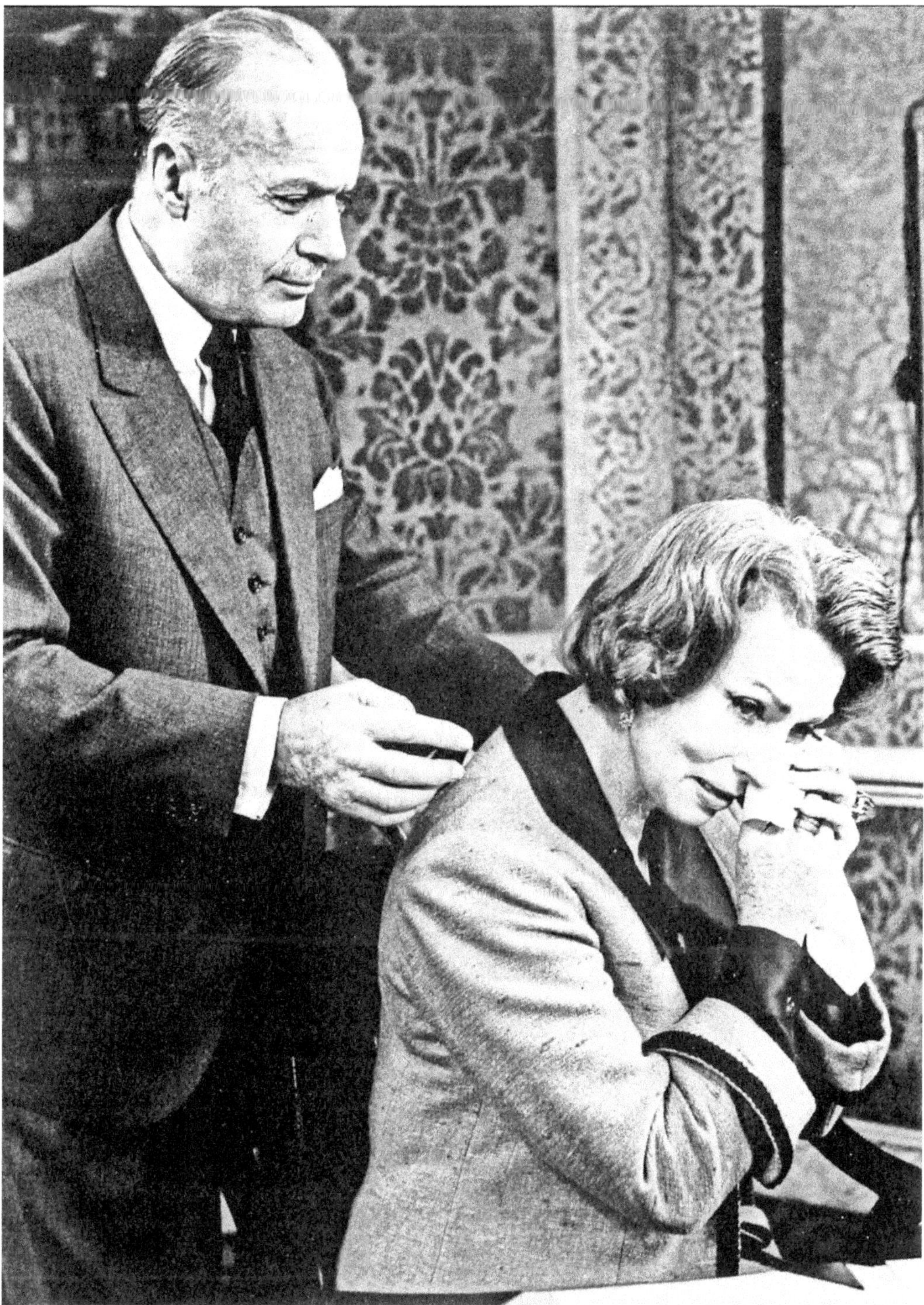

When Agnes Moorehead and Charles Boyer were reunited in *Lord Pengo* playing an art dealer and his devoted secretary, it had been ten years since they last stood on a stage together, in *Don Juan in Hell*. Unfortunately, S.N. Behrman's play was flawed in construction and a newspaper strike didn't help matters. The show only lasted five months on Broadway.

dramatic depths), but Donehue directed it as a drama and made it much heavier than it needed to be. Main would never forget what happened after the New York opening. In full hearing of the cast and guests gathered on stage, Behrman intoned to his director: "You have made me the unhappiest man in New York tonight."[26]

For Moorehead, the director became a *bête noir* from the beginning. He quickly cancelled out the good effect of the telegram he had sent her on August 6, saying he had been a fan of hers "since the old Orson Welles radio days,"[27] by insisting that she should be found on stage in the opening of Act 2 with her "derriere" to the audience rummaging around in a cupboard. This Moorehead adamantly refused to do. Gregory interceded and a solution was found where she was seated at her boss's desk when the curtain went up on her first scene. Nevertheless, she was cheated out of the middle-stage entrance she had wanted and the applause that would have accompanied it. Moorehead felt the director favored Ruth White, who got both an entrance and applause. Much as Behrman, too, began to dislike Donehue, there was no support to be had from the playwright. According to Paul Gregory, he viewed Moorehead as nothing more than a movie actress.[28]

When *Lord Pengo* opened at the Royale Theater at 242 W. 45th St. on November 19, 1962, it was Moorehead's first Broadway show in ten years. Her friends rallied round and showered her with flowers and telegrams. Among the gratulants we find Ann Sothern, Rita Hayworth, Dorothy and Alfred Strelsin, Joan Fontaine, Kathryn Grayson, Shirley Eder, Carroll Baker, Arnold Weissberger, Bea Lillie, Delmer and Mary Lou Daves, and Vincent Sardi, Jr.[29] Basil Rathbone wrote after seeing the show with his wife: "It was good to see you giving such an expert performance.... Those are the really tough roles to play. Just enough to get hold of, but not quite enough material to satisfy. I do think the author has been a little lavish with Lord Pengo + a little sketchy with the rest of his characters."[30] Moorehead's birthday only a few weeks later led to a new barrage of greetings.[31] Paul Gregory sent a telegram: "Dear Aggie, you are so clever. I know you are not as old as you say you are, but it does help in getting these character parts. Love you with all my heart. Happy birthday and many more Paul."[32] The next day, though, he had to inform her that her hairdressing expenses could not be covered: "in light of the fact that at $38,000 a week gross we only make $900 they positively will not engage one additional expenditure."[33]

Very quickly, then, *Lord Pengo* was in trouble in New York. Though the gross receipts the week of Moorehead's birthday were the highest they'd been since Detroit, they were making hardly any money. The reviews had been mixed, to say the least. The short verdict was that the play was a "two and a half hour still life" and "almost totally undramatic."[34] After seeing the first version in Philadelphia, Jerry Gaghan observed that this was a "well cast and beautifully mounted production," but "as a whole *Lord Pengo* lacks the strength of plot line and theatrical dynamics that spell 'hit.'"[35] His fellow Philadelphia critic, Henry T. Murdock, referred to the title character as "a huckster of art," adding: "As his faithful, critical, ever-loving American secretary, Agnes Moorehead gives pungency to each of her rather limited sides of dialogue."[36] Several reviewers suggested, like Murdock and UPI critic Jack Gaver, that Moorehead was "really wasted in a mediocre role."[37]

Detroit critic Josef Mossman considered the play at length in a piece titled "'Lord Pengo' Is Too Talky." Finding the quality of the play hardly on par with "the art works displayed during its course," he nevertheless thought Boyer was magnificent. The play as a whole was a "grab-bag of samplings, samplings of the finest of S.N. Behrman, samplings of superb actors in fascinating portrayals that were hardly more than bits."[38] Mossman reviewed *Lord Pengo* again after the first act revision and thought the new version was a marked improvement. The play had chiefly been strengthened by developing Brian Bedford's role as Pengo's son. As for Primrose Drury, Mossman found that "[t]he role of a millionaire art collector's wife, played by Ruth White, still was not wholly defined, but Miss White was so lovable that the vagueness of the character could almost be overlooked."[39]

In his review for the *New York Times*, Howard Taubman put his finger squarely on the problem with the play: "it lacks the indispensable ingredient needed in the theater: the development of character and a story with dramatic tension." Agnes Moorehead, he found, "plays with a gruff integrity; Ruth White ... almost makes you believe she is serving some purpose in a dramatic design." His conclusion was scathing: at the Metropolitan Museum of Art you could see the originals of the paintings on stage "for a lot less than the going rates at the Royale."[40] Another of the more acid critiques of the play was penned by Ernest Schier: "Bowing to outmoded convention, *Lord Pengo* becomes hopelessly entangled in the artificial conflicts between Boyer and his son (wouldn't you know the boy wants to be an abstract artist?) and in having Boyer play Dear Abby to his clients. People are forever wandering onto the stage and discussing so-and-so's relationship with so-and-so and what dear Daphne did to poor whatsisname. Agnes Moorehead," he added, "who hasn't more than a dozen lines, breaks down and cries near the end because, she says, the great Pengo is not long for this world. She may be right, at that."[41]

In addition to the lackluster reviews, a 114-day newspaper strike in 1962–63 coincided with *Pengo*'s run on Broadway. On April 20, 1963, after only five months, that run was over. By then Boyer had accepted a pay cut to keep the play going and director Donehue had agreed to waive his royalty when the weekly gross was $26,000 or less.[42] The gross receipts were down to $16,000.[43] Several cast members had either jumped ship or signaled their departure. Chief among these was Moorehead herself, who left at the end of March to join the cast of Jerry Lewis's new film, *Who's Minding the Store?* She was briefly replaced by her standby, Margot Stevenson, who received $400 a week.[44] In a letter to his associate producers, Jane Friedlander and Michael Parver, after it was all over, Paul Gregory pointed out that it had cost a great deal of time and money to secure Boyer and get the script: "We reached for the top—we didn't quite make it, but we have nothing to be ashamed of."[45] To a disgruntled investor, he wrote: "We had every ingredient for success and it just didn't happen."[46]

In March 1963, as she was about to leave *Pengo*, Moorehead gave an interview to *The Buff: The Magazine of the Little Theatre*. As so often in the 1960s, she took the opportunity to vent about the deterioration of standards in the theater:

> I am associated with Mr. Paul Gregory ... and while he may not always have a hit, at least he is interested in bringing to the stage something of quality and of theatrical value. He is not at the beck and call of the critics, and he is not interested in filth, simply because it makes money. I know that when I am in a show of his, I don't have to be embarrassed by the lines I say on stage, and I don't have to be ashamed of being in his production. It is always in good taste.[47]

Though Moorehead could not have known it then, these rousing words were an epitaph to her long collaboration with Paul Gregory. They never worked together again. Though Gregory was only 42 when it closed, *Lord Pengo* would be his last show on Broadway. Moorehead would not be back on the "Great White Way" for another decade. That show would be her last.

CREDITS: *Director:* Vincent J. Donehue; *Producers:* Paul Gregory, Amy Lynn; *Writer:* S. N. Behrman; *Settings:* Oliver Smith; *Costumes:* Lucinda Ballard; *Lighting:* Jean Rosenthal; *Premiere:* October 11, 1962, at the New Locust Theatre in Philadelphia, Pennsylvania

CAST: Brian Bedford (Derek Pengo), Charles Boyer (Lord Pengo), Constance Carpenter (Lady Winfield, understudy), Henry Daniell (Enoch Drury), Reynolds Evans (Johnson), Cliff Hall (Sylvester Schmitt), Claude Harz (Wilfred Oliver, replacement), Laurie Main (Filbert), Agnes Moorehead (Miss Swanson), Lee Richardson (Wilfred Oliver), Edmon Ryan (Walter Cannon Brink III), Betty Sinclair (Lady Winfield), Margot Stevenson (Miss Swanson, replacement), Ruth White (Primrose Drury)

TOURING SCHEDULE: Fisher Theatre, Detroit (October 22–November 10, 1962); Royale Theatre, New York (November 19, 1962–April 20, 1963)

18

Burke's Law (TV, 1963–65)

Agnes Moorehead gave three amusing and entertaining performances on the camp and unconventional detective series *Burke's Law*, which aired on ABC from 1963 till 1965 and starred Gene Barry as the suave, debonair police captain and homicide investigator, millionaire and ladies man, Amos Burke. The format of the series was classic "whodunnit?" Someone would be murdered or found dead in the opening scene and the remainder of the episode would be devoted to Captain Burke and his detectives going around and interviewing the various suspects until the case was solved by Burke. Sometimes, as in "Who Killed Hamlet?," there would further murders in the course of their investigations. In his inquiries, Burke was assisted by no less than three sidekicks: Regis Toomey, as the seasoned veteran detective Les Hart; Gary Conway as the young, energetic detective Tim Tilson; and Leon Lontoc as Burke's Filipino chauffeur Henry. Henry provided comic relief through various linguistic and cultural misunderstandings, while Les Hart was grumpy and not easily impressed and Tim Tilson played Robin to Burke's Batman. Despite his busy schedule, Burke nearly always found time for a dalliance with one of the female suspects.

What made the series so enjoyable was not primarily the murder mystery plotlines, but the opportunity to see a plethora of the stars and contract players of the studio era in featured roles as suspects and murder victims. *Burke's Law* is a veritable "who's who" of the American entertainment industry in the mid–1960s. Some actors rounded out their careers in the series (Zasu Pitts, Mary Astor, Ann Harding, Una Merkel, Jane Darwell, Debra Paget) and others appeared on the cusp of breakthrough TV roles (Barbara Eden, Elizabeth Montgomery, Eva Gabor, Tina Louise, David White, Nancy Kovack, Mabel Albertson, Sandra Gould, and for that matter, Agnes Moorehead). Their roles were never very large, since as many as five or six suspects might need to be interrogated in any given episode, but they afforded the older actors an opportunity to remind the world that they were still alive and available and gave the audience a welcome opportunity to spend a little time with their favorite stars and character actors of yesteryear.

In other words, this wasn't your average police drama series. With all the famous faces showing up and the luxurious Beverly Hills setting, the series constantly spoofed Hollywood and show business in subtle ways. This "industry insider" viewpoint and camp attitude to murder as entertainment was underscored by plotlines usually set among the upper crust. There was almost always a sexual undercurrent to the homicides and any female witness or suspect was fair game for aging Lothario Amos Burke. Today watching *Burke's Law* is a bigger nostalgia fest than ever, as practically all the featured players (and the regulars for that matter) have gone to that great sound stage in the sky.

Moorehead got her first call to co-star in *Burke's Law* in the fall of 1963. It was ten years since she and the star of the series, Gene Barry, had co-starred in *Those Redheads from Seattle*. The revised script among her papers is dated October 7, 1963.[1] This makes it likely that "Who Killed Beau Sparrow?," the 14th episode of Season 1, went into production in October 1963, at what was formerly Republic Studios at 4024 Radford Ave. in Studio City. It was precisely at this time Moorehead was thinking about whether or not to accept the role of Samantha's as yet unnamed mother in *Bewitched*.[2] Moorehead wrote to her friend Georgia Johnstone on October 29, 1963, that she'd been offered the part of a witch in a new series to be called *Bewitched*.[3]

In "Who Killed Beau Sparrow?," the murder victim is a playboy, toyboy, and portrait painter, who dies mysteriously after diving into a pool to retrieve a valuable ring thrown in by his cougar fiancée, the Countess Barbara Erozzi (Yvonne De Carlo). This affords us an opportunity to view Gene Barry's none too impressive physique in swimming trunks, as he in turn dives in to save Sparrow. Moorehead plays Liz Haggerty, the cosseted, invalid, and reclusive wife of hypochondriac millionaire Victor Haggerty (Jack Haley of *Wizard of Oz*/"Tin Man" fame). The couple has not spoken in five years, though they still share a home. They both have "outside interests": Mrs. Haggerty in the murder victim Beau Sparrow and Mr. Haggerty in Sparrow's fiancée, the aforementioned countess.[4]

It turns out that Sparrow was not stingy with his favors and also dated Mr. Haggerty's efficient secretary, Jean Samson, played by June Allyson. Allyson, born in 1917 and just turned 46 at the time of taping this episode, may well be the oldest romantic interest for Gene Barry, born in 1919, in the course of the series. Allyson's husband and Moorehead's director in the disastrous film *The Conqueror*, Dick Powell, had died on January 2, 1963, and this episode of *Burke's Law* was Allyson's first acting job since his death. It was no coincidence, as *Burke's Law* was produced by her late husband's production company, Four Star Productions. Allyson actually remarried on October 13, 1963, just at the time this episode was in production, and wouldn't be seen again on any screen large or small until 1968.[5]

While Allyson got to kiss the leading man in this episode of *Burke's Law*, her old friend and *Stratton Story* co-star Agnes Moorehead got two Pekingese and a lovely female secretary and companion, Ann Martin, played by Robert Stack's wife, Rosemarie Bowe. Ann has to read to her employer and the dogs from Flaubert's "Un Coeur Simple" in the original French. Mrs. Haggerty, who never leaves her bedroom and is seen in peignoir and negligee, has a modified version of Moorehead's *Lord Pengo* bouffant bob and, of course, wears her signature gold earrings. Mrs. Haggerty is very airy-fairy and spiritual and goes through a whole song and dance about Beau Sparrow being her last chance of happiness. She and Burke bond over his feigned admiration for her Pekingese and she says he should get one. She later makes a half-hearted attempt to kill herself with sleeping pills. Her second and final scene, which was not in the revised script and must have been added at the last moment,[6] is when Burke comes back to tell her what he has discovered, in an attempt to engineer a reconciliation with her husband. It turns out Sparrow was taking money both from Mrs. Haggerty and from the countess, who was getting it from Mr. Haggerty, prompting Burke's laconic comment: "They got it from both ends."

By the time Moorehead returned to *Burke's Law* for her second appearance, an episode produced in the second half of March 1964, *Bewitched* had been picked up, but had not yet started production.[7] In "Who Killed Don Pablo?," she plays Spanish American Dona Ynez Ortega y Esteban, from a prominent family that has fallen on hard times, who is hired by a socially ambitious man to lend him social cachet by pretending to be his mother. He is subsequently murdered with a sword through the heart. In her first scene, when veteran detective Les Hart (Regis Toomey) comes to ask her a few questions, she plays the mourning mother to the hilt with black mantilla and the works. When Les and Tim Tilson return unexpectedly, though, she is discovered on her way out in modern dress with jazz on the record player. Her parting words are: "Sergeant, one must live."

Casting Moorehead in this role is an example of the camp intertextuality at work in the series. At least some of her fans must have been reminded that the last time Moorehead played a Spanish "doña" was in the famous stage production of *Don Juan in Hell* with Charles Boyer, Charles Laughton, and Sir Cedric Hardwicke in the early 1950s. This is an amusing, tongue-in-cheek performance, though Moorehead doesn't look particularly well. The makeup artist on all three of her *Burke's Law* appearances was Robert Hickman. Her "up do" with the big fall of sausage curls on top is one she would also use when in mortal guise on the early episodes of *Bewitched*.

As it happens, Moorehead had two friends in the same episode, though they didn't share any scenes: Cesar Romero, her frequent escort and *The Story of Mankind* co-star; and Patricia Medina, wife of her longtime friend and colleague Joseph Cotten. Moorehead had co-starred in a play with the Cottens and Thomas Mitchell called *Prescription: Murder* in the first half of 1962. Romero would later show up on an episode of *Bewitched* in Season 7 called "Salem, Here We Come," but Moorehead wasn't in that one.

Moorehead's third and final guest role on *Burke's Law* was in a late Season 2 episode called "Who Killed Hamlet?," which was ready in script form on February 17, 1965.[8] *Bewitched* was in full production on the final episodes for Season 1, but Moorehead was not needed in all of them and was going to have some extended time off. As soon as Episode #1.28 "Open the Door, Witchcraft" (the not very funny one about the Stephens installing an automatic garage door) finished shooting on February 18, she was off to New York.[9] She wasn't back on the *Bewitched* set until March 25.[10] Given the dating of the script and the fact that the episode aired on April 7, 1965, her last episode of *Burke's Law* must have been taped during this break from *Bewitched*.

In "Who Killed Hamlet?," Moorehead plays Pauline Moss, a deliciously hammy actress in a second-rate company, who is questioned in her dressing room by Burke and Tilson after a fellow actor, Roland Trivers (Bobby Darin in an uncredited role), is murdered. Always grateful for an audience, Miss Moss grasps the opportunity relate the story of how the unpopular Trivers upstaged her one night in New Haven, as she was about to give the performance of her life as Lady Macbeth. This episode is the closest we will ever get to seeing Moorehead acting the role of Shakespeare's murderous lady, as Miss Moss manages to slip quite a few lines from *Macbeth* into her tale, though not, surprisingly, "out, damned spot!" In attendance, too, is her feisty little terrier, who keeps biting Burke's pants leg. Miss Moss is currently playing Gertrude to Trivers's Hamlet (hence the title of the episode), or she *was* until he got murdered. In her brief second scene, we find her going through her lines as Gertrude with producer Milo James (Basil Rathbone) reading Hamlet's lines. She promptly expires after drinking deeply from a poisoned cup. Burke and Tilson witness the scene from the wings and come forward to confirm that Miss Moss is very dead indeed. This was Moorehead's only common film or television credit with Basil Rathbone, though they may have acted in a Sherlock Holmes radio serial together over NBC Blue in the 1930s.[11]

The key to why Moorehead was such a good fit in these three roles and in *Burke's Law* in general lies is the combination of ambiguity and imposture that the role of a crime suspect puts into play. Moorehead often excelled in roles that involved an element of artificiality or theatricality, such as actresses, con women, hysterics, and hypochondriacs. It's almost so you can see the enjoyment she is getting out of "sending up" these usually quite unsympathetic women, yet the illusion never breaks and she keeps a straight face. Conversely, what was deadly for her as an actress was any role that was so serious or dramatic that it was bereft of this element of fun and play. I'm thinking of her forced and monotonous portrayal of Queen Elizabeth I in *The Story of Mankind* or her deadly dull impersonation of the harpsichordist Wanda Landowska. It was the witty, batty, self-involved, or downright devious characters that called out the best in her and, however briefly, she had something to work with in Liz Haggerty, Dona Inez, and Pauline Moss.

CREDITS: *Directors:* David Orrick McDearmon ("Beau Sparrow"), Richard Kinon ("Don Pedro"), Don Weis ("Hamlet"); *Producers:* Richard Newton, Aaron Spelling; *Writers:* Frank D. Gilroy (characters creator), John Meredyth Lucas ("Beau Sparrow"), Gwen Bagni ("Don Pedro"), Paul Dubov ("Don Pedro"), Albert Beich ("Hamlet"), Lewis Reed ("Hamlet"); *Music:* Joseph Mullendore; *Cinematography:* George E. Diskant ("Beau Sparrow"), Charles Burke ("Don Pablo," "Hamlet"); *Film editing:* Lyle Boyer ("Beau Sparrow"), Desmond Marquette ("Don Pablo"), Sherman Todd ("Hamlet"); *Art direction:* Bill Ross; *Set decoration:* John Burton ("Beau Sparrow," "Don Pablo"), Dorcy Howard ("Hamlet"); *Makeup department:* Robert Hickman, Scotty Rackin (hairstylist "Hamlet"); *Costume and wardrobe department:* Robert B. Harris; *Production company:* Four Star Productions/Barbety; *Air dates:* "Who Killed Beau Sparrow?," December 27, 1963; "Who Killed Don Pablo?," May 1, 1964; "Who Killed Hamlet?," April 7, 1965, on ABC

CAST (regular): Gene Barry (Amos Burke), Gary Conway (Tim Tilson), Leon Lontoc (Henry), Regis Toomey (Les Hart). "Who Killed Beau Sparrow?": June Allyson (Jean Samson), Jerry Catron (Beau Sparrow), Jacqueline D'Avril (Paula), Yvonne De Carlo (Countess Barbara Erozzi), Michael Fox (George McLeod), Jack Haley (Victor Haggerty), Linda Kennon (Giulietta), Hedley Mattingly (Crenshaw), Agnes Moorehead (Liz Haggerty), Ken Murray (Charles P. Banner), Rosemarie Bowe Stack (Ann Martin), Dan Tobin (Dr. Eric McLean), Celeste Yarnall (Marlena). "Who Killed Don Pablo?": John Cassavetes (Carlos de Vega), Cecil Kellaway (Brother Flaherty), Patricia Medina (Serena Diablo), Agnes Moorehead (Dona Ynez Ortega y Esteban), Cesar Romero (Antonio Cordoza), Forrest Tucker (Cyrus Smuts). Who Killed Hamlet?": Susan Bay (Eileen), John Cassavetes (Stephen Collins), Bobby Darin (Roland Trivers), Eddie Foy, Jr. (Dugan), Edward Everett Horton (Wilbur Starlington), Agnes Moorehead (Pauline Moss), Basil Rathbone (Milo James), Nina Shipman (Sandra Prentiss)

19

Channing: "Freedom Is a Lovesome Thing, God Wot!" (TV, 1964)

On Wednesday, January 22, 1964, Moorehead wrote to her friend Georgia Johnstone from Phoenix, Arizona. She was staying at the celebrated Jukake Inn and had just finished a "very difficult" episode of the series *Channing* on Monday before coming away: "I can't tell you how tired I am with that T.V. thing—lines, lines, lines." Moorehead was in Phoenix to see her friends Joe Cotten and Patricia Medina in a play called *Seven Ways of Love*, before doing her one-woman show in Coldwater, Michigan, on January 25 and going on to visit her mother in Reedsburg, Wisconsin.[1]

The TV drama series *Channing* was produced at Universal Studios, where Moorehead had done *Magnificent Obsession* and *All That Heaven Allows*. *Channing* was different from most of the films, plays, and TV series Moorehead acted in and a far cry from your average 1960s TV series. Set on the campus of the fictional liberal arts college Channing, the series in the words of one observer, "tried to make gripping TV drama out of that world, and the average viewer wasn't buying."[2]

The episode with the cumbersome title "Freedom is a Lovesome Thing, God Wot!" focused on the challenges of being an African American intellectual and college professor in the Civil Rights era. Moorehead was cast as Amelia Webster, an economics professor (Vassar '47), who initially is in conflict with her younger male colleague, Dr. Peter Cooke (James Earl Jones), "the new Young Turk in the Economics department" and "the first Negro to join the faculty." The two academics have a difference of opinion over the intellectual capacity of the African American undergrad and former track star Rob Ramsay (Leon Bibb). Professor Webster wants him to get the Wainwright scholarship, but Cooke is skeptical and the committee's decision must be unanimous. To Cooke, Ramsay is "just an average student." In a fraught meeting with Dean Fred Baker (Henry Jones), Webster charges Cooke with bigotry. When Webster storms out and the two men are left alone, the dean asks Dr. Cooke: "Have you ever asked yourself if you may subconsciously be applying a more severe set of standards to Ramsay than to other students?"

In this episode, Moorehead creates a touching and convincing portrait of a middle-aged, unmarried professor. In one of her best lines, she assures the college librarian: "Spinsterhood isn't a tragedy, Ruth, it's just a kind of requiem between great books." Dr. Webster is a little seedy at this point, drinks bourbon on the rocks, likes to shoot pool, and is even seen playing the saxophone in a quartet with Dr. Cooke at the piano. That is after they are reconciled and, in their mutual loneliness and isolation, begin spending a lot of time together. This gives rise to rumors on campus. A happy ending is nevertheless assured when Professor Webster brings Dr. Cooke around to her view of the African American student and prevents her brilliant young colleague from abandoning his academic career.

Moorehead plays the role with her chin down and her arms crossed over her chest a lot of the time and uses her horn-rimmed glasses to great effect. She wears "sensible" clothes: shapeless wool cardigans, white blouses, plaid skirts, and even pants in one scene. Her hair is gathered in a somewhat unkempt bun. At times, Professor Webster is given to wearing a visor, making her look more like a bank teller than an economics professor. The visor is typical of the small touches Moorehead liked to introduce to lend verisimilitude and individuality to her characters. As in countless film and TV roles, she is wearing her favorite gold filigree earrings. She admonishes Dr. Cooke: "Just because I look like one of Channing's gothic ruins, don't come to any conclusions."

In "Freedom is a Lovesome Thing, God Wot!," Moorehead co-starred with a varied roster of talented male actors, though hardly marquee names at the time. The two recurring characters in *Channing* were Dean Fred Baker, played by Henry Jones, and Joseph Howe, a professor of English, played by Jason Evers, who was little in evidence in this episode. Henry Jones was a very busy character actor on Broadway, television, and in films and had won a Tony award in 1958 for his role as FDR's confidant in *Sunrise at Campobello*. One of his most outstanding screen performances was the nefarious janitor Leroy Jessup, who meets his match in *The Bad Seed*, a role he had also played on Broadway. He would go on to play the title character's father-in-law in *Phyllis* starring Cloris Leachman, among many other roles.

James Earl Jones turned 33 while this episode was being produced. The major phase of his acting career was still ahead of him, but he had had a handful of TV roles before *Channing* and made his film debut that same year in *Dr. Strangelove*. In 1964, too, he was nominated for a Primetime Emmy award (for the first of eight times) for an episode of the drama series *East Side/West Side*, in which George C. Scott starred as a social worker in the slums of New York City.

Leon Bibb was an American folk singer born in Kentucky in 1922, who made half a dozen appearances on Broadway between 1946 and 1966 and had a smattering of film and television roles between 1964 and 1990. He was actually 42 years old when he made his television debut playing an undergraduate student on *Channing*, nine years older than James Earl Jones, who played a professor. Bibb died in 2015.

In a September 2010 question and answer session, James Earl Jones recalled working with Moorehead on this episode. He was surprised, he remembered, by the fact that when the camera was on her, she didn't need or expect him to give his part of the dialogue: "I was mystified. I'm behind the camera and I'm acting my head off and she, you know, she doesn't need me. She's got her own stuff going on." He did an imitation of her talking to the camera. "She's not even trying to reach me. And that mystified me until I learned more about film acting. Most of us are dedicated to supporting our fellow actor by getting behind the camera and giving them the best performance we can that's never seen, but she didn't need it.... She was wonderful."[3]

Ahead of its time, *Channing* only lasted one season. Moorehead's episode was the 21st out of the total of 26 that were produced, and aired on March 4, 1964. One newspaper wrote: "There are lots of gimmicks in this episode (how about that dismal title for one?)

but it holds you nevertheless. It also has some very good acting."[4] Writers Jack Guss and Edmund Morris were nominated for a WGA Award for Episodic Drama for this episode in 1965. They lost to Arnold Perl for the same episode of *East Side/West Side*, "Who Do You Kill," that led to an Emmy nomination for James Earl Jones.[5]

CREDITS: *Director:* William Hale; *Producers:* Jack Guss, Jack Laird; *Writers:* Jack Guss (teleplay), Edmund Morris (story); *Director of photography:* Richard L. Rawlings; *Film editor:* Michael J. Minth; *Art director:* Howard E. Johnson; *Makeup artist:* Bud Westmore; *Hair stylist:* Larry Germaine; *Costume supervisor:* Vincent Dee; *Production company:* Revue-Betford Prod.; *Air date:* March 4, 1964, on ABC

CAST: Leon Bibb (Rob Ramsay), Jeff Cooper (Professor Gray), Jason Evers (Professor Joseph Howe), Henry Jones (Dean Fred Baker), James Earl Jones (Dr. Peter Cooke), Agnes Moorehead (Professor Amelia Webster), Willard Sage (Reed Jackson), Evelyn Scott (Ruth Cunningham), Barbara Werle (Lydia Jackson)

20

Bewitched (TV, 1964–72)

Endora in *Bewitched* is not just wonderful company and an integral part of the success of the series, she is one of the most important comic characters in American popular culture created for and by an older woman. Long before the "Golden Girls," Julia Sugarbaker, Karen Walker, or Evelyn Harper, there was Endora. Endora is also one of the most important and interesting witches in American culture. Beyond the Wicked Witch of the West and her own daughter Samantha, it is hard to find a witch that has continued to be so memorable for so long in the minds of so many.

Where to begin? What to focus on? The "angles" on a cult series like *Bewitched* are endless, the permutations and influences vast. In this chapter, I want primarily to consider the uniqueness of Endora as a character and what made Moorehead so eminently suited to portraying her; how a draft version of the pilot laid the groundwork for Moorehead's interpretation of the role; the various functions of Endora as a character; the atmosphere on the *Bewitched* set and Moorehead's attitude to her working environment and the series itself; and finally how *Bewitched* might have been an even better series.[1]

So first of all: where did Endora come from? While her character sprung out of several familiar stereotypes of the older woman in American culture—the witch, the mother-in-law, the matriarch, the dowager—it was the unusual and unexpectedly attractive combination of so many of the mostly negative images of "women of a certain age" that made her unique. There is really no clear precedent for Endora in films or on television that I can think of, even among Moorehead's previous roles. The witches were usually hags both on the large and the small screen, the mothers-in-law terribly straight-laced and conventional, the matriarchs and dowagers likewise. These female characters were either uncompromisingly evil in the case of the witches or staunch defenders of propriety, morality, and the status quo in the case of the mortals. Even the flibbertigibbets and dizzy dames played by Billie Burke, Alice Brady, Mary Boland, and Spring Byington in all their egocentric, out of touch myopia didn't have Endora's "edge" and hedonistic tendencies. Even the two feature films that are often cited as precursors of *Bewitched*—*I Married a Witch* and *Bell Book and Candle*—contain no character resembling Endora.

In addition to the unusual combination of various older woman stereotypes, a crucial aspect of Endora's uniqueness was that she was being played by Agnes Moorehead. It's hard to overestimate the importance casting Moorehead in this role had for the success of the character and the series a whole. According to producer William Froug: "He [Sol

Saks] developed the comedic situation with a family of characters, most particularly the witch's mother, Endora, played with great gusto by the redoubtable Agnes Moorehead. It was Saks's creation of the mother as a meddling know-it-all superwitch along with the comedic talent of Elizabeth Montgomery and co-star Dick York that had catapulted the series to the highest ratings in ABC Televisions history."[2]

It is hardly surprising, then, that several people have wanted to take credit for this brilliant casting. I'm not going to adjudicate the various claims of Harry Ackerman, Elizabeth Montgomery, William Asher, and Paul Gregory here, but I do want to mention a man who has not, I think, been mentioned before in this context: Screen Gems executive William Dozier. In two separate conversations with me, Moorehead's frequent producer and close friend Paul Gregory insisted that if it hadn't been for his relationship with Dozier, which went back to when they both worked at RKO, she would not have been cast in *Bewitched*. Bill Asher did not want her, Gregory claimed, as Asher feared she would outshine Elizabeth Montgomery. Dozier had seen Moorehead as the "shade" of cosmetics queen Eleanor West in *The Pink Jungle* in 1959, which showed that she could be a glamorous ghost in addition to everything else she had done.[3] At the end of the day, though, the deciding vote was cast by Moorehead herself. Initially, she didn't want the part. If she hadn't changed her mind, no amount of influence, power, or persuasion on the part of these industry "players" would have mattered.

When you think about it, casting Moorehead as Endora was a "no-brainer." She was the obvious choice. She had the charisma and the authority that the role required. She was attractive, but also a little bit scary. She had recently delivered two tour de force witch performances on Shirley Temple's show, which, though they differed outwardly from Endora, showed to the full that she could be both funny and intimidating as a witch. William Asher had even produced one of the episodes, "The Land of Oz," where Moorehead played the comic witch Mombi. More than any other actress at the time, Moorehead could be the "bad good witch" the producers were looking for. And she would lend prestige to the production.

As one newspaper wrote when the new series was announced in the summer of 1964: "Agnes Moorehead brings her prestige as one of America's outstanding stage, screen and television actresses."[4] Another observer wrote after the series had started, that this was "a role for which she is ideally suited: Nothing personal mind you, but Agnes is a first-class witch. They don't come any better than Aggie who traces her witchcraft directly to Salem. Hardly a day goes by that somebody doesn't get the urge to burn Agnes at a stake. So it was only natural that the brass at Screen Gems should right away hire Miss Moorehead for the mother-in-law witch role in 'Bewitched.'"[5] According to Kay Gardella of the *New York Daily News*, it was "a case for sure of perfect casting."[6] *TV Guide*'s Cleveland Amory, though, voiced a dissenting view. In an article published on October 24, 1964, after the first six episodes had aired, Amory wrote: "Agnes Moorehead ... is an old meanie who is always stirring up trouble and, in our opinion, if she doesn't stop overplaying her part and witching about everything, she ought to be packed off on the next broom, to Olde Salem."[7]

Of her own preparations for the role of Endora, Moorehead said in an interview just a month before the show premiered: "Playing a convincing witch takes a bit of research.... I've looked up the old Salem business, re-read a lot of fairy stories and the Oz books. The main thing is to develop one strange, odd little thing to do that the audience does not expect."[8] Samantha certainly had her "one strange, odd little thing," but it is hard to point to a comparable tick of Endora's. Could it be what one journalist referred to as "Moorehead's instinctive touch to call the young husband anything except his right name"? According to the actress: "It adds just the right touch of disdain."[9]

In another interview, Moorehead was "Asked the chief ingredient in a witch's brew." "A mad imagination," she responded. "Good family background also helps.... I had a wonderful background.... My father told me fairy stories and he read to us. And my grandmother was Irish. She told us about 'the little people.' When I went into the forest I used to look for them."[10] Moorehead thought that one reason for Endora's popularity was that "The character I play brings order out of chaos. I don't know anybody who hasn't said at some time, 'Oh, I wish I didn't have to sweep the floor. I wish I didn't have to clean this or that. I wish I could snap my fingers and everything would be done!'"[11]

In a 1967 interview, Moorehead had an unusual explanation of what motivated Endora's behavior towards Darrin: "She's a knowing mother who doesn't really dislike her mortal son-in-law—she just brews up trouble to force her daughter into using witchcraft occasionally, lest she become a mortal too."[12] This argument is probably more subtle than the impression most of us are left with when viewing the series: that, initially at least, Endora *really* dislikes the man whose name she can never remember (or pretends to forget). Where can Moorehead have gotten this idea from? Well, it turns out she probably had it from a draft of the pilot dated September 30, 1963. In the scene between Endora (at this stage only referred to as "Mother") and Samantha (here called "Cassandra" and "Stevens" with a "v"[13]), she warns her daughter: "And do you realize the danger you're in? If you live like one of them for a year ... without practicing your trade..." Cassandra finishes her sentence: "You *become* one of them."[14] This was a portion of dialogue and a premise for the series, that didn't make it into the final version of the pilot episode, but Moorehead clearly remembered it years later and used it to understand her character's motivations. For her, Endora's animosity towards Darrin was much less important than her love and concern for the well-being of her daughter Samantha and making sure she stays a witch. Many episodes did, of course, focus on Samantha's failing powers.

Speaking of the pilot: It is interesting to note that the September 1963 revised draft contains all the basic scenes and much of the dialogue that went into the final, broadcast version *plus* a couple of scenes that ended up in #1.2 "Be It Ever So Mortgaged" (Sam's cooking and dishwasher disaster in the kitchen with Endora) and #1.4 "Mother, Meet What's His Name" (the visit of the neighborhood women and their rowdy boys, though not including Gladys Kravitz). In this version of the pilot, Endora was supposed to enter with a clap of thunder right at the end of the "teaser" before the opening credits, as part of the revelation that Samantha is a witch. She is described in the script as being "dressed in the characteristic wide-brimmed hat and flowing gown, but they are not black, as a matter of fact, rather attractive."[15]

On the cover of this script, in which she has marked her lines in a way that indicates she was expecting to use it to shoot from, Moorehead has written the following name suggestions for "Mother": Witch of Endora, Xantippe, Macadamia, Jerrabohm, Jezebel, Zenobia, Takla, Carousel, and Azza.[16] The only change she has made in the dialogue is to alter the word "Huh?" to "What?"; a change that made it into the episode as aired.[17]

What is Endora's function in the show? The basic premise for most of the episodes involving Endora is her disapproval of her mortal son-in-law, which results in her doing something to meddle in her daughter's marriage. In a typical pattern, Endora pops into the kitchen in the morning, as Samantha is cooking breakfast and Darrin is more or less in a hurry to get off to work. Darrin asks Endora to please not show up unannounced like that, they swap insults, Endora is asked not to meddle in something, she cannot resist and casts some kind of spell that creates problems and complications in the remainder of the episode, usually involving Darrin and one or more of his clients. Having done that, Endora may not be seen again or she may pop in to check on progress, remove the spell, or create further complications.

A typical example of this dynamic at work is seen in episode #2.33 "Divided He Falls" in which Endora disapproves of the fact that Darrin works so much. Her solution is to cast a spell on him that allows "fun Darrin" to take Samantha on vacation to Florida and "work Darrin" to stay home and work. This episode was remade as #6.15 "Samantha's Better Halves," which was the first episode Dick Sargent worked on, though "Sam and the Beanstalk" was the first of his episodes to air.

As mentioned, Endora's casting some kind of spell on Darrin often results in problems at work. In episode #3.23 "I Remember You.... Sometimes," she casts a spell on his wristwatch, which gives him perfect recall when he is wearing it. This turns him into a pedantic bore and irritates his client, Mr. Pennybaker (Dan Tobin), who is used to monopolizing the conversation himself with all his more or less arcane knowledge. This episode is also an example of an increasing tendency as time went on, where Endora is used to cause a problem by casting a spell and then hardly seen in the remainder of the episode.

Episode #6.13 "You're So Agreeable" is also a standard "Endora puts a spell on Darrin, which gives him trouble at work, and leaves Samantha to clean up the mess" episode. In this case, the spell first makes him annoyingly agreeable and then, after Endora reverses it, crotchety. Neither attitude goes down well at McMann & Tate.

When not casting spells to make Darrin different or his and Samantha's marriage more to her liking, Endora sometimes tries to test Darrin's marital fidelity. Examples of this type of plot twist are #1.11 "It Takes One to Know One," where Endora gets an attractive witch-cum-model to try and lead Darrin astray; #3.27 "The Crone of Cawdor," where the ancient crone of the title tries to get Darrin to kiss her, so she can be rejuvenated; #8.5 "Bewitched, Bothered and Baldoni," which is set in Rome and where Endora brings a statue of Venus to life; and #8.12 "The Eight-Year-Itch Witch," which in its testing of Darrin's fidelity contains elements of at least four previous episodes of this kind. In #6.24 "The Generation Zap," Endora has just promised "witch's honor" not to meddle in her daughter's life, so she has to get Samantha's look-alike cousin Serena involved. Here the temptress is college intern Dusty Harrison, who makes even a pencil sharpener have sexual overtones.

Beyond these typical situations involving Endora, we often find her wanting Samantha to go somewhere or do something, which Samantha won't or can't do because of Darrin. In episode #1.20 "Your Witch Is Showing," for example, Endora is annoyed because Samantha won't go to a cousin's wedding in Egypt without Darrin. In #2.13 "My Boss, the Teddy Bear," the situation is much the same only the cousin getting married is Miranda, not Mario. In neither case does Endora actually cast a spell in retaliation, but Darrin's suspicions that she has creates the comic complications.

Endora's major function, then, is primarily to serve as an antagonist who gets the ball rolling plot-wise by shaking things up in the Stephens household, but she also has other plot functions. Endora is not infrequently called on to find people, like Dr. Bombay (e.g., #4.6 "No Zip in My Zap," #5.18 "Samantha, the Bard," and #6.4 "Samantha's Curious

Cravings") or her husband, Maurice (e.g. #6.5 "And Something Makes Four" and #7.21 "Mixed Doubles"). She may also be called on to help solve problems that are not of her own creating, as in #2.4 "My Grandson, the Warlock," #5.14 "Samantha's Super Maid," #7.8 "Samantha's Old Salem Trip," and #8.6 "Paris, Witches Style." Finally, like most grandmothers, Endora may be asked to babysit, which happens for the first time in #2.26 "Baby's First Paragraph" and also in episodes like #4.25 "To Twitch or Not to Twitch," #7.17 "The Return of Darrin the Bold," #8.1 "How Not to Lose Your Head to Henry VIII (Part 1)," and #8.12 "The Eight-Year-Itch Witch." Sometimes, with all the goings on, Endora never gets the chance to babysit, as in aforementioned #3.27 "The Crone of Cawdor."

How much more interesting aren't those episodes where Endora can act on her own behalf, rather than just reacting to something Darrin or Samantha do or say. The Endora-centered episodes are, not surprisingly, some of my favorites, such as #1.4 "Mother, Meet What's His Name," where Endora and Darrin first meet; #3.29 "It's Wishcraft" with Endora and Darrin's mom Phyllis at daggers drawn yet again; #4.11 "Allergic to Macedonian Dodo Birds," where Endora loses her powers due to the proximity of a certain rare bird; and #4.18 "Once in a Vial," where a softer side of Endora is in evidence after she downs the love potion intended for Samantha. It is always highly entertaining when Endora gets to interact with other characters than her daughter and son-in-law, be it mortals like Larry Tate, Darrin's parents Frank and Phyllis Stephens, or Gladys Kravitz; or fellow witches like her husband, Maurice, Aunt Clara, or Uncle Arthur.

Agnes Moorehead in her iconic role as Endora on *Bewitched*. While her rumpled look as a witch remained basically the same throughout the eight seasons of the series, her hairstyles when passing for a mortal went through a number of permutations. Here we see the gold filigree earrings Moorehead so often used in her performances. According to a friend, they had been given to her by her father.

Despite the episodes that allowed Endora to act more on her own behalf and show new aspects of her personality, I would suggest that overall there was little change or development in Endora from the pilot to Season 8. Her character and its various functions stayed more or less the same. What did change, though, was her level of involvement. Sad to say, her presence was reduced as the years went by and there was little attempt in the final seasons to capitalize on all that Endora as a character and Moorehead as an actress could bring to the series. Thus, in the last three seasons, among the total of 44 episodes Endora was seen in, the only one I consider to be first rate is #7.14 "The Mother-in-Law of the Year." Here Endora manages to get herself elected "Mother-in-Law of the Year," but when it comes time to receive the award on a live TV show she opts to go skiing with a certain Mr. Peabody instead. Samantha has to step in and pretend to be Endora, causing a cacophony of complications when the real Endora finally shows up.

In a hit series that runs for several years, you have the opportunity to develop working and personal relationships with fellow cast members and the crew in a whole different way than if you're simple doing a guest spot on a show or even when working on a feature film. The atmosphere on the *Bewitched* set was described by one observer as follows during Season 2: "Contrary to reports in a nationwide television magazine, all is not billing and cooing and coddling on the sound stage which houses Bewitched. There is a businesslike atmosphere, sometimes broken by reprimands and sometimes by jests. Above all, there is the sweet smell of success that can come only when you are one of the most popular shows on the air."[18] According to William Froug, who produced Season 3, "The *Bewitched* set was a model of quiet probity, without bickering, animation, or joy."[19]

Moorehead's basic attitude throughout her years on *Bewitched* was to keep herself to herself as much as possible without seeming rude or antisocial. That is not to say that she wasn't friendly with several members of the cast, not least of all her co-stars Elizabeth Montgomery, Dick York, and, after a "period of adjustment," Dick Sargent. Even with them, though, I think there was always a certain reserve. Kasey Rogers, who replaced Irene Vernon as Larry Tate's wife, Louise, from the start of Season 3, told me: "While I worked with Agnes and was often a guest in her home, especially her birthday party in December (was it the 8th?), I really did not know her too well."[20] This was the experience of many I have talked to, who knew Moorehead primarily in a work-related setting. Robert F. Simon, who was the first actor to play Darrin's father, Frank Stephens, made an interesting observation about both Moorehead and Mabel Albertson, who played Darrin's mother Phyllis: "Both Mabel and Aggie were hard to know. They were both very strong-willed women. They were kind enough, but they both wanted power over everyone in their life."[21]

Maybe the best description of how Moorehead appeared to a fellow worker on *Bewitched* comes from Bill Froug. In his 2005 memoirs, he writes: "Agnes Moorehead ... let me know right off that she was a grande dame and was to be treated accordingly.... Word had obviously reached her that it was her performance as Endora that was a key element in the show's success, and she apparently wanted to make certain everyone in the series knew it." Froug continues:

> Watching her perform on our set was to see a master of her craft at work. She routinely did her often wildly outrageous scenes in one take, then soon after the director said "cut," she swiftly and silently swept off into her dressing room at the other end of the stage. She apparently needed privacy. There was no levity in Agnes Moorehead and no nonsense. One got the understanding that she did what she was paid to do, and that was the end of it.

During my year producing the series I don't believe she and I exchanged more than a passing nod. As best I could tell, she spent every moment she was not on camera in her dressing room with the door closed. The crew also tread lightly around her. There was something mysterious in her reserve."[22]

Moorehead explained the reason for her reserve in a revealing newspaper article she wrote in 1965. She began by admitting that, because she had played so many "authoritative and strong characters," some people were nervous at the prospect of meeting her for the first time. "To be frank," she wrote, "there is a certain amount of aloofness on my part at times, because an actor can so easily be hurt by unfair criticism.... I have always felt that the most successful artists are the easiest to talk to, except that they are protected by buffers—secretaries and assistants. Some kind of protection is absolutely necessary. I think an artist should be kept separated to maintain glamor and a kind of mystery."[23]

Though one might sometimes get that impression, Moorehead did not feel just negatively about *Bewitched*. Let's say she felt "ambivalent" about it. When parsing her remarks about the series, be they in public or private, it is important to consider the context of the remark. Who was she speaking to? At what point in the run of the series was she saying this? What was her agenda in making this remark? For all her vaunted forthrightness, with Moorehead there was always an agenda.

Naturally, in writing a letter to the fans not long after *Bewitched* premiered, it was all good: "The series, as you already know, is a bit hit and we couldn't be happier. I love the role of 'Endora' and feel she is a bright, new, lovable and humorous image of a witch and mother-in-law."[24] In writing to her close friend and confidante, Georgia Johnstone, on the other hand, it was a different story. On August 23, 1965, after spending the entire summer filming episodes for Season 2, Moorehead wrote: "The set [of *Bewitched*] is so dull, as far as I'm concerned, so much haggling and gossip. It's just awful—but as Paul [Gregory] says, it's an umbrella."[25] In her letters to Johnstone, who worked as her secretary and dealt with all the fan correspondence during the *Bewitched* years, Moorehead seldom had anything good to say about the series. In January 1970, though, as she neared the end of taping episodes for Season 6, she wrote jubilantly: "3 more years of 'Bewitched' without options! Can you believe it? Well one can't be choosy these days—So many are out of work—I'm very lucky!"[26]

Other people who were close to her at the time, like her personal assistant Quint Benedetti, were left with the impression that the series "wasn't enough of a challenge for her."[27] Dick York recalled in an interview with Herbie J. Pilato: "That was Aggie's big debate on the set.... When do we get to act?"[28] This was a criticism Moorehead would make of television acting in general: that it was all rush and hurry with no time for perfecting your craft. As *Bewitched* was well into its fifth season, she observed to a newspaper that she thought TV was "very difficult, very tedious: Many times I enjoy a script as I read it. But when you're on your feet doing it, you can get bogged down. The pressures are so tremendous—time is the biggest problem—that you often let something go that could be improved. That is a great deterrent to a good performance."[29]

Moorehead was not afraid to distance herself from Endora and *Bewitched*, even during the original run of the series. We've all read how reluctant she was to do the pilot; how she only took it on because it paid so well and she thought the series would never fly. Part of the explanation for her reluctance is to be found in a letter to Georgia Johnstone after she'd been offered the role of Endora: "they want me to play a witch in a series! You know this is murder for then all my work + what little talent I have would be used by others around Halloween. They have such little minds out here [in Hollywood] and I would only be thought of as a witch from now on!"[30]

In a 1965 interview, "She said she didn't want to be in a TV series at first because a series can be difficult for a versatile performer. There is the danger of falling into a groove, she said. 'Bewitched,' is the kind of groove, however, that a lot of performers would delight in falling into."[31] As we've seen above, Moorehead was always willing to recognize what a boon the series was to her from a financial standpoint.

Given the singular importance of Endora to Moorehead's posthumous reputation and continued fame, it may seem strange to find her saying straight out in an interview in 1967 that "I don't want to be identified with Endora." She goes on, though, to modify and explain that bald statement: "I don't want to be identified with any role." She has to admit, though, that she has probably been seen by "many, many more people in ... 'Bewitched' than in anything else she has ever done. 'But I'm not on every week, you know,' she says defensively. 'Only eight out of 13. I don't want that much exposure as Endora. The only thing I want to be identified with is that I'm an actress.'"[32]

The secret to any good sit com is creating as many characters as possible that the viewers want to spend time with. In this regard, *Bewitched* succeeded remarkably well. In addition to Samantha and Darrin Stevens and their two cute kids, there was Gladys Kravitz and her husband, Abner, Uncle Arthur, Aunt Clara, Dr. Bombay, Esmeralda, and Serena. There were also important antagonist figures, first and foremost Endora, of course, but also Darrin's boss Larry Tate and Samantha's father, Maurice. In addition, there were opportunities for a host of talented character actors to play McMann & Tate clients and their spouses, witches and warlocks, and various other characters the Stephens family members interact with in their daily and "other-worldly" lives.

Given the success of the series, which continues to this day in interminable reruns, it might seem unnecessary to ask how *Bewitched* might have been even better. Certainly, it would have made for a richer and complex viewing experience and less repetition and predictability, if there had been developing storylines that extended beyond the single episode. This would have created more of a sense of the characters having a history individually and with each other, rather than living in an eternal present, suffering from extensive amnesia, and starting more or less from scratch in each episode.

In reality, given the way *Bewitched* was produced, this sense of developing action over several episodes and seasons would have been very difficult to achieve. With each episode being a self-contained, completed story and very little change and development from episode to episode and season to season, you have the maximum of flexibility with regard to the order in which the episodes are produced and aired. As it turned out, *Bewitched* was absolutely dependent on this kind of flexibility, because two of the three lead actors were not always available, though for different reasons. Moorehead made it clear from the start that she did not want to be in all the episodes or even close to every episode. She settled on a standard quota of eight out of 13 episodes, which is roughly ⅔. She only reached that number of episodes in seasons 1, 3, and 5. In seasons 2, 4, 6, 7, and 8, she was seen in between 50 percent and 57 percent of the episodes; Season 8 being the season in which she was seen only in half the episodes.

As Elizabeth Montgomery explained in an interview with Herbie Pilato in 1989, they went to great lengths to accommodate Moorehead's need for time to do other things.[33] Her outside activities included going on tour with her one-woman show, doing feature films like *The Singing Nun* and *Dear Dead Delilah*, but also doing guest spots on other TV series, even those on rival networks. According to a 1965 feature article on Moorehead: "she has one of the few eat-your-cake-and-have-it-too deals among series headliners filming in California. The majority find themselves virtual gilded prisoners the week around, forty weeks a year. Not she. 'We have it clearly understood that all my scenes will be done in two days.'"[34]

While Moorehead's time off was known about in advance and could be worked into the schedule, it was different with Dick York's absences. As the years went by, his increasing back problems made it difficult to know if he could come in to work and ultimately meant he had to leave the series after Season 5. Because of the way *Bewitched* was produced, though, it was possible to work around him much longer than it would have been possible in a series with a chronological development in the characters and storylines from week to week.

Even with the limitations on production I have outlined, it is possible to imagine, for example, that Endora and Darrin's relationship could have been allowed to develop and improve to some extent. It is really rather nice to see them getting along at times, however briefly, as in #2.18 "And Then There Were Three," when Endora tells Darrin about Tabitha's birth and they actually hug; in the parts of Season 6's "Turn on That Old Charm" where Endora is under the power of an amulet that makes her charming to Darrin for a change; and in the double episode at the start of Season 8, where Darrin ends up asking for Endora's help to avoid losing his head to Henry VIII.

The series' gender dynamics have, of course, dated terribly. It's striking how many episodes begin with Samantha in the kitchen preparing some kind of food, usually breakfast. A variant is finding her in the garden gardening. In this context, Endora suggests a "witch feminist," decadent, anti-bourgeois alternative to her daughter's deadening domesticity. That aspect of Endora's character might well have been played up, as well as the interesting marital dynamics in her "open relationship" with her husband, Maurice.

In Western culture down through the ages, the witch (whether as an historical or fictional figure) has been a significant embodiment of misogyny. Yet it is possible to see the witch as potentially both liberating and empowering for women by being outside the stifling confines of femininity as defined by their culture. One feminist critic notes: "Endora made gestures of femininity that were exaggerated, like a Mardi Gras mask. But it was this defiance that gave her power, and made her such a liberatory character. She was blunt, honest, catty, and self-indulgent, and she did not waste her time trying to soothe others' feelings or placate men the way Samantha did.... Endora got to say what many women wished they could say, and her complete indifference to the approval of men was a joy and relief to watch, even as we knew we did not want to be like her."[35] According to the author of a book on witches and witchcraft: "Television witches show the power inherent in women and the conflicts modern women face in trying to balance various facets of their lives."[36]

All this is not to suggest that *Bewitched* should have taken on the socially significant trappings of a 1970s, Norman Lear sitcom. Because of the rigid limitations on the characters and the storylines, though, the series as a whole didn't have much room for growth or development. It was remarkable that they kept it going for eight seasons. Though a ninth season was in the works, it was probably a good thing that the series ended when it did.

CREDITS: *Directors:* William Asher, Richard Michaels, R. Robert Rosenbaum, etc. *Producers:* Harry Ackerman (executive producer), Danny Arnold (producer), William Asher (producer), Jerry Briskin (associate producer), Jerry Davis (producer), William Froug (producer), Ernest A. Losso (associate producer), Richard Michaels (associate producer); *Writers:* Sol Saks (creator), Richard Baer, Lila Garrett, John L. Greene, James S. Henerson, Ed Jurist, Bernie Kahn, Michael Morris, Bernard Slade, etc.; *Cinematography:* Lloyd Ahern, Sr., Frederick Gately, Robert Tobey, Robert Wyckoff, etc.; *Film editing:* Hugh Chaloupka, Aaron Nibley, Jack Ruggiero, etc.; *Art direction:* Ross Bellah, Malcom C. Bert, Robert Peterson, Robert Purcell, etc.; *Makeup department:* Ben Lane (makeup supervisor), Rolf Miller (makeup artist), Lillian Ugrin (hair stylist), etc.; *Costume and wardrobe department:* Vi Alford (costumer: women), Byron Munson (costumer: men); *Production company:* Ashmont Prod./Screen Gems Television; *Air dates:* September 17, 1964–March 25, 1972, on ABC

MAJOR CAST: Elizabeth Montgomery (Samantha Stephens), Dick York (Darrin Stephens), Agnes Moorehead (Endora), Dick Sargent (Darrin Stephens), David White (Larry Tate), Irene Vernon (Louise Tate), Kasey Rogers (Louise Tate), George Tobias (Abner Kravitz), Alice Pearce (Gladys Kravitz), Sandra Gould (Gladys Kravitz), Erin Murphy (Tabitha Stephens), Diane Murphy (Tabitha Stephens), David Mandel-Bloch (Adam), Mabel Albertson (Phyllis Stephens), Robert F. Simon (Frank Stephens), Roy Roberts (Frank Stephens), Marion Lorne (Aunt Clara), Bernard Fox (Dr. Bombay), Maurice Evans (Maurice), Paul Lynde (Uncle Arthur), Alice Ghostley (Esmeralda)

AWARDS (only Agnes Moorehead's): Primetime Emmy Award nom.—Outstanding Performance by an Actress in a Supporting Role in a Comedy (1966); Primetime Emmy Award nom.—Outstanding Continued Performance by an Actress in a Leading Role in a Comedy Series (1967); Primetime Emmy Award nom.—Outstanding Performance by an Actress in a Supporting Role in a Comedy (1968); Primetime Emmy Award nom.—Outstanding Continued Performance by an Actress in a Supporting Role in a Series (1969); Primetime Emmy Award nom.—Outstanding Performance by an Actress in a Supporting Role in Comedy (1970); Primetime Emmy Award nom.—Outstanding Performance by an Actress in a Supporting Role in Comedy (1971)

21

Alice Through the Looking Glass (TV, 1966)

While we can never see and hear *Gigi* or *The Pink Jungle* or *High Spirits*, we do have the chance to experience at least one of Moorehead's performances in a musical comedy. *Alice Through the Looking Glass*, a TV special broadcast over NBC on November 6, 1966, must be one of the most underappreciated and undeservedly forgotten TV productions Moorehead lent her many and varied talents to. I love every part of this show from the catchy tunes, to the zany costumes, to the upbeat message that people should not be afraid to "come out, come out, wherever you are" and that anyone can become a queen, if they only work hard enough and don't give in to fear.

On July 4, 1966, the *New York Times* announced that Agnes Moorehead would replace Bette Davis, "who is ill," in *Alice Through the Looking Glass*.[1] Bob McKenzie provided some more details in his column "On Television" two days later, noting that Davis had been "forced to leave the cast," because "She slipped and fell while looking at a new house a few weeks ago" and "the doctor ordered her out of the show." Clearly not a fan, MacKenzie concluded: "Agnes Moorehead will take over the role, and that won't be the same, at all."[2]

Well, of course it wouldn't be the same. Davis and Moorehead were two very different actresses with different backgrounds and different screen personas. I can't imagine, though, that Davis would have been half as effective as the Red Queen as Moorehead was. For all her undoubted talents, Davis was Davis. What you got was Bette Davis playing Bette Davis playing so and so. It was impossible to see beyond the force of her unique presence and the wattage, however much reduced by this point, of her star image. Moorehead, on the other hand, was a chameleon, adaptable to the circumstances. Audiences were used to seeing her in a wide variety of guises. So why not dressed up like a playing card or a chess piece with only her flashing eyes and patrician profile showing?[3] And that unmistakable, stentorian voice.... There was no point in paying Davis to hide her light under the bushel of huge, outrageous costumes, but that was exactly what Moorehead had often done. She could even act through several ounces of rubber if necessary, as proven by *The Lost Moment*, or inside a cocoon of a costume, as in *The Conqueror*; not two highpoints of her career from an artistic perspective, certainly, but she still delivered the goods.

Nanette Fabray revealed in an interview with Moorehead biographer Charles Tranberg, that Davis wasn't really sick: "she got a case of the nerves close to the taping."[4] The final script of the program is dated June 26, 1966, which gives us a good indication of

From left: Ricardo Montalban, Nanette Fabray, Agnes Moorehead, and Robert Coote in the "There Are Two Sides to Everything" number from *Alice Though the Looking Glass*, wearing two-sided costumes by Ray Aghayan and Bob Mackie inspired by playing cards and chess pieces. The two designers deservedly won the first Primetime Emmy Award ever given for costume design.

when it was produced.[5] Moorehead wrote to a friend that she would be back on the *Bewitched* set June 24th, after being on hiatus since March 30.[6] In fact, she didn't start taping the first episode of Season 3, "Nobody's Perfect," until July 7.[7] My guess is that production on *Alice Through the Looking Glass* was over by then.

Associated Press TV writer Cynthia Lowry describes how the show's creators "crossed 'Alice in Wonderland' with 'The Wizard of Oz' and then borrowed unblushingly from other enchanted sources." They called the resulting mix *Alice Through the Looking Glass*, "a misleading title that will infuriate Lewis Carroll lovers,"[8] Lowry claimed. Actually, she exaggerates the extent to which the program moved beyond Lewis Carroll's original story. Though this version does feature a "Blue Road" and throws the three witches from Hansel and Gretel, Snow White, and Sleeping Beauty into the mix, about 90 percent of the plot and characters here are taken from Carroll's 1871 sequel to *Alice in Wonderland*, which he called *Through the Looking-Glass, and What Alice Found There*.

In the wacky, fresh, and amusing musical that resulted, Alice was played by 19-year-old, Chicago-born Judi Rollin. Rollin's only TV credit at this point was an episode of *Bonanza* and her career went nowhere after her starring role in this program. In *Alice Through the Looking Glass*, Alice's fondest wish is to become a queen. To attain her goal, she must make her way to the palace along the perilous "Blue Road," which presents a number of challenges to her intelligence and courage. The musical numbers and guest stars performing them—from Jack Palance, in what must have been one of the most bizarre roles of his career as the menacing Jabberwock, to the Smothers Brothers as Tweedledee and Tweedledum to Jimmy Durante as Humpty Dumpty—are stationed at regular intervals along this fanciful obstacle course. There's even a love interest of sorts in the form of British comedian Roy Castle's likeable Lester the Jester. Each performer has his or her own "act." It's all as if vaudeville is reborn for a moment in a TV studio with canned laughter and raucous prerecorded applause. There are even live giraffes looking mildly dazed in the "Keep on the Grass" number. The journey ends with Alice being crowned a queen, before being woken by her father and discovering it was all a dream. Or was it?

From "Through the Looking Glass," the melodious theme song, to the rousing "Hail to the Queen," there were no less than a dozen original songs composed by Moose Charlap with lyrics by Elsie Simmons. Some of the best numbers involve the royal couples. As the Red Queen, Agnes Moorehead is teamed with Robert Coote as the Red King, while Nanette Fabray and Ricardo Montalban are the White Queen and the White King. While I love Moorehead's spirit of fun and no-holds-barred clownery in this, it must be said that Nanette Fabray as the zany, ungainly White Queen gives her a run for her money, especially in Fabray's solo "I Wasn't Meant to Be a Queen." She sings this slapstick-inspired number to Alice, all the while caught in mortal combat with her long, white silk shawl, which threatens to trip her up at every juncture.

Moorehead, funnily enough, doesn't get a solo, which makes you wonder why. I imagine it was because Davis had not felt up to singing a solo. By the time Moorehead came onboard, the production was probably so far advanced that they had to stick to their already scripted songs and dance numbers. Moorehead is in fine fettle, though, in the quartet with her three royal counterparts called "There Are Two Sides to Everything," where they are fancifully togged out like two-sided playing cards with chess-inspired headgear. In Fabray's other solo, "Alice Is Coming to Tea," Moorehead chimes in with the words "with me," often combined with a close-up. I mention this, because there aren't many close-ups in the production as a whole. Fabray is right in pointing out that the show was "badly photographed: They put a camera on the floor and had us walk in front of it—they used no imagination at all."[9] Even though the show was taped, they performed it as if it were a live performance. Due to the heavy costumes and intense lighting, Fabray remembered the whole thing as a hot and uncomfortable experience.[10]

Though Moorehead is slighted on the solo front, she does get two good spoken scenes with Alice that go some way to making up for it: a duologue with Alice in the forest and the tea party scene where the Red Queen gives Alice a test, while the White Queen makes note of the not too impressive results. Particularly resonant for many reasons is the scene set in the Queen's Forest. The Red Queen makes sure to point out to Alice that "It's just for girls, you know" and that "This one is strictly for us girls." The forest, she explains, is purposely "all done in pink," in fact, "I decided the colors me self." Given the lesbian legend surrounding Moorehead and the gay and lesbian fan base she has always appealed to, this becomes a sort of "in joke." Another queer running gag is Moorehead's repeated insistence on the fact that "I'm a queen" and the rightness of everything she does because she's a queen. The gay subcultural meaning of the word queen was, of course, well established by the 1960s and no doubt "queens" of various shapes and sizes would have been a receptive audience for this program. Indeed, what would musical comedy be without queens, as producers, performers, and audience members?

It's no wonder, then, that Lowry called this "a gay, imaginative 90 minutes of thoroughly enjoyable fantasy."[11] *Alice Through the Looking Glass* as a whole is rife with queer allusions and gay allegorical resonances. One wonders how Gloria Gaynor's 1978 megahit "I Will Survive" ever became the gay national anthem, when you had Judi Rollin singing the equally rousing tune "Come Out, Come Out, Wherever You Are" a dozen years earlier.... Timing is everything, I suppose. "Oh daddy, if you only knew," Alice sighs when it's all over.

CREDITS: *Director:* Alan Handley; *Producers:* Alan Handley, E. Jay Krause, Bob Wynn; *Writer:* Albert Simmons; *Music:* Moose Charlap; *Lyrics:* Elsie Simmons; *Art director:* E. Jay Krause; *Costume design:* Ray Aghayan, Bob Mackie; *Choreographer:* Tony Charmoli; *Musical director:* Harper McKay; *Vocal arrangements:* Don Costa; *Production company:* Alwynn Prod./Dum & Dee Prod.; *Air date:* November 6, 1966, on NBC

CAST: Iris Adrian (Tiger Lily), Roy Castle (Lester the Jester), Robert Coote (Red King), Richard Denning (Alice's Father), Jimmy Durante (Humpty Dumpty), Nanette Fabray (White Queen), Ricardo Montalban (White King), Agnes Moorehead (Red Queen), Jack Palance (Jabberwock), Judi Rollin (Alice), Tom Smothers (Tweedledum), Dick Smothers (Tweedledee)

22

The Wild Wild West: "The Night of the Vicious Valentine" (TV, 1967)

The winter of 1966 was an extremely busy time for Agnes Moorehead. Season 3 of *Bewitched* had premiered on September 15 with only 13 episodes completed and 20 remaining to be produced. Come December, they were still working fast and furiously to finish the number of episodes needed to round out the season. Despite working on *Bewitched* 24/7, or so it seemed, Moorehead was able to squeeze in an appearance on a show for a rival network. Playing the arch villainess Emma Valentine on an episode of the campy series *The Wild Wild West* was an offer she simply couldn't refuse. In direct line of descent from her Baroness Aspasia Conti in *Mrs. Parkington* and a precursor of Aunt Alicia in *Gigi*, this glamorous, humorous, and imperious demimondaine also had a lot in common with Endora. This was a type of role Moorehead could do with little effort, but a sufficiently large gap had to be found in her schedule.

Such a gap materialized towards the end of 1966. In late November, Moorehead went directly from taping her scenes for "The Super Car" episode of *Bewitched* (#3.19) at Columbia Studios to working on *The Wild Wild West* at CBS Studio Center in Studio City on the old Republic lot. Moorehead had a week off from *Bewitched*, because Endora did not appear in the episode called "The Corn Is High as a Guernsey's Eye" (#3.20). We have a *Wild Wild West* call sheet for Monday, December 5, 1966, that indicates that this was the fifth day of production on the episode that would be known as "The Night of the Vicious Valentine."[1] If we assume they weren't filming at the weekend, that means production started on Monday, November 28 and was probably done by December 5 (or Moorehead's part was).[2] As soon as she was done, she returned to the set of *Bewitched* to do "The Trial and Error of Aunt Clara" (#3.21), which finished production on December 9.[3] Before the month was out, "Three Wishes" (#3.22) and "I Remember You.... Sometimes" (#3.23) were also completed. It was truly a case of "no rest for the wicked."

Described by its creator Michael Garrison as "James Bond on horseback," *The Wild Wild West* was an unusual hybrid, being a Western spy series set during the presidency of Ulysses S. Grant in the 1870s, a period often referred to as the "Gilded Age." The series ran on CBS for four seasons from 1965 to 1969 and inspired two TV movies with the original cast in 1979 and 1980 and a 1999 feature film.[4] Robert Conrad and Ross Martin starred as Secret Service agents James T. West and Artemus Gordon, "Jim" and "Artie" among friends, who like James Bond used advanced technology in their ongoing battle against organized crime and threats towards the government. "In the tradition of James Bond, there were always beautiful women, clever gadgets, and delusional arch-enemies with half-insane plots to take over the country or the world."[5] The agents were not limited to horseback, though, as they had their own specially equipped luxury train, "The Wanderer," which included a stable car and laboratory. The series ultimately fell victim not to low ratings, but to a network crack-down on television violence, and was cancelled in mid–February 1969.[6]

The plot of "The Night of the Vicious Valentine" is unusual only in having an older woman as villain. Here the murder victims are "extra wealthy" and lonely older men, who have recently married much younger women. In the teaser, Curtis Dodd, played by J. Edward McKinley, the quintessential McMann & Tate client on *Bewitched*, appears as the fourth murder victim, who is killed at the piano right before the eyes of West and Gordon and his recent bride Elaine (Diane McBain). The fifth intended murder victim is the "beef baron of the West," Paul J. Lambert (Henry Beckman), one of Kansas City's leading citizens. He is set to marry Miss Michele LeMaster (Sherry Jackson), a former barmaid and thief whom Emma Valentine has "saved" in Paris and carefully trained to attract a man of Lambert's type.

Through the young brides and soon-to-be widows, her protégées, Emma Valentine intends to gain control over so much U.S. capital that she can also control Congress. She is a radical feminist *avant-la-lettre* and deems herself "savior of all womankind.... From domination of the spirit, economic exploitation, annihilation of the mind—in brief, all the injustices wrought by men." Her plan is ultimately to be crowned Queen Emma I for a period, before returning the United States to democracy and having a grateful populace elect her president.

Miss Valentine first appears 15 minutes into the episode, when she enters a printing shop where Jim West is interviewing the proprietor. She calls herself "a confirmed, compulsive snoop," while West describes her as "the most charming and most original of the Washington hostess corps." Emma Valentine uses a lorgnette with heart-shaped lenses to examine him and likes what she sees. In addition to fabulous frocks by some uncredited costumier, in this episode Moorehead uses all her best jewelry: the diamond starburst pin so frequently seen on *Bewitched*; another large diamond brooch in the shape of shield or coat of arms, that she also used on *Bewitched*; her cabochon star sapphire ring; and her favorite gold filigree earrings.

Most of Moorehead's scenes are with Robert Conrad, which I'm sure she didn't mind. It wasn't the first time she had acted with a male co-star who was prettier than herself and with eyes even more brilliantly blue. Their big show-down takes place in her bedroom, or maybe she would have preferred to call it her "boodwah," which is decorated in a style that almost defies description. The set decorators must have scoured the antique shops of Hollywood for cherubs. The walls and all available surfaces are laden with knick knacks or covered in textiles in shades of pink and red in a brilliant visual cacophony that includes Miss Valentine's gown. Naturally, she exercises with heart-shaped dumbbells! The Gilded Age was one of the most plush, overstuffed, tasseled, fringed, and furbelowed periods in American fashion and home decorating. This gave the art directors and costume designers on *The Wild Wild West* an opportunity to go all out on the kitsch décor, elaborate frocks for the ladies, and fancy duds for the gentlemen, including pants so tight one has to wonder where they put their equipment. In decorating Miss Valentine's abode, they outdid themselves.

As mentioned above, advanced weaponry and various futuristic machines and gadgets were a part of the show's concept and appeal. In this episode, the high tech inventions seem to be mainly in the grasping hands of Emma Valentine, as the heroes only employ such hackneyed devices as a blade in the sole of a boot and a knife literally up their sleeve. In the lengthy scene in Miss Valentine's bedroom, Jim West is held in an unwelcome embrace by a piece of furniture he ironically refers to as a "love seat." It is strictly speaking a type of day-bed the French refer to as a "duchesse"; *duchesse-brisée*, if it is in two parts, and *duchesse en bateau*, if it is in one. It is hard to tell, as the camera stays pretty close to Robert Conrad's face. More pertinent, perhaps, is the fact that this sofa is equipped with something that is not usually part of the design: two pairs of mechanical arms with bejeweled, manicured hands, that can crush the life out of poor Jim West at any moment.

Emma Valentine also has what she calls the "Love Eternal Machine" behind a sliding wall in her bedroom. After asking West a number of questions about his likes and dislikes in women and otherwise, she cuts out a pattern of hearts on a sheet of red paper and feeds West's "record" into the machine. The result, she tells him is that "Your ideal mate is a combination of Aphrodite, Helen of Troy and Lola Montez. Oh, Mr. West, I'm afraid it can't be done." He responds: "Oh, frankly, I like to do my own shopping anyway." Things end badly, when Miss Valentine makes a pass that is not well received. West quips "If I have a choice, may we go back to questions and answers?" and gets double slapped for his effrontery.

Agnes Moorehead in her memorable role as the vicious Emma Valentine in the episode of *The Wild Wild West*, for which she won a Primetime Emmy Award for in 1967. While the heart-shaped lorgnette was specially made for the occasion, the decorative brooch (minus the heart-shaped attachment) and the faintly discernible gold earrings were her own.

"The Night of the Vicious Valentine" (#2.20) was broadcast on Friday, February 10, 1967, the day after the "Three Wishes" (#3.22) episode of *Bewitched* aired and while "No More Mr. Nice Guy" (#3.28) was in production.[7] On April 28, the National Academy of Television Arts and Science wrote to inform Moorehead that she had been nominated for two Primetime Emmy awards.[8] She was nominated in the category "Outstanding Continued Performance by an Actress in a Leading Role in a Comedy Series" for *Bewitched* and in the category "Outstanding Performance by an Actress in a Supporting Role in a Drama" for *The Wild Wild West*. It was the second time she was nominated for *Bewitched*, but the first and only time she was nominated in the "Leading Role" rather than the "Supporting Role" category.

In a bi-coastal ceremony hosted by Joey

Bishop at the Century Plaza Hotel in Los Angeles and by Hugh Downs at the American Hotel in New York on Sunday, June 4, 1967, Moorehead won her first and only Primetime Emmy award for her performance on *The Wild Wild West.* This was the only Emmy awarded to that show during its four-year run. In a note to her friend Georgia Johnstone, Moorehead wrote: "It was quite a shock! I don't win, as you know—the feeling on the set is strange!"[9] Taping on the fourth season of *Bewitched* had just started with the episode "Business, Italian Style" (#4.3).[10]

CREDITS: *Director:* Irving J. Moore; *Producer:* Leonard Katzman; *Writers:* Leigh Chapman (teleplay), Michael Garrison (series creator); *Cinematography:* Ted Voigtlander; *Film editing:* Alan L. Jaggs; *Art direction:* Albert Heschong; *Production company:* Columbia Broadcasting System; *Air date:* February 10, 1967, on CBS

CAST: Henry Beckman (Paul J. Lambert), Robert Conrad (James T. West), Owen Cunningham (minister), Don Dillaway (butler), Mitzie Evans (aide), Sherry Jackson (Michele LeMaster), Diane McBain (Elaine Dodd), J. Edward McKinley (Curtis Dodd), Ross Martin (Artemus Gordon), Shephard Menken (Itnelav), Agnes Moorehead (Emma Valentine), Walter Sande (Colonel Crockett)

AWARD: Primetime Emmy Award—Outstanding Performance by an Actress in a Supporting Role in a Drama (1967)

23

Custer: "Spirit Woman" (TV, 1967)

When the episode of *Custer* titled "Spirit Woman" aired on December 13, 1967, *Bewitched* was halfway through its fourth season. Moorehead's regular role on the series limited the time available to do other shows. Apart from Endora, Watoma on *Custer* and her Emmy-winning performance as Emma Valentine on *The Wild Wild West* were her only major roles on the small screen in 1967. The final draft script with Moorehead's annotations is dated October 23, 1967, which makes it likely that her episode of *Custer* was produced by Twentieth Century–Fox Television not long after this date.[1] Moorehead had time off from *Bewitched* throughout the month of October 1967.[2]

Under the headline "A Busy Time," a local newspaper ran the following item on December 17, 1967: "Within in a space of three weeks Agnes Moorehead had done her regular role of Endora in 'Bewitched,' played an Indian witch doctor in a 'Custer' episode and guested on a 'Smothers Brothers' show as a fun-loving witch. Agnes then took off for a week in the Florida sun to bake the witchcraft out of her system."[3] The paper failed to mention that she had also celebrated her birthday on December 6 with a combined birthday and Christmas party for more than 400 guests.[4] She had turned 67, but wasn't telling.

Custer was a short-lived TV drama series inspired by the life and career of the soldier and adventurer George Armstrong Custer. It was set not long after the Civil War, when Custer was a lieutenant colonel in the Seventh Cavalry. In the series, he was stationed at Fort Hayes under the command of General Alfred Terry, played by Robert F. Simon. If that name seems familiar, it was because Simon played Darrin Stephens's father Frank Stephens during the first three seasons of *Bewitched*, before taking up this regular role on *Custer* in 1967.[5] The other regular characters were the scout California Joe (Slim Pickens), Sergeant James Bustard (Peter Palmer), and the Sioux chieftain Crazy Horse (Michael Dante). The title role was played by a 30-year-old, 6'1" Canadian with long blond hair called Wayne Ernest Maunder. Maunder turned to acting after failing to achieve a Major League baseball career and studied with Stella Adler in New York, before moving to Los Angeles. He had made his television debut on *The Monroes*, less than eight months before *Custer* premiered.

Moorehead was cast as the Sioux "Spirit Woman" Watoma, who attempts to broker a peace treaty between her people and the Yankee invaders of their lands. A local newspaper summed up the episode as follows:

Agnes Moorehead as the Sioux "Spirit Woman" Watoma is seen prophesying the violent death of George Armstrong Custer, played by the Canadian-born actor Wayne Maunder (left). She might also have prophesied the demise of Maunder's acting career. While he went on from the short-lived *Custer* to the more successful Western series *Lancer*, Maunder's film and television career was over by the early 1980s (courtesy Muskingum University Archives).

> Agnes Moorehead and James Whitmore make this episode perhaps the best of the season. The "Bewitched" star is again cast in a pseudo supernatural role, as a buckskin clad Indian seeress who sees the dangers of her warmongering Sioux tribesmen and goes to Custer to seek peace. The Sioux come after her but she is first captured by a trapper (Whitmore) who intends using her as a bargaining tool to get back his own wife, a Sioux captive.[6]

Even 100 years after the events depicted, only the Native Americans in the program are described as "warmongering."

At great risk to her own life, Watoma seeks out the military men at Fort Hayes. In her first important scene, she must convince General Terry and Custer that this is not a trick and that she has honorable intentions. Custer explains to Terry that to the Sioux people, Watoma is even more important than Chief Crazy Horse. He could be replaced, but she is unique: "She's more than a person, she's a symbol of their spirit—their soul." This begs the question: if Watoma is so important to the Sioux, why are they resolutely trying to knock her off throughout the episode? At any rate, Watoma explains to Terry and Custer: "I had vision. I looked deep into sacred smoke. I see my people gone from lands. You drive them away. I see many die. Frozen. Snow. Arms lifted sky. Must not happen."

It simplifies communication between the two parties, that Watoma can make herself understood in a classic "Indian style" English, which, like a telegram, is short on determiners and prepositions. Here are some further samples of her "idiolect." When asked to explain why she has come, she says: "I come against will of my people. End fighting between us." After telling Custer he was responsible for the death both of her husband, Black Beaver, and her son, she adds: "You soldier, Yellow Hair. For you, only battle. For me, all ends. Life. Hope." "Yellow Hair" is her name for Custer.

Watoma not only sees visions in smoke, she can read sand too. It is in sand she prophecies Custer's death at the Battle of the Little Big Horn ten years later: "Death everywhere across face of earth.... Not soon, yet not long." When General Sheridan wants to see Watoma personally at Fort Dodge, Custer has to escort her there secretly. The Sioux are not the only threats to her life. Veteran character actor James Whitmore co-stars as a deranged, drunken trapper, Eldo, whose wife Annie and son Joey were abducted by the Sioux two years earlier. Eldo manages to abduct Watoma at one point, hoping to exchange her for his family members. The two have a touching scene, when he asks her if she ever saw anyone answering to the description of his wife and son. Watoma insists that she hasn't, but you can tell from her facial expression as she is eating with her back to Eldo, that she knows something and what she knows isn't good. Eldo is finally killed by the Sioux.

As she often did in her race-crossing roles, such as Aunt Jezebel in *Adventures of Captain Fabian* and Jikiri in *Adventures in Paradise*, Moorehead looks pretty cute in this role, something along the lines of Rosa Moline's grandmother. She's having a bad hair day of epic proportions, comparable only to Velma Cruther in *Hush...Hush, Sweet Charlotte*. In fact, the hair does a lot for her characterization. I wouldn't go so far as to say that her performance is being given by the wig, but it does contribute substantially to the portrayal. Moorehead proves herself a keen "keener," too, as she mourns the Sioux dead. Maybe she got some pointers from her friend and longtime producer, Paul Gregory, who was one quarter Sioux on his mother's side. When it comes down to it, I rather like this performance. However ludicrous in some respects, however many needy Native American character actresses were kept out of a job by the casting of a white woman in this role, there is something about Watoma that works. She can certainly hold her own against similar portrayals some years later by Judith Anderson in *A Man Called Horse* and Gale Sondergaard in *The Return of a Man Called Horse.*

An article on the series in Wikipedia claims that the *Custer* was cancelled "due to wide protest of Native American tribes throughout the United States."[7] That may well be, but I imagine poor ratings also had something to do with it. Maunder went on to star in another series co-created by Samuel A. Peeples and set in the post–Civil War West, namely *Lancer,* which ran on CBS from 1968 to 1970. Moorehead showed up in a second season *Lancer* episode titled "A Person Unknown" in November 1969. Maunder married Lucia C. Maisto in Los Angeles on March 1, 1968.[8] The couple had a son, Dylan T. Maunder, on July 22, 1968, and divorced in March 1971.[9] Wayne Maunder, who is still alive as I write, has not acted in films or television since 1981.

Credits: *Director:* Laslo Benedek; *Producers:* Frank Glicksman, William Self, David Weisbart; *Writers:* William Blinn (written by), Larry Cohen (series suggested by), Samuel A. Peeples (created by), David Weisbart (created by); *Director of photography:* William W. Spencer; *Film editing:* George Gittens; *Art direction:* Russell Menzer, Jack Martin Smith; *Production company:* Twentieth Century–Fox Television; *Air date:* December 13, 1967, on ABC

Cast: Chick Casey (Ira), Mike Howden (sentry), Eugene Martin (young Sioux), Wayne Maunder (Lt. Col. George Armstrong Custer), Christopher Milo (Indian brave), Agnes Moorehead (Watoma), Read Morgan (medicine man), Peter Palmer (Sgt. James Bustard), Slim Pickens (California Joe Milner), Robert F. Simon (General Alfred Terry), James Whitmore (Eldo)

24

Don Juan in Hell (Stage, 1972–73)

George Bernard Shaw's play-within-a-play *Don Juan in Hell*, the third act of *Man and Superman*, had a way of showing up in Agnes Moorehead's life at critical junctures. In 1950, she had received an offer to star in the original American production just as her eight-year tenure as a contract player at MGM was drawing to a close. That decisive bit of casting signaled a new phase of her career as a leading lady of the American stage. At a similarly significant turning point in her life in April 1972, just as it became clear that the eighth season of *Bewitched* would be its last, Moorehead received an offer from producers Lee Orgel and William J. Griffiths to star in a revival of *Don Juan in Hell*. There would be no new beginnings this time, though.

Indeed, the 1972–73 revival was rather a reminder of all that had been lost in the 20 years since Moorehead electrified audiences across the United States with her portrayal of the "eternally feminine" granddame Doña Ana. By the early 1970s, her co-stars Charles Laughton and Sir Cedric Hardwicke were dead. Their young producer genius, Paul Gregory, was in his fifties now, had married the movie star Janet Gaynor, and settled into semi-retirement on a ranch in Palm Springs. The original Don Juan, 72-year-old Charles Boyer, had not been seen on Broadway since 1963 and was depressed after the suicide of his only child, 21-year-old Michael Charles Boyer, in 1965.

Moorehead herself was convalescing from her first battle with cancer at her mother's home in Reedsburg, Wisconsin, when she received the call to do *Don Juan in Hell* all over again. She had had to cancel all the scheduled performances of her one-woman show that spring, but needed to get back to work and start earning again, especially now that *Bewitched* was at an end. The new production of Shaw's classic "doesn't come up until Aug. + Sept.," she wrote to her friend Georgia Johnstone on April 19, 1972. The producers wanted her both to direct the production and star in it. Vincent Price and Ricardo Montalban were two names being touted to co-star. "Want approval of everything—before I take it over," she wrote to Johnstone, adding: "I'm thinking about it."[1]

Moorehead finally decided to do the revival, but she would not direct. The legendary Romanian-born actor and producer John Houseman was brought in to do that duty. Despite all his accomplishments as a distinguished producer and acting teacher, Houseman is probably best remembered today for playing the haughty and austere Professor Charles W. Kingsfield, Jr., in the law school drama series *The Paper Chase*. Houseman had known Moorehead since the 1930s, when he was closely associated with Orson Welles.

He had worked on the screenplays of two of her films, *Citizen Kane* and *Jane Eyre*, but they had never acted together.

Moorehead apparently retained some measure of control over casting the three male roles, as her letter to Johnstone suggested she would. Ricardo Montalban was to play Don Juan, the Devil was to be portrayed by Edward Mulhare, and the Commander by Paul Henreid. She knew Montalban best, having directed him in the 1955 production of *Don Juan in Hell*, which also starred Mary Astor, Kurt Kaznar, and Reginald Denny. It was Montalban's antics as Don Juan that had caused Astor to quit the show; a difficult decision she defended at length in a letter to Moorehead.[2] In 1966, Moorehead and Montalban had shared acting credits in *The Singing Nun* and *Alice Through the Looking Glass*. Critical opinion would be divided on the success of his return as Don Juan.

Austrian-born Paul Henreid, best known as Victor Laszlo in *Casablanca*, had had a small role as Cyd Charisse's manager in *Meet Me in Las Vegas*, though he and Moorehead, who played Dan Dailey's mother and Charisse's potential mother-in-law, didn't have any scenes together. Finally, Edward Mulhare was a dashing, Irish-born actor and the youngest of the four, who was known as a kind of replacement Rex Harrison, having taken over for him as Professor Higgins in the Broadway run of *My Fair Lady* and playing the same role on television that Harrison had created in the film version of *The Ghost and Mrs. Muir*. As far as I know, Mulhare and Moorehead had not acted together before.

So in place of a Frenchman and two Englishmen, there was now a Mexican, an Irishman, and an Austrian. Compared with the original production, *New York Times* critic Clive Barnes noted laconically, "Three out of four of the new cast are not, I contend, so well known as their predecessors, and the fourth has, to be gallant, aged at least five years." Moorehead had, of course, aged more than 20 years since the original run of the show in 1951–52 and, after her recent serious illness, was beginning to look her age.

According to producer Paul Gregory, who had been disappointed that she would do the show again without him, Moorehead fell into the trap of believing "all that glittered was gold." She put weak people into the 1970s production of *Don Juan*, he said, to make herself look good, but in the end it was self-defeating. Comparing later productions with the original was like "comparing platinum and silver."[3] The New York *Daily News* remarked that "It is good to find that mettlesome actress Agnes Moorehead back as Doña Ana."[4] The reviewer for the *Nation* thought that, "while it isn't up to the level of the Laughton team, it still serves the event admirably."[5] The *Toronto Star* wrote that the production "foolishly tries to resnare the past without setting any nets for the present.... What was once historic is now a relic."[6]

John Houseman recalled that they would meet and rehearse at Moorehead's home—"which so perfectly reflected the fine taste and sense of style that distinguished her"—when the stage of the Ahmanson Theatre in Los Angeles was occupied by matinees of *No, No, Nanette*. "Agnes sustained us with coffee and sandwiches and stimulated us with admonitions about the show she knew so well. She was mentor and queen bee, reminding us of what Laughton had created so brilliantly 20 years before."[7] It doesn't take a lot of imagination to perceive the potential animus between these diplomatic lines. Clearly, Houseman was a director in name only.

In a later account of their collaboration, he admitted he had taken the directing job because he was "Attracted by the quality of the text and the promise of continuing royalties from what promised to be a long tour." His production simply reproduced "the original

Sometimes one should not try to repeat a success, but that is exactly what Moorehead tried to do in 1972 when she played Doña Ana in Shaw's *Don Juan in Hell* for the second time. Her three male co-stars were new, though, including Edwin Mulhare (above) as the Devil. The production got mixed reviews.

setup of four music stands and high stools set in a semicircle in the style of a chamber-music quartet." Again, he mentions how "Agnes was there to remind us of how it had been done before, and my ego did not demand any appreciable changes."[8] Ultimately, this lack of self-assertion on the part of the director proved a mistake and made the 1972–73 revival a museum piece rather than living theater.

AP theater critic William Glover, for example, wrote: "The staging repeats the high-stool-and-music-rack artifice of the previous rendition, and has even added a few extra benches and chairs, so that one gets the feeling of having wandered into a furniture shop on a dull day."[9] To Urjo Kareda in Toronto, "a platform reading seems dated and out of touch."[10] As far as costuming was concerned, the men were still in formal evening wear, "soup and fish." Moorehead had gone to the opposite extreme of her 1951 décolleté and was insistently covered in a Nolan Miller gown, including a Renaissance ruff collar. She still wore a little crown, though, but the effect was not the same with bobbed hair.

Don Juan in Hell opened to a black-tie audience at the Civic Theatre in Fresno, California on August 28, 1972.[11] The show opened at the Ahmanson Theater at the Music Center in Los Angeles on September 5, 1972, the day 11 Israeli athletes and a German police officer were massacred by a Palestinian terrorist group at the Summer Olympics in Munich. In these difficult circumstances, Camilla Snyder found, "there was comfort as well as pleasure and wit in listening to an Austrian, a Mexican, an Irishman and a minister's daughter from Massachusetts ... discuss death and life, heaven and hell on a bare stage."[12] *Variety* gives a list of people at the Los Angeles opening, including Charles Laughton's widow, Elsa Lanchester, with the casting director David Graham; Red Buttons, Jan Murray, Eve Arden, Rose Marie, Henny and Jim Backus, Jane Withers, Dame Judith Anderson, Anne Baxter, Paul Stewart, Zsa Zsa Gabor, Virginia Graham, and Moorehead's agent Jim Jacobson and his wife.[13] "Ricardo Montalban brought 17 members of his family"; Army Archerd reported, "Paul Henried, nine. Edward Mulhare and Agnes Moorehead were solo at the Blue Ribbon Room party that followed."[14]

After closing at the Ahmanson on September 24, *Don Juan in Hell* proceeded on a lengthy tour, including Chicago ("well received"), Boston ("described in the *Globe* as 'a rare and distinguished evening in the theatre'"), Washington ("a deluge of rain in the midst of an election"), and Toronto ("made a fortune in the huge O'Keefe Auditorium").[15] In Boston, Elliot Norton, "Dean of American Theater Critics," gave them a glowing review, saying of Moorehead that she was "charming as Dona Ana, who, finding herself in Hell, wishes she had taken more advantages of her earthly opportunities to misbehave.... She is easy and elegant, and in the end, suddenly and startlingly dramatic when she turns to the audience and shouts the great key line: 'A father! A father for the Superman!'" He also had high praise for Ricardo Montalban, calling his efforts as Don Juan "one of the great performances of the year."[16]

In the nation's capital, David Richards found himself "less than totally enchanted" with the production. "If you are of a mind that appreciates the discursive tack," he wrote, "then 'Don Juan' may be just your cup of chatter." His chief criticism was that "the cast takes after Shaw's work as if it were a significant event: Now, such may be the case, but I find it a gross error to remind us constantly of the fact. Very little of the evening is allowed to pass in a minor key. Speech after speech is delivered as if it had been engraved on a stone tablet and brought, hot off the mountain, to the theater." Richards preferred Mulhare to Montalban and as for Moorehead, he thought she had "become a parody of Dona Ana.... [H]er coquetry is flagrantly false this time."[17]

Richards's remarks seemed positively benign compared with the observations of *Toronto Star* critic Urjo Kareda: "John Houseman's overcasual production, slackly paced, encourages the actors to mug and preen. Often the performance has the archness of a TV talk show, all ingratiation and no substance." But Kareda pointed his critical rapier mainly at Moorehead, "whose behavior is impossible to fathom." "Can her first Dona

Ana really have been so broad an insensitive?" he asked. The conclusion to his review is worth quoting at length, as it shows that Moorehead was still up to the old scene-stealing tricks that Paul Gregory had objected to in the original production:

> Miss Moorehead compensates for the fact that Dona Ana has little to say by making something disproportionately big out of everything she utters. Lines are overemphasized not just vocally, but with coy, artificial gestures. And when she isn't speaking, she is a very haughty upstager, shuffling her chiffons, mouthing words to the audience and at one point performing a meaningless mime of putting on her make-up. These were the kind of prima donna bad manners, that one had hoped long gone.[18]

Moorehead kept a copy of this review in her scrapbook.[19] She wrote to Georgia Johnstone on January 11, 1973, from the luxurious Sutton Place Hotel: "The crowds have been immense here in Toronto."[20]

The next and final stop of the tour was New York City, against director Houseman's "emphatic and frequently repeated advice."[21] Co-producer Lee Orgel had hoped to get the Royale Theatre for the New York run, where Moorehead had done *Lord Pengo*, but they ended up at the cavernous Palace Theatre at 1564 Broadway between 46th and 47th Street.[22] "On Broadway" columnist Jack O'Brian was gung-ho about the production, but had "a quibble: The Palace Theatre's too big, the play's intimacy screams for a straight-play house not a musical comedy hangar."[23] The Palace had over 1,700 seats compared to just over 1,000 seats at the more intimate Royale.[24] *Grease* was enjoying a long run at the Royale, which would last till 1980.

For success in New York, a positive review in the *New York Times* was important. Here *Don Juan in Hell* "ran head on into Clive Barnes's irrational detestation of Shaw and all his works."[25] As a result, Houseman recalled in 1983, "I had the dubious thrill of seeing my name in lights for a week [three weeks actually] over the marquee of the Palace Theatre on Broadway and the annoyance of receiving one of the worst notices ever given to a production in which I was involved."[26]

Houseman's memory serves him well in this case. Barnes begins his review by admitting that he is "out of joint with current dramatic history," as he does not "regard George Bernard Shaw as one of the great playwrights of this century." As for *Don Juan in Hell*, Barnes thought it "one of Shaw's most tedious exercises," but even he had to admit that "The play is not so bad as it appears to be here. The present version is by John Houseman," he continued, "and although I did not see the Laughton version, even by envisioning the former cast, one senses that it must have been better." Montalban was chided for "monotonous delivery ... whose rise and fall phrasing runs up and down Shaw's drearily antithetical phrases like a child on a roller-coaster"; Paul Henreid's "world-weary Commander" seemed "glazily cynical"; and Edward Mulhare's Devil was "decent but tamed, clubbable but foolish." Moorehead got off lightly: "though Miss Moorehead shows some excitement, it is not always sustained."[27]

William Glover, whose review for the Associated Press was reprinted in small town newspapers across America, characterized this production as "A supercast for gabby discourse about a possible superman, but not exactly superfine." He had only one line for Moorehead, writing that "The veteran actress, who in 1952 initiated the fad for galactic productions of this play..., tackles her role now in the grip of some internal gripe."[28] Internal gripe, indeed. According to Houseman, "During our six months' tour, though she was already under the shadow of the illness that finally destroyed her, she never missed a show or diminished a performance."[29]

In this connection, it is interesting to note that the three male players are listed in the program with a common understudy, Ricardo S. Ramos, while Moorehead has none.[30] As it turns out, Moorehead had an unofficial, secret understudy, even though she didn't want one, and that was the eminent actress and stage devotee Marian Seldes. Houseman, who may have been aware of Moorehead's precarious health, had made sure that Seldes would be able to step in in case Moorehead could not go on, but she was not to know about it. Seldes saw the show in Chicago, but under the circumstances didn't go round afterwards. She never went on for Moorehead as Doña Ana. "She was perfect, she was absolutely perfect," this tireless promoter of the theater recalled in 2007.[31]

CREDITS: *Director:* John Houseman; *Producers:* William J. Griffiths, Lee Orgel; *Writer:* George Bernard Shaw; *Costumes:* Nolan Miller (Moorehead's gown); *Premiere:* August 28, 1972, at the Civic Theatre in Fresno, California

CAST: Paul Henreid (Commander), Ricardo Montalban (Don Juan), Agnes Moorehead (Doña Ana), Edward Mulhare (Devil)

TOURING SCHEDULE: Ahmanson Theatre, The Music Center, Los Angeles (opening September 5, 1972); Shubert Theatre, Chicago; Shubert Theatre, Boston; National Theatre, Washington, D.C.; Shubert Theatre, Cincinnati; Forrest Theatre, Philadelphia; Nixon Theatre, Pittsburgh; Playhouse, Wilmington; O'Keefe Centre, Toronto; Palace Theatre, New York (closing February 4, 1973)

25

Gigi (Stage, 1973–74)

The embrace of *Gigi* by the American entertainment industry is really an oddity, when you consider many Americans' reticence and, Europeans might even say, prudishness about sexual matters. While Americans certainly had their own form of nostalgia about the turn-of-the-last century, it customarily took the form of classic "Americana" like Eugene O'Neill's *Ah, Wilderness!* or Thornton Wilder's *Our Town*. In Colette's novella from 1944 about the French *fin de siècle*, there is no portrayal of clean-living, resolutely Protestant and middle-class families in small, picturesque, rural towns and villages. We encounter instead a multi-generational, matriarchal family of unwed mothers and former courtesans in an emphatically urban and cosmopolitan setting.

Gigi, one reviewer reminded us, "is about a young girl in turn-of-the-century Paris who is groomed by a great aunt and her grandmother to become a high-class courtesan when she grows up. Gaston is a family friend, who suddenly realizes that little Gigi has blossomed into a beautiful woman. He and the family arrange an agreement whereby he would take care of her future whether they stay together or not. Gigi balks at the deal, and eventually Gaston decides he'll even go for marriage."[1] The basic plot remained unchanged through the story's permutations from page to stage, from stage to screen, and back to the stage again, though the five main characters went from Gigi, her mother Andrée Alvar, grandmother Inez Alvarez ("Mamita"), great aunt Alicia, and potential lover Gaston Lachaille to Gigi, Mamita, Aunt Alicia, Gaston, and Gaston's uncle Honoré Lachaille. In addition, Gaston's mistress, Liane d'Exelmans, only mentioned in the novella and stage play, puts in an appearance in the film version and the stage musical.

Maybe it was the foreignness of *Gigi*'s setting that allowed greater leeway for the decadence of "Old World" ways, and a marked tendency to forgive abroad what one might condemn at home. Also, *Gigi*, in all the different forms the story has taken as a favorite figment of the French imagination in Western culture, is genuinely funny. A lot of the comedy is the result of the inversion of conventional values in this world of courtesans and demimondaines, where marriage and mediocrity are frowned upon and where romantic love takes a back seat to "liaisons."

As Judith Thurman explains: "The charm of the tale—and its narrative tension—reside in the incongruity between the thorough and proper 'finishing' that the virginal *jeune fille* receives from her exigent Aunt Alicia, and its aim: to make her into the most desirable and expensive of kept women."[2] Ultimately, though, 16-year-old Gigi, "the century's first teenage girl,"[3] has surprisingly bourgeois ideals and ideas about her future. She turns out emphatically *not* to be the product of her environment, and marriage and domesticity win out over concubinage and materialism. This is a modern romantic comedy after all, not a nineteenth century naturalist novel.

As the papers duly noted at the time, the 1973 stage musical version of *Gigi* was significant for reteaming the long-time collaborators Alan Jay Lerner and Frederick Loewe for the first time since they "broke up" in 1960 after *My Fair Lady* and *Camelot*.[4] Ron Base pointed out that Lerner and Loewe had "teamed together 31 years," longer than Rodgers and Hart or Rodgers and Hammerstein or the Gershwins. Among other "firsts," *Gigi* was "the first musical originally conceived for the screen which reversed the route to the stage."[5]

As already mentioned, *Gigi* was originally conceived during World War II by the iconoclastic French writer Colette. That story inspired a dramatization by another free-spirited woman, Anita Loos, which premiered at the Fulton Theatre in New York on November 24, 1951, with Audrey Hepburn in her Broadway debut as Gigi and veteran British actress Cathleen Nesbitt as Aunt Alicia, Moorehead's future role. Incidentally, *Gigi* ran concurrently in late 1951 with the original Broadway production of *Don Juan in Hell* in which Moorehead starred with Charles Boyer, Charles Laughton, and Sir Cedric Hardwicke. Though not a major hit, the straight play version of *Gigi* ran for twice as many performances as the musical would 22 years later. It has never been revived on Broadway.

In 1958, the multi–Oscar-winning film version directed by Vincente Minnelli appeared with screenplay and lyrics by Alan Jay Lerner and music by Frederick Loewe. Gigi was played by Leslie Caron, who would define the role to such an extent that there has never been a successful portrayal of Gigi since. In the film, Aunt Alicia was played by the hypersophisticated, 67-year-old British actress Isabel Jeans, as her only major American film role in a sporadic screen career that went back to silent films.

From the original novella to the stage musical, Aunt Alicia is basically the same character and serves the same function: she is Gigi's instructor in the skills she will need to be a successful courtesan and a driving force in bringing Gigi and her prospective lover, the millionaire man-about-town Gaston Lachaille, together. Appearing under her full name Alicia Saint-Efflam in Colette's story, she is described as being "seventy years old," a "pretty old lady" with a "cupid's bow mouth," "her robust health concealed by a pretence of delicacy."[6] The role of Aunt Alicia is more modest in the novella than in the later versions of the story. Alicia's "arrival" is elaborately prepared, but she does not make her entrance until halfway through the story with the scene of instruction on eating ortolans and the contents of her jewel case ("a lesson in gemology," as Thurman calls it[7]). The important negotiation scene with Gaston, which became the basis for Alicia's big number "The Contract" in the stage musical, here takes place between Gigi's grandmother Mamita and Gaston instead.

Anita Loos's play version, which hews closely to the original, especially in the first act, contains a description of Alicia as "seventy years old—dainty as porcelain, but with a robust health, which she hides under affectations of frailty."[8] Alicia's part has been considerably built up at Mamita's expense: here Alicia is the one who brings news of Liane's attempted suicide; Alicia stops Gaston from taking Gigi out to a restaurant, because it might tarnish her reputation; and last but not least, Alicia conducts the "negotiation" with Gaston; all of which Mamita did in the novella. A future meeting with their respective lawyers is mentioned,[9] providing an impetus for "The Contract," probably the most successful part of the 1973 stage musical.

Mamita got her own back in the film, where the inimitable Hermione Gingold rekindles an old romance with Maurice Chevalier's Honoré Lachaille and sings the now classic duet "I Remember It Well." In the film version, the "Pygmalion" aspects of Aunt Alicia's role are heightened, as Gigi undergoes what we today would call an extreme make-over. The obligatory scene with the ortolans and the jewels is there ("Without a knowledge of jewelry a woman is lost"), but also lessons in deportment and table manners ("Bad table manners, my dear Gigi, have broken up more households than infidelity"). Alicia doesn't have any songs here, though, and doesn't get to go to fashionable Trouville with Mamita and Gigi, nor does she enter into any negotiations with Gaston.

Moorehead was canny enough to realize that Aunt Alicia was a perfect role for her and may even have seen *Gigi* on Broadway in 1951–52. She would have been sure to have seen the film, which was a major critical and popular success and won every one of the nine Oscars it was nominated for, including Best Picture and Best Director. In the many years since the 1958 film, Moorehead had not forgotten this character. According to journalist Pericles Alexander, she had said she wanted to play Aunt Alicia long before there was talk of making a stage musical out of the film. Alexander recalled just before *Gigi* was to open in St. Louis, that "Agnes Moorehead some five years ago revealed to this amusements writer that she anticipated playing—and singing in 'Gigi,' whenever that wondrously endearing Lerner and Loewe movie musical became a viable stage vehicle." These prophetic words had fallen in a conversation "at a cozy al fresco dinner at Miss Moorehead's Beverly Hills home." Alexander recalled her "keen affection for 'Gigi' and the role of Aunt Alicia: It was a role worth waiting for."[10]

Despite her many chameleon roles, where she was hidden behind more or less grotesque costumes, wigs, and make-up, Moorehead relished this kind of stylish, sophisticated, and physically attractive role. As such, Aunt Alicia was a great follow-up to Endora, sharing with her an anti-conventional attitude to sex and marriage, a healthy love of luxury, an unflinching belief in the rightness of her own viewpoint, and an unremitting need to meddle in her family members' affairs. A year after *Bewitched* had come to an end, what Moorehead's fans and admirers wanted was to spend some quality time "live" with Endora. Aunt Alicia might well have been Endora's witch ancestress or, more likely, one of her former incarnations. A friend of a friend wrote to Moorehead after seeing the show in Los Angeles: "Your incisive diction, your superb body movement and, especially, your hands—all contributed to a captivating characterization. It was such a pleasure seeing you in the beautiful gowns and in a witty part. Your heart would have been warmed by the favorable and loving comments made by the audience."[11]

Aunt Alicia also harkened back to a glamorous film role Moorehead had dearly loved. In *Gigi*, it was as if she was playing Baroness Aspasia Conti in old age. After all, didn't Aspasia go back home to lead a quiet life in Paris? Back in 1944, Moorehead had lobbied for the second lead in *Mrs. Parkington*. Nearly 30 years later, she did the same with *Gigi*, getting in direct contact with the founder and director of the San Francisco Light Opera, Edwin Lester, who had commissioned the musical and was co-producing it with Arnold Saint-Subber. In mid–February 1973, Lester wrote to her: "I am in the unusual position of having a lot of people to please beside myself. Were I operating as I normally do, I would be busy wooing you to play Aunt Alicia in *Gigi*. At this point, none of us are in agreement about anybody." He added that she was his first choice.[12] To the

Los Angeles Times, he explained that "The trouble was finding an actress who was old enough to have Alicia's authority and yet glamorous enough to be believable as an aging courtesan."[13]

Lester got his wish. A month after his letter to Moorehead, the *Pasadena Star-News* reported that she would "portray Aunt Alicia, an elegant, imperious courtesan whose earlier beauty and guile had established her as the mistress of numerous royal admirers. As Aunt Alicia, Miss Moorehead will sing and dance."[14] Moorehead was in England at the time, filming *Frankenstein: The True Story*. After a performance of her one-woman show at a festival in Jacksonville, Florida, on April 7, 1973, she returned to Los Angeles and was ready to start rehearsals.[15]

So what did Moorehead actually do in *Gigi*? What would we have seen and heard had we been in the audience at the Uris Theatre during the two months she played the role on Broadway? Moorehead played the role for eight months in total, but the script kept changing. I want to give you the final version, as seen in New York between the premiere at the Uris on November 13, 1973, and Moorehead being forced to leave the show in January 1974.

Our first meeting with Aunt Alicia is basically the same in Colette's novella, Anita Loos's play, Vincente Minelli's film, and the stage musical. In Act 1, Scene 3, Gigi goes to visit her great aunt in her elegant Paris apartment, so different from Gigi's modest and chaotic yet comfortable home with her mother and Mamita. What ensues is the scene of instruction about gemstones and other matters of importance, before Alicia and Gigi go down to have ortolans for dinner. Many lines are taken directly from the novella and some from the film, relating to such matters as why Gigi needs to avoid "ordinary people"; why women in their family instead of getting married "at once" sometimes get married "at last"; the misidentification by Gigi of "a yellow diamond of the finest quality" as a topaz ("A topaz amongst my jewels!"); why "Great kings do not give very large stones"; and the need to avoid opals, because they are bad luck.[16]

Alicia next appears in Act 1, Scene 5, which transpires early in the afternoon of the following day and is also set in her apartment. Alicia is instructing Gigi in how to offer a man a cigar, when she receives the news over the phone that Gaston Lachaille (Daniel Massey) has broken up with his mistress Liane d'Exelmans (Sandahl Bergman), after he has discovered she is seeing another man. Liane has tried to kill herself. Alicia scoffs that this is the fifth time and when Gigi asks how she did it, replies famously: "Oh, the usual way. Insufficient poison." This is a split scene with Gaston's uncle, Honoré Lachaille (Alfred Drake), on the other side of the stage getting his hair trimmed by his valet Manuel (Truman Gaige), when Gaston shows up to gripe about Liane's infidelity.

Act 1, Scene 7 (divided into 7A and 7B in the script) is a development of the film's Trouville interlude and takes place first in the lobby of the fashionable Grand Hotel and then on the beach in this "plush, seaside resort." Amusingly the stage directions say: "The period is (Hopefully) Golden Age Oliver Smith and it had better get a hand." In the film, Aunt Alicia didn't get to go to Trouville at all, but here we have her arriving with great fanfare, as five dancers-cum-porters struggle with her excessive luggage. She demands her usual suite of rooms and masseur and is annoyed that the suite is already occupied by Russian aristocrats ("a contradiction in terms") and that the masseur died last week ("How inconsiderate! Did you tell her I was coming?"). Alicia is surprised to find that her sister Mamita is there with Gigi. Later, after Gigi has sung "I Never Want to Go Home Again," Alicia and Mamita observe Gaston and Gigi together and realize that Gigi may be his new potential paramour. Alicia tells her sister that they "must at least try to save this child from following you and her mother into an unromantic, semi-precious oblivion" and gets the final line of Act 1 when she concludes: "From now on, it's work, work, work; lessons, lessons, lessons!"

Act 2, Scene 3 is "The Contract," a ten-minute tour de force of a song covering nine pages of the *Gigi* script. In "The Contract," Aunt Alicia and Gaston Lachaille's lawyer, Maître Du Fresne (George Gaynes), negotiate the terms that will secure Gigi's financial future in return for her companionship and sexual favors, while Mamita makes disapproving and ultimately futile interjections ("Alicia, *please*!") and Alicia's lawyer, Maître Duclos (John Dorrin), is entirely sidelined. "The Contract" is the theme song, if you will, of the alternative scale of values in *Gigi*. It was the one musical number that was consistently praised by the critics. According to UPI reviewer Dustin Harvey, it "proved Lerner and Loewe haven't lost their musical touch."[17] Clive Barnes of the *New York Times* concurred in a review that on the whole may not be described as a rave: "The outstanding new number is 'The Contract'.... It is this number that points up both the daring dexterity of Mr. Lerner as a lyricist ... and the musical imagination of Mr. Loewe."[18] Shirley Eder, admittedly a good friend of Moorehead's, wrote ecstatically in the *Detroit Free Press*: "'Bewitching' Agnes Moorehead is simply fantastic acting, singing and dancing in a number in 'Gigi' called 'The Contract.' She's too much! Matter of fact, 'The Contract' is one of the best staged numbers I've seen in any musical."[19] Douglas Watts from the *New York Daily News* appears to have been the only critic not to like this number, observing that "This extra emphasis on the business arrangements, clear enough in the film, seems a bit out of place."[20]

Act 2, Scene 6 is the scene in which Alicia is appalled that Gigi "doesn't want to" after all her efforts on her behalf and blames Mamita, uttering the immortal put-down: "You are a fool; your daughter is a bigger fool; and your granddaughter is the triumphant disaster of the clan. Somehow she has managed to go from puberty to senility without a stop on the way." Much to her surprise, right after Alicia has told Mamita that Gaston will never come back, he calls Gigi. Gigi sings "In This Wide, Wide World" to him over the phone and they are reconciled, giving the musical its requisite, albeit abrupt, happy ending. Aunt Alicia has the last word yet again: "That sweet child! I never lost faith in her."

From San Francisco to New York, Moorehead's performance was lauded by the critics. She must have been aware of this, though she put on a pretense of not reading reviews. She wrote to a friend in late May 1973, that "*Variety* was very kind to me I'm told."[21] Indeed, they were:

> Miss Moorehead, as Aunt Alicia, steals the show, from her vitriolic comment, delivered staccato as only Miss Moorehead can do, "Gigi has gone from puberty to senility without making a stop along the way," to taking full charge of an 11-minute vignette in the second act. This vignette, called simply "The Contract" in the program, summarizes the genius of Lerner & Loewe. It's not only a verbal jungle gym, but it is a total story within itself, this single number being worth the price of admission.[22]

Variety's critic wasn't the only one who felt that "Agnes Moorehead stole the show as Aunt Alicia."[23] Here is a smattering of critics' comments about her: "gives life to the production whenever she is on stage" (*Hollywood Reporter*); "played the part of the haughty harridan harried by the hassles of the haute monde hilariously" (*Van Nuys Valley News*); "by far the outstanding performer in this production" (columnist Jay Stanley); "a patrician of the modern theatre" (*Windsor Star*); "tartly amusing" (*Time*); "most winning" (UPI).[24]

Sometimes the less adulatory descriptions are more interesting. A reviewer in San

Francisco wrote: "Agnes Moorehead was a stately, occasionally arch set-piece of a determined Aunt Alicia, her determination largely expressed through stiffly held arms and torso."[25] Lynn Slotkin, reviewing the show in Toronto, had this thoughtful analysis:

> Agnes Moorehead as Aunt Alicia is a master of timing, the withering look (which almost always gets a laugh) and the scowl. She is not, however, a master of the understatement (in this instance anyway) and in *Gigi* it's vital. She ... has some of the best lines, yet Miss Moorehead tends to overproject on their delivery, and therefore, they miss the mark; the laugh just doesn't come. The lines will speak for itself, all one has to do is let it, understate it.[26]

But, then, what is it Aunt Alicia says again? "Only those who have no taste at all—understate—understate."

Despite its many merits, including Agnes Moorehead's personal triumph as Aunt Alicia, the lingering impression is that the 1973 stage musical version of *Gigi* was not a success. An analysis of everything that was wrong with the show can't help but sound like a litany of ills. There was certainly no lack of diagnoses of what ailed it. "The problems derive from the book itself," wrote one critic.[27] "The ensembles ... are overlong," wrote another.[28] UPI critic Dustin Harvey faulted the distracting "secondary love plot" between Honoré Lachaille and Mamita, the "talky first act," and "the play's abrupt, flat ending."[29] Rick Talcove pointed out after the world premiere in San Francisco, that "the show abounds in script and technical difficulties that are simply too glaring to overlook; mistakes that should have been corrected the first week of performances."[30] Dan Sullivan of the *Los Angeles Times* concluded that "'Gigi' on the whole lacks soul."[31]

On a more superficial level, there was no lack of derogatory descriptions, alliterative labels, and backhanded compliments either. The show was variously described during its five-month, pre–Broadway tour and after the New York opening on November 13, 1973, as "a French charmer looking a little tattered by the journey from film to stage"; "a frothy 1950s effort somewhat out of place in the '70s, with little artistic reason for existence"; "overlong, slow, repetitious, and hopelessly mired in the '50s in terms of staging and style"; "curiously unconvincing"; "a delight, even in its present unpolished state"; "a million-dollar show that has everything but charm"; and "a gorgeous flower without fragrance."[32] Jeanne Miller of the *San Francisco Examiner* concluded tersely after the world premiere in her hometown on May 15, 1973: "at this point, it simply isn't ready."[33]

Not that the show didn't have its adherents. The critic for *Variety*, who we have already seen lauding Moorehead's efforts, was optimistic, saying that *Gigi* "will probably be the smash of the year."[34] "Probably" being the operative word. Ron Base reported exuberantly that "The big, gay, fantasy, no-messages-thanks, check-your-worries-at-the-box-office musical was back and the audience lapped it up."[35] The critic for the Associated Press called *Gigi* "a musical now of dazzling enchantment: All the things that create super entertainment, from story to scenery, from melody to cast, are felicitously united in the production."[36] The AP review was reprinted in small town newspapers across America, but most smalltowners would not be buying tickets.

To return to the bad news: part of the problem may have been 44-year-old director Joseph Hardy. Hardy had helmed a revival of *The Sound of Music* for the San Francisco Civic Light Opera the previous season and had six Broadway shows under his belt, though the first and last of these had actually closed after one performance.[37] When asked by the *Oakland Tribune* in mid–March 1973, a few weeks before rehearsals started, if *Gigi* would be a "great big production," Hardy responded: "No, not one with a lot of people because the play is rather intimate, just five people. But it will be lovely to look at. It's set in a beautiful period, and the detailing will be exquisite." Lerner and Loewe had prepared a new musical score for the stage production with six new songs, which Hardy described as "delicious." The major songs from the movie would be retained.[38]

By all accounts, *Gigi* was not director Hardy's proudest hour. Few critics had anything positive to say about his efforts. The UPI critic called his direction "lackluster"[39] after the San Francisco opening. By the time the show got to New York, he could go so far as to say that the direction was "fluid most of the time."[40] Jay Stanley observed: "It would seem that this production was directed all on one level having neither highs or lows, but started in the middle and remains there throughout the presentation."[41] The AP critic wrote: "The company is spectacularly exciting under Joseph Hardy's subtly paced direction."[42] "Subtly paced" was not exactly as rousing endorsement. *Newsweek*'s review was damning: "Its production standards are simply not classical Broadway standards.... Performers like Agnes Moorehead, Maria Karnilova and Daniel Massey are simply let down by a dull continuity and flat direction."[43]

According to columnist Shirley Eder, by the time the *Gigi* company got to St. Louis, the third stop on their pre–Broadway tour, Alan Jay Lerner and choreographer Onna White had taken over the directing duties from Hardy, who "took on another assignment and could not travel with this show to work out all the new things which will be added before it goes into the Uris Theater on Broadway."[44] Lerner and Loewe said openly that they expected to "keep working on the play prior to its arrival in New York."[45] In fact, the pre–Broadway tour turned into a kind of extended rehearsal period. Moorehead wrote to her friend Georgia Johnstone in mid–October 1973, as they were about to travel from Detroit to Toronto: "It's been madness! Changes + rehearsal every day—and we've been out over 5 months."[46] Script changes were still being made during the New York previews. The last new pages of changes in Moorehead's script are dated November 11, 1973, just two days before the New York premiere.[47]

Veteran critic Walter Kerr put his finger on one central problem with *Gigi* as a stage musical. Librettist Lerner, he wrote, "seems to have forgotten how to tell the story, perhaps because he has become so used to it."[48] Thus he faulted the "book," which didn't create a clear enough storyline to bind the various songs and production numbers together. "Gigi herself is a bit lost in the shuffle," he said, as too much time was spent getting rid of Gaston's former lover Liane, leaving the audience wondering when the story was going to start.[49]

Then there were technical problems. Hardy and White had aimed to recreate some of the fluidity of the film version on stage. As the director explained:

> What we're doing, choreographer Onna White and I, is moving the show as well as we possibly can. In a movie you can cut from one scene to another, but of course on the stage you need some transition. In this day and age, with the equipment available, we can move quickly. We're not using turntables, but one thing revolutionary is that our sets can break apart and move diagonally, as well as horizontally and vertically. One set can be moving in while another is moving out.[50]

This concept resulted in 13 sets that changed no less than 26 times.[51] According to one reviewer, there was "More scenery than Switzerland."[52]

From a purely aesthetic standpoint, the sets met with approval. AP critic Williams Glover observed: "The settings by Oliver Smith give everything a touch of Renoir glamor and long-ago extravagance rarely dared by today's production budgets."[53] The reviewer for UPI found *Gigi* "a stunning show to look at."[54] According to Ron Base in the *Detroit*

Sunday Sun: "The scenery was ersatz Toulouse-Lautrec swinging in and out of place onstage with a precision that was breathtaking. It was all larger than life, sumptuously garish."[55] Yet the precision wasn't always breathtaking. Rick Talcove complained that "The technical difficulties—stuck curtains, hard to move scenery, ties falling off—are simply inexcusable at Music Center prices."[56]

In this connection, dancer Russ Beasley relates an amusing story:

> Agnes Moorehead's first appearance on stage was on a settee or divan that tracked on into her boudoir or apartment—I can't remember which exactly, and involved quite a big scene change, as *Gigi* was one of the first big shows to use electronically controlled winches rather than having stage hands pushing a lot of scenery around (if memory serves me). One evening, there was a slight malfunction that caused a delay both in her arrival and with the set change and when she finally arrived to much applause and the set pieces had finally settled in place, she looked out into the audience and said: "Bewitching, Isn't it?" and brought down the house.

"This was at the Uris in NYC, which is now called the Gershwin, where the production *Wicked* is playing."[57]

Speaking of dancers: opinions on choreographer Onna White's efforts were divided, being variously described as "a champagne bubbly assortment of delights,"[58] "pedestrian"[59] and "not overwhelming."[60] Shirley Eder thought the choreography was "superb," but meant that "The lighting leaves a lot to be desired."[61]

Gigi wasn't all bad. As we've already seen, Moorehead was a major asset to the show. Lerner's secretary, Judy Insel, recalled: "We had a lot of Broadway stars in *Gigi*, but Agnes was the big draw. Everybody knew her from *Bewitched*, & the crowd at the stage door was generally there to see her. Especially out-of-town before we got to NYC."[62] The rest of the cast surrounding Gigi was also strong. According to Richard Styles: "It is worth seeing not so much for the music as for the captivating smoothness of troupers Drake and Moorehead, who can still deliver the most subtly telling lines with flawless timing, for the spirit and charm of Karnilova, and for the class and style with which Daniel Massey plays Gaston."[63] "As things now stand, the production's strong points are all of Oliver Messel's colorful costumes, most of Oliver Smith's beautiful sets, and the engaging performances of Alfred Drake and Agnes Moorehead, plus those famous songs," wrote Rick Talcove in the *Van Nuys Valley News*.[64] He felt compelled to add that "The low points are Joseph Hardy's wooden direction, Onna White's uninspired choreography and the bad handling of Terese Stevens and Daniel Massey, not to mention the almost total neglect of wonderful Maria Karnilova."[65]

Naturally, the review in the *New York Times* counted the most. Ten months after he'd panned *Don Juan in Hell*, Clive Barnes characterized *Gigi* as "enormously charming, but … a little long-winded." "That the show for all its incidental sparkle, never quite takes off," he considered "partly a matter of changing tastes, but also seems due to a staging by Joseph Hardy … that lacks vitality. The dances by Onna White proved pallid, and even the normally admirable Oliver Smith (scenery) and Oliver Messel (costumes) seem unduly subdued except in an enchanting scene in Maxim's."[66] Barnes thought both Karnilova and Moorehead were "perfect."[67]

On the negative side, then, we have noted poor direction, lackluster choreography, technical problems with the sets, and last but not least, problems with Lerner's book, including too much emphasis on the Gaston-Liane subplot and a too abrupt ending. The final and decisive weakness in the production was that they never found the right girl to play Gigi.

The cast of *Gigi* from left: Alfred Drake (Honoré Lachaille), Agnes Morehead (Aunt Alicia), Teresé Stevens (Gigi), Maria Karnilova (Mamita), and Daniel Massey (Gaston Lachaille). So much talent, so much experience, but somehow the show never quite came together. Teresé Stevens, a young British actress, turned out to be miscast, and was replaced by Karin Wolfe during the Los Angeles run.

The first Gigi to be cast, Teresé Stevens, was "a 19-year-old English singer who was spotted by Katharine Hepburn in London in a rock version of 'Carmen.'" "Miss Stevens has never before appeared in this country," wrote columnist Robert Taylor, "but she's been singing since she was 11":

> While entertaining in a restaurant run by a friend of her father's, she came to the attention of agent Sandy Lloyd, who discovered Shirley Bassey and Shani Wallis. Since then she has appeared at the Palladium, made several records, appeared on most major English television variety shows, and starred

> in a stage production of "The L-Shaped Room." "We were beginning to despair," said Edwin Lester, the Civic Light Opera's director. "The part was most difficult to cast because so few girls in their late teens have the experience required for the role. Gigi must sing, dance and act and still be able to project the vivacity and innocence of a 16-year-old. Terese, at 19, already has a wealth of experience."[68]

One imagines, though, that Stevens didn't have "a wealth of experience" with getting panned by the critics. Dustin Harvey put it plainly in his UPI review after the San Francisco premiere: "Miss Stevens, 20, displayed a gamin charm, a throaty-voiced singing talent, almost no dancing ability and little stage presence. She wasn't helped at all by Onna White's pedestrian choreography and Joseph Hardy's lackluster direction."[69] Richard Styles was even more critical, calling Stevens "the show's biggest disappointment." She "simply does not have the class or experience to fit in with her four veteran colleagues," he went on. "She is like A.A. Milne's 'Tigger,' a bit too bouncy."[70] Rick Talcove thought Stevens seemed "ill-at-ease with Gigi: She's mostly made to stand down stage cupping her hands."[71] Jay Stanley found her "only adequate" and thought she probably got the role because she "strongly resembles Leslie Caron."[72] Described as a "junior Ethel Merman,"[73] it was clear to everyone, including Stevens herself, that she had been miscast. A replacement needed to be found.

Enter Karin Wolfe. Wolfe was born in Dallas, Texas, in 1944 and had acted since childhood, getting her first stage role at six and a half in a Paper Mill Playhouse production in New Jersey. Wolfe was 29 when she was asked to replace Teresé Stevens's understudy in San Francisco, after auditioning first for director Joseph Hardy and choreographer Onna White and then for producer Edwin Lester. "I'd been away from the theater for several years," she said in a 1973 interview, "and I didn't realize how much I'd missed it."[74] During those years, Wolfe had worked mostly in television, including spending the last year and half as Mary Anderson, one of the lead characters on *Days of Our Lives*. She took over the lead in *Gigi* after only two weeks as an understudy. "Terry wasn't happy in the role," she said in the interview. "It was a mutual decision for her to leave."[75] *Gigi* was not Wolfe's Broadway debut, as she had played one of the two "sad girls" in the musical *Bye Bye Birdie* at age 16 and even had her own song with Dick Van Dyke called "Put on a Happy Face." Off Broadway, she had starred with Liza Minnelli in *Best Foot Forward* at Stage 73 in 1963 and played the title role in Jo, the musical version of *Little Women*, at the Orpheum Theatre in 1964.[76]

Unfortunately, Wolfe didn't fare much better with the critics than Stevens had. Ron Base felt that she "tended to get lost in the reviews playing with veterans like Alfred Drake as Honore and Agnes Moorehead as Aunt Alicia."[77] Clive Barnes thought "Karin Wolfe was very pretty, with a bright, well-controlled voice—but she did lack individuality."[78] According to Douglas Watt, "The unhappy fact is that neither the Gigi, Karin Wolfe, who seems a competent performer, nor the Gaston, Daniel Massey, an able enough actor, possesses an ounce of charm. And charm is everything here."[79] *Newsweek* quipped: "As the pubescent Gigi, Karin Wolfe is a square loaf of Silvercup, not a seductively elliptical little French bread," Silvercup being a then famous type of American bread made by the Gordon Baking Co. in Long Island City.[80] AP critic William Glover felt that Alfred Drake "almost steals the show from the titular heroine: That assignment is handled competently by Karin Wolfe, even though she's a bit beyond the implied teens."[81] Shirley Eder felt that "Karin Wolfe's American accent needs to sound a little more Continental to mesh with the other major players on the stage."[82] Finally, the UPI critic had a good word for her, writing that Wolfe "experienced but little known here, is a delight as Gigi."[83]

At the end of the day, it is better to be a character actress than an ingénue. There is more of a future in it. While Agnes Moorehead lives on in our popular imagination more than 40 years after her death, where are Teresé Stevens and Karin Wolfe today, I wonder? Well, I actually know where Karin Wolfe is, as I was able to track her down. My search started in January 2007. Working from the assumption that New York actors tend to stay in New York even if they are no longer acting and having been told that Wolfe worked as a waitress in a Greenwich Village restaurant, I checked the phone book and wrote to the two Karin Wolfes I found there: one on the Upper East Side and one in the Village. No response. At the same time, I contacted Actors Equity Association, but they wrote back that Wolfe had no agent listed. I wrote again. Still no response. I let the matter rest for more than four years, while I did other research and followed up other leads. Having become a competent "googler" during that time and with Karin Wolfe having a relatively unusual spelling of both her names, I googled her in May 2011 and discovered that there was a real estate agent called Karin V. Wolfe working in New York City. I shot off an e-mail to Ms. Wolfe and had an answer the following week. Yes, she was *the* Karin Wolfe. Yes, she would be willing to be interviewed.

On my next trip to New York in June 2011, I met Karin Wolfe for lunch at a restaurant on West Houston Street, three blocks south of Washington Square Park. Wolfe proved to be an attractive, thoughtful, and down-to-earth woman, who looked younger than her 67 years. If she was not instantly recognizable to me as Gigi, it was because all the press photos I'd seen were of Teresé Stevens. When I met Wolfe, it was 38 years since she was in *Gigi*, but she remembered the experience vividly.

Karin Wolfe was 29 and had recently played a leading role in the soap opera *Days of Our Lives*, when she took over the title role in *Gigi* with very little rehearsal time or advance preparation. This was only possible because of her extensive stage experience, which included productions both on and off Broadway. Unfortunately, by the time she came onboard it was too late to fix the show, which only had a three-month run on Broadway.

It all started when Wolfe had gone to see the show in San Francisco, because she had friends who were in it.[84] Not long after, a friend called and asked if she wanted to audition to replace Teresé Stevens's understudy. She did and got the job the next day. When the show transferred to Los Angeles, Wolfe asked to be able to sit in on rehearsals at the Ahmanson Theatre and, in her own words, "basically learned the show 'out front.'" She had two understudy rehearsals the second week in Los Angeles and went on for Stevens early in the third week, as she recalled. The stage manager had telephoned the same day to say "You're going on tonight." After that, Wolfe was asked to take over the role permanently and accepted with alacrity. As she remembered it, she was called into producer Ed Lester's office on a Wednesday between shows with the Lerner and Loewe present and offered the role. Stevens ostensibly had laryngitis. She never returned to the show. The official reason for her withdrawal was problems with income tax. Stevens went home to England and Wolfe never heard from her or about her again. As Wolfe remembered her, Stevens was a big-boned actress, not a dancer, whom Hepburn had seen in a rock opera version of *Carmen* and recommended for the role. She was a brunette with a huge voice and as such miscast.

There was panic in the cast when Wolfe had to step in. Agnes Moorehead in particular seemed flustered. Wolfe suspects it was because Moorehead knew she had only had two rehearsals. Yet Wolfe knew what she was doing from the start, even though she "never had a director." Joe Hardy was off at the Guthrie Theatre in Minneapolis doing *Cyrano* with Richard Chamberlain. When he finally returned to Los Angeles and Wolfe met him, he said: "So this is the little wonder child." He had no notes for her, only that she should change her hairstyle from the unbecoming pigtails she was wearing. If she had it all to do over again, she wishes she could have had some help with making the role less American.

Wolfe remembered that in their first scene together, Moorehead had moved her a little from her position so that Wolfe would not upstage her. She was glad to defer to Moorehead. Even though Wolfe was a seasoned actor herself at this point, she had a lot of respect for veteran actors like Moorehead and Alfred Drake. On her first night, Drake and Moorehead had brought her forward to accept the final ovation. It was a nice gesture, she thought. The nicest gesture, though, was when for Christmas Moorehead gave her a small pillow with a white Irish linen sham delicately embroidered with flower detail and a note with the words: "Rest, my dear Gigi, rest!" Wolfe still has the pillow and the note.

Generally, Moorehead remained aloof throughout the run and Wolfe really only saw her when they were working on stage. Her only personal memory was knocking on the door of Moorehead's dressing room to give her a Christmas present, hoping her dresser Dolores would answer. Moorehead answered herself and was not happy to have been awakened.

Moorehead was bone tired and seemed to do everything with great effort. Wolfe only learned later that she was ill. She remembered hearing about Moorehead's death from a friend at CBS. CBS had called to ask for her reaction to Moorehead's passing.

Wolfe felt that by the time she got into the show "It was too late to fix it." Her part had been reduced to cover up for Stevens's failings and the show no longer seemed to be about Gigi, but mostly about Honoré and Gaston Lachaille. The show was "exquisitely beautiful," but the balance was off. Wolfe felt the New York audience had appreciated it, but not the intelligentsia. *Gigi* came about two years before the nostalgia craze and some thought it was nothing new.

Wolfe told me she had been married twice and had lived with someone longer than any of her marriages. Today she is single and lives in New York City and Westchester with her two Collies. She has been working in real estate since 1998. She realized she had to be realistic about her acting career, she said, but is still interested in acting and doing workshops of her friends' plays and things like that.

Wolfe sent me an e-mail about ten days after our meeting, which I want to share. "I must say," she wrote, "it was a little odd returning to my life as it is today after that stroll down memory lane. Not that my life is so bad, it's just not what I thought it would be. But then, I guess I am not alone in that! As I thought back over some of the things you shared with me about Agnes, I was fascinated to learn of her sense of who she was or wasn't; and what she felt she had achieved or not achieved. She was to me and I guess all those around her, the grand lady, the movie star, the woman who had shared space with Orson Welles. I never would have thought she experienced the basic emotions of insecurity and dissatisfaction. Perhaps my naivety at the time and now; or perhaps the recognition that the journey, though individual, is the same for all, isn't it?"[85]

The journey for Moorehead would soon be over. The newspapers reported in mid–January 1974, that she was leaving *Gigi* for a week to get a checkup. Stand-by Louise Kirtland was taking over.[86] When it became clear Moorehead was not returning to the show, her friend Arlene Francis was brought in as Aunt Alicia.[87] Judy Insel recalled that Francis decided to go in an entirely different direction from Moorehead in her performance. She was more fragile, feminine, and nurturing in her relationship with Gigi. "She was very good," Insel said, "she just wasn't Agnes and never could be. There was nothing fragile about Agnes. She looked like she could lift a car!"[88] Francis only had about three weeks as Aunt Alicia, as *Gigi* closed on February 10, 1974.[89] Agnes Robertson Moorehead died on April 30, only three and a half months after leaving the show. She was 73.

CREDITS: *Director:* Joseph Hardy; *Producers:* Edwin Lester, Arnold Saint-Subber; *Book and lyrics:* Alan Jay Lerner (based on a novella by Colette); *Music:* Frederick Loewe; *Choreography:* Onna White; *Scenic production design:* Oliver Smith; *Costume design:* Oliver Messel; *Lighting:* Thomas Skelton; *Premiere:* May 15, 1973, at the Curran Theatre in San Francisco, California

CAST: Sandahl Bergman (Liane d'Exelmans), Howard Chitjian (Maître Duclos), Alfred Drake (Honoré Lachaille), Arlene Francis (Aunt Alicia, replacement), George Gaynes (Maître Du Fresne), Maria Karnilova (Mamita), Louise Kirtland (Aunt Alicia, understudy), Daniel Massey (Gaston Lachaille), Carmen Mathews (Mamita, replacement), Agnes Moorehead (Aunt Alicia), Teresé Stevens (Gigi), Karin Wolfe (Gigi)

TOURING SCHEDULE: Dorothy Chandler Pavilion, The Music Center, Los Angeles (opening July 3, 1973); Municipal Open-Air Theatre, Forest Park, St. Louis; Fisher Theatre, Detroit; O'Keefe Centre, Toronto; Uris Theatre, New York (closing February 10, 1974)

Appendix: Moorehead's Appearances on *Bewitched*

This episode guide only contains the 148 episodes of *Bewitched* in which Moorehead appeared as Endora. The "*What's up?*" section gives a brief summary of what happens in the episode; the "Style guide" focuses on what Endora is wearing or how she looks in the episode; the "Winged words" are spoken by Endora in the episode, unless another speaker is indicated; and the "Day in the life" section focuses on production information or on what was happening in Moorehead's life at the time the episode was being produced or aired. Given the nature of this book, observations are biased towards Endora and her fabulous apparition as an integral part of *Bewitched* during its entire eight-year run.

Season 1

#1.1 "Pilot: I, Darrin, Take This Witch Samantha" (Sept. 17, 1964)

What's up? On their honeymoon, Samantha tells Darrin she is a witch, Endora stops by to try to save her daughter from her mortal marriage, and the newlyweds attend a dinner party hosted by Darrin's fashionable former fiancée, Sheila.

Style guide: Looks awful in an unruly, tired, oversized wig and a nondescript, long nightgown-like dress and wears her favorite gold filigree earrings, as so often on the small and the large screen.

Winged words: "Don't talk to your mother like that. I'll tell you when you're happy."

Day in the life: The pilot episode of *Bewitched* finished taping on December 6, 1963, which was Moorehead's 63rd birthday.[1]

#1.2 "Be It Ever So Mortgaged" (Sept. 24, 1964)

What's up? Darrin and Samantha find their dream home and Samantha and Endora have fun experimenting with how it might look, which does not go unobserved by nosy neighbor Gladys Kravitz.

Style guide: In the opening scene, it's the witch's garb from the pilot with signature gold earrings, which she also wears when she changes into mortal garb for the first time to look at the new house, wearing a medieval style cloth coat with an elaborate diamond brooch in the form of a coat of arms.

Winged words: "Just because you married a human, Samantha, that's no reason to overdo this grubby little housewife role."

Day in the life: The day this episode aired, *Detroit Free Press* gossip columnist Shirley Eder wrote that Moorehead could not play a part in *The Loved One* due to the delay in filming *Hush...Hush, Sweet Charlotte,* where Joan Crawford had just been replaced by Olivia de Havilland.[2]

#1.3 "It Shouldn't Happen to a Dog" (Oct. 1, 1964)

What's up? Samantha turns a sexually aggressive client into a dog.
Style guide: Pops in and out in witch's garb.
Winged words: "I'm not like other people, Samantha, and neither are you."
Day in the life: By the time this episode and three others from the first season finished production on September 11, 1964, Moorehead was back on the set of *Hush...Hush, Sweet Charlotte.*[3]

#1.4 "Mother, Meet What's His Name" (Oct. 8, 1964)

What's up? Samantha receives a neighborly visit from three nosy local ladies, including Gladys Kravitz, and Endora has a disastrous first meeting with her son-in-law Darrin.
Style guide: The black headband and Tina Turner style wig Endora wears for her first meeting with Darrin is never seen again, but the dress shows up in #1.10 "Just One Happy Family."
Winged words: "Typical! Typical! That's a human being for you. Spending most of their lives running around in circles for a series of nothing" (Endora's definition of baseball).
Day in the life: Moorehead may well have taped Endora's cataclysmic first meeting with Darrin on August 27, 1964, as she wore the headband, wig and gown from that scene to the black tie premiere of *Mary Poppins* at Grauman's Chinese Theatre.[4]

#1.5 "Help, Help, Don't Save Me" (Oct. 15, 1964)

What's up? Darrin refuses Samantha's help on the Caldwell Soup advertising campaign that he is struggling with, because he thinks her ideas are generated by witchcraft and he doesn't want to become dependent on it for success in his career.
Style guide: Still stuck in what is sometimes referred to as her "flying suit."
Winged words: "Any man with a wife like you, who spends every night with a can of soup, must be even less than human."
Day in the life: One of four early episodes to finish shooting September 11, 1964.[5]

#1.9 "Witch or Wife" (Nov. 12, 1964)[6]

What's up? With Darrin working at all hours, Endora convinces Samantha to go on a flying trip to Paris and there they run into Larry and Louise Tate.
Style guide: After being stuck in her flying suit for most of the first five episodes, Endora finally finds her mortal style, so to speak, wearing a large picture hat decked out with tulle for lunch at the Parisian bistro and with her hair in an attractive "updo," with bangs and a large "fall" of curls on top, at dinner with the Tates (what I will refer to below as her "Mike Douglas" style, because she has her hair that way in several attractive promotional shots for that talk show).
Winged words: "It's the only way to fly" (the motto of now defunct Western Airlines).
Day in the life: On October 3, 1964, the week this episode was being produced, Moorehead gave a dinner at her home for 40 guests, including Bette Davis, Olivia de Havilland, Joseph Cotten and Patricia Medina, Robert Aldrich, Paul Gregory and Janet Gaynor, Greer Garson and Buddy Fogelson, Hedda Hopper, Charles and Pat Boyer, and Kay Gable.[7]

#1.10 "Just One Happy Family" (Nov. 19, 1964)

What's up? Samantha's father Maurice makes his first visit since her marriage and discovers she has married a mortal, which greatly impacts the crockery and other fixtures of the interior before Darrin and Maurice finally and explosively meet.

Style guide: The black satin and chiffon gown with the shawl collar from Endora's first meeting with Darrin makes a reappearance and the witch wig is the same old.

Winged words: "Well, here we are: just one big, happy family."

Day in the life: The week this aired, Moorehead was at work on #1.17 "A is for Aardvark."[8]

#1.11 "It Takes One to Know One" (Nov. 26, 1964)

What's up? Endora questions Darrin's fidelity and gets an attractive witch cum model to try to lead him astray.

Style guide: Another restaurant lunch with Samantha and the Mike Douglas "fall" is still doing service, as is the large diamond brooch like a coat of arms or shield and her favorite earrings.

Winged words: "Well, well, well, all dressed up and nowhere to go."

Day in the life: Four days before this aired, shooting finally ended on *Hush…Hush, Sweet Charlotte*.[9]

#1.17 "A Is for Aardvark" (Jan. 14, 1965)

What's up? When Darrin twists his ankle and drives Samantha crazy with his demands, she makes the house cooperate with him and he gets to like the change a little too much.

Style guide: Stuck in her witch's nightie and tired old wig throughout.

Winged words: "Well, well, well, it's Adam and the apple all over again."

Day in the life: Ida Lupino directed this episode and this was probably the only time in Moorehead's entire film and TV career that she was directed by a woman.

#1.18 "The Cat's Meow" (Jan. 21, 1965)

What's up? When Darrin has to travel to Chicago at the behest of an attractive female client, Darrin suspects Samantha is keeping an eye on him in the guise of a Siamese cat.

Style guide: Has no reason to change out of her flying suit, as all her scenes are with her daughter.

Winged words: "You forbid me? Oh, isn't that divine!"

Day in the life: Two days before this aired, columnist Dick Kleiner wrote that Moorehead was a "favorite for the supporting Oscar for *Hush…Hush, Sweet Charlotte*" and that she and Bob Aldrich were "a mutual admiration society."[10]

#1.19 "A Nice Little Dinner Party" (Jan. 28, 1965)

What's up? Endora meets Darrin's parents for the first time and Frank Stephens takes quite a shine to her, creating discord with his wife, Phyllis.

Style guide: With her hair swept up, as we've seen all season, she arrives in a luxurious mink wrap over an ornate brocade jacket and matching long skirt to the dinner with Darrin's parents.

Winged words: "You know, I always thought my son-in-law was handsome and now I can see where he gets his good looks."

Day in the life: Moorehead's celebrated her 64th birthday on Sunday, December 6, 1964, just as production on this episode was underway.[11]

#1.20 "Your Witch Is Showing" (Feb. 4, 1965)

What's up? Darrin suspects, wrongly as it turns out, that the shady young assistant who is upstaging him at work is a warlock planted by Endora.

Style guide: Wears three different cloth coats and the leopard print is the nicest.

Winged words: "You really mean to set yourself against me?"

Day in the life: Taping on this episode was scheduled to end on December 16, 1964, but additional scenes were taped on January 5, 1965, together with #1.22 "Eye of the Beholder."[12]

#1.22 "Eye of the Beholder" (Feb. 25, 1965)

What's up? When Endora plants a picture of Samantha as the "Maid of Salem" dated 1682, it raises a range of anxieties in Darrin's mind about how old Samantha really is and how they are aging at a different rate and Endora doesn't make matters better by giving him the internal frailties and habits of an old man.

Style guide: As chic as ever in a two-piece, wool suit, her hair piled high, in the antique store overture.

Winged words: "So it's come to that. You forsake your mother for a mere mortal."

Day in the life: Two days after this aired, on Saturday, February 27, 1965, Moorehead hosted a wedding celebration at her home for her friend and long-time producer Paul Gregory and Janet Gaynor, who had married on Christmas Eve, 1964.[13]

#1.23 "Red Light, Green Light" (March 4, 1965)

What's up? Samantha and Endora have fun using both mortal and magical means to get a traffic light at a busy intersection on Morning Glory Circle, while Gladys Kravitz keeps "seeing things" that are gone by the time her husband, Abner, gets there.

Style guide: Witch's gear for her scenes with Samantha and mortal clothing for her appearance at the rally.

Winged words: "Oh, Samantha, you do have an annoying way of putting a damper on my *divertissements*."

Day in the life: This episode finished shooting on New Year's Eve 1964. Moorehead was invited to a celebration at the home of Dr. Donn Beeman and Mr. Julio Alvarez at 505 Monterey Rd. in Palm Springs.[14]

#1.24 "Which Witch Is Which?" (March 11, 1965)

What's up? Endora doubles for Samantha at a dress fitting while the latter is doing the marketing and ends up meeting a best-selling author, who just happens to be an old friend of Darrin's.

Style guide: Spends most of the episode as Samantha with only the eye make-up (and voice quality) to give her away.

Winged words: "It might be interesting to see how the other half amuse themselves."

Day in the life: On January 15, 1965, while this episode was in production, the Golden Globe nominations were announced. Moorehead was nominated and later won the award for Best Supporting Actress for *Hush…Hush, Sweet Charlotte*.[15]

#1.26 "Driving Is the Only Way to Fly" (March 25, 1965)

What's up? Samantha tries to learn to drive from nervous nelly Harold Harold, as Endora pops in and out of the back seat of the car.

Style guide: Isn't in this long enough to change out of her witch costume.

Winged words: "He *is* high strung, isn't he?"

Day in the life: The day this episode aired, Moorhead finished taping her scenes for #1.33 "A Change of Face" on Stage #4 at Columbia Studios.[16]

#1.28 "Open the Door, Witchcraft" (April 8, 1965)

What's up? The Stephens are forced to install an automatic garage door, when Gladys Kravitz sees Samantha twitch it open.

Style guide: Pops in and out in her flying suit.

Winged words: "If I were starved for entertainment, I certainly could come up with something more amusing than that."

Day in the life: The day this episode finished production, Moorehead received a "Celebrity Key" to the New York Playboy Club at 5 E. 59th St. in New York.[17]

#1.30 "George the Warlock" (April 22, 1965)

What's up? Endora encourages George the Warlock to throw a spanner into her daughter's marital works, but he ends up being more attracted to the Stephens's young, unmarried next door neighbor and wannabe model, Danger O'Riley.

Style guide: The two-piece suit she wears for the showdown with Darrin has a floral pattern rather like wallpaper.

Winged words: "You have personally set back the mother-in-law business 200 years!" (Darrin).

Day in the life: At 8 p.m. on the Saturday this episode wrapped, which was April 3, 1965, Moorehead was invited to dinner at the Jimmy Stewarts.[18]

#1.33 "A Change of Face" (May 13, 1965)

What's up? Endora and Samantha have fun changing Darrin's face while he's asleep, bringing out all his insecurities when he wakes up and discovers what they've done.

Style guide: Still having a bad hair day in the big, curly witch wig from the pilot.

Winged words: "What a lovely looking couple except for him."

Day in the life: The week after this aired, taping began on Season 2 with #2.1 "Alias Darren Stephens."[19]

#1.34 "Remember the Main" (May 20, 1965)

What's up? Samantha and Endora collaborate to unmask a corrupt councilman, who is too shrewd to be foiled by conventional methods.

Style guide: Still favors wool suits for mortal dress and the big coat of arms diamond pin makes a reappearance.

Winged words: "What was that incantation you were gyrating through?"

Day in the life: This episode was scheduled to finish production February 1, 1965, but an additional scene with Samantha and Endora in corrupt councilman John C. Cavanaugh's office had to be shot on Thursday, April 8, together with scenes from the season finale "Bewitched: Cousin Edgar."[20]

#1.35 "Eat at Mario's" (May 27, 1965)

What's up? Samantha and Endora wreak havoc with Darrin's advertising campaign for a pizza manufacturer when they take out a full-page ad and manipulate a TV broadcast to support their favorite Italian restaurant Mario's, so they have to give Darrin's client some magical publicity as well to save Darrin's reputation.

Style guide: Looking posh in a different cloth coat with a large fur collar than we saw her don for shopping with Samantha in #1.24 "Which Witch Is Which?"

Winged words: "This is the best Italian food I've had this century."
Day in the life: Four days after this aired, Moorehead started rehearsals in Dallas for a production of *High Spirits*, the musical version of Noël Coward's comedy *Blithe Spirit*, in which she played Madame Arcati.[21]

#1.36 "Cousin Edgar" (June 3, 1965)

What's up? Samantha's impish yet bashful elf cousin Edgar comes to visit and plays a series of pranks on Darrin, whom he's jealous of.
Style guide: In her traditional witch's garb for her brief appearance.
Winged words: "A witch who is on the wagon is no match for an elf who is on the war path."
Day in the life: The reading and first rehearsal for this episode was held in the Screen Gems board room on April 5, 1965. That evening Moorehead attended the 37th Annual Academy Awards hosted by Bob Hope in the Santa Monica Civic Auditorium and lost the Best Supporting Actress Oscar to Lily Kedrova for *Zorba the Greek*. Moorehead had been nominated for her performance in *Hush…Hush, Sweet Charlotte*. After the ceremonies, she and her escort, make-up man Tony Lloyd, went to the Governors Ball in the International Ballroom of the Beverly Hilton. She wore the Mike Douglas "updo" and her mink stole from episode #1.19 "A Nice Little Dinner Party."[22]

Season 2

#2.1 "Alias Darrin Stephens" (Sept. 18, 1965)

What's up? On the Darrin and Samantha's first wedding anniversary, Aunt Clara mistakenly turns Darrin into a chimpanzee and the next day Samantha finds out she is pregnant.
Style guide: Starts off the new season wearing her favorite earrings both with and without the pearl attachment.
Winged words: "He's probably hanging around here somewhere."
Day in the life: When this season premiere aired, Moorehead had just finished taping #2.13 "My Boss, the Teddy Bear." Production on the series wouldn't resume until December due to Elizabeth Montgomery's maternity leave.[23]

#2.2 "A Very Special Delivery" (Sept. 23, 1965)

What's up? Endora is pleased despite herself to discover she is going to be a grandmother and makes Darrin feel all the symptoms of a pregnant woman when he doesn't treat Samantha right, including mood swings, exhaustion, back ache, and a sudden urge for certain kinds of food.
Style guide: From traditional flying suit to mortal garb, more specifically the "updo" with the fall she used in the *Mike Douglas Show* publicity shots and a striped blue cotton dress with short sleeves and later a beautiful brown two-piece suit (in the colorized version).
Winged words: "That's right! That's right! Twist the knife."
Day in the life: The day this episode aired, Alice Pearce sent Moorehead a postcard from Hawaii to tell her that her husband, Paul Davis, had given her two weeks on Maui as an anniversary present and that she was going to be in the film *The Glass Bottom Boat*.[24]

#2.4 "My Grandson, the Warlock" (Oct. 7, 1965)

What's up? Maurice thinks the Tates' newborn baby is his grandson and abducts him, because he fears he won't be raised right.

Style guide: "Mike Douglas" style hair and a purple wool cape for Endora's brief scenes helping to look for the baby.

Winged words: "You know your father. Always looking for fun places."

Day in the life. On the day this aired, Moorehead was invited by Shirley Temple to be a guest star at the opening of the 9th Annual San Francisco Film Festival on Oct. 21.[25] She couldn't go, as she was shooting *The Singing Nun* that day.[26]

#2.5 "The Joker Is a Card" (Oct. 14, 1965)

What's up? Uncle Arthur comes to visit and plays a series of practical jokes on Darrin and the others until he is hoist by his own petard.

Style guide: Endora has taken a leaf out of Scarlett O'Hara's book and is wearing a green, flouncy curtain in the dinner party scene.

Winged words: "Be careful, Tinkerbell."

Day in the life: Production on this episode ended July 16, 1965. That day Moorehead was a guest on *Celebrity Game* with Bob Newhart, Allan Sherman, Abby Dalton, Stephen Boyd, Mel Brooks, Jayne Meadows, Steve Allen, Raymond Massey, and host Carl Reiner. The show aired August 2, 1965.[27]

#2.7 "Trick or Treat" (Oct. 28, 1965)

What's up? When Samantha refuses to go to the Sacred Volcano on Halloween, Endora turns herself back into a child and casts a spell on Darrin so he turns into a werewolf.

Style guide: In the scene in Darrin's office, she wears an attractive robin blue cloth coat with large buttons that perfectly matches her eye shadow (at least in the colorized version) and later a gown with a large rose in the cleavage, that a fellow dinner guest mistakes for a Halloween costume.

Winged words: "This is the black day for us, Samantha. This is Halloween."

Day in the life: This episode was produced April 26–29, 1965.[28]

#2.9 And Then I Wrote" (Nov. 11, 1965)

What's up? When Samantha gets stuck having to write the script for a Civil War pageant, her characters come to life and Gladys Kravitz seeks out a psychiatrist after running into them.

Style guide: In the colorized version, her raspberry red gown clashes terribly with the orange bead necklaces, not to mention her signature red hair, still in the Mike Douglas style.

Winged words: "Do you realize the war might take longer to write than it did to fight?"

Day in the life: Two days after this aired, Moorehead attended the Imperial WAIF Ball in honor of Princess Margaret and the Earl of Snowdon at the Hollywood Palladium.[29]

#2.10 "Junior Executive" (Nov. 18, 1965)

What's up? Samantha is curious about what Darrin looked like as a boy and Endora turns him back into one, so they can find out.

Style guide: The big witch wig from the pilot is still in use.

Winged words: "Ambitious little rascal, isn't he? I'd say he'd grow up to be president, if I didn't know better."

Day in the life: Moorehead completed her short scene in the opening before she went off to play Madame Arcati in the musical version of Noël Coward's *Blithe Spirit*, called *High Spirits*, for two weeks at the Dallas State Fair in June 1965.[30]

#2.11 "Aunt Clara's Old Flame" (Nov. 25, 1965)

What's up? Despite her initial reluctance, Aunt Clara is reunited with an old beau, warlock Hedley Partridge, and in that connection Gladys Kravitz is exposed to more witchcraft.

Style guide: Get a load of that gorgeous old rose outfit Endora wears as she plays the fiddle for Aunt Clara and Hedley to dance to.

Winged words: "Endora, haven't you a house to haunt or something?" (Aunt Clara).

Day in the life: At the time this episode was in production in early August 1965, Moorehead published an article in *Guideposts* magazine titled "My Favorite Script" about her faith and hard times as an actress in Depression era New York."[31]

#2.13 "My Boss, the Teddy Bear" (Dec. 9, 1965)

What's up? Darrin thinks Endora has turned Larry Tate into a teddy bear, because he's prevented Samantha from going to a family wedding.

Style guide: The sea green brocade suit with braiding looks a bit like a luxuriously upholstered sofa, albeit a slim and trim sofa.

Winged words: "You know the trouble with your mother? She's here today and here tomorrow" (Darrin).

Day in the life: While this episode was being recorded in the second week of September 1965, Moorehead's maid Freddie Logan Jones was visiting family and friends in the South.[32]

#2.14 "Speak the Truth" (Dec. 16, 1965)

What's up? Endora secretly gives Darrin a little "truth god" statue that makes everyone who gets near it speak the truth, which creates complications at a dinner party for a client.

Style guide: Looks young and modern in a pink top and matching skirt with equally trendy bead necklaces.

Winged words: "You see, they just can't stand the truth any of them."

Day in the life: Scheduled to finish taping August 27, 1965, this episode was still in production on September 2. Moorehead fired her agent Paul Kohner at this time and signed with Fred Briskin.[33]

#2.18 "And Then There Were Three" (Jan. 13, 1966)

What's up? Tabitha is born, Darrin thinks Serena is an adult version of his newborn daughter, and Nurse Kelton thinks she is going round the bend with all the strange goings on at the hospital.

Style guide: The powder blue Chanel suit nicely matches the signature eye shadow this time.

Winged words: "You know how it is. Every family has one."

Day in the life: This episode finished taping on Friday, December 10, 1965, and that evening Moorehead did her one-woman show at Marymount College in Palos Verdes, California.[34]

#2.22 "The Dancing Bear" (Feb. 10, 1966)

What's up? Phyllis and Frank Stephens come to see their granddaughter for the first time and it materializes that both Phyllis and Endora have brought the same teddy bear for Tabitha, with the difference that Endora's bear can dance.

Style guide: Looks regal in an emerald green, knee-length dress and a diamond brooch in the shape of a shield or coat of arms, which is not the one we've seen so often before.

Winged words: "Never judge a gift by its wrapping."

Day in the life: Scheduled to finish taping December 29, 1965, this episode was still in production (with #2.23 "Double Tate") on December 30. On New Year's Eve, Moorehead was invited to a white tie "dinner and dancing" celebration at Mrs. Harry Robinson's.[35]

#2.23 "Double Tate" (Feb. 17, 1966)

What's up? On his birthday, Endora gives Darrin three wishes without telling him and he wishes he was Larry Tate for a day, which leads to numerous complications.
Style guide: Stuck in her flying suit for her flying visits.
Winged words: "I'll give him something precious and see what use he makes of it."
Day in the life: Two days before this aired, Moorehead wrote to fan club president Roy Buchanan that she had recently held auditions for her new drama school.[36]

#2.24 "Samantha the Dressmaker" (Feb. 24, 1966)

What's up? Samantha gets in trouble when the designer of the "Paris original" dresses she has twitched up for Darrin's client's wife and her sister, and Gladys Kravitz turns out to be another of Darrin's clients.
Style guide: Is wearing a wool suit to so broadly knit she looks like a woolly mammoth.
Winged words: "Mother, this charming little French restaurant is in France" (Samantha).
Day in the life: While this episode was in production, Moorehead was invited to attend Don Bachardy's first show of paintings at the Rex Evans Gallery in Los Angeles held on January 7, 1966. Bachardy was the longtime companion of the writer Christopher Isherwood and did several sketches of Moorehead in 1960 and 1964.[37]

#2.26 "Baby's First Paragraph" (March 10, 1966)

What's up? Endora gets carried away by her competitive spirit when Mrs. Kravitz comes over with her nephew, and makes Tabitha speak like an adult, making the child an instant celebrity.
Style guide: Stylish in lavender and pearls.
Winged words: "You didn't leave Tabitha alone with that, that broom jockey?" (Darrin).
Day in the life: A week before this aired, on March 3, 1966, Alice Pearce died in Hollywood at the age of 49. Though not her last episode to air, which was #2.38 "Prodigy," this episode was the last one she taped, ending production on January 21, 1966.[38]

#2.29 "Disappearing Samantha" (April 7, 1966)

What's up? An authority on witchcraft accidentally casts a spell at one of his lectures that makes Samantha disappear.
Style guide: From Japanese kimono to black dress and pearls.
Winged words: "She certainly gets around" (Darrin).
Day in the life: At this time, Moorehead enrolled her foster son Sean in the church school of the Beverly Hills Presbyterian Church.[39]

#2.33 "Divided He Falls" (May 5, 1966)

What's up? Endora casts a spell so Samantha can go on vacation to Florida with "fun Darrin" while "work Darrin" stays at home.
Style guide: Appears for the first time with the bobbed hairstyle with bangs that, with variations in length, would persist for the remainder of the series. Also wears her diamond starburst pin for the first time, which she would leave to Elizabeth Montgomery in her will.
Winged words: "Do you have four mice and a pumpkin around?"

Day in the life: When this episode aired, Moorehead was at her mother's home in Reedsburg, Wisconsin recovering from an operation.[40]

#2.35 "The Catnapper" (May 19, 1966)

What's up? Endora suspects Darrin is being unfaithful to Samantha and turns an attractive client into a cat and a shady private investigator tries to blackmail them.
Style guide: Wears a caftan for the first time on a visit to Tibet. Even the diamond shield pin can't improve the ugly trilby she wears to the restaurant.
Winged words: "Your mortal roommate seems to be getting the seven year itch five years early."
Day in the life: When this aired, Moorehead was still in Reedsburg, Wisconsin, with her mother.[41]

#2.36 "What Every Young Man Should Know" (May 26, 1966)

What's up? Endora convinces Samantha to go back in time and see what would have happened if she had told Darrin she was a witch before they were married.
Style guide: Regulation flying suit and big witch wig, and later a rather fabulous, partially see-through, lilac gown, seed pearl necklace, the favorite earrings with the pearl attachment, and a chic bob.
Winged words: "When you go back to the past, it will be exactly as it would have been."
Day in the life: The day after production ended on this episode March 30, 1966, Moorehead was in Denver, Colorado, to promote *The Singing Nun*, which was released April 2.[42]

#2.37 "The Girl with the Golden Nose" (June 2, 1966)

What's up? Darrin mistakenly thinks Samantha has cast a spell on him, so that he is living a charmed life and can do no wrong.
Style guide: Endora's basic witch wear and wig is unaltered after two seasons of *Bewitched*.
Winged words: "By the time Darwin can afford a mink, mink will be extinct."
Day in the life: On April 7, 1966, the day after production on this episode ended, Moorehead gave her one-woman show at a Brentwood–Bel Air Woman's Club luncheon.[43]

Season 3

#3.1 "Nobody's Perfect" (Sept. 15, 1966)

What's up? Samantha and Endora have quite different reactions to the discovery that Tabitha is a witch, while Darrin remains in the dark.
Style guide: Has got a new witch wig, but it's still big.
Winged words: "Is that a way to greet your daughter's grandmama?"
Day in the life: The day before this episode aired, Moorehead wrote to her longtime friend and personal assistant Georgia Johnstone that *Bewitched* was "The usual treadmill—just ghastly everyday—until I'm really quite tired—I'd love to get on a train and go somewhere!"[44]

#3.3 "Witches and Warlocks Are My Favorite Things" (Sept. 29, 1966)

What's up? Endora and Samantha's aunts Clara, Enchantra, and Hagatha convene for a coven to test and evaluate Tabitha's powers and Maurice sends Enchantra, Hagatha, and Endora to Mount Everest for trying to "witchnap" the child.

Style guide: Looks well in this one with a becoming bob and chic, knee-length mortal dress in shades of red, pink, and orange with a touch of lavender.

Winged words: "Keep smiling, Endora!" (Maurice).

Day in the life: Two days after she finished her scenes for this episode on August 2, 1966, Moorehead travelled to Akron, Ohio for the Soap Box Derby. Elizabeth Montgomery and Dick York also took part in the Recreation Day Parade on Friday, August 5. Moorehead didn't return to Los Angeles till August 7.[45]

#3.5 "A Most Unusual Wood Nymph" (Oct. 13, 1966)

What's up? To lift the curse on Darrin, Samantha has to go back to 15th-century Ireland to prevent his ancestor Darrin the Bold from killing Rufus the Red.

Style guide: No need to dress up for this one.

Winged words: "Did you ever see a human who could do weaving like that?"

Day in the life: The day this aired, Moorehead may have attended a surprise party to celebrate Jane Darwell's 87th (and, as it turned out, last) birthday and 60th anniversary in show business.[46]

#3.6 "Endora Moves in for a Spell" (Oct. 20, 1966)

What's up? Endora and Uncle Arthur feud over Tabitha's upbringing, but decide to temporarily suspend their sibling rivalry after Samantha puts her foot down.

Style guide: Looks smashing in a purple two-piece wool suit with plenty of plastic bead necklaces and an attractive bouffant hairstyle.

Winged words: "Endora! The Madame La Farge of all time" (Uncle Arthur).

Day in the life: Moorehead had played Madame La Farge in a CBS *DuPont Show of the Month* live telecast of Charles Dickens's *A Tale of Two Cities* on March 27, 1958, and got some of the worst reviews of her career. The day before this episode of *Bewitched* aired, Moorehead came in third place for a Golden Laurel Award for *The Singing Nun.*

#3.7 "Twitch or Treat" (Oct. 27, 1966)

What's up? When Darrin objects to Endora giving a Halloween party in the house she's zapped onto the vacant lot across the street, he has to agree to allow her to hold it at their place and Gladys Kravitz sends their local councilman to investigate the strange goings on.

Style guide: The witch costume is looking a little tired at this point and the braided twist perched on top of her head in the party scene looks equally moth-eaten.

Winged words: "Anybody who would knock anybody out of a tree is sick" (Uncle Arthur).

Day in the life: Three days after this episode aired, Moorehead did her one-woman show at Mission Mountain College in Missoula, Montana.[47]

#3.8 "Dangerous Diaper Dan" (Nov. 3, 1966)

What's up? The diaper delivery man turns out to be a spy for a rival advertising agency, who plants a bug in a rattle he gives Tabitha and Samantha and Endora wreak a terrible revenge when they discover it.

Style guide: Her bobbed hairstyle with a fringe is becoming.

Winged words: "The fountain of trivia runneth over."

Day in the life: At 4 p.m. on the Thursday this episode aired, Moorehead attended the dedication ceremony of the Jules Stein Eye Institute at UCLA.[48] Jules C. Stein was a physician and businessman who founded the Music Corporation of American (MCA) and he and his wife, Doris, were friends of Moorehead's, as were Doris's son from a former marriage, Gerald Oppenheimer, and his wife, Virginia.

#3.10 "I'd Rather Twitch Than Fight" (Nov. 17, 1966)

What's up? Louise and Larry Tate try a little amateur psychology on Darrin and Samantha after Sam has given away Darrin's beloved hounds tooth sport coat and only succeed in making matters worse.

Style guide: Looks stylish in a hot pink two-piece suit.

Winged words: "Oh, a psychiatrist! My own daughter! Where did I go wrong?"

Day in the life: The day after this aired, Moorehead got Orson Welles's home address in Madrid from a mutual friend.[49]

#3.11 "Oedipus Hex" (Nov. 24, 1966)

What's up? Endora casts a spell on a bowl of popcorn, that makes everyone who eats it, including Darrin, Larry, their uptight client, the local milkman, the TV repairman, a policeman, and three committee women, forget their troubles and responsibilities and "hang loose" enjoying each other's company.

Style guide: As a natural redhead, Moorehead had freckled skin and this is quite noticeable in the opening scene in the kitchen.

Winged words: "Oh, dear, without work, men are nothing. They are like little children."

Day in the life: On Friday, August 12th, the day after production ended on this episode, Rock Hudson hosted a 100th birthday party for Lynn Bowers and Kurt Kasznar at his home at 9402 Beverly Crest Dr. in Beverly Hills, which Moorehead probably attended.[50]

#3.12 "Sam's Spooky Chair" (Dec. 1, 1966)

What's up? Adelaide Cosgrove, the particularly demanding wife of a client, falls in love with an old chair Samantha has just bought, that is not just any kind of chair and turns out to be a boy who once had a crush on her.

Style guide: Pops in and out in her flying suit, as she tries to figure out who the chair might be.

Winged words: "What do you want me to do, darling, referee?"

Day in the life: This episode was produced September 26–29, 1966.[51]

#3.17 "Sam in the Moon" (Jan. 5, 1967)

What's up? When Darrin irritates Samantha by demanding to know where she's been and what she's been doing, she tells him she's been to the moon, rather than the truth, that she and Endora popped out for a shopping trip to Tokyo.

Style guide: Wears an attractive powder blue two-piece suit with enormous buttons, three strands of pearls, and her diamond starburst pin for the shopping trip.

Winged words: "Really, Samantha, it's getting harder and harder to tell the difference between you and a regular household drudge."

Day in the life: When this aired, Moorehead was invited to attend Ronald Reagan's inauguration as governor of California, but was probably not able to do so due to working on *Bewitched* #3.24 "Art for Sam's Sake."[52]

#3.18 "Hoho the Clown" (Jan. 12, 1967)

What's up? Endora casts a spell on Hoho the clown, star of Tabitha's favorite TV show, so that he falls in love with Tabitha and she wins the show's big prize, which creates problems for Darrin, who has the show's sponsor as a client.

Style guide: The diamond starburst pin is ubiquitous at this point.
Winged words: "Adios, *muchacha!*"
Day in the life: This episode wrapped November 11, 1966, and that evening Moorehead attended a benefit performance of *Is Paris Burning?* at the Warner Hollywood Theater.[53]

#3.19 "Super Car" (Jan. 19, 1967)

What's up? In an attempt to mend fences with Darrin, Endora gives him a futuristic car, only it turns out she's stolen it from the manufacturers in Detroit.
Style guide: Wears a colorful print blouse with an abstract pattern and matching, old rose skirt in the opening. When she is called back from the New Orleans Mardi Gras, she is wearing a full-length, sea green, caftan-like silk dress.
Winged words: "What do you think? The stork brought it?"
Day in the life: Production finished on #3.25 "Charlie Harper, Winner" the day this episode aired.[54]

#3.21 "Trial and Error of Aunt Clara" (Feb. 2, 1967)

What's up? A witch's coven is convened to determine if Aunt Clara is to be earthbound and Clara requests that Samantha defend her before Judge Bean.
Style guide: Surrounded by witches, there is no reason for her to get out of her witch costume.
Winged words: "Mother, would you please stop bouncing around like Tinkerbell and tell me what all this is about?" (Samantha).
Day in the life: Moorehead got the final draft of this episode while she was taping her episode of *The Wild Wild West*, titled "Night of the Vicious Valentine."[55]

#3.22 "Three Wishes" (Feb. 9, 1967)

What's up? Endora gives Darrin three wishes without telling him and for a while it looks to Samantha as if he's using them to have an affair with a bikini model.
Style guide: Endora's far out wig to attend the Kasbah seems inspired by Ona Munson's Mother Gin Sling in *The Shanghai Gesture*.
Winged words: "He'll never win an Oscar for that performance."
Day in the life: At this time, Moorehead was being courted by Tino Balio, the new director of the Wisconsin Center for Film and Theater Research, in the hope that she would donate her papers to the center. She would ultimately give them most of her papers, including her scripts and more than 70 scrapbooks.[56]

#3.23 "I Remember You…Sometimes" (Feb. 16, 1967)

What's up? Endora gives Darrin total recall and he becomes unbearably pedantic, irritating everyone, including a know-it-all client.
Style guide: Paisley print dress and a new fall on top of her regular bob.
Winged words: "Total recall can only be handled by a strong, mature mind."
Day in the life: Production on this episode was scheduled to end December 22, 1966, but Endora's brief scenes in the kitchen and living room weren't taped until January 10, 1967.[57]

#3.24 "Art for Sam's Sake" (Feb. 23, 1967)

What's up? Endora switches Samantha's still life with a landscape by an up and coming French painter in the local art exhibit and she wins first prize, which complicates things when one of Darrin's clients buys the painting at a charity auction.

Style guide: Wears a mauve cloth coat in the gallery scene. Moorehead used to say mauve was pink trying to be purple.[58]

Winged words: "Remember, anything less than a masterpiece will be a disgrace to the family name."

Day in the life: In mid- to late February 1967, Moorehead was busy taping three of her four last episodes of Season 3: #3.28 "No More Mr. Nice Guy," #3.29 "It's Wishcraft," and #3.30 "How to Fail in Business with All Kinds of Help."[59]

#3.25 "Charlie Harper, Winner" (March 2, 1967)

What's up? Samantha gets carried away by a game of one-upmanship with the wife of Darrin's vastly successful college friend Charlie Harper, including zapping up a luxurious mink coat, but ultimately reaffirms that everything most valuable in life cannot be bought.

Style guide: She's not in this long enough to change out of her flying suit.

Winged words: "You know what they say: starve a success, feed a frustration."

Day in the life: When this episode aired, Moorehead was taping her second episode for Season 4, "Toys in Babeland."[60]

#3.27 "The Crone of Cawdor" (March 16, 1967)

What's up? Samantha's trust in Darrin is put to the test when the ancient Crone of Cawdor impersonates an attractive young female client to get Darrin to kiss her and be able to become young again, while he in turn would become 500 years old.

Style guide: When Endora pretends to be Miss Travisrod, copywriter at McMann & Tate, we can see how thin Moorehead's own hair really is. The bun is a hairpiece.

Winged words: "If he kisses her, he'll be 500 years older, but no wiser."

Day in the life: Dorothy Neumann, who plays the crone, took the minor role in the film version of *Sorry, Wrong Number* that Moorehead had been offered when the lead went to Barbara Stanwyck.

#3.28 "No More Mr. Nice Guy" (March 23, 1967)

What's up? When Endora and Samantha disagree about Darrin's likeability, Endora casts a spell to make everyone take an instant dislike to him.

Style guide: Wears an unusual, heavy gold necklace in the opening scene.

Winged words: "Just keep that harpy away from my daughter—and me!" (Darrin).

Day in the life: Two days before this episode aired, fan club president Roy Buchanan wrote to Moorehead detailing his plans for writing her biography.[61] It remained unfinished when he died, just a month and a half after Moorehead, at the age of 46.

#3.29 "It's Wishcraft" (March 30, 1967)

What's up? Darrin's parents come for a visit and Samantha, anxious that Tabitha will reveal her magic powers, asks Endora to help out, though she ultimately does more harm than good.

Style guide: What I call the Christmas tree ornament earrings, shaped like two bells, make their debut.

Winged words: "In case she's up, we wouldn't want her to be startled by an unfamiliar face, now would we?" (Endora to Phyllis Stephens).

Day in the life: On February 16, 1967, as this episode was about to go into production, Moorehead attended a benefit and press preview for the opening of the new European health Spa at 18039 Sherman Way in Reseda to benefit the Eye Dog Foundation.[62]

#3.30 "How to Fail in Business with All Kinds of Help" (April 6, 1967)

What's up? Highly doubtful about Darrin being able to achieve career success on his own and, more specifically, get a bonus sufficient for a holiday in Bermuda, Endora casts a spell on a client that means Darrin can do no wrong in his eyes.

Style guide: In full blown caftan mode and still using a hairpiece to adorn the crown of her head on special occasions.

Winged words: "Mother, speaking of wind, why don't you blow?" (Samantha).

Day in the life: The evening this was first televised, Moorehead was doing her one-woman show at Walt Whitman High School in Bethesda, Maryland.[63]

#3.33 "There's Gold in Them Thar Pills" (May 4, 1967)

What's up? Endora calls in Dr. Bombay to cure Darrin's cold and he and Larry Tate want to market his pills as a miraculous cure for the common cold that will make them all rich.

Style guide: Looks bewitching in the same hot pink two-piece suit she wore in #3.10 "I'd Rather Twitch Than Fight." She wore the white fox fur cap from this episode in private life as well, including at a *Holiday on Ice* premiere she attended with her mother in 1968.

Winged words: "Endora, some women can get away with being coy. You are not among their number" (Dr. Bombay).

Day in the life: The evening this episode aired, Moorehead attended the black tie Lenox Hill Hospital Spring Dinner-Dance in the Savoy Room of the Plaza Hotel in New York, as the guest of her friend, the banker Mary Roebling.[64]

Season 4

#4.1 "Long Live the Queen" (Sept. 7, 1967)

What's up? Samantha is crowned Queen of the Witches after Ticheba retires, but finds it difficult to restrict working hours till after midnight as she has promised Darrin.

Style guide: The Christmas tree ornament earrings are back.

Winged words: "Samantha, I will not stand here and be insulted by something that is 94% water."

Day in the life: This episode was produced July 24–27, 1967. On August 3, Ruth McDevitt, who played Ticheba, wrote to Moorehead to thank her for her hospitality on the set.[65]

#4.2 "Toys in Babeland" (Sept. 14, 1967)

What's up? Endora leaves a toy soldier to babysit Tabitha when it turns out she's double-booked, Tabitha brings several more toys to life, and Larry Tate suspects Darrin is planning to open his own ad agency.

Style guide: Witch's garb for her only scene.

Winged words: "Did anyone ever tell you that you are impossibly endearing?" (Samantha).

Day in the life: This was the first and only episode of Season 4 to be produced in the spring of 1967. It was scheduled to wrap March 6, 1967.[66]

#4.3 "Business Italian Style" (Sept. 21, 1967)

What's up? When Larry demands that Darrin learn Italian to please an Italian client, Endora casts a spell that makes him not only fluent but unable to speak or understand English.

Style guide: Resplendent in the opening in an apple green cocktail dress with gold earrings, a double strand of pearls, her diamond starburst pin and large cabochon sapphire ring and later manages to wear all that jewelry even when taking a bubble bath.

Winged words: "What do you expect at this hour, darling? Poetry?"

Day in the life: Endora's scenes in the kitchen, den, and living room were taped on Wednesday, June 7, 1967, on Stage #4 at Columbia Studios. She was picked up at 8 a.m., was in makeup at 8:30, and on the set at 10:00.[67]

#4.4 "Double, Double, Toil and Trouble" (Sept. 28, 1967)

What's up? After Darrin interrupts Samantha's nightly audience with her subjects, Endora gets Serena to double as Sam to give voice to her frustration over his lack of support for her queenly career and hopefully break up their mixed marriage.

Style guide: Wears the same black and gold metallic caftan, earrings, and hairstyle as she wore to Samantha's crowning as queen.

Winged words: "Any minute we should hear him slamming out suitcases in hand."

Day in the life: The day after this episode finished taping, Moorehead was invited to Rock Hudson's party for Carol Burnett at his home at 9402 Beverly Crest Dr. in Beverly Hills.[68]

#4.5 "Cheap, Cheap!" (Oct. 5, 1967)

What's up? Endora casts a spell on Darrin to make him even more of the cheapskate she thinks he is, which ironically makes him the perfect match for a tightwad new client, that is until Samantha tries to remedy the situation and accidentally cures the client of his parsimony.

Style guide: Now also dressed like an Arabian princess in gauzy light blue veils.

Winged words: "That's right, he's a careful cheapskate."

Day in the life: At this time, Moorehead was reported to be learning sign language, so she could use it in her one-woman show.[69]

#4.6 "No Zip in My Zap" (Oct. 12, 1967)

What's up? Dr. Bombay is called in when Samantha loses her powers, while Darrin thinks she has turned herself into a fly to help him close a deal with a girl he jilted in college, who is now a business leader and potential client.

Style guide: For once I'm at a loss how to describe what she's wearing!

Winged words: "Will you kindly ask little Miss Muffet to get her tuffet outta here?" (Darrin).

Day in the life: While this episode was in production in mid–August 1967, Moorehead and her escort Murray Matheson went to a party for Ethel Merman hosted by socialite Dorothy Strelsin at her Doheny Estates home.[70]

#4.7 "Birdies, Bogies and Baxter" (Oct. 19, 1967)

What's up? Endora casts a spell and Samantha helps out on the green, so Darrin instantly becomes a champion golfer and saves a client's marriage by trouncing the formerly unbeatable husband.

Style guide: Endora is in and out so fast in this one, you hardly notice what she's wearing.

Winged words: "Mother, the elephants are in the starting gate. Hadn't you better get back to India?" (Samantha).

Day in the life: At the time this episode aired, Eva Gabor was taking acting lessons from Moorehead.[71]

#4.11 "Allergic to Macedonian Dodo Birds" (Nov. 16, 1967)

What's up? Endora temporarily loses her powers when, unbeknownst to herself, she comes in contact with a Macedonian Dodo bird that Tabitha has conjured up.

Style guide: Is having a bad hair day worthy of Phyllis Diller.
Winged words: "I'll have to live out my life in a climate of hatred."
Day in the life: It was about the time this episode was in production in mid–September 1967, that Moorehead's foster son Sean disappeared from home.[72]

#4.13 "The Solid Gold Mother-in-Law" (Nov. 30, 1967)

What's up? McMann & Tate client Mr. Gregson is impressed that Darrin has a picture of his mother-in-law on his desk and offers to set him up with his own advertising agency.
Style guide: Wears a black caftan richly embroidered with silver thread in the dinner party scene that makes her look as big as a house.
Winged words: "He isn't likely to come home and see a pony stomping around. *He is the pony.*"
Day in the life: Moorehead celebrated Thanksgiving with Debbie Reynolds and her family in Palm Springs this year.[73]

#4.14 "My, What Big Ears You Have" (Dec. 7, 1967)

What's up? Endora casts a spell so that Darrin's ears grow when he tells an untruth.
Style guide: Looks like someone attacked her with a curling iron and a cattle prod at the same time. The episode should have been titled "My, What Big Hair You Have"...
Winged words: "Oh, don't be such a spoil sport!"
Day in the life: This episode aired the day after Moorehead's 67th birthday and her annual Christmas party.[74]

#4.15 "I Get Your Nannie, You Get My Goat" (Dec. 14, 1967)

What's up? Darrin is persecuted by a warlock, Lord Montdrako, who accuses him of having stolen Tabitha's new nanny, Elspeth, from the lord's employ, until Samantha finds a different solution to assuage the lord's loneliness.
Style guide: Looks smashing in a black riding habit.
Winged words: "That baggage has got to go!"
Day in the life: According to a news item, Moorehead had a busy start to the month of December when, in addition to *Bewitched,* she had a featured role on the TV series *Custer*, guested on the Smothers Brothers' show, and still found time to take a week off in the Florida sun. She finished taping her last episode of *Bewitched* for the year on December 11, 1967 (#4.22 "Prince of a Guy") and didn't return to the set until late February (for #4.32 "Man of the Year").[75]

#4.18 "Once in a Vial" (Jan. 4, 1968)

What's up? Endora tries to get Samantha's former beau Rollo to tempt her away from Darrin, but is hoist by her own petard when she drinks Rollo's love potion by mistake and almost gets married to a churlish client of Darrin's.
Style guide: Wears an unbecoming, short-sleeved dress with a colorful abstract pattern to the evening party and her near nuptials.
Winged words: "She'd be perfect. Smart dresser, sophisticated, still pretty good-looking" (Bo Callahan).
Day in the life: The evening this aired, Moorehead gave a reading at a dinner dance held by the Leukemia Society of America's Southern California division at El Caballero Country Club in Tarzana in honor of Dr. William Dameshek, a blood disease expert.[76]

#4.19 "Snob in the Grass" (Jan. 11, 1968)

What's up? Darrin is reunited with his former fiancée Sheila when Larry wants the firm to try and capture her father's account and Samantha is subjected to yet another one of Sheila's snobbish evening parties, before taking a terrible revenge.

Style guide: Appears briefly in waitress gear when spying on Darrin and Sheila at lunch.

Winged words: "Why in the name of all that's witchly are you massaging that rug?"

Day in the life: Moorehead's brief scenes in this episode nevertheless meant that she had to be on the set on Monday, July 3, 1967, for the read through and rehearsal; Thursday, July 6 to tape her brief appearances in the living room, when she blows the rug clean, and in the kitchen; and on Friday, July 7 for her appearance as a waitress in the restaurant where Darrin and Sheila are having lunch. The shooting schedule shows she was originally to have dumped the plate of food in Sheila's lap rather than Darrin's.[77]

#4.20 "If They Never Met" (Jan. 25, 1968)

What's up? After Darrin and Samantha have a spat, sparked, as is often the case, by Endora, she takes Samantha back to see what Darrin's life would have been like if they had never met.

Style guide: The witch costume and wig has changed very little in four seasons.

Winged words: "Oh, it kills me to think of you going back to this miserable, bourgeois existence!"

Day in the life: Georgia Johnstone wrote to Moorehead on January 16, 1968, that she hoped she wasn't worrying too much about Sean.[78] This was the last mention of Moorehead's runaway foster son in their correspondence and, as far as we know, she never saw him again.

#4.22 "Prince of a Guy" (Feb. 8, 1968)

What's up? When Tabitha's "wishcraft" conjures up Prince Charming from the fairy tale, Louise Tate, Darrin's cousin Helen, and various other women throw themselves at him and Samantha has quite a challenge getting him back between two covers.

Style guide: More décolleté than usual in a high-waisted, filmy evening gown in purple, blue, and green with huge faux ruby cabochon earrings and a matching brooch.

Winged words: "Oh, gad, you're beautiful. If only you were a little more inhuman."

Day in the life: While this episode was in production, Moorehead's guest spot on Season 2 of *The Smothers Brothers Comedy Hour* aired on December 10, 1967.[79]

#4.25 "To Twitch or Not to Twitch" (March 14, 1968)

What's up? Samantha and Darrin have an epic fight about her using witchcraft, which culminates in Samantha taking Tabitha "home to mother" and, as so often happens, impacts on Darrin's client relations.

Style guide: The colorful plastic disk earrings were first seen in #4.13 "The Solid Gold Mother-in-Law" and will be seen again.

Winged words: "Look how well she sleeps up here. It's the lovely, smog-free air."

Day in the life: Production on this episode ended February 5, 1968.[80]

#4.27 "Tabatha's Cranky Spell" (March 28, 1968)

What's up? When Louise Tate's Aunt Harriet comes over with her crystal ball to babysit Tabitha, it sets in motion a chain of more or less supernatural events and ultimately convinces a recalcitrant McMann & Tate client to update his company's image.

Style guide: Appears first in witch costume and later in a gold embroidered, white caftan over a powder blue turtleneck that matches her eye shadow.

Winged words: "Oh, Samantha, you're bringing this child up in the wrong environment!"

Day in the life: When this aired, Moorehead was making personal appearances in Chicago before going to Reedsburg to visit her mother.[81]

#4.32 "Man of the Year" (May 2, 1968)

What's up? Endora casts a spell so that everyone is charmed and impressed by Darrin, adversely affecting the innate modesty Samantha likes so much.

Style guide: Wears a coat in her first scene that looks like a plaid woolen blanket.

Winged words: "Oh, you're a wicked witch!" (Samantha).

Day in the life: The day this aired, Moorehead started on her tour of American army bases in Europe judging plays written by GIs as part of the 1968 USAREUR Tournament of Plays.[82]

Season 5

#5.1 "Samantha's Wedding Present" (Sept. 26, 1968)

What's up? Endora slowly shrinks Darrin after yet another one of their morning spats.

Style guide: Looks divine in the opening scene in an orange two-piece Chanel suit to match her becomingly bobbed hair and later in a filmy lavender and silver hostess gown with elaborate costume jewelry, including gypsy style gold earrings, a heavy necklace with a green stone, and several gold bracelets.

Winged words: "Mother, you make the Wicked Witch of the West look like Shirley Temple" (Samantha).

Day in the life: At this time, Moorehead's East coast secretary, Georgia Johnstone, responded to a fan that Moorehead didn't have time to write the story of her life herself, but that her fan club president, Roy Buchanan, was doing it.[83]

#5.3 "Samantha on the Keyboard" (Oct. 10, 1968)

What's up? Endora casts a spell on Tabitha, so she becomes a child prodigy at the piano.

Style guide: The witch wig has undergone a make-over and the gypsy earrings from #5.1 are back, this time with a colorful, zigzag-patterned gown.

Winged words: "And by the way, she gets her talent from her mother's side."

Day in the life: This month, Moorehead was up for the role of Molly Fletcher in *The Maltese Bippy*, which ultimately went to Mildred Natwick.[84]

#5.4 "Darrin Gone! And Forgotten?" (Oct. 17, 1968)

What's up? Carlotta makes Darrin disappear, because she wants Samantha to marry her sissy son Juke.

Style guide: Love that scuba gear! Beyond that, this is one of the few times Endora wears pants.

Winged words: "She does have a good side. All you have to do is find it and get on it" (Samantha).

Day in the life: The first episode Moorehead did for Season 5.[85]

#5.5 "It's So Nice to Have a Spouse Around the House" (Oct. 24, 1968)

What's up? Serena agrees to substitute for Sam for a few hours, to allow her to attend a witches' council meeting, the same day Darrin decides it's time to put the romance back in their marriage by returning to the inn where they spent their honeymoon.

Style guide: Looks divine in a powder blue gown with rhinestone beading.

Winged words: "I'm sure he'd rather do without you for a few hours, than wind up a bird perch."
Day in the life: The *Bewitched* filming schedule indicates that this episode was completed July 25, 1968, but there were in fact additional scenes in the living room, kitchen, and bedroom taped on Friday, August 16, 1968, together with #5.6 "Mirror, Mirror, on the Wall."[86]

#5.6 "Mirror, Mirror, on the Wall" (Nov. 7, 1968)

What's up? Endora zaps a vanity spell on Darrin, which turns out, after several twists and turns, to make him just the man for the new suntan lotion account.
Style guide: The Christmas tree ornament earrings are back! Last seen in #4.1 "Long Live the Queen."
Winged words: "Oh, Samantha, you're so blind when it comes to that mortal nothing!"
Day in the life: After this episode, Endora was not seen in the next six, her longest continuous absence during the entire series.

#5.13 "Instant Courtesy" (Dec. 26, 1968)

What's up? Endora casts a courtesy spell over Darrin and his elaborate politeness drives Larry Tate around the bend to the extent that he fires him, but impresses a client who wants to start Darrin up in his own ad agency.
Style guide: We've seen those brightly colored, plastic disk earrings before (starting with #4.13 "The Solid Gold Mother-in-Law"), but the ultra-loud, multi-colored caftan is new.
Winged words: "Endora, you're a one woman invasion of privacy" (Darrin).
Day in the life: Moorehead was invited to the Ashers for champagne two days before this aired, but was visiting her mother in Reedsburg, Wisconsin.[87]

#5.14 "Samantha's Super Maid" (Jan. 2, 1969)

What's up? Samantha's mother-in-law Phyllis thinks she should have a maid and Amelia is so hard-working and devoted, Sam and Darrin don't have the heart to fire her.
Style guide: Appears first and last in a voluminous blue metallic caftan and the massive gold necklace with the green stone worn in #5.1 "Samantha's Wedding Present," but changes to a cloth coat with an abstract zebra-like pattern to meet the elder Mrs. Stephens.
Winged words: "I'm hooked on his hookah."
Day in the life: When this episode aired, Moorehead was making a visit to New York, where she socialized with the entertainment lawyer Arnold Weissberger and his partner Milton Goldman and her old friend, the singer Margaret Whiting.[88]

#5.17 "One Touch of Midas" (Jan. 23, 1969)

What's up? Endora casts a spell on Darrin so the furry doll he invests in becomes a fabulous success and he goes off the rails buying everything he thinks his family should have.
Style guide: Her witch wig is bigger than ever and so, incidentally, is Samantha's hair. We also get to see Endora in a fashionable, furry Eskimo costume and slalom gear.
Winged words: "What a soggy bore, but he does have a fascinating igloo."
Day in the life: At this time, Moorehead spent two Sundays in San Francisco, where they held a festival dedicated to her films.[89]

#5.18 "Samantha, the Bard" (Jan. 30, 1969)

What's up? Samantha wakes up one morning speaking in rhymes and is diagnosed with "primary vocabularyitis" by Dr. Bombay, who finally cures her after several attempts and a rather trying dinner with a client, but not before Endora is infected.

Style guide: Mostly wears a tomato red coat dress with a large, chain link, faux gold necklace and the faux ruby cabochon earrings and brooch from #4.22 "Prince of a Guy."

Winged words: "Good old mother. She's like no other" (Samantha).

Day in the life: Moorehead was invited to attend the wedding of her and her mother's Reedsburg friend Gordon Emery to Dale Lee Smith on Saturday, February 1, 1969, but was unable to attend due to work on *Bewitched.* Mollie Moorehead attended the nuptials in the United Methodist Church of Lime Ridge, Wisconsin and her daughter sent china.[90]

#5.19 "Samantha, the Sculptress" (Feb. 6, 1969)

What's up? When Samantha starts sculpting in clay so she can teach Tabitha the mortal way, Endora goes her one better by whipping up two talking busts of Darrin and Larry that make the two men and their hard-drinking client not believe their eyes and ears.

Style guide: Wears the same embroidered ivory silk caftan that she wore to the Emmy awards on June 4, 1967, when she won for her episode of *The Wild Wild West.*

Winged words: "A bust of Durwood? He's already a bust."

Day in the life: The reading and rehearsal for this episode was on Friday, November 22, 1968, and taping took place November 25–27.[91]

#5.22 "Going Ape" (Feb. 27, 1969)

What's up? Samantha turns a runaway chimpanzee into a man to find out where he belongs, he is "discovered" in Samantha's backyard, and becomes a model for the men's cologne "Brawn."

Style guide: This time the gypsy earrings and the faux gold chain link necklace accompany a heavily embroidered, knee-length, apple green silk dress.

Winged words: "Oh, you're a regular little swinger, aren't you?"

Day in the life: Three days after this aired, H.R.H. Princess Grace of Monaco wrote to Moorehead from Gstaad to say how sorry she was Moorehead couldn't make it to the TV festival and thanking her for the gifts for the children.[92] Moorehead had been slated to be a judge at the festival in Monaco, but had to cancel when Dick York fell ill and she was needed to fill in till Dick Sargent could start work on the series.

#5.23 "Tabitha's Weekend" (March 6, 1969)

What's up? Frank Stephens convinces Samantha to let him and Phyllis have Tabitha for the weekend and Samantha's attempt to stop Tabitha from revealing her powers to her grandparents is only a partial success.

Style guide: Runs through a myriad of outfits from a low cut medium blue velvet dress with a rhinestone band around the bodice (also used in publicity shots for the show) via full jockey gear (including the horse) to one of her garish cloth coats like a plaid blanket.

Winged words: "Oh, the modern generation just doesn't swing."

Day in the life: On February 2, 1969, while working on this episode, Moorehead wrote to her friend Georgia Johnstone that Dick York was to leave *Bewitched*, that she had to cancel her trip to Monaco, and that she'd gotten everything she asked for in her new contract.[93]

#5.24 "The Battle of Burning Oak" (March 13, 1969)

What's up? Through the patronage of a wealthy client, Darrin and Samantha have the chance to become members of the exclusive Burning Oak Country Club, but both are skeptical and Endora and Samantha manage to scotch the plan by making Darrin outsnob the snobs and letting some skeletons out of the existing members' closets.

Style guide: Wears a paisley cotton gown over a ribbed blue turtleneck with her diamond pin and gypsy gold earrings in the opening scene and her flying suit for the rest.

Winged words: "There are no important mortals, my darling, you are wasting your time."

Day in the life: The same Thursday that this episode aired, Moorehead was a guest on *That Show*, a syndicated daytime talk show hosted by Joan Rivers that was her first show on television.[94]

#5.25 "Samantha's Power Failure" (March 20, 1969)

What's up? The witches' council strips Samantha of her powers for not renouncing her mortal marriage and likewise Arthur and Serena when they show up to support her; they have to get regular jobs until Samantha's appeal is heard and their powers are restored.

Style guide: The witch's wig is bigger than ever.

Winged words: "A mother's work is never done."

Day in the life: Three days after this episode aired, TV columnist Barney Glazer wrote that Moorehead and Ingrid Bergman "frequently visit each other's set."[95] Bergman, who was 15 years younger than Moorehead, was filming *Cactus Flower* at Columbia.

#5.26 "Samantha Twitches for UNICEF" (March 27, 1969)

What's up? Samantha "haunts" a millionaire businessman, who has reneged on his promise to support the local ladies' charity drive for UNICEF, making him seek out a psychiatrist and ultimately getting back his $10,000 donation.

Style guide: The giant faux ruby cabochon earrings and matching brooch from previous episodes turn out to have a twin set in faux amethyst.

Winged words: "Samantha, it depresses me no end to see you engaging in such disgustingly mortal activity."

Day in the life: The day after this aired, Moorehead was invited to the West Coast premiere of the film *Sweet Charity*, starring Shirley McLaine, at the Pantages Theatre.[96]

#5.27 "Daddy Does His Thing" (April 3, 1969)

What's up? Maurice turns Darrin into a jackass on his birthday when Darrin refuses his gift of a magic lighter.

Style guide: Wears a cloth coat in pale orange with a large fox fur collar and matching fur at the cuffs and hem.

Winged words: "Imagine that, at your age to take them on two at a time."

Day in the life: On Monday, February 24, 1969, at 7 p.m., while this episode was in production, Moorehead attended the Golden Globe Awards at the Cocoanut Grove of the Ambassador Hotel.[97] She was not a nominee that year.

#5.28 "Samantha's Good News" (April 10, 1969)

What's up? Despite having an "informal marriage," Endora is incensed by Maurice having an affair with his new private secretary, Abigail Beecham, and she and Samantha concoct a plan to make Maurice jealous in turn by Endora going on a date with the charming Australian warlock, John Van Millwood.

Style guide: More fur in this episode in the form of a big silver fox hat and matching muff when she shows up with Van Millwood.

Winged words: "Abigail, don't live dangerously. My mother has the most powerful one-two punch in the cosmos" (Samantha).

Day in the life: The Australian actor Murray Matheson, who played Van Millwood, was

Moorehead's dear friend and often escorted her to parties and openings. This episode of *Bewitched* was their only common credit.

#5.29 "Samantha's Shopping Spree" (April 17, 1969)

What's up? Samantha's prankster and punster cousin Henry wreaks havoc on a visit to a department store and turns the store owner's son into a mannequin on his first day at work.

Style guide: Wears a slate grey cape with matching skirt, a mauve turtleneck, bead necklace, and her favorite earrings for the shopping expedition.

Winged words: "Well, well, well, the clown king of the cosmos."

Day in the life: When this episode aired, Moorehead was going on a shopping spree of her own—in Charleston, South Carolina—where she also gave a lecture and had dinner with members of the Junior League.[98]

#5.30 "Samantha and Darrin in Mexico City" (April 24, 1969)

What's up? Darrin and Samantha have to go to Mexico to placate a disgruntled Mexican client. Endora babysits Tabitha and casts a spell on Darrin, so he disappears when he speaks Spanish.

Style guide: Endora appears in full surfing gear.

Winged words: "I think it's a multi-million dollar bore."

Day in the life: As soon as the cast and crew went on hiatus in April 1969, Moorehead went on tour with her one-woman show and started building her new house on the Moorehead family farm "Kitchen Middens" near New Concord, Ohio. She wouldn't return to the *Bewitched* set until late August 1969.[99]

Season 6

#6.1 "Sam and the Beanstalk" (Sept. 18, 1969)

What's up? When Tabitha gets the impression that Darrin would rather have a baby boy than a girl, she zaps Jack out of the fairy tale and climbs up the beanstalk, so Samantha has to go looking for her in the Giant's castle.

Style guide: In patriotic colors of red, white, and blue in her first episode to air with the new Darrin, Dick Sargent.

Winged words: "Oh, I just remembered I have a pressing engagement I have to iron out."

Day in the life: Three days before this episode aired, Moorehead may have attended the wedding of Kathryn Grayson's daughter Patricia Kathryn to Robert Lewis Towers.[100]

#6.2 "Samantha's Yoo Hoo Maid" (Sept. 25, 1969)

What's up? Endora finds a witch maid, Esmeralda, for Samantha and Darrin, who has lost most of her powers, but is subject to "involuntary witchcraft" when she sneezes.

Style guide: Looks elegant in a filmy pastel gown with matching costume jewelry.

Winged words: "Tell me Endora, what was it like at the Tower of Babel?" (Darrin).

Day in the life: After this episode finished production on April 9, 1969, Moorehead was to have gone for cocktails at the home of socialite George G. Frelinghuysen, but he cancelled due to the death of his aunt.[101]

#6.4 "Samantha's Curious Cravings" (Oct. 9, 1969)

What's up? Dr. Bombay gets called into help stop Samantha's strong cravings for food, but only makes matters worse, before Sam gets taken to the hospital to have the baby in what turns out to be a false alarm.

Style guide: Pops in briefly in a gorgeous ruffled lavender dress.
Winged words: "With me it was hummingbird wings."
Day in the life: The Saturday morning after taping ended on this episode on April 25, 1969, Moorehead gave her one-woman show in Fox Chris-Town Theater in Phoenix as part of the "Phoenix YWCA Spotlight Series."[102]

#6.5 "And Something Makes Four" (Oct. 16, 1969)

What's up? Maurice casts a spell so everyone at the hospital falls in love with Samantha and Darrin's newborn baby boy, including Larry Tate.
Style guide: What's with the spit curls on Endora's forehead?
Winged words: "I thought for a moment mortal taste was improving."
Day in the life: Two days after the episode aired, Moorehead's drama school started classes for the 1969–70 school year at the Morgan Theater in Santa Monica.[103]

#6.6 "Naming Samantha's New Baby" (Oct. 23, 1969)

What's up? Samantha's father Maurice takes offense at his new grandson being named after his paternal grandfather Frank, but ultimately agrees that Adam would be a better name than his own.
Style guide: Doesn't look very well and the flat hair doesn't help matters.
Winged words: "It seems like you and Endora are hoping that little Frank will grow up to be a florist" (Frank Stephens).
Day in the life: When Moorehead returned to Columbia Studios to tape this episode in late August 1969, she hadn't been on the *Bewitched* set since production ended on #6.4 "Samantha's Curious Cravings" in late April.[104]

#6.7 "To Trick-or-Treat or Not to Trick-or-Treat" (Oct. 30, 1969)

What's up? Blaming Darrin for Samantha's involvement in a local Halloween charity drive for UNICEF, Endora turns him into a stereotypical witch.
Style guide: The flat hair and the spit curls on the forehead persist until she shows up dressed like Robin Hood.
Winged words: "Your mother always does unto others what they do unto her" (Darrin).
Day in the life: The day this episode aired, Moorehead's *Mayor of the Town* co-star, Conrad Binyon, wrote to ask if she could send a letter to a dying child called Judith Ann Guerra in San Antonio, Texas.[105]

#6.9 "Samantha's Secret Spell" (Nov. 13, 1969)

What's up? After Darrin forbids Endora from entering the house, Samantha has to get him through a three part "anti spell" without his knowing it to prevent him from being turned into a mouse by his mother-in-law.
Style guide: Endora is dressed up like a playing card, but the spit curls in the forehead are still there.
Winged words: "There is an annoying vibration somewhere in this house and I wish it would go away."
Day in the life: The day after this aired, Moorehead was a special observer and honorary "technical advisor" at the launching of the manned Apollo 12 spacecraft at Cape Kennedy in Florida.[106]

#6.13 "You're So Agreeable" (Dec. 11, 1969)

What's up? Endora first casts a spell that makes Darrin sickeningly agreeable and then reverses it in the opposite direction, making him cantankerous, while he manages in turn to lose his job, find a new one, and get rehired in his old one.

Style guide: The colorful dress with a large, abstract swirly pattern in shades of purple and blue is very Endora, as are all the white bead necklaces of various lengths and sizes. The square gold earrings are new.

Winged words: "You lay a lip on me and I'll put you in orbit for the rest of your life."

Day in the life: Two days before this aired, Moorehead appeared for the second time on *The Red Skelton Show* on CBS. In her sketch, she played Bertha Bluenose crusading against drink and corruption and threatening to close a saloon run by crooked Sheriff Deadeye (Skelton), who retaliates by reminding her that she once posed for the provocative painting over his bar. This episode of the show was taped November 10–12, 1969.[107]

#6.15 "Samantha's Better Halves" (Jan. 1, 1970)

What's up? While under siege from Larry to go to Chicago on business for him rather than on a well deserved vacation, Darrin and Samantha reminisce about the time he was so torn between going on a business trip to Japan and taking care of his pregnant wife, that Endora splits him into "business Darrin" and "domestic Darrin."

Style guide: We've seen that paisley dress before, this time with a baby blue turtleneck and plenty of gold bangles and baubles, before she changes to a royal blue caftan over a white turtleneck.

Winged words: "If your mother was really interested in my welfare, she'd migrate—to another planet" (Darrin).

Day in the life: Though it didn't air till nine months later, this was the first episode of Season 6 to be taped (ending March 31, 1969) and thus the first time Moorehead played Endora to Dick Sargent's Darrin.[108]

#6.17 "The Phrase is Familiar" (Jan. 15, 1970)

What's up? Endora turns Darrin into a veritable "encyclopedia of clichés," thinking it will help his career, while Tabitha gets a warlock for a tutor, who introduces her to Dickens's Artful Dodger from *Oliver Twist*.

Style guide: Still very much in the flowing multi-colored gown over turtleneck sweater with "big" costume jewelry mode.

Winged words: "Why don't you call those phrases what they really are? Clichés."

Day in the life: Two days after this episode went on the air, Moorehead was invited to a cocktail party at the home of her local Republican congressman, Alphonzo E. Bell, Jr., at 9551 Hidden Valley Rd. in Beverly Hills.[109]

#6.18 "Samantha's Secret Is Discovered" (Jan. 22, 1970)

What's up? Samantha is stripped of her powers when she reveals to her mother-in-law Phyllis that she is a witch, so she has to engineer a ruse to make Phyllis think she's been taking hallucinogens rather than tranquilizers to explain all the strange things she's been seeing.

Style guide: Is seen with the chin-length bob that she retained for the remainder of the series.

Winged words: "You could be living in the lap of luxury instead of on the bony knees of poverty."

Day in the life: On January 24–25, 1970, Moorehead taped *Easter with Oral Roberts* at NBC.

The program, where Moorehead gave a dramatic reading of the resurrection of Jesus Christ as observed by Mary Magdalen, aired March 27 in some areas and March 28 in others.[110]

#6.21 "What Makes Darrin Run?" (Feb. 12, 1970)

What's up? Insisting that he is going nowhere, Endora gives Darrin a "good, strong dose of ambition" and he becomes a scheming, power-hungry egomaniac, who nearly manages to displace Larry Tate at work.

Style guide: Wears a kind of two-piece cotton print peasant dress in earth tones, before she returns from Venus in full astronaut gear and from bronco-busting in fringed leather cowgirl gear.

Winged words: "While everyone is at the ball, Cinderella toils."

Day in the life: The day after this episode aired, Moorehead attended the Valentine Ball of the Beverly Hills Chamber of Commerce and Civic Association in the International Ballroom of the Beverly Hilton Hotel, as a guest of the philanthropist and activist Sybil Brand. She was escorted by her friend Cesar Romero.[111]

#6.24 "The Generation Zap" (March 5, 1970)

What's up? After she promises "witch's honor" not to meddle, Endora gets Serena to cast a love spell on a female college intern in Darrin's office to test his fidelity.

Style guide: Has very big hair in this one, where she wears her witch's garb throughout the episode.

Winged words: "Samantha, blind faith is unbecoming to you."

Day in the life: While this episode was in production, Moorehead attended Mrs. Harry Robinson's *Twelfth Night* costume ball on January 6, 1970, dressed as an Elizabethan lady with a conical cap and veil.[112]

#6.25 "Okay, Who's the Wise Witch?" (March 12, 1970)

What's up? Darrin, Samantha, and later Endora and Esmeralda, are suddenly and unexpectedly housebound and powerless to get out, until Dr. Bombay comes to the rescue and explains that Samantha's failure to use her powers regularly has resulted in a vapor lock around the house.

Style guide: Yet a new gown, this one with a floral pattern on a black background, a bright green sash, and worn with a yellow and orange plastic necklace to heighten the colorful effect.

Winged words: "How about that? You have an unexpected house guest."

Day in the life: The evening this episode was shown, Moorehead was invited to a reception and buffet supper in honor of David Frost at the home of British Consul General Andrew Franklin.[113]

#6.27 "If the Shoe Pinches" (March 26, 1970)

What's up? Tired of casting spells herself, Endora strongarms a leprechaun into giving Darrin some leather shoes that make him lazy.

Style guide: No need to dress for a leprechaun. The flying suit will do.

Winged words: "I never interfere in my daughter's marital life."

Day in the life: On February 9, 1970, as this episode was in production, Moorehead and her mother Mollie attended a reception and dinner held by Pepperdine College to honor Ronald Reagan in the LA Room of the Century Plaza Hotel.[114]

#6.28 "Mona Sammy" (April 2, 1970)

What's up? When Endora gives Samantha a portrait of her great aunt Cornelia painted by Leonardo da Vinci as an anniversary present and says Darrin has painted it, he is forced to paint a portrait of Louise Tate which intermittently does not flatter her.

Style guide: Dressed to the nines in a geometrically patterned lavender evening gown in a shimmering material with matching costume jewelry.

Winged words: "Well, if it isn't the ever glamorous, popular Endora!" (Larry Tate).

Day in the life: On Saturday, February 14, 1970, while this episode was being produced but she was not needed on the set, Moorehead did her one-woman show *An Evening with Agnes Moorehead* at the Central Presbyterian Church in Eugene, Oregon. This meant that she missed the luncheon given in honor of Debbie Reynolds by the Variety Club of Southern California.[115]

#6.29 "Turn on That Old Charm" (April 9, 1970)

What's up? Samantha gives Darrin an amulet which makes Endora behave charmingly towards him and Endora retaliates by making Darrin and Samantha bicker constantly.

Style guide: Beyond the dune buggy outfit, the focus is not on fashion and Endora appears in her classic witch's garb throughout.

Winged words: "He sounds huffy to me. Does he sound huffy to you?"

Day in the life: The day after this episode aired, Moorehead wrote to Georgia Johnstone that she would be filming *Bewitched* in Salem the first week of June, thus she could not go in for Katharine Hepburn in the Broadway musical *Coco* about Coco Chanel.[116]

Season 7

#7.1 "To Go or Not to Go, That Is the Question" (Sept. 24, 1970)

What's up? Samantha is summoned to a witch convention in Salem, Massachusetts and when she refuses to go without Darrin, Hepzibah, "Empress and High Priestess of the Witches," moves in to observe their marriage.

Style guide: Endora is sporting yet more billowing housedresses in loud colors and vibrant patterns with equally large-scale jewelry.

Winged words: "I took basic training in weird from your mother" (Darrin).

Day in the life: The day this aired, there was a big interview with Moorehead's mother Mollie in a Minneapolis newspaper under the title "Your Friends and Neighbors in Review: Life Exciting for Mother of Actress."[117]

#7.3 "The Salem Saga" (Oct. 8, 1970)

What's up? Samantha, Darrin, and Endora travel to Salem for the witches' convention and Sam is pursued by a bed warmer in the House of the Seven Gables.

Style guide: Wears her flying suit for flying on the wing and mortal dress for the rest.

Winged words: "One thing I can say for your mother. She's a real mother-in-law" (Darrin).

Day in the life: Sam and Darrin visit the House of the Seven Gables in this episode. Moorehead had played Hepzibah Pyncheon in a TV version of Nathaniel Hawthorne's tale as part of *The Shirley Temple Show*, which aired December 11, 1960.

#7.4 "Samantha's Hot Bedwarmer" (Oct. 15, 1970)

What's up? Darrin is arrested for stealing the bed warmer and to get him out Endora has to send Serena back to old Salem to remember the spell she used to turn a warlock lover into the bed warmer.

Style guide: As chairwoman of the convention in her flying suit, Endora has even bigger hair than usual.

Winged words: "Look what the atmospheric continuum blew in!"

Day in the life: While this episode was in production, Moorehead's friend, composer and MGM musical producer Roger Edens, died of cancer aged 64 on July 13, 1970.[118]

#7.7 "Samantha's Bad Day in Salem" (Nov. 5, 1970)

What's up? Samantha's childhood friend Waldo casts a spell to pretend Sam is in love with him; and Larry, observing the pair in the garden of the House of the Seven Gables, thinks they are having an affair.

Style guide: Endora is in full flying gear for her scenes as the chairwoman of the witches' convention.

Winged words: "If she's the chairman, it should be called the 'ways to be mean' committee" (Darrin).

Day in the life: After she returned from her trip to Salem, Moorehead wrote to a friend: "Back at the films—Salem was frightening—the crowds about tore our clothes off and our hair out!"[119]

#7.8 "Samantha's Old Salem Trip" (Nov. 12, 1970)

What's up? When Esmeralda mistakenly sends Samantha back to 17th-century Salem, Endora sends Darrin back in time to rescue her.

Style guide: Endora's hair is a bit longer than usual and very attractive, but how much of it is her own?

Winged words: "Endora, believe it or not I am genuinely glad to see you" (Darrin).

Day in the life: At this time, Moorehead was wearing copper bracelets against arthritis.[120]

#7.9 "Samantha's Pet Warlock" (Nov. 19, 1970)

What's up? Ashley Flynn, a dashing warlock enamored of Samantha, turns himself into a dog to get close to her and to observe Darrin, who is working on a dog food account.

Style guide: Togged out in a psychedelic, sparkling gown and heavy on the costume jewelry.

Winged words: "My oatmeal has curdled. I wonder why" (Darrin).

Day in the life: The evening before this episode finished production on Aug. 20, 1970, there was dinner and dancing at Mrs. Harry Robinson's palatial mansion at 1008 Elden Way in Beverly Hills, only a few blocks from Moorehead's home.[121]

#7.10 "Samantha's Old Man" (Dec. 3, 1970)

What's up? When Endora ages Darrin, he is forced to pretend he is his own grandfather, which disconcertingly makes him a good match for Louise Tate's Aunt Millicent, until Samantha shows up as his equally aged wife.

Style guide: The second time Endora appears as a playing card. The first time was in #6.9 "Samantha's Secret Spell."

Winged words: "Endora, no offense, but I think you need a shave" (Darrin).

Day in the life: This episode was produced August 24–27, 1970, and Moorehead's scenes were all shot on Stage 4 on the 27th.[122]

#7.11 "The Corsican Cousins" (Dec. 10, 1970)

What's up? When Darrin insists they join a country club to please a client, Endora casts a spell on Samantha so she feels everything her more unconventional cousin Serena is feeling, which causes a stir when two members of the ladies admission committee come to call.

Style guide: Decked out like an entire counter of long white plastic bead necklaces.

Winged words: "Sam, don't expect your mother to be gracious. She doesn't do imitations" (Darrin).

Day in the life: At the time this episode was in production, Moorehead attended Rod McKuen's concert at the Hollywood Bowl with Rock Hudson, Sue Lyon, and Cesar Romero.[123]

#7.12 "Samantha's Magic Potion" (Dec. 17, 1970)

What's up? When Darrin suffers a crisis of confidence at work, Samantha pretends to give him a magic potion to make him master of every situation that restores his confidence.

Style guide: In addition to her favorite earrings, she is looking resplendent in a necklace of antique gold coins which may be the same one she wore in a publicity shot from the 1940s.

Winged words: "Have you been fooling around with Darrin?" (Samantha).

Day in the life: This episode finished taping the day Season 7 premiered with "To Go or Not to Go, That Is the Question" on September 24, 1970.[124]

#7.14 "The Mother-in-Law of the Year" (Jan. 14, 1971)

What's up? Endora manages to get herself elected "Mother-in-Law of the Year" as part of the new advertising campaign for Bobbins Bonbons, but complicates matters when she fails to show up to receive her award on the TV show *Sweetheart Parade*.

Style guide: Still has the attractive bob she's worn all season and still wearing caftans and plenty of colorful bead necklaces when she's not dressed to go skiing.

Winged words: "I had a lovely evening with her and I can tell you something: She is not shy" (Bernard Bobbins).

Day in the life: As soon as this episode was completed October 1, 1970, Moorehead returned to the set of *Dear Dead Delilah* in Nashville, Tennessee.[125]

#7.17 "The Return of Darrin the Bold" (Feb. 4, 1971)

What's up? At Endora's behest, Serena goes back in time and gives Darrin's ancestor Darrin the Bold a magic potion, so that Darrin in turn begins to have the powers of a warlock.

Style guide: Is wearing a beautiful paisley print dress in shades of red, orange, and robin's egg blue with gold embroidery.

Winged words: "Oh, Endora, how infinite are thy gifts."

Day in the life: At the time this episode aired, production had just ended on *What's the Matter with Helen?*[126]

#7.20 "This Little Piggie" (Feb. 25, 1971)

What's up? Endora first casts a spell of indecisiveness over Darrin and later turns him into a pig.

Style guide: The pattern of Endora's housedress in oranges and browns is positively painful to look at.

Winged words: "Personally, I think I'd make a rather dashing hood ornament."

Day in the life: Production on Season 7 ended in mid–February 1971.[127]

#7.21 "Mixed Doubles" (March 4, 1971)

What's up? Because of a metaphysical, molecular disturbance, Samantha wakes up one morning as Louise Tate, while Louise wakes up as Samantha, though only Sam realizes what has happened until she tells Darrin.

Style guide: Suddenly looks much older in this episode, at least in some lights, and her hair color is faded.

Winged words: "Forget it, sawbones."

Day in the life: On the Thursday evening this aired, Moorehead attended "campaign cocktails" at Debbie Reynolds's and Harry Karl's home at 813 Greenway Dr. in honor of their candidate for re-election to the Beverly Hills Board of Education, Dr. Martin H. Prince.[128]

#7.23 "Money Happy Returns" (March 18, 1971)

What's up? Darrin finds a bundle of money in the back of a cab and suspects Endora has had a hand in it, but the cash is stolen and the gangsters want it back.

Style guide: Is wearing her full set of black jet jewelry in this one, which may well be plain plastic.

Winged words: "No one seems to appreciate me."

Day in the life: Three days before this aired, Moorehead wrote to her seven-year-old fan, Judith Ann Guerra. Guerra died just a few weeks later.[129]

#7.24 "Out of the Mouth of Babes" (March 25, 1971)

What's up? Endora turning Darrin into a boy indirectly leads to a client being sold on marketing his Irish stew as dog food.

Style guide: That zebra inspired gown in black and white (and mustard yellow) is out of this world.

Winged words: "Now your appearance has caught up with your mentality."

Day in the life: The day production ended on this episode, which was February 5, 1971, Lucille Ball wrote to Moorehead inviting her to stay in her new condo in Aspen.[130]

#7.27 "Laugh, Clown, Laugh" (April 15, 1971)

What's up? Tired of what she perceives of as Darrin's lack of a sense of humor, Endora first turns him into an inveterate teller of bad jokes and then makes him giggle at things that are no laughing matter.

Style guide: Makes her most unusual entrance of the series atop a camel in full polo gear.

Winged words: "Face it, Samantha, that man simply has no sense of humor."

Day in the life: This episode was produced February 8–11, 1971.[131]

Season 8

#8.1 "How Not to Lose Your Head to Henry VIII (Part 1)" (Sept. 15, 1971)

What's up? When Samantha releases a 16th-century nobleman and warlock from a painting in the Tower of London, the witch who put him there zaps her back in time to the court of Henry VIII, where the lecherous king takes a liking to her.

Style guide: Liver spots on Moorehead's throat are visible in the opening scene.

Winged words: "Oh, don't get your giblets in an uproar!"

Day in the life: The week this aired, Moorehead was at work on #8.13 "Three Men and a Witch on a Horse."[132]

#8.2 "How Not to Lose Your Head to Henry VIII (Part 2)" (Sept. 22, 1971)

What's up? Endora sends Darrin back in time to rescue Samantha from the clutches of Henry VIII and ends up going to Hampton Court herself to help him out.

Style guide: Endora's conical cap when she time travels belongs more to the Middle Ages than the 16th century, but she sure looks funny.

Winged words: "Maybe she's tired of just watching television in the evening" (Samantha after Endora has taken the warlock from the painting and back to the future with her).

Day in the life: What's the Matter with Helen? was released the day after this double episode finished shooting on June 29, 1971.[133]

#8.5 "Bewitched, Bothered and Baldoni" (Oct. 13, 1971)

What's up? Endora brings a statue of Venus to life to tempt Darrin into infidelity on a combined business and pleasure trip to Rome and Samantha animates a statue of Adonis as a counter move.

Style guide: In her scene in the museum, Endora is wearing a knee-length dress for a change, rather than a floor-length gown.

Winged words: "Now that's what I call bad casting. Your mother as a doll" (Darrin).

Day in the life: Two days after this episode aired, Moorehead appeared as a grandmother in the TV movie *Marriage: Year One* on NBC.

#8.6 "Paris, Witches Style" (Oct. 20, 1971)

What's up? Maurice is offended that Samantha and Darrin haven't visited him in London on their trip to Europe and Endora tries to placate him by conjuring up a more compliant Darrin.

Style guide: Is looking old and unwell in this one.

Winged words: "Don't worry, it's a dummy Darwin. Not too different from the real thing."

Day in the life: A few days after this episode aired, Moorehead flew to Orlando, Florida, to attend the dedication ceremony of Walt Disney World.[134]

#8.9 "A Plague on Maurice and Samantha" (Nov. 10, 1971)

What's up? Having caught a bug and temporarily lost his powers, Maurice accompanies Darrin to work and helps out with ideas on how to advertise a client's chili.

Style guide: The zebra dress gets a reprise, as does the twinkly black jet jewelry.

Winged words: "Endora, you have all the charm of a tsetse fly" (Maurice).

Day in the life: The evening this aired, Moorehead was present at the premiere benefit performance of the film *Fiddler on the Roof* at the Northland Theatre in Southfield, Michigan, escorted by her friend, the Detroit millionaire industrialist Charles Gershenson.[135]

#8.11 "The Warlock in the Gray Flannel Suit" (Dec. 1, 1971)

What's up? When Darrin refuses to go with Samantha to her cousin Panda's wedding in Hong Kong, Endora sends the far out hippie warlock Alonzo to McMann & Tate to give Darrin some competition and Darrin responds by starting his own company.

Style guide: Wears a broadly striped, brightly colored caftan faintly reminiscent of a Bedouin tent in the opening scene.

Winged words: "One thing you can say about my mother: She's a mother-in-law" (Samantha).

Day in the life: On Saturday, December 4, 1971, three days after this aired, Moorehead gave what would prove to be her last Christmas party for 220 guests.[136]

#8.12 "The Eight-Year-Itch Witch" (Dec. 8, 1971)

What's up? Endora tries to tempt Darrin with another woman yet again, this time the cat familiar Ophelia, who gets cast as model in a campaign for tractors.

Style guide: No longer wears the big curly wig with her flying suit.
Winged words: "Don't you care if Durwood's briefcase contains a gaggle of centerfolds?"
Day in the life: The day this aired, Moorehead was sent an invitation to a special screening of *What's the Matter with Helen?* from director Curtis Harrington.[137]

#8.13 "Three Men and a Witch on a Horse" (Dec. 15, 1971)

What's up? Darrin receives a horse racing tip on the "daily double" from the Tabitha's rocking horse, after Endora casts a spell that makes him an avid gambler.
Style guide: Still very much in the long, loud gown and long plastic bead necklace mode.
Winged words: "By this spell that's oh so droll, you'll receive a gambler's soul. Double, double, toil and trouble, to Tabitha's room for the daily double."
Day in the life: This episode was produced September 13–16, 1971.[138]

#8.14 "Adam, Warlock or Washout" (Dec. 29, 1971)

What's up? Maurice and Endora and the witches Grimalda and Enchantra arrive for the testing of Adam's powers and Darrin, returning unexpectedly from playing golf, objects vociferously to the proceedings.
Style guide: Looks puffy eyed, drawn, and pale in the opening scene and is having a bad hair day all through the episode. Her hair was fairly thin at this point and in Season 8 she seldom used a wig.
Winged words: "Thank you, Endora, your charm is ageless. So sad about the rest of you" (Maurice).
Day in the life: The day this episode aired, the final draft script of *Charlotte's Web* was completed.[139]

#8.18 "Samantha on Thin Ice" (Jan. 29, 1972)

What's up? Endora casts a spell on Tabitha, so she becomes an expert ice skater.
Style guide: Can hardly get more '70s than this.
Winged words: "How would you like to be a carrot growing in a field of rabbits?"
Day in the life: After production ended on this episode September 30, 1971, Moorehead travelled to her mother Mollie's home town of Reedsburg, Wisconsin, and presided at the opening of the $700,000 Reedsburg Center Municipal Complex before about 250 Reedsburgians on October 3. Mollie Moorehead held the ribbon with Mayor John Bernien and Moorehead cut it.[140]

#8.23 "School Days, School Daze" (March 4, 1972)

What's up? Endora casts a spell over Tabitha so she passes her test at school with flying colors and her teacher, Mrs. Peabody, is convinced she has discovered a genius.
Style guide: Is wearing a distinctive necklace with little white dog pendants and matching earrings, that we haven't seen before. Or could they be polar bears?
Winged words: "Give her knowledge, all ye muses, all the knowledge that she chooses. Aristotle, Shakespeare, Plato, all the languages in NATO. Science back to Galileo, medicine from the brothers Mayo. You'll know it all from A to Z. Awake now, my little chickadee."
Day in the life: The day after this aired, Moorehead checked out of the Methodist Hospital in Rochester, Minnesota, where she had undergone an operation for cancer.[141]

#8.24 "A Good Turn Never Goes Unpunished" (March 11, 1972)

What's up? Darrin refuses Samantha's help on the Benson mattress advertising campaign that he is struggling with, because he thinks her ideas are generated by witchcraft.

Style guide: For some odd reason, the blue make-up on her right eye is smudged in her final scene.

Winged words: "If you leave him on his own, the closest you will get to Bermuda will be an onion."

Day in the life: By the time this episode aired, Moorehead was recuperating as an out-patient in Rochester, Minnesota, before going to her mother's home in Reedsburg, Wisconsin, at the end of March.[142]

#8.26 "The Truth, Nothing but the Truth, So Help Me, Sam (March 25, 1972)

What's up? Endora casts a spell so that everyone who comes near a unicorn pin Darrin has bought for Samantha has to speak the truth and this indirectly reestablishes a client's marriage on a more honest and equal footing.

Style guide: For the final episode of *Bewitched,* Endora first wears a capacious, wildly patterned gown in reds and oranges with large blue stars, heaps of red and white bead necklaces and enormous cabochon ruby red earrings; followed by her flying suit when she casts the spell in Darrin's office; and finally, a more fitted gown with large flowers in shades of blue on a black background, piles of pearls, and elaborate diamond and pearl drop earrings for the dinner party scene.

Winged words: "The baloney in this place could supply a delicatessen for a year."

Day in the life: Due to her illness, Moorehead had to cancel several performances of her one-woman show in April 1972.[143]

Chapter Notes

The Agnes Moorehead Papers at the Wisconsin Center for Film and Theater Research are abbreviated WCFTR.

Introduction

1. Axel Nissen, *The Films of Agnes Moorehead* (Lanham, MD: Scarecrow, 2013).
2. The exception is *High Spirits*, the musical version of Noël Coward's comedy *Blithe Spirit*, in which Moorehead played Madame Aracati for three weeks at the Dallas State Fair in June 1965.
3. See the theater annuals titled "The Best Plays of..." edited by Burns Mantle and www.ibdb.com for information on the original casts of these Broadway shows.
4. Hilda Cole, "Chameleon of the Air," *Radio Guide* [October 14, 1933], no page.
5. Agnes Moorehead to Georgia Johnstone [1960s], (Box 1, NYPL).
6. Earl Wilson, "Hattie Winston Is Getting Used to the Dog's Room," *Wichita Falls Times*, January 21, 1973, p. 14.
7. Phyllis Scott Carlin, "Agnes Moorehead," *Notable Women in the American Theatre: A Biographical Dictionary*, ed. Alice M. Robinson, et al. (New York: Greenwood, 1989), p. 664.
8. Interview with Paul Gregory, February 16, 2007.
9. "Mini-Interview," *Newark Advocate*, November 30, 1968, p. 7.
10. Chuck Schaden, *Speaking of Radio: Chuck Schaden's Conversations with the Stars of the Golden Age of Radio* (Morton Grove, IL: Nostalgia Digest, 2003), pp. 378–79.

Chapter 1

1. "'Blue Coal' Radio Program Off to Fine Start," *Blue Coal News* (November 1938) (Box 140, WCFTR). *The Shadow* may also have been broadcast during its first season from the Mutual Broadcasting System's flagship radio station in New York, WOR, which was located for many years at 1440 Broadway.
2. https://en.wikipedia.org/wiki/The_Shadow.
3. Chris Steinbrunner, "Preface," *The Shadow Scrapbook*, ed. Walter B. Gibson (New York: Harcourt Brace Jovanovich, 1979), no page.
4. Frank Brady, *Citizen Welles: A Biography of Orson Welles* (London: Hodder and Stoughton, 1990), p. 78.
5. "Ethel Clarks' Radio Flashes," *Ogden Standard-Examiner*, June 9, 1940, p. 14A. Ellipses in original.
6. "Ethel Clarks' Radio Flashes," p. 81.
7. Schaden, *Speaking of Radio*, p. 377.
8. Anthony Tollin, "The Invisible Shadow," *The Shadow Scrapbook*, ed. Walter B. Gibson (New York: Harcourt Brace Jovanovich, 1979), p. 78.
9. Brady, *Citizen Welles*, p. 78; John Dunning, *On the Air: The Encyclopedia of Old-Time Radio* (New York and Oxford: Oxford University Press, 1998), p. 607.
10. Orson Welles and Peter Bogdanovich, *This Is Orson Welles*, ed. Jonathan Rosenbaum (London: HarperCollins, 1992), p. 11.
11. Simon Callow, *Orson Welles: The Road to Xanadu* (London: Vintage, 1996), p. 321.
12. Tollin, "The Invisible Shadow," p. 79.
13. Quoted in "'Blue Coal' Radio Program Off to Fine Start."
14. Paul Heyer, *The Medium and the Magician: Orson Welles, the Radio Years, 1934–1952* (Lanham, MD: Rowman and Littlefield, 2005), p. 25.
15. Tollin, "The Invisible Shadow," p. 79.
16. Dunning, *On the Air*, p. 608.
17. https://en.wikipedia.org/wiki/Margo_Lane.
18. Heyer, *The Medium and the Magician*, p. 26.
19. I strongly suspect, though, that it is not Moorehead playing Margo in the 24th episode of the season, titled "Sabotage by Air" (March 6, 1939), as the voice quality is different.
20. Tollin, "The Invisible Shadow," p. 80.
21. Dunning, *On the Air*, p. 609; Charles Tranberg, *I Love the Illusion: The Life and Career of Agnes Moorehead* (Boalsburg, PA: BearManor, 2005), p. 52.
22. Show creator Walter B. Gibson reproduces the only extant script of the premiere episode of *The Shadow*, "The Death House Rescue," in *The Shadow Scrapbook*. While the storyline resembles the episode as aired, Margo Lane does not appear in this script by Edward Hale Bierstadt. See Walter B. Gibson, ed., *The Shadow Scrapbook* (New York: Harcourt Brace Jovanovich, 1979), pp. 94–11.
23. Bruce Weber, "Margot Stevenson, Prolific Broadway Actress, Dies at 98," *New York Times*, January 7, 2011, www.nytimes.com. A quarter of a century after her stint on *The Shadow*, Stevenson would replace Moorehead

again, this time as Lord Pengo's devoted secretary Miss Swanson, when Moorehead quit the Broadway show to do *Who's Minding the Store?* with Jerry Lewis. Stevenson lived to be 98 and died in 2011.

24. www.findagrave.com.

25. Burns Mantle, ed., *The Best Plays of 1937–38* (New York: Dodd, Mead, 1938), p. 389.

26. Moorehead's scrapbook contains correspondence to this address starting in 1935 and ending in 1938 (Box 143, WCFTR).

27. Mary Jacobs, "She Admits She Doesn't Like Her Work," *Oakland Tribune*, February 2, 1936, p. 14.

28. Unidentified clipping [September 1937], (Box 140, WCFTR).

Chapter 2

1. Dunning, *On the Air*, p. 443. In the first season, Marilly's surname was Appleton.

2. www.zillow.com. This building was razed in 2009 to make way for a new house. Moorehead's two other homes in Cheviot Hills are still standing and externally unchanged since her day.

3. www.zillow.com.

4. Conrad Binyon told me about Frank, whose surname he thought may have been Silva. Frank sometimes spent time at the studio during rehearsals and broadcasts. Binyon recalled that he would do double duty as a cook. (Conrad Binyon to Axel Nissen, June 4, 2007, and February 11, 2016.) There is a picture of Frank, who was Mexican, with Moorehead and Jack Lee in the kitchen of the Forrester Drive house. See "Agnes Moorehead," *Radio Life*, May 12, 1946 (Box 142, WCFTR).

5. James Robert Parish and Ronald L. Bowers, *The MGM Stock Company: The Golden Era* (New York: Bonanza, 1972), p. 66.

6. Parish and Bowers, *The MGM Stock Company*, p. 67; Margot Peters, *The House of Barrymore* (New York: Alfred A. Knopf, 1990), p. 505.

7. Barrymore would reprise his *On Borrowed Time* role on radio on April 1, 1946, with Moorehead playing his nemesis Demetria Riffle, a role memorably created on the screen by Eily Malyon.

8. Parish and Bowers, *The MGM Stock Company*, p. 70.

9. Peters, *The House of Barrymore*, pp. 438–39, 495.

10. Peters, *The House of Barrymore*, p. 601.

11. Tranberg, *I Love the Illusion*, p. 93.

12. Jerry Franken, review of *Mayor of the Town*, *The Billboard*, November 29, 1947, p. 12.

13. "Lionel Barrymore Is Dead at 76; Actor's Career Spanned 61 Years," *New York Times*, November 16, 1964, www.nytimes.com; Peters, *The House of Barrymore*, p. 391, 394.

14. "United States Census, 1940," database with images, *Family Search* (https://familysearch.org/pal:/MM9.1.1/K9HJ-5S3, accessed 24 February 2017), Lionel Barrymore, Councilmanic District 1, Los Angeles, Los Angeles Township, Los Angeles, California, United States; citing enumeration district (ED) 60–5, sheet 2A, line 14, family 28, Sixteenth Census of the United States, 1940, NARA digital publication T627. Records of the Bureau of the Census, 1790–2007, RG 29. Washington, D.C.: National Archives and Records Administration, 2012, roll 374; Margot Peters, *The House of Barrymore*, pp. 440–41; Virginia Watson, "Oscar Special: Movie Personalities Lived in Chatsworth," www.patch.com.

15. "United States Census, 1940," database with images, *Family Search* (https://familysearch.org/ark:/61903/1:1:K974-CJQ, accessed 24 February 2017), Lionel Barrymore, Tract 381, Beverly Hills, Beverly Hills Judicial Township, Los Angeles, California, United States; citing enumeration district (ED) 19–37, sheet 3A, line 27, family 38, Sixteenth Census of the United States, 1940, NARA digital publication T627. Records of the Bureau of the Census, 1790–2007, RG 29. Washington, D.C.: National Archives and Records Administration, 2012, roll 220; Peters, *The House of Barrymore*, p. 394, 441. The house is now no. 800 N. Roxbury Dr. According to the census, it was valued at $100,000 in 1930, but only $25,000 in 1940, reflecting the fall in property values during the 1930s. See "United States Census, 1930," database with images, *Family Search* (https://familysearch.org/ark:/61903/1:1:XCFX-DG7, accessed 24 February 2017), Lionell [sic] Barrymore, Beverly Hills, Los Angeles, California, United States; citing enumeration district (ED) ED 819, sheet 1B, line 93, family 21, NARA microfilm publication T626 (Washington D.C.: National Archives and Records Administration, 2002), roll 124; FHL microfilm 2,339,859.

16. "Lionel Barrymore Is Dead."

17. "Lionel Barrymore Is Dead."

18. Peters, *The House of Barrymore*, p. 488.

19. Peters, *The House of Barrymore*, pp. 438–39.

20. Peters, *The House of Barrymore*, p. 439, 482.

21. Peters, *The House of Barrymore*, p. 438.

22. Warren Sherk, *Agnes Moorehead: A Very Private Person* (Philadelphia: Dorrance, 1976), p. 30.

23. See Peters, *The House of Barrymore*, pp. 437–38.

24. Peters, *The House of Barrymore*, p. 439. See also Conrad Binyon, "Mayor of the Town," http://www.geocities.ws/conradab.geo/MOTGallery.htm.

25. Dunning, *On the Air*, p. 443.

26. Peters, *The House of Barrymore*, p. 601.

27. Binyon to Nissen, February 11, 2016.

28. Hutton Wilkinson to Axel Nissen, November 26, 2007.

29. "California Death Index, 1940–1997," database, *Family Search* (https://familysearch.org/ark:/61903/1:1:VP7S-L3P, 26 November 2014), Susan Oneill, 28 February 1949; Department of Public Health Services, Sacramento.

30. Quoted in Tranberg, *I Love the Illusion*, p. 90.

31. Franken, review of *Mayor of the Town*, p. 12.

32. "Agnes Moorehead," *Radio Life*.

33. Conrad Binyon to Axel Nissen, July 21, 2007.

34. Parish and Bowers, *The MGM Stock Company*, p. 71.

35. Tranberg, *I Love the Illusion*, p. 91.

36. Sherk, *Agnes Moorehead*, p. 30.

37. Sherk, p. 31.

38. Clair C. Stebbins, "Farm in Rich Hill Township Holds Fond Memories for Famous Actress," *Zanesville Sunday Times-Signal*, June 8, 1947, p. 1.

39. Peters, *The House of Barrymore*, pp. 439–40, 506.

40. All information in this section is from my interview with Conrad Binyon in Los Angeles, May 10, 2007, unless otherwise indicated.

41. "California Birth Index, 1905–1995," database, *Family Search* (https://familysearch.org/ark:/61903/1:1:VG3Q-ZBN, 27 November 2014), Conrad Ambress Binyon, 30 Jan 1931; citing Los Angeles, California, United States, Department of Health Services, Vital Statistics Department, Sacramento.

42. Binyon to Nissen, February 11, 2016.

43. Binyon to Nissen, February 11, 2016.

44. "California, Southern District Court (Central) Naturalization Index, 1915–1976," database with images, *Family Search* (https://familysearch.org/ark:/61903/1:1:KX3B-5J1, 28 November 2014), Ann Dorothy or Anna Binyon, 1943; citing Los Angeles, Los Angeles, California, United States, National Archives and Records Service, Los Angeles Branch, Laguna Niguel; FHL microfilm 1,561,839.

45. "California, County Marriages, 1850–1952," database with images, *Family Search* (https://familysearch.org/ark:/61903/1:1:K8NB-CSP, 28 November 2014), William Ambress Binyon and Ann Dorothy Zelichckovies, 02 Apr 1930; citing Los Angeles, California, United States, county courthouses, California; FHL microfilm 2,074,790.

46. https://en.wikipedia.org/wiki/One_Man's_Family.

47. Binyon to Nissen, February 11, 2016.

48. Binyon to Nissen, February 11, 2016.

49. Binyon to Nissen, February 11, 2016.

50. Binyon to Nissen, February 11, 2016. There is a similar account of Conrad helping Barrymore on his "Mayor of the Town" website, http://www.geocities.ws/conradab.geo/MOTGallery.htm.

51. Tranberg, *I Love the Illusion*, p. 91.

52. Binyon to Nissen, February 11, 2016.

53. Binyon to Nissen, February 11, 2016.

54. This film from 1948 starred Merle Oberon and Robert Ryan. Lee played an uncredited role as a captain.

55. He sent Moorehead an invitation to the ceremony at Laredo Air Force Base in Laredo, Texas (Box 150, WCFTR), which she was unable to attend, as she was performing her one-woman show at the Jewish Community Center in Scranton, Pennsylvania, that day (see contract in Box 4, AHC).

56. See Scrapbook Vol. 7 (January-March 1963) (Box 69, WCFTR).

57. See itinerary in Box 14, AHC.

58. About his tour in Vietnam, see Conrad Binyon to Agnes Moorehead, September 24, 1965 (Box 80, WCFTR).

59. Conrad Binyon to Agnes Moorehead, June 17, 1967 (Box 100, WCFTR).

60. Conrad Binyon to Agnes Moorehead, October 30, 1969 (Box 123, WCFTR).

61. Binyon to Nissen, February 11, 2016.

Chapter 3

1. Dunning, *On the Air*, p. 648.

2. Louella O. Parsons, "Fred Astaire May Return to Movies," *Charleston Gazette*, April 8, 1947, p. 13.

3. "Radio Review: Follow-Up," unidentified clipping, August 25, 1943, (Box 2, NYPL).

4. *Variety*, February 24, 1944, (Box 141, WCFTR).

5. *Bakersfield Californian*, November 18, 1948, p. 35; *Mason City Globe-Gazette*, November 18, 1948, p. 2.

6. Bill Doudna, "Bill Doudna's Spotlight: The Badger Beat," *Wisconsin State Journal*, September 5, 1951, p. 6.

7. See *Don Juan in Hell* itinerary (Box 6, AHC).

8. See *The Rivalry* itinerary (Box 11, AHC).

9. James Robert Parish, *Good Dames: Virtue in the Cinema* (South Brunswick, NJ, and New York: A.S. Barnes, 1974), p. 88.

10. "She's 'Girl Next Door' in Fact," unidentified clipping [July 1934], (Box 140, WCFTR).

11. Quoted in Heyer, *The Medium and the Magician*, p. 165.

12. Laughton quoted in an article for the press book to Moorehead's one-woman show "That Fabulous Redhead" in 1954 (Box 12, AHC).

13. There is an undated, nine-page typescript with Moorehead's handwritten changes among the Agnes Moorehead Papers at the Wisconsin Center for Film and Theater Research. This is surely a version she used in her one-woman show, as it is somewhat shorter than the original and only includes her lines.

14. Lotte Lehmann to Agnes Moorehead, July 20, 1948 (Box 145, WCFTR).

15. Parsons, "Fred Astaire May Return," p. 13.

16. Norman Nadel, "Attained Fame in Many Roles," *Columbus Citizen*, March 16, 1949 (Box 145, WCFTR).

17. Dunning, *On the Air*, p. 649.

18. Schaden, *Speaking of Radio*, pp. 378–79.

19. Sam Irvin, *Kay Thompson: From Funny Face to Eloise* (New York: Simon and Schuster, 2010), p. 103.

20. Dunning, *On the Air*, p. 648.

21. I have included only Moorehead's documented roles and other types of credits below that are found in the actual broadcast or in reliable sources. It was not until about 1950 that supporting cast members were routinely given credit, so it is possible, though not likely, that Moorehead played uncredited supporting roles on *Suspense* that have not yet been identified. Some modern sources, for example, indicate that Moorehead had an uncredited role as the screaming woman of the title in "The Screaming Woman" (November 25, 1948), starring Margaret O'Brien, but I have not found any historical evidence to support this claim. See Lynn Kear, *Agnes Moorehead: A Bio-Bibliography* (Westport, CT: Greenwood, 1992), p. 212; Tranberg, *I Love the Illusion*, p. 407.

Chapter 4

1. Accounts vary of how long the 1951–52 version of *Don Juan in Hell* took to perform. See, for example, "Famous Actors Give Shaw Play at UNC," *Rocky Mountain Evening Telegram*, February 17, 1951, p. 7; and Agnes Moorehead, speech to the 25th Annual Convention of the Western Speech Association at Hotel Californian, Fresno, California [November 28, 1953] (Box 2, NYPL).

2. "Four-Star Troupe Brings 'Don Juan' to Town March 4," *Syracuse Herald-American*, January 7, 1951, p. 24.

3. "Talent Will Abound at NTSC Wednesday with Drama Four," *Denton Record-Chronicle*, February 11, 1951, p. 1.

4. "Famous Actors Give Shaw Play at UNC," p. 7.

5. "Famous Actors Give Shaw Play at UNC," p. 7.

6. Laughton quoted in "Famous Actors Give Shaw Play at UNC," p. 7.

7. Wood Soanes, "Curtain Calls: 'Don Juan in Hell' Opens Geary Run," *Oakland Tribune*, October 20, 1955, p. E29.

8. Simon Callow, *Charles Laughton: A Difficult Actor* (London: Methuen, 1987), p. 212; Larry Swindell, *Charles Boyer: The Reluctant Lover* (London: Weidenfeld and Nicholson, 1983), p. 223.

9. Cedric Hardwicke, *A Victorian in Orbit: The Irreverent Memories of Sir Cedric Hardwicke, as Told to James Brough* (London: Methuen, 1961), p. 227.

10. Interview with Paul Gregory, August 21, 2006.
11. Walter Winchell, "Shaw Was Doubtful His Play Would Be Broadway Success," *Lubbock Journal*, June 11, 1952, p. 8.
12. Hardwicke, *A Victorian in Orbit*, p. 228.
13. Hardwicke, p. 229.
14. Moorehead, speech to the 25th Annual Convention of the Western Speech Association.
15. "Talent Will Abound," p. 1.
16. Swindell, *Charles Boyer*, p. 222.
17. Hardwicke, *A Victorian in Orbit*, p. 230.
18. Frank Morriss, "Here, There, and Hollywood," *Winnipeg Free Press*, September 13, 1950, p. 5.
19. "University Theater Offers Shaw Play in February," *Salt Lake Tribune*, January 7, 1951, p. B7.
20. Kurt Singer, *The Laughton Story: An Intimate Story of Charles Laughton* (Philadelphia and Toronto: John C. Winston, 1954), p. 260.
21. Interview with Paul Gregory, May 11, 2007.
22. Quoted in Frank Morriss, "Four Film Stars in Shaw Show," *Winnipeg Free Press*, August 18, 1951, p. 13.
23. Quoted in Tranberg, *I Love the Illusion*, p. 153.
24. Quoted in Morriss, "Four Film Stars in Shaw Show," p. 13.
25. Quoted in Callow, *Charles Laughton*, p. 211.
26. John Gielgud, *Gielgud's Letters*, ed. Richard Mangan (London: Weidenfeld and Nicolson, 2004), p. 163.
27. Louise Faulk, "Moorehead Vitality Impresses Ruston Audience," *Ruston Daily Leader*, March 3, 1954, p. 1.
28. Carlin, "Agnes Moorehead," p. 664.
29. Some of the more detailed accounts of the production are as follows (in chronological order): Singer, *The Laughton Story*, pp. 257–63; Hardwicke, *A Victorian in Orbit*, pp. 227–32; Charles Higham, *Charles Laughton: An Intimate Biography* (London: W.H. Allen, 1976), pp. 155–68; Elsa Lanchester, *Elsa Lanchester: Herself* (New York: St. Martin's, 1983), pp. 211–19; Swindell, *Charles Boyer*, pp. 221–25; Callow, *Charles Laughton*, pp. 210–15. For an account of Vincent Price taking over Charles Laughton's role on the final tour, see Victoria Price, *Vincent Price: A Daughter's Biography* (New York: St. Martin's Griffin, 1999), pp. 204–5. See also the useful summary in Kear, *Agnes Moorehead*, pp. 220–24.
30. Tranberg, *I Love the Illusion*, p. 138; Lanchester, *Elsa Lanchester*, p. 213.
31. Interview with Paul Gregory, October 22, 2006. See also Higham, *Charles Laughton*, p. 166, where Higham writes that "although she might be acceptable as the crone Doña Ana at the beginning of the dream-play, she would be absurd as the twenty-seven-year-old Doña Ana whom the Devil evokes in later passages." Bondi was 61 years old at this time and had specialized in playing old ladies from the beginning of her acting career.
32. Interview with Paul Gregory, October 22, 2006.
33. Quoted in Tranberg, *I Love the Illusion*, p. 138.
34. Moorehead, speech to the 25th Annual Convention of the Western Speech Association.
35. Higham, *Charles Laughton*, p. 165.
36. Quoted in Tranberg, *I Love the Illusion*, p. 138.
37. Quoted in Tranberg, p. 138.
38. Quoted in Singer, *The Laughton Story*, p. 257.
39. Swindell, *Charles Boyer*, p. 223.
40. Higham, *Charles Laughton*, p. 166.
41. Quoted in Tranberg, *I Love the Illusion*, p. 138.
42. Tranberg, *I Love the Illusion*, p. 141.
43. Moorehead, speech to the 25th Annual Convention of the Western Speech Association.
44. Interview with Paul Gregory, August 1, 2006.
45. [George] Bernard Shaw, *Man and Superman: A Comedy and a Philosophy* (Harmondsworth: Penguin, 1971), p. 173.
46. Quoted in Mary Daniels, "Personality Profile," *Chicago Tribune*, October 1, 1972 (Box 137, WCFTR).
47. Interview with Paul Gregory, January 9, 2007.
48. Interview with Paul Gregory, September 26, 2006.
49. Interview with Paul Gregory, August 21, 2006.
50. George E. Perry, "Agnes as I've Known Her," *Versatility* (1965), p. 15 (Box 385, Muskingum). Doña Ana is actually transformed by the Devil from 77 to 27.
51. John Houseman, *Final Dress* (New York: Simon and Schuster, 1983), p. 475. This description is a slight revision of a passage towards the end of his eloquent obituary of Moorehead from 1974. See John Houseman, "Agnes Moorehead: 1906–1974," *Los Angeles Times*, May 5, 1974, p. 34.
52. Quoted in Pilato, *Bewitched Forever*, p. 61.
53. Quoted in Pilato, *Bewitched Forever*, p. 61.
54. William Hawkins quoted from the *New York World Telegram*, October 23, 1951, in Carlin, "Agnes Moorehead," p. 664.
55. Quoted on the back of a handbill for "That Fabulous Redhead."
56. Quoted on the back of a handbill for "That Fabulous Redhead."
57. Quoted in Tranberg, *I Love the Illusion*, p. 152.
58. Quoted in Carlin, "Agnes Moorehead," p. 664.
59. Quoted in an article for the press book to "That Fabulous Redhead" [1954] (Box 12, AHC).
60. Ruth E. Thompson, "'Bewitched' Co-Star Has Her Cake, Eats It Too," *Leader-Times*, March 20, 1965, no page.
61. Anne Lloyd-Williams, "Fashion—Make Your Own Rules," unidentified Birmingham paper [1951] (Box 147, WCFTR). The designer's name is given in a press book article for "That Fabulous Redhead" (Box 12, ACH).
62. Interview with Paul Gregory, August 1, 2006.
63. Swindell, *Charles Boyer*, p. 222.
64. Moorehead, speech to the 25th Annual Convention of the Western Speech Association.
65. "Drama Quartet Here," *Wisconsin State Journal*, October 14, 1951, p. 7.
66. Quoted on the back of a handbill for "That Fabulous Redhead."
67. Quoted on the back of a handbill for "That Fabulous Redhead."
68. Mary Daniels, "Personality Profile," *Chicago Tribune*, October 1, 1972 (Box 137, WCFTR).

Chapter 5

1. Tranberg, *I Love the Illusion*, p. 172.
2. Francis M. Nevins, Jr. *Cornell Woolrich: First You Dream, Then You Die* (New York: Mysterious, 1988), p. 511.
3. Tim Brooks and Earle Marsh, *The Complete Directory of Prime Time Network and Cable TV Shows, 1946-Present* (New York: Ballantine, 1995), p. 865.
4. Nevins, *Cornell Woolrich*, pp. 582–85.

Chapter 6

1. Charles Laughton to Agnes Moorehead, June 5, 1949 (Box 145, WCFTR).

2. Laughton to Moorehead, July 11, 1949 (Box 145, WCFTR).
3. Hedda Hopper, "Hedda Hopper Writes from Hollywood," *Altoona Mirror*, August 31, 1950, p. 14.
4. See the numerous contracts for "That Fabulous Redhead" in Box 4 of the Paul Gregory Papers (AHC).
5. Erskine Johnson, "In Hollywood," *Portsmouth Herald*, January 22, 1953, p. 13.
6. Sheilah Graham, "Hollywood Today," *San Antonio Express*, October 30, 1953, p. 10.
7. Handbill for "That Fabulous Redhead" [1954] (Box 12, AHC). Robert Gist's name has been crossed out by hand.
8. See telegrams from Julian Olney, Gregory Associates to Mrs. Archer E. Linde, Phoenix, AZ, January 7, 1954 (Box 4, AHC); Olney to Lloyd Jones, Chico State College, January 7, 1954 (Box 4, AHC); Olney to Gail Plummer, University of Utah, January 7, 1954 (Box 4, AHC); and Olney to Mrs. Sam T. Clarke, Reno Ballet Guild, January 7, 1954 (Box 4, AHC) about Gist dropping out.
9. Dorothy Olney, Gregory Associates, to Mrs. Archer E. Linde, Phoenix, AZ, November 11, 1953 (Box 4, AHC).
10. See, for example, Paul Gregory to Gail Plummer, January 27, 1954 (Box 4, AHC). The same letter was sent in late January and early February 1954 to all the sponsors, who took this change in the contract surprisingly well.
11. "Agnes Moorehead Appearance Here Being Postponed," *Nevada State Journal*, January 13, 1954, p. 16.
12. "Moorehead Show Tonight," *Ruston Daily Leader*, March 2, 1954, p. 1.
13. This was the same fee as Charles Laughton was getting at the time. See Lloyd S. Jones, Chico State College, to Arthur Kennard, Gregory Associates, April 22, 1953 (Box 4, AHC). Charles Higham writes that on his first reading tour, Laughton was earning "between one thousand and fifteen hundred a performance" and that Paul Gregory later "managed to increase the appearance fees for many engagements to four thousand dollars a performance." See Higham, *Charles Laughton*, p. 157.
14. "La Moorehead Shows Friday in Berkeley," *Oakland Tribune*, September 26, 1954, p. B1.
15. "Agnes Moorehead Plays Monterey," *San Mateo Times*, July 23, 1960, p. 7A.
16. Mel Heimer, "My New York," *New Castle News*, June 2, 1970, p. 11.
17. See information in Scrapbook Vol. 73 (Dec. 1972-Summer 1973) (Box 139, WCFTR); Georgia Johnstone to Jill Lehmann, April 2, 1973, included in Jill Marie, *With Every Good Wish...: Agnes Moorehead and Me, 1965–1973*, p. 109 (Nissen); and Sherk, *Agnes Moorehead*, p. 90.
18. See Paul Gregory to Professor John Pick, Marquette University, December 2, 1963 (Box 7, AHC), where he writes: "Her fee ranges from $1,000 to $2,000 per date depending on the kind of presentation, i.e., if a date is a straight promotion on a strictly commercial basis her fee is $2,000. If the presentation is on a series, convocation or educational, then the fee varies based on seating capacity, size of school and considers also the policy of each interested party."
19. Quint Benedetti (*My Travels With) Agnes Moorehead: The Lavender Lady—More Bewitching than Endora* (N.p.: Xlibris, 2010), p. 126.
20. http://kingsburyhall.utah.edu/history-and-mission/.
21. http://kingsburyhall.utah.edu/spaces/.
22. "University Theatre Offers Shaw Play in February," *Salt Lake Tribune*, January 7, 1951, p. B7.
23. Gail Plummer to Paul Gregory, no date (Box 4, AHC).
24. Charles Laughton to Agnes Moorehead [January 1954] (Box 150, WCFTR); Gail Plummer to Gregory Associates, January 28, 1954 (Box 4, AHC).
25. Frank Morriss, "'Fabulous' Actor Arrives: Life Keeps Laughton Hopping," *Winnipeg Free Press*, February 5, 1954, p. 1.
26. Press book article for "That Fabulous Redhead" [1954] (Box 12, AHC).
27. Bayard F. Ennis, "Miss Moorehead's Versatile Show Charms Audience," *Charleston Gazette*, March 18, 1954, p. 8; "Agnes Moorehead Brings Dramatic Treat to 2,000," unidentified Oklahoma City paper [March 1, 1954] (Box 150, WCFTR).
28. For a detailed account of the program as I present it here, see "Reno Audience Enthralled by Moorehead Performance," *Reno Evening Gazette*, April 21, 1954, p. 13.
29. "Agnes Moorehead Brings"; Virgil Miers, "Evening of Agnes Is a Grand Treat," *Dallas Times Herald* [April 6, 1954] (Box 150, WCFTR).
30. Ennis, "Miss Moorehead's Versatile Show," p. 8.
31. Ralph Green, "Fine Evening of Moorehead at Coliseum," *Daily Argus-Leader*, February 3, 1954 (Box 12, AHC); Louis Sheaffer, "Agnes Moorehead Gives an Enjoyable Solo Show," *Brooklyn Eagle*, March 15, 1954 (Box 150, WCFTR).
32. "Agnes Moorehead Brings."
33. Green, "Fine Evening"; Sheaffer, "Agnes Moorehead."
34. "Reno Audience Enthralled," p. 13.
35. Sheaffer, "Agnes Moorehead."
36. "Agnes Moorehead Brings."
37. Sheaffer, "Agnes Moorehead."
38. Green, "Fine Evening."
39. "Agnes Moorehead Brings."
40. Sheaffer, "Agnes Moorehead."
41. Ennis, "Miss Moorehead's Versatile Show," p. 8.
42. Quoted in Dixie Gilliland, "Tour Is Grind, Actress Finds," unidentified Oklahoma paper, February 27, 1954 (Box 150, WCFTR).
43. See, for example, Virginia Shaw, "Agnes Moorehead Gives Fascinating Performance at Wharf," unidentified clipping, July 28, 1960 (Box 153, WCFTR).
44. "Agnes Moorehead Brings."
45. Sheaffer, "Agnes Moorehead."
46. Miers, "Evening of Agnes."
47. Helen Henry, "Readings by Miss Moorehead Thrills Filled Auditorium," *Middlesboro Daily News*, April 13, 1954 (Box 150, WCFTR).
48. "Reno Audience Enthralled," p. 13.
49. Louise Faulk, "Moorehead Vitality Impresses Ruston Audience," *Ruston Daily Leader*, March 3, 1954, p. 1.
50. Sheaffer, "Agnes Moorehead."
51. Wood Soanes, "Curtain Calls," *Oakland Tribune*, September 22, 1954, p. E33.
52. Shaw, "Agnes Moorehead."
53. Wade Crookham to Axel Nissen, July 24, 2012.
54. Ennis, "Miss Moorehead's Versatile Show," p. 8.
55. Charles Nolte, "The Caine Years: An Actor Recalls the Professional Theatre of the Fifties," unpublished typescript, p. 123 (Nissen).
56. "Agnes Moorehead's Menu Too Sugary for One Viewer," *Playground Daily News*, December 4, 1967, p. 6.

57. Interview with Paul Gregory, August 1, 2006.
58. Interview with Paul Gregory, January 9, 2007.
59. *Agnes Moorehead: The Lavender Lady* (Oceanside, CA: House of Quinto Music/Quinto Productions, 2002).
60. Claire Baker, "My Unforgettable Earful," *The Call Board* 6 (May-June 1964), pp. 3–4.
61. Herb Larson, "Agnes Moorehead Proves Charming in Reading," *Portland Reporter*, November 2, 1963, p. 8. Another article described the audience as "disappointingly small." See Peter Thompson, "Agnes Delivered 'Earful'—But to Small Audience," *Portland Journal*, November 2, 1963 (Box 7, AHC).
62. Thompson, "Agnes Delivered 'Earful.'"
63. Tranberg, *I Love the Illusion*, p. 162.
64. First mentioned in a review from 1960: Shaw, "Agnes Moorehead."
65. Benedetti, *My Travels*, p. 113.
66. George E. Perry, "Agnes on the Stage," *Scrapbook* Item #3 (January 1972), p. 4 (Box 2, NYPL).
67. These texts are mentioned in the following reviews: William Trubner, "Star Scores Mershon Hit," *Ohio State University Lantern*, July 20, 1961 (Box 7, AHC); Thompson, "Agnes Delivered 'Earful'"; Larson, "Agnes Moorehead Proves Charming," p. 8; Peggy May, "'Americana,' Agnes Moorehead Pleases Large Audience Here," *Playground Daily News*, December 1, 1967, p. 4; "Agnes Moorehead's Menu," p. 6. Also Jeanne Tro Williams, "Audience Bewitched," *Arizona Republic*, April 26, 1969, p. 48; Robert Batdorff, "Agnes Moorehead Gives Superb Performance in One-Woman Show," *Traverse City Record-Eagle*, July 16, 1969, p. 10; Deron Mikal, "Actress Dazzles Audience," *Zanesville Times Recorder*, April 25, 1970, p. 1.
68. See "Versatile Agnes Great, Be It Chaucer or Shaw," *Dayton Daily News*, October 27, 1961 (Box 7, AHC) and the reviews cited in the preceding footnote.
69. Bob Rose, "She's Only a Part-Time Witch," *Corpus Christi Caller-Times*, August 6, 1967, p. 6F.
70. In a note to Perry, "Agnes on the Stage," p. 4.
71. Kear, *Agnes Moorehead*, p. 224.
72. This overview contains only performances that the author has been able to document through primary sources.
73. For two 75-minute performances.
74. For two performances the same day.
75. Paul Gregory refunded $250 after a complaint from the sponsor about their vast disappointment in the performance and the performer.
76. Double bill with Christopher Fry's *A Phoenix Too Frequent* starring Joseph Cotten.
77. Double bill with *A Phoenix Too Frequent*.
78. Double bill with *A Phoenix Too Frequent*.
79. And return airfare for 6 performances.
80. Including lecture and seminar with theater students.
81. This is when Quint Benedetti made a sound recording of the performance, that was later released as a record (1975) and a CD (2002) under the title *Agnes Moorehead: The Lavender Lady*.

Chapter 7

1. Nelson Gidding, "The Life You Save May Be Your Own" script, October 8, 1956 (Box 39, WCFTR).
2. https://en.wikipedia.org/wiki/Republic_Pictures.
3. Brooks and March, *Prime Time Network and Cable TV Shows*, p. 908.
4. Flannery O'Connor, *A Good Man Is Hard to Find and Other Stories* (New York: Harcourt, Brace, 1955), p. 54.
5. O'Connor, p. 55.
6. O'Connor, p. 59.
7. I use the character names and the spelling of names from the televised version. In the printed story, Lucy Nell is spelled Lucynell and, as mentioned, Ma Crater is only referred to as "the old woman."
8. O'Connor, *A Good Man Is Hard to Find*, p. 57.

Chapter 8

1. Agnes Moorehead to Paul Gregory [January 11, 1958] (Box 7, AHC).
2. In this connection, it is worth recalling something Fred Carmichael told Warren Sherk in the mid-1970s: "Her talks of the people she worked with were all the more remarkable because there was never anything vindictive. If she ever did say anything the least bit negative, she would omit their names" (quoted in Sherk, *Agnes Moorehead*, p. 13). This indicates that with more distant friends, acquaintances, and fans, Moorehead behaved with more restraint. It was clearly not part of her granddame persona to speak ill of others, however much she enjoyed making barbed remarks to her confidantes.
3. T.C.O., "'The Rivalry' Re-Creates Vivid Chapter in History," *Emporia Gazette* [October 18, 1957] (Box 55, WCFTR).
4. See Agnes Moorehead to Paul Gregory [April 1958] (Box 7, AHC).
5. Willard E. Josephy to Paul Gregory, September 6, 1957 (Box 14, AHC); interview with Paul Gregory, May 11, 2007.
6. Gloria Safier to Paul Gregory, September 5, 1957 (Box 11, AHC); Martin Gabel's contract dated September 7, 1957 (Box 15, AHC).
7. Paul Gregory to Brian Donlevy, January 23, 1957 (Box 11, AHC); Brian Donlevy's contract dated August 23, 1957 (Box 14, AHC).
8. Paul Gregory to Agnes Moorehead, January 24 and February 6, 1957 (Box 11, AHC); Moorehead's contract dated August 23, 1957 (Box 14, AHC). She was also paid $50 a week in living expenses and had her transportation costs covered.
9. Kathy Ellis's contract dated September 12, 1957 (Box 14, AHC).
10. Interview with Norman Corwin, March 10, 2008.
11. Paul Gregory to Agnes Moorehead, August 22, 1957 (Box 11, AHC).
12. Paul Gregory to Agnes Moorehead, November 22, 1957 (Box 14, AHC). See also Paul Gregory to Irvin Feld (and other investors), November 15, 1957, where he mentions that "We are encountering considerable difficulty in arranging for the proper theatre in New York City" (Box 14, AHC).
13. T.C.O., "'The Rivalry.'"
14. *Vancouver Province* review quoted in "More Reviews of 'Rivalry' on its Tour," *Freeport Journal Standard*, October 12, 1957, p. 4.
15. Paul Gregory to Agnes Moorehead, September 17, 1957 (Box 11, AHC).
16. Claudia Cassidy, "On the Aisle: Neither Rivalry Nor Drama in This Lincoln-Douglas Debate," *Chicago Herald Tribune*, October 31, 1957, p. 3.
17. Elizabeth Yager and Olga Gize Carlisle, "Cast of

'Rivalry' Greeted by 275 at Party in Hotel," *Freeport Journal Standard*, November 7, 1957, p. 8.

18. T.C.O., "'The Rivalry.'"

19. "Curtain Will Not Be Lowered When Actress Dons Costumes," *Lubbock Evening Journal*, October 2, 1957, p. 4.

20. *Vancouver Sun* review quoted in "More Reviews of 'Rivalry' on its Tour," *Freeport Journal Standard*, October 12, 1957, p. 4.

21. Frank G. Schmidt, "Fine Acting Puts Spark In 'Rivalry,'" *South Bend Tribune* [November 11, 1957] (Box 55, WCFTR).

22. T.C.O., "'The Rivalry.'"

23. Fred Weterick, "Esteemed Cast Can't Lift 'Rivalry's Heavy Script," *Indiana Daily Student*, November 13, 1957 (Box 151, WCFTR).

24. Boston review dated January 19, 1958, quoted in Parish, *Good Dames*, p. 114.

25. Elisabeth Yager, "'The Rivalry' Is Stirring, Memorable," *Freeport Standard Journal*, November 7, 1957, p. 8.

26. *Variety* review dated September 24, 1957, quoted in Parish, *Good Dames*, p. 114.

27. Ralph Green, "Timeliness of 'Rivalry' Impressive," *Sioux Falls Argus-Leader* [October 26, 1957] (Box 55, WCFTR).

28. Quoted in Tranberg, *I Love the Illusion*, p. 182. See also John Finlayson, "'Rivalry' Revives Era of Lincoln and Douglas," unidentified Detroit paper [October 17, 1957] (Box 151, WCFTR).

29. Richard Bacon to Paul Gregory, October 12, 1957 (Box 11, AHC).

30. Interview with Paul Gregory, May 11, 2007.

31. Interview with Norman Corwin, March 10, 2008.

Chapter 9

1. Brooks and March, *Prime Time Network and Cable TV Shows*, p. 1103.

2. "California, County Marriages, 1850–1952," database with images, *Family Search* (https://familysearch.org/ark:/61903/1:1:K86M-LTC, 28 November 2014), Jerry Lee Alten and Carole Arlyn Johnson, 26 Jul 1952; citing Los Angeles, California, United States, county courthouses, California; FHL microfilm 1,283,810.

3. *Wagon Train* draft script, July 19, 1957 (Box 42, WCFTR).

4. *Wagon Train* shooting schedule, August 19–23 and 26, 1957 (Box 42, WCFTR).

5. Paul Gregory to Agnes Moorehead, August 22, 1957 (Box 11, AHC).

6. Brooks and March, *Prime Time Network and Cable TV Shows*, p. 1103; *The Rivalry* itinerary (Box 151, WCFTR); *The Rivalry* itinerary (Box 11, AHC).

7. "California Death Index, 1940–1997," database, *Family Search* (https://familysearch.org/ark:/61903/1:1:VGYN-4MG, 26 November 2014), Jerry Lee Alten, 19 Nov 1958; Department of Public Health Services, Sacramento; "Rising Actor Meets Fate of James Dean," *Milwaukee Journal* (November 20, 1958), p. 1.

Chapter 10

1. Pauline Bartel, *Spellcasters: Witches and Witchcraft in History, Folklore and Popular Culture* (Dallas: Taylor Trade, 2000), p. 217.

2. https://en.wikipedia.org/wiki/Campanula_rapunculus.

3. Bartel, *Spellcasters*, p. 217.

4. Hal Humphrey, "Neurotic-Proof Fairytales for Sensitive Parents," *Los Angeles Mirror News*, October 25, 1958 (Box 152, WCFTR).

5. Humphrey, "Neurotic-Proof Fairytales."

6. Humphrey, "Neurotic-Proof Fairytales."

7. "Tube," *Shirley Temple's Storybook*: "Rapunzel" review [*Variety*], October 29, 1958 (Box 152, WCFTR).

8. William Ewald, "Television in Review," *Kittanning Leader-Times*, October 28, 1958, p. 14.

9. Lillian S. Small to Agnes Moorehead, October 28, 1958 (Box 7, AHC).

10. Matt Messina, "Fair-Haired 'Rapunzel' on Shirley Temple Storybook," *New York Daily News*, October 28, 1958, p. 52.

11. "TV Today," *Hutchinson News*, October 27, 1958, p. 5.

12. Hank Grant, *Shirley Temple's Storybook*: "Rapunzel" review, *Hollywood Reporter*, October 29, 1958 (Box 151, WCFTR).

13. "Tube," "Rapunzel" review.

14. John P. Shanley, "Queens to Witches: Agnes Moorehead Takes All Roles in Stride," *New York Times*, September 18, 1960, p. 19.

15. Shanley, "Queens to Witches," p. 19.

16. Speaking of third times: Moorehead made a third appearance on Shirley Temple's show on November 11, 1960, when she played Hepzibah Pyncheon in an adaptation of Nathaniel Hawthorne's *The House of the Seven Gables*. There is no magic in this episode in which Temple plays Phoebe Pyncheon and runs the gamut of emotion from A to B. Robert Culp, Martin Landau, and Jonathan Harris co-starred.

Chapter 11

1. "Ginger Rogers to Return to Broadway for Paul Gregory," press release, May 14, 1959 (Box 3, AHC).

2. Paul Gregory had tried to interest Gig Young in the role. See Paul Gregory to Gig Young, August 6, 1959 (Box, AHC). In the letter, Gregory mentions that "It was very good seeing you, your wife and your pretty new house." Young's wife at the time was Elizabeth Montgomery.

3. Harold R. Williams to Paul Gregory, June 24, 1959 (Box 14, AHC); Moorehead's contract dated August 28, 1959 (Box 14, AHC). In comparison, Ginger Rogers was paid $5,000 a week and had 15 percent of the net profits and Leif Erickson was paid $2,000 a week. See rider to Rogers's undated contract and Gordon E. Youngman to Paul Gregory, August 13, 1959 (Box 1, AHC) and overview of "The Pink Jungle Company Contracts" dated December 4, 1959 (Box 14, AHC).

4. A stipulation in the rider to Moorehead's contract stated that "her name shall occupy that of first position subservient to the name Ginger Rogers, in the same size type as that of Ginger Rogers" (Box 14, AHC).

5. Interview with Paul Gregory, September 26, 2006.

6. Interview with Paul Gregory, May 11, 2007.

7. See Sherk, *Agnes Moorehead*, p. 15.

8. Interview with Paul Gregory, September 26, 2006.

9. Interview with Paul Gregory, May 11 and March 8, 2008. Rogers's dance-in, Carmen Clifford, had not

been stipulated in Roger's contract and had cost the production money that was not in the original budget. In addition to her salary of $400 a week, Clifford required her own costumes, hotel room, and transportation. See Paul Gregory to Ginger Rogers, September 9, 1959 (Box 1, AHC) and Paul Gregory to Gordon Youngman, January 11, 1960 (Box 2, AHC).

10. Interview with Paul Gregory, May 11, 2007.

11. On the photostat of Paul Gregory to Ginger Rogers, September 9, 1959, Gregory has handwritten "Lela had said to build up Ginger" (Box 1, AHC); Paul Gregory to Ginger Rogers, January 19, 1960 (Box 2, AHC).

12. Theresa Loeb Cone, "Talent Wasted in 'The Pink Jungle,'" *San Francisco Tribune* [October 15, 1959] (Box 153, WCFTR).

13. "Steif.," "Legit Review: 'The Pink Jungle,'" *Variety*, October 16, 1959 (Box 153, WCFTR).

14. Emilia Model, "'Pink Jungle' Looks Like Hit," *San Francisco News-Call Bulletin*, undated (Box 153, WCFTR).

15. Quoted in Parish, *Good Dames*, p. 114.

16. Elliot Norton, "'The Pink Jungle' Brings Ginger Rogers to Hub," *Boston Daily Record* [December 8, 1959] (Box 153, WCFTR).

17. Paul Gregory to Robert Rapport, November 10, 1959 (Box 3, AHC).

18. Leslie Stevens to Paul Gregory, December 5, 1959 (Box 2, AHC).

19. Peggy Doyle, "Ginger Rogers Hoping Her 'Pink Jungle' Improves," *Boston Evening American*, December 8, 1959 (Box 153, WCFTR).

20. Paul Gregory to Ginger Rogers, January 19, 1960 (Box 2, AHC).

21. Paul Gregory to members of the *Pink Jungle* company, December 7, 1959 (Box 3, AHC).

22. Bob Thomas, "Cast Friction Reported: Ginger Blames Author for New Play's Failure," *Schenectady Star*, January 14, 1960 (Box 153, WCFTR).

23. Ginger Rogers, *Ginger: My Story* (London: Headline, 1991), pp. 306–9; Doyle, "Ginger Rogers Hoping."

24. Gregory to Youngman, January 11, 1960 (Box 2, AHC).

25. Paul Gregory to Ginger Rogers, January 19, 1960 (Box 2, AHC).

26. Paul Gregory to Edd X. Russell, February 3, 1960 (Box 2, AHC).

27. Cone, "Talent Wasted."

28. See two undated typescripts of *The Pink Jungle* in the Agnes Moorehead Papers (Box 55, WCFTR). One of them is bound in a black velvet folder with gold lettering, indicating it is a final version (to the extent that any version of this script was final).

29. Interview with Paul Gregory, May 11, 2007.

30. Helen Bower, "Agnes Moorehead Is Tops at the Boxoffice," *Detroit Free Press*, December 5, 1959 (Box 153, WCFTR). Fleming's novel was made into a film in 1963. It was titled *55 Days at Peking*, starred Eva Gardner and Charlton Heston, and was directed by Nicholas Ray. It was hoped that Greta Garbo would make a long-awaited return to the screen in the role of the Dowager Empress Tzu-Hsi, but it ultimately went to Flora Robson.

Chapter 12

1. https://en.wikipedia.org/wiki/The_Millionaire_(TV_series).

2. *The Millionaire* revised script, March 8, 1960 (Box 40, WCFTR).

3. https://en.wikipedia.org/wiki/Culver_Studios#RKO-Path.C3.A9_studios.

4. www.imdb.com.

Chapter 13

1. William Froug, *How I Escaped from Gilligan's Island and Other Misadventures of a Hollywood Writer-Producer* (Madison: University of Wisconsin Press, 2005), p. 108.

2. Gardner McKay, *Journey Without a Map: A Memoir* (Honolulu: Shiptree, 2013), p. 164.

3. McKay, p. 165.

4. William Froug, *How I Escaped*, p. 108; James Rosin, *Adventures in Paradise: The Television Series* (Philadelphia: Autumn Road, 2009), p. 11.

5. McKay, *Journey Without a Map*, p. 177.

6. Rosin, *Adventures in Paradise*, p. 17.

7. *Adventures in Paradise* shooting schedule, September 7, 1960 (Box 37, WCFTR).

8. Rosin, *Adventures in Paradise*, p. 27.

9. Dominick Dunne, *The Way We Lived Then: Recollections of a Well-Known Name Dropper* (New York: Crown, 1999), p. 48.

10. Froug, *How I Escaped*, pp. 110–11.

11. *Adventures in Paradise*: "The Krismen," revised final script, September 6, 1960, p. 2 (Box 37, WCFTR).

12. Blake was the mother of Meredith Baxter and went on to co-create *One Day at a Time* with her third husband, Allan Manings.

13. Ruscio was married to future actress Kate Williamson and the son-in-law of veteran character actress Nydia Westman.

14. Dunne, *The Way We Lived Then*, p. 48.

15. Froug, *How I Escaped*, p. 112.

16. Froug, p. 114.

17. McKay, *Journey Without a Map*, p. 170.

18. Froug, *How I Escaped*, p. 117.

Chapter 14

1. https://en.wikipedia.org/wiki/Rawhide_(TV_series).

2. https://en.wikipedia.org/wiki/Rawhide_(TV_series).

3. https://en.wikipedia.org/wiki/Rawhide_(TV_series); http://www.classictvhits.com/tvratings/1960.htm.

4. Clint Eastwood, "Beauties Brighten Lives of Drovers," *Syracuse Herald-American*, July 25, 1965, p. 17.

Chapter 15

1. Hedda Hopper, "Looking at Hollywood," *Rocky Mountain Telegram*, October 19, 1960, p. 4B.

2. Don Presnell and Marty McGee, *A Critical History of Television's* The Twilight Zone, *1959–1964* (Jefferson, NC: McFarland, 2008), p. 19, including quote from Clemens.

3. As measured by votes from users of the Internet Movie Database (IMDb) in 2017.

4. Presnell and McGee, *A Critical History*, p. 83.

5. https://en.wikipedia.org/wiki/The_Twilight_Zone_(1959_TV_series).

6. Presnell and McGee, *A Critical History*, p. 19.
7. Richard Matheson, *The Twilight Zone*: Script Forty-Six "The Invaders," August 6, 1960, no page (Box 42, WCFTR). Matheson's original script is reproduced in Richard Matheson, *Richard Matheson's the Twilight Zone Scripts: Volume One*, ed. Stanley Wiater (Springfield, PA: Edge, 2001), pp. 211–45.
8. Quoted in Presnell and McGee, *A Critical History*, p. 83. See also Stewart T. Stanyard, *Dimensions Behind the Twilight Zone: A Backstage Tribute to Television's Groundbreaking Series* (Toronto: ECW, 2007), p. 166; Jean-Marc Lofficier and Randy Lofficier, *Into the Twilight Zone: The Rod Serling Programme Guide* (Lincoln, NE: Mystery Writers of America Presents, 2003), p. 219.
9. Quoted in Marc Scott Zicree, *The Twilight Zone Companion: Second Edition* (Los Angeles: Silman-James, 1992), p. 176.
10. Matheson, *The Twilight Zone*, no page.
11. Quoted in Presnell and McGee, *A Critical History*, p. 83.
12. Quoted in Matheson, *The Twilight Zone Scripts*, p. 209. Matheson expresses the same reservations about the "little roly-poly dolls," the condensation of the action, and the drawing out of the opening scene in Zicree, *The Twilight Zone Companion*, p. 176.
13. Noel Murray, "10 Episodes that Take Viewers into the Depths of *The Twilight Zone*" (February 13, 2013), www.avclub.com.
14. Matheson, *The Twilight Zone*, p. 25. In the teleplay, the lettering on the side of the space ship reads "U.S. Army Air Force—Mars I" (rather than "U.S. Air Force Space Probe No. 1" in the episode as recorded).
15. Douglas Brode and Carol Serling, *Rod Serling and The Twilight Zone: The 50th Anniversary Tribute* (Fort Lee, NJ: Barricade, 2009), p. 173.
16. Quoted in Presnell and McGee, *A Critical History*, p. 20.
17. Quoted in Zicree, *The Twilight Zone Companion*, p. 176.
18. Dave Thompson, *The Twilight Zone FAQ: All That's Left to Know About the Fifth Dimension and Beyond* (Milwaukee, WI: Applause, 2015), no page. See also Zicree, *The Twilight Zone Companion*, p. 172; Tranberg, *I Love the Illusion*, pp. 197–98.
19. Quoted in Stanyard, *Dimensions Behind the Twilight Zone*, p. 166.
20. Hedda Hopper, "Looking at Hollywood," *Colorado Springs Gazette Telegraph* (February 5, 1961), p. 7.

Chapter 16

1. Joseph Cotten, *Vanity Will Get You Somewhere: An Autobiography* (San Jose, CA: toExcel, 2000), p. 147.
2. Interview with Paul Gregory, September 26, 2006.
3. Cotten, *Vanity Will Get You Somewhere*, p. 125.
4. Agnes Moorehead to Paul Gregory, Saturday [October 1961] (Box 14, AHC). Directed by Norman Taurog, *The Pink Fuzzy Nightgown* starred Jane Russell and Keenan Wynn.
5. Paul Gregory to Agnes Moorehead, October 18, 1961 (Box 7, AHC).
6. Paul Gregory to Agnes Moorehead, August 11, 1961 (Box, AHC).
7. Gregory to Moorehead, October 18, 1961.
8. Agnes Moorehead's contracts dated October 18 and December 19, 1961; Joseph Cotten's contract dated November 20, 1961; Patricia Medina's contract dated November 20, 1961; and Thomas Mitchell's contract dated October 13, 1961 (Box 2 and 14, AHC).
9. Tranberg, *I Love the Illusion*, p. 206.
10. Paul Gregory to Karl Bernstein, December 22, 1961 (Box 14, AHC).
11. Landon Laird, "Fine Cast Sparkles in Suspense Tale," *Kansas City Star*, February 7, 1962 (Box 3, AHC).
12. Paul Gregory to Joseph Cotten and Patricia Medina, October 12, 1961 (Box 14, AHC). The play was made into a TV movie that aired on NBC in 1968 and established Peter Falk as the definitive Columbo. Gene Barry played Dr. Flemming, Nina Foch his murdered wife, and Katherine Justice his lover and accomplice.
13. Cotten, *Vanity Will Get You Somewhere*, p. 149.
14. Powell Lindsay, "Gregory Assails 'Phonies': Maverick Producer Likes Life on 'Road'" [*Knoxville Journal*] [April 13, 1962] (Box 8, AHC).
15. Cotten, *Vanity Will Get You Somewhere*, p. 149.
16. Robert Rapport to Agnes Moorehead, May 14, 1962 (Box 64, WCFTR).
17. Paul Gregory to limited partners, June 20, 1962 (Box 14, AHC).
18. See Agnes Moorehead's signed souvenir program for *Prescription: Murder* in Scrapbook Vol. 2 (Spring 1962) (Box 64, WCFTR); Patricia Medina Cotten, *Laid Back in Hollywood Remembering* (Los Angeles: Belle, 1998), p. 126; William Link and Richard Levinson to Paul Gregory, March 5, 1962 (Box 8, AHC).
19. William Link and Richard Levinson to Paul Gregory [February 1962] (Box 8, AHC).
20. Frank Morriss, "Old-Fashioned Mystery: When Actress Died, So Did Play," *Toronto Globe and Mail* [May 1962] (Box 64, WCFTR).
21. Norman Houk, "Prescription: Murder Provides Formula for Electric Evening," *Minneapolis Morning Tribune*, February 13, 1962 (Box 3, AHC); Marjory Rutherford, "'Prescription: Murder' a Tense Spellbinder," unidentified Atlanta newspaper [April 10, 1962] (Box 8, AHC).
22. David L. Owens, "Filled Auditorium Pleased by Play," *Greensboro Daily News*, March 16, 1962 (Box 3, AHC).
23. Henry H. Schulte, "Needs Polishing: Play Prescription for Pleasant Time," unidentified Savannah newspaper [April 15, 1962] (Box 8, AHC).
24. Parish, *Good Dames*, p. 117.
25. Denman Kountze, Jr., "Suspense the Biggest Lack in *Prescription: Murder*," *Omaha World-Herald*, February 9, 1962 (Box 3, AHC).
26. Bob Goddard, "'Prescription: Murder' Good Stage Medicine," *St. Louis Globe-Democrat* [April 3, 1962] (Box 8, AHC).
27. Elliot Norton, "Need to Speed Up 'Murder'Drama," *Boston Daily Record*, May 22, 1962 (Box 64, WCFTR).

Chapter 17

1. Laurie Main died in Los Angeles on February 8, 2012, at the age of 89. Brian Bedford died on January 13, 2016, at the age of 80. Claude Harz (b. 1936), who replaced Lee Richardson as Wilfred Oliver towards the end of the New York run, is at present the sole surviving cast member of *Lord Pengo*.
2. Dramatic production contract for *Lord Pengo* dated March 1953 (Box 14, AHC).

3. Paul Gregory to Agnes Moorehead, June 9, 1961 (Box 7, AHC).

4. See Charles Boyer's contract dated May 9, 1962 (Box 14, AHC).

5. Interview with Paul Gregory, September 26, 2006; Swindell, *Boyer*, p. 247.

6. Swindell, *Boyer*, p. 247; Charles Boyer to Paul Gregory, July 25, 1962 (Box 14, AHC).

7. See contract with the Royale Theatre dated June 5, 1962 (Box 14, AHC).

8. Paul Gregory to Agnes Moorehead, June 20, 1962 (Box 7, AHC).

9. Peter Glenville to Paul Gregory, June 22, 1962 (Box 14, AHC).

10. Paul Gregory to Vincent Donehue, July 5, 1962 (Box 14, AHC).

11. Paul Gregory to Agnes Moorehead, July 10, 1962 (Box 7, AHC).

12. Paul Gregory to Charles Boyer, July 20, 1962 (Box 14, AHC).

13. Interview with Laurie Main, May 19, 2007.

14. Interview with Laurie Main, May 19, 2007.

15. *Lord Pengo* script dated August 23, 1962 (Box 55, WCFTR).

16. Paul Gregory to Charles Boyer, July 20, 1962 (Box 14, AHC).

17. Gregory to Boyer, July 20, 1962.

18. John Disborough to Mrs. U. Frandsen, September 7, 1962 (Box 14, AHC).

19. Interview with Laurie Main, May 19, 2007.

20. Interview with Paul Gregory, March 8, 2008; Agnes Moorehead's contract dated September 6, 1962 (Box 14, AHC). In comparison, Charles Boyer was paid $6,000 a week, Henry Daniell and Brian Bedford $750, Ruth White $600, Laurie Main $350, and Betty Sinclair $250. See contracts dated May 9, August 27, September 1, September 3, and September 8, 1962 (Box 14, AHC).

21. William Glover, "Boyer Gives Play a Glow as Suave Portrait Seller," *Racine Journal-Times*, Nov. 20, 1962, p. 6B.

22. Interview with Laurie Main, May 19, 2007.

23. Interview with Paul Gregory, January 9, 2007.

24. Agnes Moorehead to Paul Gregory, June 17, 1962 (Box 7, AHC).

25. See Scrapbook Vol. 7 (Winter 1963) (Box 69, WCFTR).

26. Interview with Laurie Main, May 19, 2007.

27. Vincent Donehue to Agnes Moorehead, August 6, 1962 (Box 64, WCFTR).

28. Interviews with Laurie Main, May 19, 2007, and Paul Gregory, January 9, 2007. On Moorehead's dislike of Donehue, see also Georgia Johnstone to Agnes Moorehead, October 30, 1963 (Box 1, NYPL).

29. See Scrapbook Vol. 3 (Summer and Fall 1962) (Box 65, WCFTR).

30. Basil Rathbone to Agnes Moorehead, November 25, 1962 (Box 65, WCFTR).

31. See Scrapbook Vol. 3 (Summer and Fall 1962) and Vol. 4 (Fall 1962) (Box 65 and 66, WCFTR).

32. Paul Gregory to Agnes Moorehead, December 7, 1962 (Box 66, WCFTR).

33. Paul Gregory to Agnes Moorehead, December 8, 1962 (Box 66, WCFTR).

34. Unidentified review quoted in Parish, *Good Dames*, p. 118; *New York Post* review quoted in Kear, *Agnes Moorehead*, p. 228.

35. Jerry Gaghan, "'Lord Pengo' Opens at Locust," *Philadelphia Daily News*, October 12, 1962 (Box 14, AHC).

36. Henry T. Murdock, "At the Locust: Boyer Plays Behrman's Pengo with Polished Art," *Philadelphia Inquirer*, October 12, 1962 (Box 14, AHC).

37. Jack Gaver, "Broadway: Boyer Draws Patrons," *News Texan*, December 23, 1962, p. 4.

38. Josef Mossman, "'Lord Pengo' Is Too Talky," *Detroit News*, October 23, 1962 (Box 65, WCFTR).

39. Josef Mossman, "New 1st Act Improves Fisher's 'Lord Pengo,'" *Detroit News*, October 31, 1962 (Box 14, AHC).

40. Howard Taubman, "Behrman's New Play, 'Lord Pengo,' Opens," *New York Times*, November 20, 1962 (Box 65, WCFTR).

41. Ernest Schier, "At the New Locust: Comedy Portrays Life of Art Dealer," *Philadelphia Evening Bulletin*, October 12, 1962 (Box 14, AHC).

42. Peter Witt to Irving Cooper, February 13, 1963 (Box 14, AHC); Lucy Kroll to Paul Gregory, February 4, 1963 (Box 14, AHC).

43. *Lord Pengo* financial statement for week ending April 20, 1963 (Box 14, AHC). The highest grosses had been $40,000 in the week ending October 27, 1962, at the New Fisher Theatre in Detroit and $39,000 in the week ending December 8, 1962, in New York (Box 14, AHC).

44. Margot Stevenson's contract dated April 1, 1963 (Box 14, AHC).

45. Paul Gregory to Jane Friedlander and Michael Parver, July 11, 1963 (Box 14, AHC).

46. Paul Gregory to George Patrick, December 11, 1963 (Box 14, AHC).

47. "Community Theatre Needs Discipline," *The Buff: The Magazine of the Little Theatre* (March 1963), p. 4.

Chapter 18

1. *Burke's Law*, revised script, October 7, 1963 (Box 37, WCFTR).

2. The revised draft of the *Bewitched* pilot script with Moorehead's handwritten ideas for a name for her character is dated September 30, 1963. See *Bewitched*, revised draft of pilot script, September 30, 1963 (Box 43, WCFTR).

3. Agnes Moorehead to Georgia Johnstone, October 29, 1963 (Box 1, NYPL).

4. Moorehead and Jack Haley would play a married couple again in an episode of *Marcus Welby, M.D.* titled "He Could Sell Iceboxes to the Eskimos," which aired on October 17, 1972.

5. She describes this disastrous "rebound" marriage briefly in her autobiography. See June Allyson with Frances Spatz Leighton, *June Allyson* (New York: G.P. Putnam, 1982), pp. 235–36.

6. *Burke's Law*, revised script.

7. See *Burke's Law*, revised scripts, March 10 and 12, 1964 (Box 37, WCFTR).

8. *Burke's Law*, revised script, February 17, 1965 (Box 37, WCFTR).

9. *Bewitched* filming schedule (www.bewitched.net); Scrapbook Vol. 16 (Spring 1965) (Box 78, WCFTR); Tranberg, *I Love the Illusion*, p. 244.

10. *Bewitched* call sheet, March 25, 1965 (Box 44, WCFTR); *Bewitched* filming schedule (www.bewitched.net).

11. See Kear, *Agnes Moorehead*, p. 191; Tranberg, *I Love the Illusion*, p. 396.

Chapter 19

1. Agnes Moorehead to Georgia Johnstone, January 22, 1964 (Box 1, NYPL); contract with Tibbits Opera House, Coldwater, Michigan, dated January 19, 1964 (Box 7, AHC).

2. www.imdb.com.

3. https://www.youtube.com/watch?v=ybEBHRuh75Q.

4. "Today's Video Tips," *Arizona Republic*, March 4, 1964, p. 27.

5. This outstanding drama series ran concurrently on CBS with *Channing* on ABC, though on different nights, and like *Channing* only lasted one season (from September 23, 1963, till April 27, 1964). Yet its 26 episodes resulted in seven Primetime Emmy Award nominations and one win in 1964, mostly for the episode "Who Do You Kill" with James Earl Jones and Diana Sands, about a young married couple struggling to make ends meet whose infant daughter dies from a rat bite.

Chapter 20

1. The appendix to this book contains an "Episode Guide to Agnes Moorehead's Appearances on *Bewitched*."

2. Froug, *How I Escaped*, p. 230.

3. Interviews with Paul Gregory, January 9, 2007, and March 8, 2008.

4. "'Bewitched' to Be Fall TV Comedy," *Rocky Mountain Telegram*, July 12, 1964, p. 5B.

5. Joseph Finnigan, "Agnes Makes an Ideal Witch," *Mansfield News Journal*, October 16, 1964, p. 10.

6. Quoted in Tranberg, *I Love the Illusion*, p. 238.

7. Quoted in Kear, *Agnes Moorehead*, p. 153.

8. Cynthia Lowry, "In Chilly Studio, Chic Witch Explains Art of TV Sorcery," *Des Moines Sunday Register*, August 23, 1964, no page.

9. Jean Henniger, "Actress Has Strong Beliefs," *The Oregonian*, March 31, 1967 (Box 99, WCFTR).

10. Finnigan, "Agnes Makes an Ideal Witch," p. 10.

11. Mike Steen, *Hollywood Speaks: An Oral History* (New York: G.P. Putnam, 1974), p. 110.

12. Henniger, "Actress Has Strong Beliefs."

13. Sol Saks, "Bewitched: A Half Hour Comedy—Pilot Script," revised draft, September 30, 1963, p. 28 (Box 43, WCFTR).

14. Saks, "Bewitched," revised draft, p. 10.

15. Saks, "Bewitched," revised draft, p. 5.

16. Saks, "Bewitched," revised draft, no page.

17. Saks, "Bewitched," revised draft, p. 6.

18. Joan E. Vadeboncoeur, "Bewitching Business," *Syracuse Herald-American*, November 14, 1965, p. 20.

19. Froug, *How I Escaped*, p. 239.

20. Kasey Rogers to Axel Nissen, August 5, 2003.

21. Quoted in Herbie J. Pilato, *Bewitched Forever: The Immortal Companion to Television's Most Magical Supernatural Situation Comedy*, 2d ed. (Irving, TX: Summit, 2001), p. 84.

22. Froug, *How I Escaped*, p. 232.

23. Agnes Moorehead, "Actors Easily Hurt by Unfair Criticism," *Newark Advocate*, July 13, 1965, p. 12.

24. "Miss Moorehead Writes," *Call Board* no. 8 (December 1964), p. 5 (Box 36, WCFTR).

25. Agnes Moorehead to Georgia Johnstone, August 23, 1965 (Box 1, NYPL).

26. Agnes Moorehead to Georgia Johnstone [postmarked January 16, 1970] (Box 1, NYPL).

27. Benedetti, *My Travels*, p. 40. See also p. 121.

28. Quoted in Pilato, *Bewitched Forever*, p. 58.

29. "Mini-Interview," *Newark Advocate*, November 30, 1968, p. 7.

30. Agnes Moorehead to Georgia Johnstone, October 29, 1963 (Box 1, NYPL).

31. "Modern Witch Uses a Plane," *Dallas News*, May 31, 1965 (Nissen).

32. Bob Rose, "She's Only a Part-Time Witch," *Corpus Christi Caller-Times*, August 6, 1967, p. 6F.

33. Herbie J. Pilato, *Twitch Upon a Star: The Bewitched Life and Career of Elizabeth Montgomery* (Lanham, MD: Taylor Trade, 2012), p. 190.

34. Ruth E. Thompson, "'Bewitched' Co-Star Has Her Cake, Eats It Too," *Leader-Times*, March 20, 1965, no page.

35. Susan J. Douglas, *Where the Girls Are: Growing Up Female with the Mass Media* (New York: Times/Random House, 1995), p. 132.

36. Bartel, *Spellcasters*, p. 239.

Chapter 21

1. *New York Times*, July 4, 1966 (Box 2, NYPL).

2. Bob MacKenzie, "On Television," *Oakland Tribune*, July 6, 1966, p. 8A.

3. Incidentally, Ray Aghayan and 26-year-old Bob Mackie won the first Primetime Emmy ever awarded for costume design for this production.

4. Quoted in Tranberg, *I Love the Illusion*, p. 268.

5. "Alice Through the Looking Glass," final script, June 26, 1966 (Box 37, WCFTR).

6. Agnes Moorehead to Georgia Johnstone, June 19, 1966 (Box 1, NYPL).

7. *Bewitched* filming schedule (www.bewitched.net); "Nobody's Perfect" shooting schedule (Box 45, WCFTR).

8. Cynthia Lowry, "'Alice' Provides Happy Time," *Big Spring Herald*, November 7, 1966, p. 3A.

9. Quoted in Tranberg, *I Love the Illusion*, p. 268.

10. Tranberg, p. 269.

11. Lowry, "'Alice' Provides Happy Time," p. 3A.

Chapter 22

1. *The Wild Wild West* call sheet, December 5, 1966 (Box 42, WCFTR).

2. We can be sure she didn't work on Saturday, December 3, as that day she held her annual Christmas party, the first important social event of the film colony's holiday season. See Scrapbook Vol. 27 (Fall-Christmas 1966) (Box 92, WCFTR).

3. *Bewitched* filming schedule (www.bewitched.net).

4. https://en.wikipedia.org/wiki/The_Wild_Wild_West.

5. https://en.wikipedia.org/wiki/The_Wild_Wild_West.

6. https://en.wikipedia.org/wiki/The_Wild_Wild_West.

7. *Bewitched* filming schedule (www.bewitched.net).

8. See Scrapbook Vol. 31 (Spring 1967) (Box 97, WCFTR).

9. Agnes Moorehead to Georgia Johnstone [June 1967] (Box 98, WCFTR).

10. *Bewitched* call sheet, June 7 and 8, 1967 (Box 46, WCFTR); *Bewitched* filming schedule (www.bewitched.net).

Chapter 23

1. *Custer*: "Spirit Woman" final draft script, October 23, 1967 (Box 38, WCFTR).
2. *Bewitched* filming schedule (www.bewitched.net).
3. "A Busy Time," *Express and News*, December 17, 1967, p. 7.
4. Jack Bradford, "Hollywood Report," *Arizona Republic*, December 18, 1967, p. 44.
5. The elder Mr. Stephens was played in Seasons 4 through 6 by Roy Roberts. Simon returned to play Frank Stephens in the character's final appearance, which was the Season 7 episode "Samantha and the Antique Doll."
6. "Television Tonight," *Valley Independent*, December 13, 1967, p. 31.
7. https://en.wikipedia.org/wiki/Custer_(TV_series).
8. "California Marriage Index, 1960–1985," database, *Family Search* (https://familysearch.org/ark:/61903/1:1:V6XK-L9K, 27 November 2014), Wayne E Maunder and Lucia C Maisto, 01 Mar 1968; from "California, Marriage Index, 1960–1985," database and images, *Ancestry* (http://www.ancestry.com: 2007); citing Los Angeles City, California, Center of Health Statistics, California Department of Health Services, Sacramento.
9. "California Birth Index, 1905–1995," database, *Family Search* (https://familysearch.org/ark:/61903/1:1:VGZN-29T, 27 November 2014), Dylan T Maunder, 22 Jul 1968; citing Los Angeles, California, United States, Department of Health Services, Vital Statistics Department, Sacramento; "California Divorce Index, 1966–1984," database, *Family Search* (https://familysearch.org/ark:/61903/1:1:VPBK-N6D: 15 May 2014), Lucia C Maisto and Wayne E Maunder, Mar 1971; from "California Divorce Index, 1966–1984," database and images, *Ancestry* (http://www.ancestry.com: 2007); citing Los Angeles City, California, Health Statistics, California Department of Health Services, Sacramento.

Chapter 24

1. Agnes Moorehead to Georgia Johnstone, April 19, 1972 (Box 1, NYPL).
2. The original of this entertaining letter is to be found in Folder 2, Box 150 of the Agnes Moorehead Collection at the Wisconsin Center for Film and Theater Research. Tranberg reprints it in its entirety in *I Love the Illusion*, pp. 168–69.
3. Interviews with Paul Gregory, August 26, 2006, and January 23, 2007.
4. The *Daily News* review from January 16, 1973, quoted in Carlin, "Agnes Moorehead," p. 665.
5. The *Nation* review from February 5, 1973, quoted in Kear, *Agnes Moorehead*, p. 229.
6. Urjo Kareda, "Don Juan in Hell: Burden Falls on Ricardo Montalban," *Toronto Star* [January 2, 1973] (Box 137, WCFTR).
7. John Houseman, "Agnes Moorehead: 1906–1974," *Los Angeles Times*, May 5, 1974, p. 34.
8. Houseman, *Final Dress*, p. 475.
9. William Glover, "Supercast Flat in Drama's Opener," *Lima News*, January 17, 1973, p. C5.
10. Kareda, "Don Juan in Hell."
11. See information in Scrapbook Vol. 68 (March–Sept. 1972) (Box 134, WCFTR); Houseman, *Final Dress*, p. 475.
12. Camilla Snyder, "Vignettes of the Don Juan Opening," *Los Angeles Herald-Examiner*, September 7, 1972 (Box 137, WCFTR).
13. Army Archerd, "Hollywood Scene," *Variety* [September 1972] (Box 137, WCFTR); Snyder, "Vignettes of the Don Juan Opening."
14. Archerd, "Hollywood Scene." There is no longer any Blue Ribbon Room in the Music Center complex, but it would appear to have been located in the Dorothy Chandler Pavilion.
15. Quotes from Houseman, *Final Dress*, p. 475.
16. Elliot Norton, "A Four-Star Triumph: Don Juan in Hell," *Boston Herald Traveler*, October 25, 1972 (Box 137, WCFTR).
17. David Richards, "Don Juan in Hell: Over-Selling Show," *Washington Star-News* [November 7, 1972] (Box 137, WCFTR).
18. Kareda, "Don Juan in Hell."
19. See Scrapbook Vol. 71 (Fall 1972) (Box 137, WCFTR).
20. Agnes Moorehead to Georgia Johnstone, January 11, 1973 (Box 1, NYPL).
21. Houseman, *Final Dress*, p. 475.
22. Archerd, "Hollywood Scene."
23. Jack O'Brian, "On Broadway," *Mansfield News Journal*, January 22, 1973, p. 27.
24. www.ibdb.com.
25. Houseman, *Final Dress*, p. 475.
26. Houseman, p. 475.
27. Clive Barnes, "Shaw's 'Don Juan in Hell' at 70," *New York Times*, January 16, 1973, www.nytimes.com.
28. Glover, "Supercast Flat in Drama's Opener," p. C5.
29. Houseman, "Agnes Moorehead: 1906–1974," p. 34.
30. *Don Juan in Hell* program, O'Keefe Centre, Toronto, Canada,[January 1973] (Nissen). See also www.ibdb.com.
31. Interview with Marian Seldes, October 6, 2007.

Chapter 25

1. "Courageous Pair," *Zanesville Times Recorder*, November 17, 1973, p. 7B.
2. Judith Thurman, "Introduction," *Gigi* by Colette, trans. Roger Senhouse (New York: Farrar, Straus and Giroux, 2001), p. xxiii.
3. Thurman, p. xi.
4. Dustin Harvey, "'Gigi' a Lukewarm Play of Lerner and Loewe Film," *Bucks County Courier Times*, May 19, 1973, p. 14.
5. Harvey, p. 14.
6. Colette, *Gigi*, trans. Roger Senhouse (New York: Farrar, Straus and Giroux, 2001), p. 35.
7. Thurman, "Introduction," p. xxiv.
8. Anita Loos, *Gigi: A Comedy in Two Acts* (New York: Samuel French, 1953), p. 21.
9. Loos, p. 77.
10. Pericles Alexander, "Broadway Bound Musical, 'Gigi' Winds Up St. Louis Muny Season," *Lawton Constitution*, August 23, 1973, p. 2C.
11. John Edward Dorand to Agnes Moorehead, July 9, 1973 (Box 4, NYPL).
12. Edwin Lester to Agnes Moorehead, February 15, 1973 (Box 138, WCFTR); quoted in Tranberg, *I Love the Illusion*, p. 7.
13. "Behind the Scenes in Making of a Musical," *Los Angeles Times*, May 18, 1973 (Box 4, NYPL).
14. "Moorehead Signed for Role in 'Gigi,'" *Pasadena Star-News*, March 18, 1973, p. C7.

15. Sherk, *Agnes Moorehead*, p. 90. See also Georgia Johnstone to Jill Lehmann, April 2, 1973, included in Jill Marie, *With Every Good Wish*, p. 109 (Nissen).
16. All quotes and summary in this and the following four paragraphs from the typescript of Alan Jay Lerner and Frederick Loewe, *Gigi: A Musical Play* (October 13, 1973) (Box 54, WCFTR).
17. Harvey, "'Gigi' a Lukewarm Play," p. 14.
18. Clive Barnes, "'Gigi' Is Here Again as Stage Musical," *New York Times*, November 14, 1973, www.nytimes.com.
19. Shirley Eder, "Coming-Out Party to Welcome Sinatra Back," *Detroit Free Press*, September 16, 1973 (Box 4, NYPL).
20. Douglas Watt, "'Gigi' Returns as a Stage Musical," *New York Daily News*, November 14, 1973 (Box 4, NYPL).
21. Agnes Moorehead to Fred Carmichael, May 30, 1973 (Nissen).
22. "Edwa.," "Legit Review: Gigi," *Variety*, May 17, 1973 (Box 4, NYPL).
23. Barney Glazer, "Televents," *Oxnard Press-Courier*, May 27, 1973, p. 6.
24. Ron Pennington, "Play Review: Gigi," *Hollywood Reporter*, July 6, 1973 (Box 4, NYPL); Carol Thornton, "Gigi Cast Feted at After-Theater Party," *Van Nuys Valley News*, July 10, 1973, no page; Jay Stanley, "Jay Walking—From Hollywood," unidentified clipping, August 2, 1973 (Box 4, 1973); Jack Meredith, "Gigi Passes Test as Stage Musical," *Windsor Star*, September 12, 1973 (Box 4, NYPL); *Time* review of November 26, 1973, quoted in Kear, *Agnes Moorehead*, p. 230; "Courageous Pair," p. 7B.
25. Charles Shere, "'Gigi' Returns to the Stage," unidentified San Francisco paper, May 17, 1973 (Box 4, NYPL).
26. Lynn Slotkin, "Will Gigi Stop Her Trembling at the Brink?," *Canadian Jewish News*, November 2, 1973 (Box 4, NYPL).
27. Shere, "'Gigi' Returns to the Stage."
28. Shere, "'Gigi' Returns to the Stage."
29. Harvey, "'Gigi' a Lukewarm Play," p. 14.
30. Rick Talcove, "Musical 'Gigi' Lacks Professionalism: Needs More Rehearsing," *Van Nuys Valley News*, July 10, 1973, no page.
31. Dan Sullivan, "Stage Review: 'Gigi' Makes Transition from the Screen," *Los Angeles Times*, July 5, 1973 (Box 4, NYPL).
32. Harvey, "'Gigi' a Lukewarm Play," p. 14; "Har.," "Show Out Of Town," unidentified clipping, May 23, 1973 (Box 4, NYPL); Jeanne Miller's *San Francisco Examiner* review quoted under "Capsule Comments," *Bucks County Courier Times*, May 19, 1973, p. 14; Sullivan, "Stage Review: 'Gigi'"; Shirley Eder, "'Gigi' Delightful Despite Faults," *Detroit Free Press*, September 15, 1973 (Box 4, NYPL); *The Nation* review of December 3, 1973, quoted in Kear, *Agnes Moorehead*, p. 230 (final two quotes).
33. Miller's *San Francisco Examiner* review quoted under "Capsule Comments," p. 14.
34. "Edwa.," "Legit Review: Gigi."
35. Ron Base, "Check Your Worries at the Box Office: Here Comes Gigi," *Detroit Sunday Sun*, October 14, 1973 (Box 4, NYPL).
36. William Glover, "'Gigi' Goes Big on Broadway," *San Francisco Examiner*, November 14, 1973 (Box 4, NYPL).
37. Robert Taylor, "Stage and Screen: 'Gigi' Pays Another Visit," *Oakland Tribune*, March 14, 1973, p. 31; www.ibdb.com.
38. Taylor, "Stage and Screen," p. 31.
39. Harvey, "'Gigi' a Lukewarm Play," p. 14.
40. "Courageous Pair," p. 7B.
41. Stanley, "Jay Walking—From Hollywood."
42. Glover, "'Gigi' Goes Big."
43. *Newsweek* review of November 26, 1973, quoted in Kear, *Agnes Moorehead*, p. 230.
44. Eder, "'Gigi' Delightful Despite Faults."
45. Harvey, "'Gigi' a Lukewarm Play," p. 14.
46. Agnes Moorehead to Georgia Johnstone [mid-October 1973] (Box 1, NYPL).
47. Lerner and Loewe, *Gigi*, p. 1-5-35 (Box 54, WCFTR). These last-minute changes were in the scene where Aunt Alicia hears over the phone that Liane d'Exelmans has tried to commit suicide.
48. Walter Kerr, "Thank Heaven for Alfred Drake," unidentified clipping [1973] (Box 4, NYPL).
49. Kerr, "Thank Heaven for Alfred Drake."
50. Quoted in Taylor, "Stage and Screen," p. 31.
51. Tranberg, *I Love the Illusion*, p. 8.
52. Sylvie Drake, "'Gigi' Has Opening on West Coast," *Phoenix Arizona Republic*, May 8, 1973, p. N9.
53. Glover, "'Gigi' Goes Big."
54. "Courageous Pair," p. 7B.
55. Base, "Check Your Worries at the Box Office."
56. Talcove, "Musical 'Gigi' Lacks Professionalism."
57. Russell Beasley to Axel Nissen, June 11, 2011.
58. Glover, "'Gigi' Goes Big."
59. Harvey, "'Gigi' a Lukewarm Play," p. 14.
60. "Courageous Pair," p. 7B.
61. Eder, "'Gigi' Delightful Despite Faults."
62. Judy Insel to Axel Nissen, September 19, 2007.
63. Richard Styles, "Light Opera Review 'Gigi': Beautiful People See Beautiful Show," *Pasadena Star-News*, July 18, 1973, p. F9.
64. Talcove, "Musical 'Gigi' Lacks Professionalism."
65. Talcove, "Musical 'Gigi' Lacks Professionalism."
66. Barnes, "'Gigi' Is Here Again."
67. Barnes, "'Gigi' Is Here Again."
68. Taylor, "Stage and Screen," p. 31.
69. Harvey, "'Gigi' a Lukewarm Play," p. 14.
70. Styles, "Light Opera Review 'Gigi,'" p. F9.
71. Talcove, "Musical 'Gigi' Lacks Professionalism."
72. Stanley, "Jay Walking—From Hollywood."
73. Base, "Check Your Worries at the Box Office."
74. Molly Abraham, "'Trembling on the Brink' of Stardom," *Detroit News*, September 16, 1973 (Box 4, 1973).
75. Abraham, "'Trembling on the Brink' of Stardom."
76. Biographical information on Karin Wolfe from www.imdb.com, www.ibdb.com, www.lortel.org, and Abraham, "'Trembling on the Brink' of Stardom."
77. Base, "Check Your Worries at the Box Office."
78. Barnes, "'Gigi' Is Here Again."
79. Watt, "'Gigi' Returns as a Stage Musical."
80. *Newsweek* quoted in Kear, *Agnes Moorehead*, p. 230.
81. Glover, "'Gigi' Goes Big."
82. Eder, "'Gigi' Delightful Despite Faults."
83. "Courageous Pair," p. 7B.
84. The remainder of this subsection is based on my interview with Karin Wolfe, June 12, 2011.
85. Karin Wolfe to Axel Nissen, June 21, 2011.
86. Earl Wilson, "It Happened Last Night," *Dover Times-Reporter*, January 14, 1974, p. B5.
87. Earl Wilson, "Confessions of a Non-Celebrity," *Lowell Sun*, January 21, 1974, no page.
88. Interview with Judy Insel, October 4, 2007.
89. www.ibdb.com.

Appendix

1. *Bewitched* filming schedule (www.bewitched.net).

2. See clipping of Shirley Eder's column of September 24, 1964, in Scrapbook Vol. 10 (Summer 1964) (Box 72, WCFTR).

3. *Bewitched* filming schedule (www.bewitched.net).

4. See ticket folder and invitation in Scrapbook Vol. 10 (Summer 1964) (Box 72, WCFTR) and a black and white photo of Moorehead and her son Sean from the premiere in Scrapbook Vol. 11 (Fall 1964) (Box 73, WCFTR).

5. *Bewitched* filming schedule (www.bewitched.net).

6. The Internet Movie Database (IMDb) and the DVD has switched the original air dates and episode numbers on "The Girl Reporter" and "Witch or Wife," but all other sources, including the *Bewitched* filming schedule, give November 12, 1964, as the original air date of "Witch or Wife," making it episode 9.

7. See *Bewitched* call sheet, October 2, 1964 (Box 43, WCFTR) and Moorehead's handwritten guest list (Box 61, WCFTR).

8. *Bewitched* call sheet, November 20, 1964 (Box 43, WCFTR). Thus production on this episode was delayed, as the filming schedule claims the episode was completed on November 18, 1964 (www.bewitched.net).

9. Alain Silver and Elizabeth Ward, *Robert Aldrich: A Guide to References and Resources* (Boston: G.K. Hall, 1979), p. 40; www.imdb.com.

10. Dick Kleiner, "Hollywood Today," *Benton Harbor News-Palladium* (January 19, 1965), p. 19.

11. See final draft of "A Nice Little Dinner Party" dated December 2, 1964 with revisions of December 4–8, 1964 (Box 43, WCFTR) and *Bewitched* filming schedule (www.bewitched.net).

12. *Bewitched* filming schedule (www.bewitched.net); *Bewitched* call sheet, January 5, 1965 (Box 43, WCFTR).

13. See invitation and other documents relating to the party in Scrapbook Vol. 15 (Winter-Spring 1964–65) (Box 77, WCFTR).

14. *Bewitched* filming schedule (www.bewitched.net); see invitation in Scrapbook Vol. 12 (Christmas 1964) (Box 74, WCFTR).

15. Tranberg, *I Love the Illusion*, p. 246.

16. *Bewitched* call sheet, March 25, 1965 (Box 44, WCFTR).

17. See Scrapbook Vol. 15 (Winter-Spring 1964–65) (Box 77, WCFTR).

18. *Bewitched* filming schedule (www.bewitched.net); invitation in Scrapbook Vol. 16 (Spring 1965) (Box 78, WCFTR).

19. *Bewitched* filming schedule (www.bewitched.net).

20. *Bewitched* call sheet, April 8, 1965 (Box 44, WCFTR).

21. See *High Spirits* production schedule (Box 55, WCFTR).

22. *Bewitched* call sheet, April 5, 1965 (Box 44, WCFTR); UPI press photo (Nissen).

23. *Bewitched* filming schedule (www.bewitched.net).

24. Alice Pearce to Agnes Moorehead, September 23, 1965 (Box 80, WCFTR).

25. See invitation in Scrapbook Vol. 22 (December 1963–March 1966) (Box 87, WCFTR).

26. *The Singing Nun* call sheet, October 21, 1965 (Box 26, WCFTR).

27. *Bewitched* filming schedule (www.bewitched.net). Her cue cards for the show with her handwritten notes on them are in Scrapbook Vol. 17A (Spring-Summer 1965) (Box 80, WCFTR).

28. "Trick or Treat" shooting schedule (Box 44, WCFTR).

29. See invitation in Scrapbook Vol. 17A (Spring-Summer 1965) (Box 80, WCFTR).

30. *Bewitched* filming schedule (www.bewitched.net); *High Spirits* production schedule (Box 55, WCFTR).

31. Agnes Moorehead, "My Favorite Script," *Guideposts* (August 1965), 9–10. A substantial part of the article is excerpted in Parish, *Good Dames*, p. 80.

32. *Bewitched* filming schedule (www.bewitched.net); Freddie Logan Jones to Agnes Moorehead, September 11, 1965 (Box 80, WCFTR).

33. *Bewitched* filming schedule (www.bewitched.net) and final draft of "My Boss, the Teddy Bear" dated August 25, 1965, with revisions of September 2, 1965 (Box 44, WCFTR); Agnes Moorehead to Georgia Johnstone, August 31, 1965 (Box 1, NYPL).

34. *Bewitched* filming schedule (www.bewitched.net); "Moorehead at Marrymount," *Independent Press-Telegram*, December 5, 1965, p. C9.

35. *Bewitched* filming schedule (www.bewitched.net); *Bewitched* call sheet, December 30, 1965 (Box 44, WCFTR); see invitation in Scrapbook Vol. 19 (Christmas 1965) (Box 82, WCFTR).

36. Agnes Moorehead to Roy Buchanan, February 15, 1966, reprinted in the fan publication *Call Board* 11 ([March] 1966), p. 5 (Box 385, Muskingum).

37. *Bewitched* filming schedule (www.bewitched.net); *Bewitched* call sheet, January 6, 1966 (Box 44, WCFTR); invitation in Scrapbook Vol. 21A (Christmas 1965-Winter 1966) (Box 86, WCFTR); Don Bachardy to Axel Nissen, September 7, 2007.

38. *Bewitched* filming schedule (www.bewitched.net).

39. See letter from the pastor of the church, Samuel R. Allison, to Agnes Moorehead, January 20, 1966 (Box 87, WCFTR).

40. See letters and get well cards in Scrapbook Vol. 23 (Spring 1966) (Box 88, WCFTR).

41. See Fred Briskin to Agnes Moorehead, May 19, 1966, Scrapbook Vol. 23 (Spring 1966) (Box 88, WCFTR).

42. *Bewitched* filming schedule (www.bewitched.net); see itinerary in Scrapbook Vol. 24 (Spring 1966) (Box 89, WCFTR); Frances Melrose, "Each Role a Challenge to Actress," *Rocky Mountain News*, April 1, 1966, p. 21A.

43. See invitation in Scrapbook Vol. 22 (December 1963-March 1966) (Box 87, WCFTR).

44. Agnes Moorehead to Georgia Johnstone, September 11, 1966 (Box 1, NYPL).

45. See *Bewitched* call sheet, August 2, 1966 (Box 45, WCFTR) and items related to the Akron visit in Scrapbook Vol. 25 (Summer-Fall 1966) (Box 90, WCFTR).

46. See invitation in Scrapbook Vol. 29 (Christmas 1966) (Box 94, WCFTR).

47. See materials in Scrapbook Vol. 26 (Fall-Christmas 1966) and Scrapbook Vol. 27 (Fall-Christmas 1966) (Box 91 and 92, WCFTR).

48. See invitation in Scrapbook Vol. 27 (Fall-Christmas 1966) (Box 92, WCFTR).

49. Alan Foshko to Agnes Moorehead, August 26, 1966 (Box 90, WCFTR).

50. See invitation in Scrapbook Vol. 35 (Fall 1967) (Box 101, WCFTR).

51. "Sam's Spooky Chair" shooting schedule (Box 45, WCFTR).

52. *Bewitched* filming schedule (www.bewitched.net);

see invitation in Scrapbook Vol. 29A (Christmas 1966) (Box 95, WCFTR).

53. *Bewitched* filming schedule (www.bewitched.net); see invitation in Scrapbook Vol. 28 (Fall-Christmas 1966) (Box 93, WCFTR).

54. *Bewitched* filming schedule (www.bewitched.net).

55. See final draft of "The Trial and Error of Aunt Clara" dated December 5, 1966 (Box 46, WCFTR); and *The Wild Wild West* call sheet, December 5, 1966 (Box 42, WCFTR).

56. See Tino Balio to Agnes Moorehead, February 9, 1967 (Box 96, WCFTR).

57. *Bewitched* filming schedule (www.bewitched.net); *Bewitched* call sheet, January 10, 1967 (Box 46, WCFTR).

58. Interview with Dr. Roderick Bladel, May 25, 2006.

59. *Bewitched* filming schedule (www.bewitched.net).

60. *Bewitched* filming schedule (www.bewitched.net).

61. Roy Buchanan to Agnes Moorehead, March 20, 1967 (Box 96, WCFTR).

62. "Plan Benefit for Opening of Health Spa," *Van Nuys Valley News*, January 29, 1967, no page.

63. See materials relating to the performance in Scrapbook Vol. 33 (Spring 1967) (Box 99, WCFTR).

64. See invitation in Scrapbook Vol. 33 (Spring 1967) (Box 99, WCFTR).

65. "Long Live the Queen" shooting schedule (Box 46, WCFTR); Ruth McDevitt to Agnes Moorehead, August 3, 1967 (Box 101, WCFTR).

66. *Bewitched* filming schedule (www.bewitched.net).

67. *Bewitched* call sheet, June 7, 1967 (Box 46, WCFTR).

68. *Bewitched* filming schedule (www.bewitched.net); invitation in Scrapbook Vol. 35 (Fall 1967) (Box 101, WCFTR).

69. Jack Ward, "Broadcasting Backstage," *Elk Grove Daily Herald*, October 1, 1967, no page.

70. Florabel Muir, "Looking at Hollywood," *Colorado Spring Gazette Telegraph*, August 16, 1967, p. 6D.

71. Hal Humphrey, "Television and Radio," *Portsmouth Times*, October 18, 1967, p. 23.

72. *Bewitched* filming schedule (www.bewitched.net); Agnes Moorehead to Georgia Johnstone [after September 11, 1967] and September 20, 1967 (Box 1, NYPL).

73. Agnes Moorehead to Georgia Johnstone [1967] (Box 1, NYPL).

74. For the dating of the party, see Agnes Moorehead to Georgia Johnstone [1967] (Box 1, NYPL); and Jack Bradford, "Hollywood Report," *Arizona Republic*, December 18, 1967, p. 44.

75. "A Busy Time," *San Antonio Express and News*, December 17, 1967, p. 7; *Bewitched* filming schedule (www.bewitched.net).

76. "Will Honor Expert on Blood Ills," *Van Nuys Valley News*, January 4, 1968, no page.

77. "Snob in the Grass" shooting schedule (Box 46, WCFTR).

78. Georgia Johnstone to Agnes Moorehead, January 16, 1968 (Box 1, NYPL).

79. *Bewitched* filming schedule (www.bewitched.net).

80. *Bewitched* filming schedule (www.bewitched.net).

81. Tranberg, *I Love the Illusion*, p. 286.

82. See materials in Scrapbook Vol. 55 (Spring 1969) (Box 121, WCFTR) and the itinerary in Sherk, *Agnes Moorehead*, pp. 104–5.

83. Georgia Johnstone to Harry Browne, August 10, 1968 (Nissen).

84. See *The Maltese Bippy* script dated October 23, 1969 (Box 22, WCFTR).

85. *Bewitched* filming schedule (www.bewitched.net).

86. *Bewitched* filming schedule (www.bewitched.net); *Bewitched* call sheet, August 16, 1968 (Box 47, WCFTR).

87. See invitation in Scrapbook Vol. 52 (Christmas 1968) (Box 118, WCFTR).

88. See L. Arnold Weissberger, *Famous Faces: A Photograph Album of Personal Reminiscences* (New York: Harry N. Abrams, 1973), p. 306; Milton Goldman to Agnes Moorehead, January 17, 1969 and an invitation from Margaret Whiting, both in Scrapbook Vol. 53 (December 1968-January 1969) (Box 119, WCFTR).

89. Agnes Moorehead to Georgia Johnstone, November 13, 1968 (Box 1, NYPL).

90. See invitation in Scrapbook Vol. 54 (Spring 1969) (Box 129, WCFTR).

91. "Samantha, the Sculptress" shooting schedule (Box 47, WCFTR).

92. Princess Grace to Agnes Moorehead, March 2, 1969 (Box 120, WCFTR).

93. Agnes Moorehead to Georgia Johnstone, February 2, 1969 (Box 1, NYPL).

94. See materials in Scrapbook Vol. 54 (Spring 1969) (Box 120, WCFTR).

95. Barney Glazer, "The TV Scene," *Oxnard Press-Courier*, March 23, 1969, p. 7. There is a copy of this article in Scrapbook Vol. 56 (Spring-Summer 1969) (Box 122, WCFTR).

96. See invitation in Scrapbook Vol. 54 (Spring 1969) (Box 120, WCFTR).

97. See invitation and other materials in Scrapbook Vol. 54 (Spring 1969) and Scrapbook Vol. 60 (Christmas 1969) (Box 120 and 126, WCFTR).

98. Ann Griffith, "Now, What Can You Do on a Rainy Afternoon in Charleston? Follow Agnes Moorehead," *Charleston Daily Mail*, April 17, 1969, p. 23.

99. *Bewitched* filming schedule (www.bewitched.net).

100. See invitation in Scrapbook Vol. 57 (Summer-Fall 1969) (Box 123, WCFTR).

101. See invitation in Scrapbook Vol. 54 (Spring 1969) (Box 120, WCFTR).

102. See materials in Scrapbook Vol. 54 (Spring 1969) and Scrapbook Vol. 55 (Spring 1969) (Box 120 and 121, WCFTR); and Jean Tro Williams, "Audience Bewitched," *Arizona Republic*, April 26, 1969, p. 48.

103. See schedule for the 1969–70 school year in Scrapbook Vol. 60 (Christmas 1969) (Box 126, WCFTR).

104. *Bewitched* filming schedule (www.bewitched.net).

105. Conrad Binyon to Agnes Moorehead, October 30, 1969 (Box 123, WCFTR).

106. See invitation and other materials relating to the launch in Scrapbook Vol. 59 (Christmas 1969) (Box 125, WCFTR).

107. There are materials relating to this show, including photographs, in Scrapbook Vol. 59 (Christmas 1969) (Box 125, WCFTR). The Agnes Moorehead collection at the Wisconsin Center for Film and Theater Research (WCFTR) also contains the script for this sketch (Box 41). See also "Highlights of TV Shows," *Troy Record*, December 6, 1969, p. B3.

108. *Bewitched* filming schedule (www.bewitched.net).

109. See invitation in Scrapbook Vol. 60 (Christmas 1969) (Box 126, WCFTR).

110. See "Oral Roberts Presents Look at Springtime," *Florence Morning News*, March 21, 1970, p. 3; and "Easter

Special Friday Truly Family-Oriented," *Lowell Sun*, March 22, 1970, p. 6. There is a copy of the script of this original monologue, written especially for Moorehead by the show's director-producer Dick Ross, in the Agnes Moorehead collection at WCFTR (Box 38) and the performance is available at www.youtube.com.

111. See invitation in Scrapbook Vol. 60 (Christmas 1969) (Box 126, WCFTR).

112. See invitation and photograph in Scrapbook Vol. 58 (Christmas 1969) (Box 124, WCFTR).

113. See invitation in Scrapbook Vol. 60 (Christmas 1969) (Box 126, WCFTR).

114. See invitation in Scrapbook Vol. 60 (Christmas 1969) (Box 126, WCFTR).

115. Materials relating to both events in Scrapbook Vol. 60 (Christmas 1969) (Box 126, WCFTR).

116. Agnes Moorehead to Georgia Johnstone, April 10, 1970 (Box 1, NYPL).

117. "Your Friends and Neighbors in Review: Life Exciting for Mother of Actress," unidentified clipping (Box 129, WCFTR).

118. *Bewitched* filming schedule (www.bewitched.net).

119. Agnes Moorehead to Georgia Johnstone [late June 1970] (Box 1, NYPL).

120. Patricia Barham, "Poking Around Showbiz," *Van Nuys Valley News*, November 19, 1970, no page.

121. *Bewitched* filming schedule (www.bewitched.net); see invitation in Scrapbook Vol. 62 (Spring-Summer 1970) (Box 128, WCFTR).

122. "Day out of days" overview and shooting schedule for "Samantha's Old Man" (Box 49, WCFTR).

123. Dick Kleiner, "Show Beat," *Victoria Advocate*, September 6, 1970, p. 11.

124. *Bewitched* filming schedule (www.bewitched.net).

125. See Fred Carmichael to Agnes Moorehead, September 28, 1970, and Tilla Marshall to Agnes Moorehead, November 6, 1970 (Box 127, WCFTR).

126. www.tcm.com.

127. *Bewitched* filming schedule (www.bewitched.net).

128. See invitation in Scrapbook Vol. 63 (January 1971) (Box 129, WCFTR).

129. The letter is reprinted in Tranberg, *I Love the Illusion*, pp. 299–300. Judith Ann Guerra died April 11, 1971, and has a memorial at www.findagrave.com.

130. *Bewitched* filming schedule (www.bewitched.net); Lucille Ball to Agnes Moorehead, February 5, 1971 (Box 135, WCFTR).

131. "Day out of days" overview and shooting schedule for "Laugh, Clown, Laugh" (Box 49, WCFTR).

132. *Bewitched* filming schedule (www.bewitched.net).

133. *Bewitched* filming schedule (www.bewitched.net); *Bewitched* call sheet, June 29, 1971 (Box 49, WCFTR).

134. See invitation in Scrapbook Vol. 64 (Spring-Summer 1971) (Box 130, WCFTR).

135. See invitation and other materials relating to the visit in Scrapbook Vol. 64 (Spring-Summer 1971) and Scrapbook Vol. 69 (Christmas 1970–71) (Box 130 and 135, WCFTR).

136. See Army Archerd, "Just for Variety," *Variety*, December 7, 1971 (Box 131, WCFTR) and Norma Lee Browning, "Hollywood Today," *Chicago Tribune* December 7, 1971 (Box 132, WCFTR).

137. Curtis Harrington to Agnes Moorehead, December 8, 1971 (Box 135, WCFTR).

138. "Three Men and a Witch on a Horse" shooting schedule (Box 49, WCFTR).

139. *Charlotte's Web* final draft script dated September 29, 1971 (Box 13, WCFTR).

140. *Bewitched* filming schedule (www.bewitched.net); Vivian Waixel, "Municipal Complex Dedication Bewitches Reedsburg Residents," *Wisconsin State Journal*, October 4, 1971, p. 2–1; photos in Scrapbook Vol. 64 (Spring-Summer 1971) (Box 130, WCFTR).

141. "Agnes Moorhead at Rochester," *Cedar Rapids Gazette*, March 7, 1972, p. 18A. The news article does not state the cause of the illness, which is given in Tranberg, *I Love the Illusion*, pp. 302–3.

142. Agnes Moorehead to Georgia Johnstone, March 16, 1972 (Box 1, NYPL); Agnes Moorehead to Tanya Hills, March 18, 1972 (Nissen).

143. Agnes Moorehead to Georgia Johnstone, March 16, 1972, and April 19, 1972 (Box 1, NYPL).

Bibliography

Allyson, June, with Frances Spatz Leighton. June Allyson. New York: G.P. Putnam, 1982.

Bartel, Pauline. *Spellcasters: Witches and Witchcraft in History, Folklore and Popular Culture.* Dallas: Taylor Trade, 2000.

Benedetti, Quint. *(My Travels with) Agnes Moorehead: The Lavender Lady—More Bewitching Than Endora.* N.p.: Xlibris, 2010.

Brady, Frank. *Citizen Welles: A Biography of Orson Welles.* London: Hodder and Stoughton, 1990.

Brode, Douglas, and Carol Serling. *Rod Serling and The Twilight Zone: The 50th Anniversary Tribute.* Fort Lee, NJ: Barricade, 2009.

Brooks, Tim, and Earle Marsh. *The Complete Directory of Prime Time Network and Cable TV Shows, 1946–Present.* New York: Ballantine, 1995.

Callow, Simon. *Charles Laughton: A Difficult Actor.* London: Methuen, 1987.

_____. *Orson Welles: The Road to Xanadu.* London: Vintage, 1996.

Carlin, Phyllis Scott. "Agnes Moorehead." In *Notable Women in the American Theatre: A Biographical Dictionary,* edited by Alice M. Robinson, et al., 663–66. New York: Greenwood, 1989.

Colette. *Gigi.* Trans. Roger Senhouse. New York: Farrar, Straus and Giroux, 2001.

Cotten, Joseph. *Vanity Will Get You Somewhere: An Autobiography.* San Jose: toExcel, 2000.

Cotten, Patricia Medina. *Laid Back in Hollywood Remembering.* Los Angeles: Belle, 1998.

Douglas, Susan J. *Where the Girls Are: Growing Up Female with the Mass Media.* New York: Times/Random House, 1995.

Dunne, Dominick. *The Way We Lived Then: Recollections of a Well-Known Name Dropper.* New York: Crown, 1999.

Dunning, John. *On the Air: The Encyclopedia of Old-Time Radio.* New York and Oxford: Oxford University Press, 1998.

Froug, William. *How I Escaped from Gilligan's Island and Other Misadventures of a Hollywood Writer-Producer.* Madison: University of Wisconsin Press, 2005.

Gibson, Walter B., ed. *The Shadow Scrapbook.* New York: Harcourt Brace Jovanovich, 1979.

Gielgud, John. *Gielgud's Letters.* Ed. Richard Mangan. London: Weidenfeld and Nicolson, 2004.

Hardwicke, Cedric. *A Victorian in Orbit: The Irreverent Memories of Sir Cedric Hardwicke, as Told to James Brough.* London: Methuen, 1961.

Heyer, Paul. *The Medium and the Magician: Orson Welles, the Radio Years, 1934–1952.* Lanham, MD: Rowman and Littlefield, 2005.

Higham, Charles. *Charles Laughton: An Intimate Biography.* London: W.H. Allen, 1976.

Houseman, John. *Final Dress.* New York: Simon & Schuster, 1983.

Irvin, Sam. *Kay Thompson: From Funny Face to Eloise.* New York: Simon & Schuster, 2010.

Kear, Lynn. *Agnes Moorehead: A Bio-Bibliography.* Westport, CT: Greenwood, 1992.

Lanchester, Elsa. *Elsa Lanchester: Herself.* New York: St. Martin's, 1983.

Lofficier, Jean-Marc, and Randy Lofficier. *Into the Twilight Zone: The Rod Serling Programme Guide.* Lincoln, NE: Mystery Writers of America Presents, 2003.

Loos, Anita. *Gigi: A Comedy in Two Acts.* New York: Samuel French, 1953.

Mantle, Burns, ed. *The Best Plays of 1937–38.* New York: Dodd, Mead, 1938.

Matheson, Richard. *Richard Matheson's The Twilight Zone Scripts: Volume One.* Ed. Stanley Wiater. Springfield, PA: Edge, 2001.

McKay, Gardner. *Journey Without a Map: A Memoir.* Honolulu: Shiptree, 2013.

Nevins, Francis M., Jr. *Cornell Woolrich: First You Dream, Then You Die.* New York: Mysterious, 1988.

Nissen, Axel. *The Films of Agnes Moorehead.* Lanham, MD: Scarecrow, 2013.

O'Connor, Flannery. *A Good Man Is Hard to Find and Other Stories.* New York: Harcourt, Brace, 1955.

Parish, James Robert. *Good Dames: Virtue in the Cinema.* South Brunswick, NJ, and New York: A.S. Barnes, 1974.

Parish, James Robert, and Ronald L. Bowers. *The MGM Stock Company: The Golden Era.* New York: Bonanza, 1972.

Peters, Margot. *The House of Barrymore.* New York: Alfred A. Knopf, 1990.

Pilato, Herbie J. *Bewitched Forever: The Immortal Companion to Television's Most Magical Supernatural Situation Comedy,* 2d ed. Irving, TX: Summit, 2001.

_____. *Twitch Upon a Star: The Bewitched Life and Career of Elizabeth Montgomery.* Lanham, MD: Taylor Trade, 2012.

Presnell, Don, and Marty McGee. *A Critical History of Television's* The Twilight Zone, *1959–1964.* Jefferson, NC: McFarland, 2008.

Price, Victoria. *Vincent Price: A Daughter's Biography.* New York: St. Martin's Griffin, 1999.

Rogers, Ginger. *Ginger: My Story*. London: Headline, 1991.

Rosin, James. *Adventures in Paradise: The Television Series*. Philadelphia: Autumn Road, 2009.

Schaden, Chuck. *Speaking of Radio: Chuck Schaden's Conversations with the Stars of the Golden Age of Radio*. Morton Grove, IL: Nostalgia Digest, 2003.

Shaw, George Bernard. *Man and Superman: A Comedy and a Philosophy*. Harmondsworth: Penguin, 1971.

Sherk, Warren. *Agnes Moorehead: A Very Private Person*. Philadelphia: Dorrance, 1976.

Silver, Alain, and Elizabeth Ward. *Robert Aldrich: A Guide to References and Resources*. Boston: G.K. Hall, 1979.

Singer, Kurt. *The Laughton Story: An Intimate Story of Charles Laughton*. Philadelphia and Toronto: John C. Winston, 1954.

Stanyard, Stewart T. *Dimensions Behind the Twilight Zone: A Backstage Tribute to Television's Groundbreaking Series*. Toronto: ECW, 2007.

Steen, Mike. *Hollywood Speaks: An Oral History*. New York: G.P. Putnam, 1974.

Steinbrunner, Chris. "Preface." *The Shadow Scrapbook*. Ed. Walter B. Gibson. New York: Harcourt Brace Jovanovich, 1979.

Swindell, Larry. *Charles Boyer: The Reluctant Lover*. London: Weidenfeld and Nicholson, 1983.

Thompson, Dave. *The Twilight Zone FAQ: All That's Left to Know About the Fifth Dimension and Beyond*. Milwaukee, WI: Applause, 2015.

Thurman, Judith. "Introduction." *Gigi* by Colette. Trans. Roger Senhouse. New York: Farrar, Straus and Giroux, 2001. vii-xxiv.

Tollin, Anthony. "The Invisible Shadow." *The Shadow Scrapbook*. Ed. Walter B. Gibson. New York: Harcourt Brace Jovanovich, 1979. 75–80.

Tranberg, Charles. *I Love the Illusion: The Life and Career of Agnes Moorehead*. Boalsburg, PA: BearManor, 2005.

Weissberger, L. Arnold. *Famous Faces: A Photograph Album of Personal Reminiscences*. New York: Harry N. Abrams, 1973.

Welles, Orson, and Peter Bogdanovich. *This Is Orson Welles*. Ed. Jonathan Rosenbaum. London: HarperCollins, 1992.

Zicree, Marc Scott. *The Twilight Zone Companion: Second Edition*. Los Angeles: Silman-James, 1992.

Index

Numbers in ***bold italics*** indicate pages with illustrations

www.ingramcontent.com/pod-product-compliance
Ingram Content Group UK Ltd.
Pitfield, Milton Keynes, MK11 3LW, UK
UKHW060611180726
13836UKWH00012B/2507

9 781476 667584